Social Welfare in Canada

Understanding Income Security

Second Edition

For Vaida, Justin, and Kristina

For the liberation of all people and communities from
institutionalized greed, ill will, and unawareness.

Social Welfare in Canada

Understanding Income Security

Second Edition

Steven Hick
Carleton University

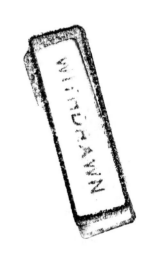

TEP

Thompson Educational Publishing, Inc.
Toronto

Information on how to obtain copies of this book is available at:

Website: http://www.thompsonbooks.com
E-mail: publisher@thompsonbooks.com
Telephone: (416) 766-2763
Fax: (416) 766-0398

Library and Archives Canada Cataloguing in Publication

Hick, Steven F.
        Social welfare in Canada : understanding income security / Steven Hick. – 2nd ed.
Includes bibliographical references and index.

ISBN 978-1-55077-168-8

1. Social security–Canada–Textbooks. 2. Income maintenance programs–Canada–Textbooks. I. Title.

HV105.H5 2007   362.5'820971   C2007-901159-4

Publisher: Keith Thompson
Managing Editor: Jennie Worden
Senior Editor: Rachel Stuckey
Copy Editing: Andy Carroll
Proofreading: Claudia Forgas
Indexing: Katy Harrison
Composition: Tibor Choleva
Photo Research: Crystal J. Hall
Permissions Research: Megan Moore Burns
Cover and Interior Design: Bruce Campbell, BeeMCee Consulting

Every reasonable effort has been made to acquire permission for copyrighted materials used in this book and to acknowledge such permissions accurately. Credits for re-printed material can be found on page 386. Any errors called to the publisher's attention will be corrected in future printings.

We acknowledge the support of the Government of Canada through the Book Publishing Industry Development Program for our publishing activities. We also acknowledge the support of the Government of Ontario through the Ontario Media Development Corporation Book Initiative.

Printed in Canada.

3 4 5   11 10

Brief Contents

Contents

Preface

This book fills a need for a Canadian text on social welfare. While providing a historical background, the book also gives a detailed overview of the many programs that exist in Canada today. Combined with information and data on the socio-economic and political context of social welfare, this book enables readers to form their own views about the nature and character of social welfare in Canada. This text is intended for students who are relatively new to social policy analysis, social work, and other human service disciplines, who need a broad survey of the field. It is also appropriate for students in public administration, social work, economics, political science, or sociology who may not be familiar with the various welfare programs in Canada.

The Second Edition

The content of this book is divided into two main parts. The first part (Chapters 1–9) introduces the theory and approaches to social welfare. Chapter 1 introduces the basic concepts and sets the context; Chapter 2 surveys the origins and emergence of income security; and Chapter 3 unravels the assortment of theories and approaches that underlie much of the discussion of Canadian income security.

Chapters 4–9 each take a different angle in looking at the issues: Chapter 4 focuses on the labour market and employment; Chapter 5 examines the impacts of globalization on social welfare and the potential of human rights; Chapter 6 looks at women's issues in relation to welfare services; Chapter 7, new to this edition, examines Aboriginal social welfare issues; Chapter 8, also new to this edition and written by Purnima Sundar, unravels issues related to immigration, race, and income security; and Chapter 9 looks at poverty in Canadian society and the world.

Both the beginner and the veteran social policy analyst or practitioner need to understand the multiplicity of perspectives on these issues. The remaining chapters (Chapters 10–14) present how specific income security programs are organized, how they operate, and some of the debate around social welfare reform. Chapter 10 focuses on Employment Insurance and Workers' Compensation; Chapter 11 concentrates on Social Assistance or Welfare; Chapter 12 focuses on families and children's benefits; Chapter 13, new to this edition, is on programs for people with disabilities; and Chapter 14 looks at programs for the elderly and retired.

This book does not dictate a particular standpoint on the nature of Canadian social welfare. My philosophy is that people must explore and discover this for themselves. I have seen the suffering and pain that people experience because of the inadequacies of our social welfare systems, and at the same time, I have been involved – through social activism, policy work, and research – in trying to move governments toward action that might ameliorate this. I have also met with people in other countries who were dying – or seeing their family members and neighbours die – due to war or the lack of the basic necessities of life. Throughout all of this, I have come to the conclusion that our current social and economic systems are extremely unhealthy, oppressive, and unjust to both people and the planet. But this is only my conclusion. I would like for you to question and discuss the issues, with the facts at hand, and arrive at your own conclusions. I hope that this book might be a small part of that journey.

Instructor and Student Supplements

This text is accompanied by an Instructor's Manual and PowerPoint slides, as well as online quizzes and the Test Builder program. Also, Social Welfare and Social Work in Canada at www.socialpolicy.ca, provides online support for both this text and *Social Work in Canada*, including a Social Work Glossary, and an online introductory course: *Canada's Unique Social History*.

Acknowledgments

Crafting textbooks such as this one, and its sister publication *Social Work in Canada: An Introduction,* involves the work of a large number of people — not least of which are the many students that have read the first edition and provided valuable feedback and suggestions. From the outset, I have intended to make these books accessible to a wide audience — providing information and analysis in a clear and succinct manner. This would not have been possible without the generous feedback of the students in my introductory social work and social welfare courses. I cannot count the number of times that a student asked for clarification on some section of the book, which would spur me to dash home and write a paragraph. For their generosity and insight, I thank them all.

The first edition of this book owes a debt of gratitude to Allan Moscovitch and Keith Thompson for their guidance. The idea for the book came from Allan, and it was Keith who believed that it could be done. His editing and feedback were invaluable. I would like to thank the graduate students that provided feedback and ideas, including Cheryl Parsons, Amy McGee, Kate Belcher, Teresa Raposo, Monica Reinvall, Carole Bourque, and Erin Brown. Their ideas still affect how the material is organized and presented in the second edition. Finally, I thank Rachel Stuckey, Megan Moore Burns, Crystal J. Hall, and Katy Harrison at Thompson Educational Publishing for their persistent and excellent work. As is typical in our new technological age, I worked closely with the editorial team, but never met them in person.

The significant changes to this edition, especially the addition of Chapters 7, 8, and 13, were inspired by several peer reviewers, including David Hannis at Grant MacEwan College and Shelley Rempel at McMaster University. The book is greatly improved due to their feedback and I thank them all for their astute suggestions.

Thanks must also go to Purnima Sundar at Carleton University for her contribution; the racialization of poverty is something that this country cannot afford to ignore, and Purnima illustrates this issue very well in Chapter 8.

My family – Vaida, my partner, Justin, my son, and Kristina, my daughter – must certainly be acknowledged. The early phases of the "second edition project" occurred while I was recovering from a serious head injury. I was skeptical that I would ever be able to complete the work, but their support and encouragement kept me going forward. They also provided numerous ideas that contributed directly to my writing.

Finally, my whitewater kayaking friends whom I met through the Ottawa paddling club, Coureurs de Bois, and my dragon boating friends on the Fleet of Foote team should be recognized for their input. Conversations while paddling down rivers provided me with invaluable insight into how "average Canadians" will identify with and understand my ideas.

Steven Hick
Carleton University

1 Introducing Social Welfare

What This Book Is About

Social welfare is a defining feature of Canadian society. The social services and income security programs available to citizens, provided or funded by the various levels of government, affect nearly every Canadian at some point in his or her life. Indeed, in view of its scope and importance, it is perhaps a little surprising that few citizens are aware of the components of the system, the history of social welfare provision in Canada, or the current issues and concerns surrounding it.

Income security programs are at the centre of the welfare state in Canada. These programs do much more than protect the poor from destitution; income security programs are used by all sectors of society. Over the course of our lives, almost everyone benefits from Canada's income security system. For example, according to Statistics Canada (2006, 13) 75 percent of non-senior Canadians and 99 percent

> *"We're in a giant car heading towards a brick wall and everyone's arguing over where they're going to sit."*
>
> *David Suzuki*

SOCIAL WELFARE

What's in a Definition?

The term *social welfare* has numerous usages, but we often see four basic themes:

- Social welfare as a philosophical concept — an abstract set of principles that enable society to seek solutions to social problems.
- Social welfare as a product — the legislated documents that prescribe how income security and social services are to be carried out.
- Social welfare as a process — a series of changes that is never fully developed due to shifting contexts.
- Social welfare as a framework for action — both a product and a process.

In fact, social welfare is all of these. Social welfare provides solutions to problems, but it also pertains to the quality of life and social well-being. It is therefore intertwined with politics, economics, and culture.

of all seniors received some income from income security programs in 2004. Some people retire and draw retirement benefits, some become incapacitated and draw on income support benefits, while others may become unemployed and require Employment Insurance (EI). In short, income security programs provide social protection for all Canadians, if and when they need it.

Unfortunately, our "social safety net," as it has come to be called, has been seriously eroded in recent years. The causes are many and varied, but this has happened so quietly that some staunch defenders have termed this process a form of "social policy by stealth." All the more reason, then, for citizens to be aware of the history of social welfare in our country and the current threats it faces.

This textbook examines the role of income security in our society and economy, and reviews the current state of affairs. It will enable you to become familiar with the income security concepts and issues in Canada today.

Analyzing Social Welfare Problems

It is common to feel overwhelmed when confronted with the prospect of analyzing a social welfare problem. Many students see social problems as too complicated, with no clear solutions, and related subjects, such as economics and sociology, can be somewhat abstract and perplexing. Social problems are indeed usually very complex, but a systematic analysis can provide extensive insights and lead to solutions.

For the purposes of this textbook, we will define a social problem as a situation that is incompatible with some standard or norm held by a significant number of people in society, who agree that action is needed to alter the situation. In many cases, this standard is already expressed in human rights codes or social policy legislation. Armed with a basic knowledge of social issues and how society works, it is possible to analyze social problems and point to possible solutions.

Consider the social problem of homelessness. If you ask a group of Canadians to think of a list of all the factors that cause or contribute to homelessness, you would end up with a long and varied list. The factors that arise from the discussion can be categorized according to internal factors and external factors. Internal factors are aspects that are personal or internal to the individual. External factors exist in society and are of a policy, systemic, or structural nature.

Once they completed the list, the group could discuss how each factor plays out in the particular context and discuss possible solutions. Certain solutions may be emphasized over others. Often, a group will emphasize solutions to the individual factors, as they are frequently easier to address than the overall problem. In relation to homelessness, for example, which is often associated with alcohol or drug addiction, individual counselling might seem like a practical solution, since a wholesale change in the federal and provincial government's policy in relation to providing low-cost housing may seem daunting. However, a comprehensive program of affordable housing would have a much larger impact in the long run on homelessness than a particular counselling activity with an individual who is homeless. Often it is necessary to address the internal and external factors simultaneously.

Figure 1.1 offers a typical list of factors that are likely to contribute to homelessness; some could be said to be individual problems, whereas some pertain more to the way our society operates.

When analyzing social problems, external factors are those influences that are located in the wider society and are systemic or structural. Internal factors, on the other hand, refer to things more personal to the individual and the immediate situation.

Figure 1.1: External and Internal Factors Contributing to Homelessness

External Factors	Internal Factors
Low income, unemployment, economic recession	Mental illness
Lack of affordable housing, low vacancy rates	Alcohol and drug addictions
Discrimination	Disabilities, either physical or mental
Low rates of social assistance	Lack of job skills
Lack of social support systems, cutbacks in welfare	Laziness
Lack of educational opportunities	Family trouble

There are several factors that lead to the social problem of homelessness, and various social welfare programs that attempt to alleviate it.

The Canadian Welfare System

The **social welfare system** consists of a combination of income security programs and social services. Although it is not always easy to distinguish between an income security provision and a social service, there is a difference.

Income security provides monetary or other material benefits to supplement income or maintain minimum income levels (e.g., Employment Insurance, Social Assistance, Old Age Security, and Workers' Compensation). Members of our society need a stable income to survive. If everyone could meet his or her income needs through wages from employment, investment income, or inheritance, the need for income security programs would be drastically reduced or eliminated. Without income security programs, Canadians would be much more financially vulnerable.

Social services (personal or community services), on the other hand, help people improve their well-being by providing non-monetary aid to persons in need. Offered by social workers, services include probation, addiction treatment, youth drop-in centres, parent-child resource centres, child care facilities, child protection services, shelters for abused women, and counselling.

Income security programs and social services are provided to citizens through social policies. Social policies are the overall rules and regulations, laws, and other administrative directives that set the framework and objectives for state social welfare activity. The government and specific social programs develop the policies (e.g., the Canada/Quebec Pension Plan). Social programs are specific initiatives that implement and follow social welfare policies.

The Welfare State

Taken together, the range of programs and services available to Canadian citizens is commonly referred to as the *welfare state*. A **welfare state** is a system in which the state protects the health and well-being of its citizens, especially those in social and financial need. The key functions of the welfare state are (1) using state power to achieve desired goals (powers include government, bureaucracy, the judiciary, and political parties); (2) altering the normal operation of the private marketplace; and (3) using grants, taxes, pensions, social services, and minimum-income programs such as welfare and social insurance.

The basic purpose of Canada's social welfare system is straightforward: to help people through difficult times until they can rebuild their lives. The system helps people face a variety of contingencies or difficulties, such as retirement, unemployment, loss of income, disability, illness, violence, homelessness, addiction, racism, warfare, death, separation, divorce, aging of family members, and responsibilities associated with additional children. These contingencies can be grouped into three interrelated categories: (1) contingencies that threaten economic survival, (2) contingencies that threaten the integrity of the person, and (3) contingencies that affect the family. Welfare can be produced by a variety of mechanisms: by purchase (markets), by reciprocity of kin (family), by private solidarity (voluntary associations), and finally by solidarity among citizens (governments).

In Canadian society, income from employment is by far the largest source of income for survival. To help individuals and families face contingencies that affect their income, the Canadian governments at various levels provide a wide range of income security programs, and these are the subject of this volume.

Tax Expenditures as Social Welfare

Textbook treatments of income security in Canada often miss the tax expenditure side of the public system. The principal function of the tax system is to raise the revenues necessary to fund government expenditures. However, the tax system is also an instrument of policy that serves to advance a wide range of economic, social, environmental, cultural, and other public policy objectives.

Tax expenditures are foregone tax revenues resulting from special exemptions, deductions, rate reductions, rebates, credits, and deferrals that reduce the amount of tax that would otherwise be payable. Tax expenditures include deductions for pension and Registered Retirement Savings Plan (RRSP) contributions, credits for charitable donations, and benefits for families with children. Tax expenditures are often designed to encourage certain kinds of activities or to serve other objectives, such as providing assistance to lower-income or elderly Canadians. While this is not often thought of as income security, it can dramatically affect the income of Canadians. By not collecting taxes from those who have a taxable income, an individual's income is effectively increased.

The use of tax expenditures for income security purposes is increasing in Canada. The Canada Child Tax Benefit (CCTB) is an example of an income security program that uses the tax system to distribute income, rather than using an expenditure benefit system. The main benefits of this approach are that (1) the programs do not bring the stigma of collecting welfare benefits, as the money is redistributed anonymously; (2) eligibility is determined on the basis of income as reported on the income tax return, rather than through an intrusive needs test; (3) tax-based income-tested programs are less costly to administer, as they use an already existing administrative structure (the tax system) and do not require the hiring of social workers

Social Welfare System

■ **Income security**: provides monetary or material benefits to supplement income or maintain income levels
■ **Social services**: provide non-monetary aid to help people improve their well-being

Tax expenditures

■ revenue returned to taxpayers for various exemptions, deductions, and credits (RRSP contributions, GST refund, etc.); should be viewed as income security to implement a needs test; and (4) the programs have a low profile and therefore may be more secure and less likely to be cut for political reasons.

Tax expenditure–based income security programs do not only benefit low-income Canadians. The programs have an appeal for higher-income Canadians who appreciate the low profile and non-stigmatizing nature of this type of income security. The CCTB provided $5.5 billion in benefits to 3.1 million families, or 82 percent of all families in Canada, in the government's 2003/04 fiscal year. The RRSP program, with both RRSP deductions for contributions and non-taxation of RRSP investment income, provided $16 billion in benefits to higher-income Canadians in 2002.

Approaches to Social Welfare

People differ in their views about income security and how to provide social protection to individual citizens and eliminate poverty, but the idea of providing income security to citizens in need is no longer a controversial one in Canada. Major disputes do arise, however, in determining which groups are in need and to what extent they need state assistance. Different approaches to social welfare are represented in these disputes. In Canada, successive governments have moved back and forth between these two approaches to social welfare: the *residual view* and the *institutional view.*

In the residual view, social welfare is a limited, temporary response to human need, implemented only when all else fails. It is based on the premise that there are two natural ways through which an individual's needs are met: through the family and the market economy. The residual model is based on the idea that government should play a limited role in the distribution of social welfare. The state should only step in when these normal sources of support fail and individuals are unable to help themselves. Residual social welfare is highly targeted to those most in need. Additionally, residual social welfare tends to provide benefits at a low level in order to discourage use and make social welfare appear undesirable. Canadian public social welfare programs, from early history to the Depression of the 1930s, can be characterized as residual in nature. In the past two decades, we have moved back to this view.

In the institutional view, social welfare is a necessary public response that helps people attain a reasonable standard of life and health. Within this view, it is accepted that people cannot always meet all of their needs through family and work. Therefore, in a complex industrial society, it is legitimate to help people through a set of publicly funded and organized systems of programs and institutions. The institutional model attempts to even out, rather than promote, economic stratification or status differences. The period after World War II saw the beginning of the rise of the institutional view.

Approaches to Social Welfare

■ **Residual view approach**: In this view, social welfare is a limited, short-term, and temporary response to human need. The approach is based on the idea that individuals' needs should be met through the market and the family.

■ **Institutional view approach**: This approach holds that social welfare is a necessary measure to help all people attain a minimum standard of living. It is based on the idea that individuals cannot not always meet all needs through family and work.

■ **Structural approach**: This approach considers market-based economic structures to be essentially exploitative and oppressive, and argues that while social welfare is necessary for survival, it also perpetuates the current system.

The structural approach considers the operation of economic markets to be tied to private concentrations of ownership, and therefore essentially exploitative. The welfare state, in the structural view, is one of the contradictions of capitalism. While social welfare provides benefits for people in need, it does not directly address the exploitative nature of capitalist markets. Since this approach sees social problems and inequalities as a constituent or built-in feature of society, it calls for society itself to change. Working directly with many disadvantaged people throughout the world has lead me to believe that economic globalization, as well as Canada's economic and social structures, are exploitative and oppressive to both people and the planet. The structural approach has never underlined Canada's social policy, but it is increasingly being vocalized by a variety of groups and organizations.

There are additional and more complex ways to distinguish between approaches to social welfare. (See Chapter 3 for an in-depth examination of how people differ on what to do about income security.) These varied approaches to social welfare capture the political controversy and economic debate surrounding social welfare today. It is useful to think about and understand the different approaches and theories, because each conveys a different sense of what social welfare is and how extensive it should be.

The Provision of Social Welfare

Government participation in income security varies widely: the government provides cash benefits for disabilities, old age, survivors of the death of a spouse, occupational injuries and illness, sickness, families, and unemployment. However, the direct government cash benefits do not reflect the entire spectrum of income security expenditures. There are several different methods of categorizing the social welfare available to Canadians. But before we explore the public welfare categories, note the distinction between public programs and private programs.

Public welfare takes place at the three levels of government: the federal or national government, the provincial and territorial governments, and the regional and municipal governments. The various levels of government fund and deliver monetary benefit programs. The government also enforces employment-related policies and legislation, such as labour standards and minimum wage legislation, as well as policies that affect the quantity and distribution of employment and employment equity programs. These policies and legislation can affect the income of Canadians, and therefore can be considered a part of our income security framework.

Private welfare can be non-profit or for-profit, and provides "in-kind" benefits to those lacking income. In-kind benefits include such things as food, emergency shelter, and other bare necessities. By law, organizations that provide these benefits are often registered, and rules and regulations govern their activities. Typically, these agencies are incorporated as non-profit corporations and receive funds from government and private sources. These agencies rarely charge money, given that they generally provide services to the destitute. Consider the Salvation Army. It receives its principal funding from individual donations, and it also receives funds to support its community activities from different levels of government. It is registered as a non-profit organization, and its boards of directors are composed of private citizens who are elected annually.

Income security is provided by for-profit organizations in certain areas, such as retirement pensions, dental and optical plans, and private long-term disability insurance. These for-profit companies provide insurance, but their purpose is to generate a profit for the owner of the organization. Some countries, such as Norway, the Netherlands, and Denmark, have substantial mandatory employer-paid income security programs. Canada does not.

The government is still the largest supplier of income security. However, with government cutbacks in recent years, more and more sources of income security protection are being provided by **non-profit and for-profit welfare agencies**. Food banks and emergency shelters are increasingly helping people with low incomes, while people with more material means are turning to private (for-profit) pensions and insurance programs to ensure their economic security in the future. All three organizations – public, private non-profit, and for-profit – are part of the income security system in Canada today.

Four Types of Programs

Public income security programs fall into the following four broad categories:

SOCIAL INSURANCE. These are programs that follow the insurance principle of shared risk. People contribute to insurance plans with the understanding that not everyone will need to access the benefits. Insurance-based programs are generally linked to employment. All workers contribute, and only those who contribute become eligible for benefits, should the need arise. Employment Insurance, Workers' Compensation, and the Canada/Quebec Pension Plan are social insurance programs.

MINIMUM INCOME. These are programs that provide monetary assistance to those with no other source of income. They are primarily geared towards those deemed to be living in poverty, and the quantity of assistance tends to be determined by the minimum amount necessary to meet basic needs. Social Assistance, also called *welfare* or *workfare*, is a minimum income program.

DEMOGRANTS. These are universal flat-rate payments made to individuals or households on the sole basis of demographic characteristics, such as number of children or age, rather than on the basis of proven need (as in minimum income programs) or contributions (as in social insurance programs). The Old Age Security (OAS) paid to all persons aged 65 and over was a universal program before a clawback was implemented. Now it is considered an income supplementation program. The former 1944 Family Allowance program, benefiting all families with children under the age of 18, was Canada's first widespread universal program.

INCOME SUPPLEMENTATION. These are programs that, as the name suggests, supplement income that is obtained elsewhere, whether through paid employment or through other income security programs. They are not intended to be the primary source of income. These programs may have a broad entitlement, in that they may be available to everyone within a very broad category, or they may be targeted to those most in need. The National Child Benefit Supplement (NCBS) and the Guaranteed Income Supplement (GIS) are income supplementation programs.

Public Income Security Programs

Canada's income security programs are in the newspaper headlines on a daily basis, and the effectiveness and affordability of such programs are frequent topics of discussion. The emphasis is often on the need to cut spending and to reduce the deficit, but the host of benefits that these programs bring to families, society, and the economy are rarely mentioned. Nevertheless, many Canadians rely on the following income security programs to bring some economic stability to their lives, without which they would not be able to regroup and again be able to participate fully in society.

EMPLOYMENT INSURANCE (EI). This federally administered program, originally called Unemployment Insurance (UI), dates back to 1940. Since then, UI has undergone numerous changes, including its name change to Employment Insurance. EI provides a level of income replacement to workers who are temporarily unemployed and meet strict eligibility conditions. Sickness, maternity, and parental benefits are included in this program. Also included in EI are benefits for those whose livelihood depends on the fishing industry. Claimants are eligible for a range of skills development programs. EI is paid for through employer and employee contributions. Recently, the program has become restricted, providing coverage for fewer and fewer workers.

WORKERS' COMPENSATION. Workers' Compensation programs provide provincially administered benefits and are designed to protect individuals against income loss due to workplace injury or disease. Employers fund the programs. In return for participation in the provincial programs, workers waive their rights to sue their employers in the case of a work-related injury or disease. The first Workers' Compensation program was instituted in Ontario in 1914. This was the first social insurance type of program in Canada.

SOCIAL ASSISTANCE, OR WELFARE. Social Assistance programs have their roots in early municipal and provincial relief programs that were designed to provide minimal support to the deserving poor or those deemed unable to work because of age or infirmity. Gradually expanded to include those in need but without resources, Social Assistance has remained a residual program of last resort for those with no other source of income or savings. Social Assistance programs, also called *welfare* or *workfare*, have remained a provincial responsibility with some funding coming from the federal government. The provinces are free to design their own programs and set the level of benefits. In some provinces, "employable" recipients must participate in work placements. This is known as *workfare*. In 2007 budget the federal government proposed the Working Income Tax Benefit (WITB). The benefit aims to offset the disincentives of moving from welfare to work, for example, higher income taxes and the loss of social benefits such as drug plans.

CANADA CHILD TAX BENEFIT (CCTB), NATIONAL CHILD BENEFIT SUPPLEMENT (NCBS), UNIVERSAL CHILD CARE BENEFIT (UCCB). There is a long history in Canada of providing benefits to families with children. Some of these benefits have been and continue to be delivered through the tax system in the form of tax credits and exemptions, and others have been direct cash transfers. In 1944, a universal benefit called the Family Allowance was instituted, and this benefit went to all families with children, regardless of income. Over time, this benefit became targeted towards middle- and low-income families. In 1993, this benefit was eliminated completely.

The Canada Child Tax Benefit (CCTB) includes two aspects: the CCTB basic benefit and the National Child Benefit Supplement (NCBS). The CCTB provides a tax credit to those who qualify, based on an income test, as low- and middle-income families with children. Currently, up to 80 percent of families receive some portion of the CCTB. Some low-income families are eligible for an additional benefit – the NCBS. An interesting aspect of this federal benefit is that provinces are allowed to claw back the benefit from families on Social Assistance. All provinces take all or part of the benefit away from Social Assistance families, except for Newfoundland and New Brunswick. With the monies taken, the provinces are expected to reinvest in programs to help alleviate child poverty and its effects.

In 2006 the newly elected federal Conservative government announced the Universal Child Care Benefit (UCCB). The UCCB payment is paid on behalf of children under the age of 6 years in instalments of $100 per month per child. It is a taxable benefit (unlike the CCTB, which is a tax credit).

CANADA/QUEBEC PENSION PLAN (C/QPP). The Canada/Quebec Pension Plan (C/QPP) is a national contributory and earnings-related pension program introduced in 1966. It provides benefits in the case of retirement, death, and long-term disability. Employees and employers jointly finance the CPP and QPP, with current contributions supporting current beneficiaries. In this sense, the plan is a pay-as-you-go system. Any funds not paid out are invested for the purpose of creating a larger reserve fund. The plan consists of Retirement, Disability, and Survivor's and Orphan's Death Benefits. Eligibility for this benefit begins at 60 years of age, with maximum benefits paid out after age 65. The pension is earnings-related, so there is a maximum amount for which claimants are eligible. It should also be noted that periods of low earnings, because of caring for young children, illness, unemployment, or retraining, are considered exempt from the calculation. This provision is particularly significant for women, who often take time out of the labour force to provide caregiving.

DISABILITY. Severe and prolonged disability resulting in the inability to participate in the labour force qualifies one for a disability pension. This pension consists of both an earnings-related portion and a basic flat-rate portion, which is unrelated to the earnings one had while employed. Recipients may also qualify for supplemental child benefits if there are dependants. People with disabilities may be eligible to receive benefits through provincial Social Assistance programs, Workers' Compensation, the Canada/Quebec Pension Plan, and, in some cases, through the Veterans Disability Pension. Because there is no reason to assume that persons with disabilities are unable to work, eligibility is based upon a determination of their ability to work and the severity of the disability. Tax credits and exemptions play an important income security role for people with disabilities.

SURVIVOR AND DEATH BENEFITS. In the case of a contributor's death, surviving family members may be eligible for benefits. These benefits are intended to provide support to both the surviving spouse and children.

OLD AGE SECURITY (OAS), GUARANTEED INCOME SUPPLEMENT (GIS), SPOUSE'S ALLOWANCE (SPA), REGISTERED RETIREMENT SAVINGS PLAN (RRSP). Between 1952 and 1989, all elderly Canadians received a universal monthly benefit called Old Age Security (OAS) — an income security program financed and administered by the federal government. Prior to 1952, this benefit was targeted to the very low-income elderly population. Since 1989, the benefit has again become targeted, with only those who qualify because of low or modest income being eligible for benefits. OAS benefits are quite low in relation to the cost of living. Without another source of income upon retirement, such as C/QPP or Registered Retirement Savings Plans (RRSPs), many seniors would still live in poverty.

Human Resources and Social Development Canada

www.hrsdc.gc.ca

For more information on the income security program offered in Canada, see the Human Resources and Social Development Canada website.

To further assist those who do not have access to these programs, there are two related programs, the Guaranteed Income Supplement (GIS) and the Spouse's Allowance (SPA). The SPA is now called the *Allowance*. These benefits supplement the OAS for the low-income elderly. From 1966 until today, the GIS has provided a politically popular add-on to the OAS for those pensioners with little or no other income.

VETERANS DISABILITY PENSION. Income security programs for veterans specifically recognize the service of war veterans. A Veterans Disability Pension is available to those who apply to Veterans Affairs Canada, provided they have a service-related permanent disability resulting from an injury or disease. Income and assets are not considered as eligibility criteria; the benefit is based solely on the extent of the disability and the fact that it is military service-related. As is the case with disability benefits, what constitutes a disability and its extent is not always easily determined or agreed upon by all interested parties.

OCCUPATIONAL BENEFITS. In addition to publicly administered benefits, private benefit plans also exist. These plans may be directly tied to one's workplace and include both retirement plans and other insurance-based benefits such as dental and drug plans, or they may be savings plans with tax-supported provisions, such as RRSPs. While individuals save and invest this money for future use, the government foregoes the collection of tax on this saved money. The lost revenue not collected by government amounts to billions of dollars per year.

Government Spending on Income Security

The expenditure for government-funded income security benefits covers just over one-quarter of government expenditures at all levels of government. Statistics Canada figures for 2002/03 show that the total expenditure for all levels of government on income security programs was $118 billion out of the total government expenditure (all levels) of $468 billion. In their publications, the government refers to this expenditure as a social security expenditure, which equates to what we are calling income security. Compare this figure to the $81.2 billion spent on health, and the $58.1 billion spent on education (see Figure 1.2). Clearly, the various levels of government in Canada spend a considerable amount on income security.

These figures only include direct government spending on pensions and benefits for the elderly, Employment Insurance, Social Assistance, child benefits, and Workers' Compensation. The figure does not include mandatory private social benefits provided by employers, voluntary private social benefits provided by charities, or tax breaks for social purposes.

A more detailed breakdown of statistics shows that the largest expenditure of income security funding went to pensions and benefits

Organisation for Economic Co-operation and Development

www.oecd.org

Founded in 1960, the Organisation for Economic Co-operation and Development (OECD) is a global organization committed to furthering democratic government and the market economy across the globe. Canada is among the thirty member states and is one of the founding members.

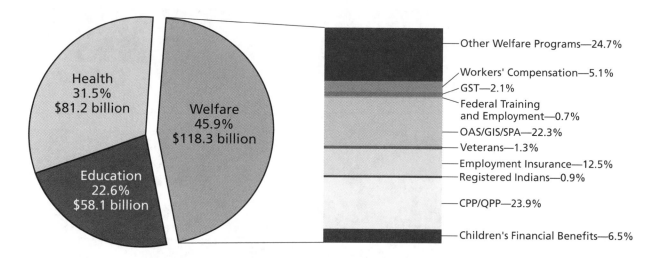

Health
31.5%
$81.2 billion

Welfare
45.9%
$118.3 billion

Education
22.6%
$58.1 billion

Other Welfare Programs—24.7%
Workers' Compensation—5.1%
GST—2.1%
Federal Training
and Employment—0.7%
OAS/GIS/SPA—22.3%
Veterans—1.3%
Employment Insurance—12.5%
Registered Indians—0.9%
CPP/QPP—23.9%
Children's Financial Benefits—6.5%

for the elderly. Canada/Quebec Pension Plan spending totalled $28.3 billion and the Old Age Security expenditure was $26.3 billion, for a total of $54.6 billion, or 45 percent of the total of income security spending (Human Resources and Social Development Canada, 2006). It is interesting to note that the government social security statistics do not include Registered Retirement Savings Plans (RRSPs), which primarily benefit the more well-off. The RRSP is a tax deduction-based program similar to the GST and child benefit tax credit programs, except the latter programs benefit people on low incomes. Our demographic trends show that the elderly population in Canada will increase in the years ahead, which will no doubt increase government income security expenditures.

At first glance, these big numbers may suggest that Canada is a rather generous welfare state, but, in fact, the numbers are much lower than those for most other developed countries. A 1995 ranking of income security expenditures for countries in the Organisation for Economic Co-operation and Development (OECD) places Canada tenth among twelve countries, outranking only the United States and Australia (Adema 1999, 32). We fall behind even more if compared to the more generous social welfare regimes. Our social expenditure of 11.4 percent of gross domestic profit (GDP) hardly compares with the 22.9 percent of GDP for Finland and 21.4 percent of GDP for Denmark and Sweden (Adema 1999, 15).

Total government revenue from taxation for all levels of government was $351 billion in 1996/97. In his book *Social Policy in Canada,* University of Toronto professor Ernie Lightman sheds light on the tax revenue sources of the Canadian government. The data reveals that corporations pay a relatively minimal 7.6 percent share of total taxes. Personal income taxes account for 32 percent of total taxes paid, and sales taxes account for 19.8 percent (2003, 170–71). In short, individual Canadians are picking up a large share of the taxation tab.

**Figure 1.2
Social Security
Expenditures
and Welfare
Expenditures,
Canada, 2002–03**

Source: Human Resources and Social Development Canada. Social Security Statistics Canada and Provinces 1978–79 to 2002–03. *Reproduced with the permission of Her Majesty the Queen in Right of Canada 2006.*

In July of 2003 this small group of anti-Olympic bid protesters set up tents at Victory Square in Vancouver's east side, vowing to stay until there were changes to welfare policy and more social housing.

Caledon Institute of Social Policy

www.caledoninst.org

The Caledon Institute of Social Policy is an independent, non-profit organization that completes research and analysis to help encourage public awareness and debate on the role of social policy in Canadian society.

Revenue Canada reports that Canadians with a taxable income between $30,000 and $40,000 paid 15 percent of their earnings in income tax in 1996. To determine whether this is too high, we can compare the amount of taxes Canadians pay as a percentage of GDP with that of other countries. In Canada, the equivalent of 35.1 percent of GDP is paid in taxes to all levels of government. According to OECD data from 1994, this percentage of GDP is in the low range when compared to other developed countries. The majority of countries have higher tax loads, including Denmark (49.9 percent of GDP), Finland (46.7 percent of GDP), and Norway (41.3 percent of GDP).

Debating Welfare

The amount of taxes we pay is invariably an issue in political debates about income security expenditures and government spending in general. Often, the discussions misleadingly portray us as the most overtaxed population in the industrialized world. Politicians focus on the tax burden to gain favour with concerned Canadians. They imply that Canadians are overtaxed, and argue that a decrease in taxes will make consumers consume more and investors invest more. The economy will grow, and this will result in more jobs and prosperity — or so the argument goes. However, the premise of this argument is questionable. Canadians are not taxed more than residents of most other industrialized countries, and a reduction in taxes does not automatically affect the economy in some magical way.

Another argument is that taxes stifle economic growth. Again, evidence from the OECD shows that Canada's economic growth rate was lower than that of countries with a higher tax load, so there seems to be more to stimulating economic growth than just lowering taxes. Moreover, some studies suggest that public spending on programs such as income security can have a greater impact on economic growth than tax cuts, because part of the tax cut will flow into savings and an increase in imports.

It is important to keep in mind that the role of taxation policy in redistributing wealth and fostering economic growth underlies many social welfare policy debates. However, the currently prevailing view that tax cuts will automatically lead to economic growth, which is held not so much by social work practitioners on the frontlines as by governments, economists, and policymakers, is a highly oversimplified one.

The Beneficiaries of Income Security

As previously mentioned, most Canadians will draw benefits from the income security system at some time in their lives. We can divide the population into groups of 20 percent, or quintiles. According to their total income, we see that, in 1980, the poorest quintile of the population received 46.5 percent of their income from government income security programs. This number increased to 59 percent in 1996. In 1980, the middle quintile of income earners received 6.9 percent of their income from government income security programs, and this was up to 12.8 percent in 1996.

Income security programs are key factors in shaping income distribution in Canada. These cash benefits are an important source of income for at least 60 percent of the population, and have become even more so since 1980. They also provide some benefits for the other 40 percent of the population. Beyond cash benefits, all Canadians benefit from programs involving tax deductions and tax credits.

In other words, all sectors of Canadian society benefit from income security programs, although different programs affect different sectors of society and different income groups. The Child Tax Benefit is spread across all income categories. Social Assistance is directed towards those who live in poverty with little other income, so it is of benefit to the lowest-income earners. Other programs, such as pension plans and Employment Insurance, provide social insurance funded through individual contributions. Since benefit levels are generally proportionate to earnings, middle-income households usually receive more from these programs than do low-income households.

Selective and Universal Programs

When designing income security programs, a key distinction is made as to whether they are universal or selective.

Universal programs are available to everyone in a specific category (such as people aged 65 and over or children), on the same terms

Income Quintiles

Income quintiles are a common way that researchers categorize and analyze income distribution. There are five quintiles, each measuring 20 percent of the population, usually referred to as the lowest, second, third (or middle), fourth, and highest quintiles. Quintiles are used to provide a window into the income levels of people at various levels of society.

Income Security Programs

■ **Universal**: programs available to everyone in a particular category, such as seniors

■ **Selective**: programs limited to those people who are determined to be in need based on a means test or a needs test

and as a right of citizenship. The idea is that all persons are equally eligible to receive program benefits, regardless of income and financial situation.

Selective programs target benefits at those who are found to be in need or eligible, based on a means test (sometimes called an *income test*) or a needs test. A means test determines eligibility based on the income of the prospective recipient. The benefit is reduced according to income level, and there is always a level at which no benefit is granted. A needs test determines eligibility based on the income and the need of the prospective recipient. Eligibility criteria define need, which is then compared to the prospective recipient's life situation.

In the postwar era, universal programs were seen as a way to build national solidarity. More recently, they have been viewed as too expensive and have all but disappeared. The foremost objection to universal programs is their cost. Giving a benefit to everyone, regardless of income, means that even the wealthy get a benefit. On the other side of the issue, universal programs are less expensive to administer, as government workers are not required to scrutinize each person's situation. Selective programs are often viewed as more efficient and less costly, as the government provides benefits only to those most in need. However, identifying eligible recipients using means or needs tests can be administratively complex and costly and take money out of the system that could be directed towards benefits. In some cases, the higher administrative costs are partially avoided by using the tax system as a method of determining eligibility and dispensing benefits. Increasingly, social policy experts are seeing that some selective programs are necessary for tackling poverty and inequality.

Universal program supporters maintain that universal income security promotes a sense of citizenship, solidarity, and nationhood. They claim that selective programs for the needy tend to be punitive and stigmatizing, are more susceptible to cutbacks, and lack necessary mass public support. If services are only for the poor, they are likely to be poor services. Finally, many believe that universal income security programs can fulfill various economic functions, such as economic stabilization, investment in human resources, and development of the labour force.

Over the years, Canada has had a mix of selective and universal programs. Governments have moved away from a focus on citizenship rights and inclusion, to an anti-poverty strategy geared towards promoting attachment to the labour force.

With the recent introduction of the Universal Child Care Benefit (UCCB) Canada now has one officially defined universal income security program. This is a universal benefit, much like the Family Allowance program available from 1944 to 1993. Health care and education are examples of universal social services, but are not strictly defined income security programs. Other programs such as the Canada Child Tax Benefit are approaching universality in their coverage, but still contain an income test.

All of Canada's other income security programs offer selective entitlements. Most have complex selection criteria based on income, work history, or the willingness to find a job. Employment Insurance is based on an insurance principle with eligibility tied to employment and income levels. Everyone within the broad category of "employee" pays into the program, and in this sense it is comprehensive, but a strict set of criteria determines who is eligible to receive benefits, and the level of benefits depends on the earnings and contributions one has made. In recent years, eligibility for Employment Insurance has become more restrictive.

Other selective programs are based solely on how much money one has and whether this meets one's needs. To be eligible for Social Assistance or Ontario Works (as it is referred to in Ontario), one must pass through a means test, proving that income and assets fall below a certain specified maximum level. In provinces with workfare, such as Ontario and Alberta, applicants must also comply with an employment or training placement. The benefit is then calculated by a social worker. Those wishing to access these programs must complete forms and possibly have an interview with a social worker in order to prove that they are in need and do not have the means to meet their needs.

Canadian Federalism and Income Security

Canadian federalism has always influenced income security policy in Canada. Federalism is a system of government in which a number of smaller states (in this case, provinces and territories) join to form a larger political entity while still retaining a measure of political power.

When Canada was formed in 1867, social welfare was largely a private responsibility of the individual, family, and church. The *British North America Act* (1867) said little about jurisdiction over income security or social services. The terms, in fact, did not even exist at the time. This omission caused Canada political misery, as it attempted to determine which level of government had the legislative jurisdiction to fund and deliver income security programs. Political wrangling, informal side-deals between the federal government and the provinces, and non-stop constitutional amendments formed the basis for our income security system. Throughout this process, income security slowly emerged as an area of federal authority. The provinces, on the other hand, largely prevailed in the delivery of social services. The *Constitution Act* of 1982 did not change these arrangements.

The various side-deals and amendments that enabled the federal government to deliver programs such as EI and CPP remained unchanged with the *Constitution Act* of 1982. An important point to note is that, while the provinces have responsibility for social services and income security programs such as social assistance, the federal government has always been responsible for services and programs for "registered Indians," as defined by the *Indian Act*. The provision of social welfare to Aboriginal people is, therefore, somewhat different than for the rest of the population.

Reforms to the Social Welfare System

Reforms to Social Welfare

■ Canada Assistance Plan (CAP), 1966
■ Canada Health and Social Transfer (CHST), 1996
■ Social Union Framework Agreement (SUFA), 1999
■ Canada Health Transfer (CHT) and Canada Social Transfer (CST), 2004

Prior to 1996, federal government contributions to Social Assistance and social services had been funded through the **Canada Assistance Plan (CAP)**, established in 1966. One of the most significant changes to Canada's social welfare system arose with the introduction of the **Canada Health and Social Transfer (CHST)** in 1996. Federal government contributions to health care services and post-secondary education had been funded through Established Programs Financing (EPF) since 1977. Both CAP and EPF were replaced with the CHST. In its first two years, CHST paid the provinces $7 billion less than they would have received under CAP and EPF.

CAP was a 50/50 cost-shared program – the federal government shared 50 percent of the cost of eligible Social Assistance and social services spending with the provinces. With CAP, federal transfers rose as provincial social welfare expenditures increased, so CAP provided an economic stabilizing function. Federal transfers increased in economic recessions, thereby stimulating the economy through social spending. Conversely, CHST is a fixed per-capita or per-person amount based on the population of the province, which means federal transfers are not connected to either the needs of the people or the state of the economy. Many believe that it is the economic stabilizing effect of social spending that has prevented a depression-style drop-off in the Canadian economy since the Great Depression of 1930, and that with CHST this stabilizing effect is greatly reduced.

The national standards, as set out in CAP, are almost absent in CHST. CAP stipulated that the provinces must establish eligibility for Social Assistance based on need as determined by a means test, make services available for all those eligible regardless of when they established residency in the province, establish an appeals procedure, and require no community service or other work (also known as *workfare*) in return for social benefits. The regulations associated with CAP were removed except for the ban on residency requirements, and funding regulations associated with medicare were retained. Many policy analysts fear that, with the removal of national standards, provinces will establish very different benefit levels and eligibility criteria.

Another recent welfare reform is the **Social Union Framework Agreement (SUFA)** of 1999 between the Government of Canada and the provinces and territories, with the exception of Quebec. According to the federal government, the social union initiative is the umbrella under which governments will concentrate their efforts to renew and modernize Canadian social policy. The objective of SUFA is to reform and renew Canada's system of social services and to reassure Canadians that their pan-Canadian social programs are strong and secure. So far, several welfare initiatives have been established under this framework, such as the National Child Benefit, the National Children's Agenda for child care, and employability services for persons with disabilities.

The social union was largely a result of disapproval on the part of provincial governments over the unilateral cancellation of CAP and its replacement with CHST. The provinces wanted to be notified of and participate in formulating any future funding changes. They wanted the federal government to agree that, if it initiated any new social programs, even ones for which it paid the total costs, any province could opt out and take the cash instead with virtually no strings attached. The province would only be required to spend the money in the same general area as the national plan. The provinces also made it clear that they wanted more future influence over the federal government's actions when stepping into provincial jurisdictions.

While most social commentators have applauded SUFA's potential for collaborative positive change, there have been criticisms. Perhaps the most common concerns are the lack of inclusion of Aboriginal governments and the lack of a role for municipal governments. The latter is seen as a serious omission because municipal governments are increasingly responsible for implementing and partially funding SUFA-related social programs.

In 2004, the CHST was divided into the **Canada Health Transfer (CHT)**, in support of health, and the **Canada Social Transfer (CST)**, in support of post-secondary education, Social Assistance, and social services (including early childhood development).

Globalization and Social Welfare

Canada does not exist apart from the rest of the world. This is especially true as the era of globalization increasingly takes hold.

Economic globalization is the growing integration of international markets for goods, services, and finance. It is the latest expression of market liberalism and the latest stage in the development of advanced capitalist economies. This globalization includes the expansion of free trade and investment, the expansion of trade in goods and services between countries, the geographical expansion and increase in power of transnational corporations (TNCs), and the use of agreements between nations and international bodies such as the World Trade Organization (WTO) to protect the rights of TNCs.

Globalization generally means that national and local governments have increasingly less freedom to act on behalf of their citizens, especially on big economic and social questions of the day. In view of this, in the future, income security provisions aimed at creating greater equality of income and opportunity among individuals will likely become

World Trade Organization

www.wto.org

Founded in 1995, the World Trade Organization deals with the rules of trade between nations.

intertwined with the issue of global human rights. Indeed, what might be called global social welfare (a concern with justice, social regulation, social provision, and redistribution between nations) is already a part of the activities of various supranational organizations or international governmental organizations, such as the United Nations. The fight to gain and maintain global human rights in the face of economic globalization is, in many respects, today's epic struggle. Advocacy for equality within and between nations is an integral part of social welfare.

The economic pressures of globalization will continue to have a direct effect on income security policy and practice in this country. In many nations, especially poorer ones, economic restructuring and cutbacks to social programs have been imposed by international agencies, such as the World Bank and the International Monetary Fund, in the form of so-called "structural adjustment" (see Chapter 5 for details). The Canadian government is not immune to these pressures, and adjusts its own income security programs to meet the new economic order and to battle with other nations to be the most "investor friendly."

Unfortunately, the impact of globalization on Canada's income security programs at this point is being felt mainly by the most disadvantaged in our society, and they are also the ones who are least able to fight back. Cutbacks and strict eligibility criteria mean that many are often left without even the bare necessities. The rise in the number of people who are homeless, the growing number of food banks, and the persistence of child poverty are signs of this. But it is not only the very poor that suffer. The middle class is increasingly finding that high-paying jobs are moving offshore to corporate tax havens or export-processing zones. Income security increasingly affects them as well, insofar as welfare cutbacks will mean that ordinary working Canadians may not be able to depend on the traditional social protection offered by such programs as Employment Insurance and Old Age Security.

Conclusion

The multi-faceted area known as social welfare includes two major components: income security (or programs that provide financial or material assistance) and social services (which provide personal and community services to help people improve their well-being). This text deals with income security, but this should not negate the importance of understanding social services and the work that social workers do. (A companion book entitled *Social Work in Canada: An Introduction* examines this other aspect of social welfare.)

Most citizens of Canada will face social or economic difficulties at some point in their lives. In an ideal world, income security allows all citizens to share the risk of events such as poverty, unemployment, disability, and old age. Income security also helps to regulate and stabilize our economic and social system by putting money into the hands of consumers, which in turn stimulates the economy.

Canadians disagree about whether income security programs should be extended and strengthened, or whether they should be reduced. At the root of the debate are political ideologies, economic theories, and basic notions about the role of income security in our society. Meanwhile, as the debate continues, federal, provincial, and municipal governments have continued to make social spending cuts, and our social welfare system has been more closely aligned with those of countries that have eroded their welfare systems to a bare minimum.

This is not the only course open to us. Other countries in Europe, notably Denmark and Finland, have continued to support and even expand their social welfare commitments, and they continue to have good productivity and economic growth. As we look ahead, we must decide which direction we want to take as a society.

Chapter Summary

Key Concepts

- ■ Canada Assistance Plan (CAP)
- ■ Canada Health and Social Transfer (CHST)
- ■ Canada Health Transfer (CHT)
- ■ Canada Social Transfer (CST)
- ■ Demogrants
- ■ Economic globalization
- ■ Federalism
- ■ Income security
- ■ Income supplementation
- ■ Institutional view
- ■ Minimum income
- ■ Non-profit and for-profit welfare agencies
- ■ Private welfare
- ■ Public welfare
- ■ Residual view
- ■ Selective programs
- ■ Social insurance
- ■ Social problem
- ■ Social services
- ■ Social Union Framework Agreement (SUFA)
- ■ Social welfare system
- ■ Structural approach
- ■ Tax expenditures
- ■ Universal programs
- ■ Welfare state

Review Questions

1. What are the main components of the social welfare system in Canada?

2. Define and compare the following sets of terms: (1) "social policy" and "social program," and (2) "public welfare" and "private welfare."

3. What is meant by the "residual" and "institutional" approaches to welfare?

4. What is the division of responsibilities between the federal and provincial governments, and what are the major changes brought about by the CHST of 1996 and the SUFA of 1999?

Exploring Social Welfare

1. As discussed in the chapter, social problems are due to a combination of internal and external factors. Research the social problem often referred to as "addictions" or "substance abuse," and create your own list of internal and external factors. Create a diagram with the internal factors inside a circle and the external factors outside of the circle. Using this diagram as a base, discuss a social policy that might resolve the problem at both levels.

2. Pick one social welfare topic from the thematic list of links on the Canadian Social Research Links website (www.canadiansocialresearch. net). Using the resources listed under the chosen theme, define the issue and discuss the major groups and organizations (including governments) that are working towards a solution. Explore the challenges in resolving the issue.

Websites

Canadian Council on Social Development (CCSD)
www.ccsd.ca

CCSD is one of Canada's most authoritative voices promoting better social and economic security for all Canadians. A national, self-supporting, non-profit organization, the CCSD's main product is information, and its main activity is research. It focuses on concerns such as income security, employment, poverty, child welfare, pensions, and government social policies. Check out the "Links" section for a variety of excellent resources.

Canadian Social Research Links
www.canadiansocialresearch.net

This is Gilles Séguin's virtual resource centre for Canadian social program information. His purpose in creating and maintaining this site is to provide a comprehensive, current, and balanced collection of links to Canadian social program information for those who formulate Canadian social policies and for those who study and critique them.

Social Union
www.socialunion.gc.ca

The federal government's Social Union website has information about child benefits, the National Children's Agenda, and disability benefits.

References

Adema, W. 1999. *Net Social Expenditure: Labour Market and Social Policy, Occasional Papers No. 39.* Paris: Organisation for Economic Co-operation and Development. www.oecd.org.

Health Canada. 2002. *Canada's Aging Population.* Ottawa: Health Canada, Division of Aging and Seniors. www.hc-sc.gc.ca/seniors-aines/pubs/fed_paper/pdfs/fedpager_e.pdf.

Human Resources and Social Development Canada. 2006. *Social Security Statistics Canada and Provinces 1978-79 to 2002-03,* Table 3 *Expenditure Analyses of Social Security Programs, Canada, 1978/1979 to 2002/2003.* www.hrsdc.gc.ca/en/cs/sp/sdc/socpol/tables/table3a.shtml.

Lightman, Ernie. 2003. *Social Policy in Canada.* Don Mills, Ontario: Oxford University Press.

Statistics Canada. 2006. *Income in Canada: 2004.* Ottawa: Statistics Canada. Cat. no. 75-202-XIE. http://dsp-psd.pwgsc.gc.ca/Collection/Statcan/75-202-XIE/75-202-XIE.html.

The History of Social Welfare

Emergence and Decline of the Welfare State

ncome security in Canada was created in the twentieth century and became an important social and economic tool after World War II. Early colonial practices in Canada mirrored the laws and ideas in England and France. This colonial inheritance brought distinctions between the "deserving" and "undeserving" poor and the belief that public assistance should be demeaning and punishing. These are ideas that still find their way into social welfare practices today.

A number of key historic events influenced the path of development of our public income security programs. Among these are confederation, industrialization, two world wars, the Great Depression, urbanization, and the acceptance of Keynesian economic ideas in the post-World War II period.

The charitable practices adopted by the provinces, and later by the nation, were strongly influenced by British law and practice, such as

"People must know the past to understand the present, and to face the future."

— Nellie McClung (1873–1951), Canadian writer and early women's rights activist

This man would have been eligible to beg under the Elizabethan Poor Laws.

the English Poor Laws. Distinctions between the deserving and undeserving poor were imported in colonial practices. The notion of workhouses and indoor relief, which were first established in the English Poor Laws, also found their way into Canadian legislation and into the practices of most provinces. Quebec was the exception because of the singular role that the Catholic Church played in the history of charity in the province.

It is for these reasons that we have to look back into the history of British law and practice to understand the origins of modern Canadian social welfare. In fact, we have to look as far back as the fourteenth century to trace the rise of the system of social and economic organization called modern capitalism.

The Rise of Capitalism

The concept of social welfare developed in England and France when society shifted from feudal relations to capitalism. The shift began in the 1300s and culminated during the Industrial Revolution in the early 1800s. Prior to the fourteenth century, society was based largely on a system of obligations in a primarily agricultural society. This kind of social organization was known as feudalism. Feudalism was both an economic and a social system in which the owner of the property was responsible for the peasants working on the land. The lord was obligated to provide for the peasants' welfare, ensuring that everyone on his land had food and shelter. Peasants, in return, were tied to the land on which they lived and worked. Technically, land in the form of private property did not exist — land was held as a trust from the monarch and ultimately as a divine entrustment. Feudalism in France was similar to the system in England.

With the shift from feudalism, lords were no longer obligated to ensure the economic security of peasants. As the shift advanced, many people found themselves poor and homeless. A long series of legislative acts, such as the Poor Laws, were enacted to address this new economic insecurity. A new economic system came into being known as **capitalism**, an economic and social system based on a monopoly of the ownership of capital rather than the ownership of land, as in the case of feudalism. Ownership of or access to capital (machinery and equipment, private property, and money) provided the new industrialists with the basis for employing workers at a wage.

Several developments were key parts of what became known as the *industrial capitalist system*. First, the factory system began to develop in the late eighteenth century, bringing the production and assembly of products under one roof. The growth of the factory system led to other changes. As factories developed in the towns and cities, potential workers had to go to the cities to find work; it did not come to them. Factory work required the existence of what came to be called *free workers* — workers who were no longer obligated to a feudal lord, but were mobile and free to sell their labour.

New technology also emerged in this period, in the form of complex and expensive mechanical means of production — machines that could do the work of several people. From steam power driven by coal, industry rapidly progressed to the use of other fuels, such as natural gas, electricity, and gasoline, and to other machinery, including electric and gasoline engines.

The period that saw the rise of industrial capitalism was filled with new and rapidly changing ideas. The ideas of individual ownership, portable money, and storable wealth emerged in this period, as did the modern concept of the family. Women were seen as weak and subordinate and responsible for the home; men worked for wages at employment located outside of the home. Childhood began to be seen as a separate part of life requiring special care.

The nineteenth century was also a period of rapid European and American colonization of other peoples and societies. Much of Africa, Asia, and the Americas were divided up between the European powers and the United States in their search to conquer and exploit the earth's natural resources and available labour. Colonization provided the resources on which European industrialization was built. Canada emerged in the last third of the nineteenth century — a country built on first the French and then the English desire for the wealth of the North American lands. This desire to conquer lands and extract wealth had a profound impact on the Aboriginal peoples of Canada, which we will discuss in subsequent sections. It is in the era of industrial capitalism that the modern system of public and private social welfare was born. By the twentieth century, private markets and prices had become the key method of organizing economic and social life in

Canada's Unique Social History

www.socialpolicy.ca/cush

This website offers an overview of social history in Canada, with audio and video clips, as well as links to activities and supplemental readings.

Canada. Most individuals and households were dependent on the sale of their labour, and unemployment became the key insecurity. This new form of social organization created both wealth and financial uncertainty. A gradual transition took place for the unemployed as they moved from dependence on private charity to dependence on publicly organized and administered assistance.

Early English Social Welfare: *The Statute of Labourers*

The plague in Europe between 1347 and 1349 (known as the "Black Death") killed one-third of the British population, and many people survived by living off the land as vagabonds or by begging for food. The deaths and the need to survive by begging resulted in a severe labour shortage – there were not enough workers for the emerging factories, such as those used by the weaving industry. It was the labour shortage that prompted the first piece of English social welfare legislation – the first example of social policy – known as the *Statute of Labourers*.

In attempting to address the problems of begging, vagrancy, and the shortage of labour, the *Statute of Labourers* originated four ideas. It put forth the concepts that:

1. as long as beggars can live from begging they will not work for wages but will remain idle,
2. those who are idle will also become involved in crime and vice,
3. beggars should not be supported so that they are compelled to work for their living, and
4. people who give charity are contributing to the problem and should be prevented from doing so.

Income security today remains linked to the past by many of these same ideas. Many people believe that charity or social programs encourage idleness, and that workers will not work unless they are compelled to do so. At the root is the belief that humans are lazy by nature and will only work if they are forced to work due to lack of food and shelter. It is a belief still held by many Canadians, although the experience of mass unemployment in the 1930s convinced others that, more likely, it is the lack of employment, not the lack of initiative, that accounts for the inactivity of many of the able-bodied unemployed.

The *Statute of Labourers* originated the concepts of the deserving poor and the undeserving poor, notions that persist to this day. Six hundred years ago, the goal was to ensure that those who were able to work did so and to allow relief for those unable to work. The ultimate goal was to ensure a supply of cheap labour. Those physically able to work were forced to work by law. Those not physically able to work were considered the deserving poor or paupers. As the notion developed, it became a problem to identify the deserving poor and control begging. Again, this is an issue that is still relevant.

From these early origins, the present welfare system developed, and several themes contained in the *Statute of Labourers* remain in our current social welfare legislation and practices. First, the notions of idleness and work as expressed in the statute are largely intact. Second, the contradiction between the impetus to help people and the impetus to punish them for not working when society considers that they should is a view that remains with us. Third, just as the statute took the point of view of the employer in search of cheap labour, and not necessarily the point of view of the welfare of the individual, today's legislation places priority on incentives to work.

The dislocation of the old feudal order provided a new freedom to the individual to sell his or her labour, but it also created instability. Many of these instabilities and insecurities have since shifted, but they still exist. The history of modern social welfare has been a history of dealing with such insecurities and instabilities.

The Colonial Inheritance

Denis Guest, the first Canadian social work author to provide a comprehensive history of social security in Canada, traces the origins of modern social security legislation to the late sixteenth century in England and France (1999, 11). Until the sixteenth century, there were few resources for people without land or employment, and people resorted to illegal begging, private charities and foundations, churches, and craft organizations where employed workers helped those less fortunate. But in 1531, an important change took place in the legislation with respect to beggars and vagabonds, and that change has become a fundamental aspect of social welfare in Canada today. The famous Elizabethan Poor Law of 1601 provided the bedrock of the modern welfare states in England, the United States, and Canada.

In sixteenth-century England, during the reign of Henry VIII, begging was legalized for all aged poor and "impotent persons." Herein lies the origin of the contemporary distinction between the able-bodied and the aged and disabled poor. The disabled poor were given permission to beg, and the citizenry were given sanction to provide charity. The able-bodied poor were still compelled to work. The lazy able-bodied were required by that same law to be tied to a cart and whipped until bloody, and then forced to work in the area from which they had most recently come.

The early Poor Laws were passed in 1597 and reiterated in 1601. They contained five basic principles:

- The local government was responsible for the poor.
- The local government was responsible for apprenticing children. Courts could place a child with a local family so he or she could learn a craft.
- A distinction was made between the able-bodied unemployed and those deemed to be unemployable.

Punishment for Illegal Begging

Before the institution of the Elizabethan Poor Law of 1601, King Henry VIII, father of Elizabeth I, licensed begging to ensure that the undeserving poor, or those people who were considered able to work, would not be able to beg. He also instituted punishment for those who were caught begging illegally (or without a licence). An undeserving beggar was to be "tied to the end of a cart naked and beaten with whips . . . till his body be bloody . . . after which [he] shall oath to return to the place he was born . . . and there put himself to labour."

In 1547, Henry's son, King Edward IV, increased the punishment. He decreed that idlers and wanderers would have a "'V' marked with a hot iron in the breast" and be enslaved for two years. On their second offence, they would be marked with an "S" on the forehead and be enslaved forever. Their third offence brought a sentence of death.

■ The construction of hospitals and almshouses for the poor was to be done locally using local or parish funds (there was no national government responsibility at the time).

■ Impoverished parents and children were responsible for each other.

Two key principles were established with the introduction of the Poor Laws. First, the **principle of less eligibility** stipulated that the amount of assistance had to be less than the lowest paying job. This is described in more detail shortly. The less-eligibility principle continues today as a key idea in income security. The second principle dealt with the demarcation between outdoor and indoor relief. **Outdoor relief** was provided in their place of residence to a select category of recipients: the sick, the aged, the disabled, the orphaned, or the widowed — all groups that were seen as deserving of aid. The relief generally came in kind, meaning it was in the form of food, second-hand clothing, or fuel. In contrast, **indoor relief** was provided to able-bodied men who were deemed employable. These recipients were obligated to live in a workhouse and undertake work duties in order to receive assistance. The objective was to limit relief and use work as a form of punishment.

In the seventeenth century, **workhouses** were erected as private enterprises, with the aim of making a profit. Although the houses were officially called *almshouses*, the public referred to them as *workhouses* or *poorhouses*. In order to receive relief, the poor were required to undertake mandatory work in a centralized institution. Early in the nineteenth century, there were more than 4,000 workhouses populated by about 100,000 people, out of a population of 9 million (Webb and Webb 1927, 215). The work was supposed to make the ventures profitable, but little profit was being made, and the workhouses were an economic failure.

The Elizabethan Poor Laws drew a strict distinction between the unemployable and the employable poor. The employable poor were put to work so they could learn discipline. At the same time, the work they did was seen as a punishment for laziness. In addition, the work was meant to train beggars so they would have the skills to pull themselves out of their "disgraceful" state. Women's eligibility was largely dependent on their relationship to a man. Deserted and unmarried mothers were often denied support, while widows were deemed deserving of relief.

The three concepts of work in the Poor Laws were discipline, punishment, and training. When you listen to debates about workfare today, there are clear echoes of the Poor Laws. The key principle is that in a society where people are free to sell their labour, they are not to test this freedom by refusing to do so. This ensures that employers have a steady supply of labour, and it reduces the benefits of being idle or not working.

In the seventeenth century, it was believed that the poor could be trained and employed and the surplus labour could be used for the prosperity of the nation. At the same time, there was a growing belief in the responsibility of the individual for his or her own poverty. Poverty was understood as a defect in character. Because of this, charity to the poor was thought to increase idleness and dependency, and contribute to the growth of pauperization. In other words, the long-standing debate over individual versus social responsibility for poverty was resolved: it was the individual's fault. This is evident in the advent of the workhouse, a place where people were virtually incarcerated for their poverty as a form of punishment.

The Poor Law of 1834

In 1834, a complete review of the existing Poor Law was undertaken in Britain. English poor taxes increased twofold between 1803 and 1818 and threefold by 1832 (Webb and Webb 1927, 1,037). Harsh criticism by the elite of the Poor Law and the rising poor rates led Parliament to appoint an investigative commission. The commission began with a biased agenda, believing that the Poor Law was a path to indolence and vice, and that it needed a relief-rates cut and drastic reforms. The report presented an immense shift in thinking about the poor in English society — rapid population growth, industrialization, and the emergence of a new ethos of individualism culminated in recommendations for fundamental changes to the Poor Law. Several Poor Law reforms were introduced in 1834, which affected social thinking in England and continue to affect social thinking in present-day Canada.

The rather harsh new **Poor Law of 1834** had three main features. First, it forbade outdoor relief for able-bodied persons and their families. The able-bodied (contemporary welfare institutions use the term "employable") were only to receive relief in a workhouse. Second, the new law aimed to dramatically cut relief rates. However, placing the poor in workhouses or poorhouses proved difficult, as it was expensive — costing almost twice as much as outdoor relief. Finally, the new law aimed to tighten administrative rules and clean up what it saw as abuses of the system.

The dominant beliefs at the time were anchored in Reformation Protestant theology. Pauperism was thought to be a result of personal or family defects, and individuals were seen as responsible for their poverty. Idleness, worldly temptations, and moral decline resulted in poverty. At the same time, the Protestant work ethic dictated that people could lift themselves out of poverty through discipline and hard work.

Major Free Market Thinkers

Adam Smith, 1723–90

Smith is one of the early founders of the science of political economy. In 1776 he published *The Wealth of Nations*, a book that laid the theoretical basis for the modern capitalist or "free-market" economy.

Jeremy Bentham, 1748–1832

As a social reformer, Bentham advocated for individual and economic freedom, the rights of women, the end of slavery, and the separation of church and state. He is also the father of utilitarianism, which argues for the greatest good to the greatest number.

Thomas Malthus, 1766–1834

Malthus was a political economist who argued that, if unchecked, the world's population would outgrow its resources, leading to famine and poverty. This theory was very influential, but was later proved false, as it overlooked the inevitable improvements in technology for production, distribution, and infrastructure.

John Graham, Karen Swift, and Roger Delaney, three prominent Canadian social policy professors, outline how the ideas of several key theorists of the day reinforced Poor Law ideas: Thomas Malthus, Adam Smith, and Jeremy Bentham (2003, 29). Malthus believed that if the poor were coddled, they would multiply too quickly and threaten society's limited material wealth. Smith, known as the architect of capitalism, believed that the pursuit of individual well-being and wealth would benefit all people in society. Finally, Bentham's utilitarian beliefs proposed that society should promote the greatest possible good for the greatest number of people. These beliefs tended to leave the poor with minimal benefits.

Key Historic Debates

There have been continuing debates about the best way to accomplish social welfare goals. These historical debates continue to this day.

Deserving versus Undeserving Poor

Anchored in the *Statute of Labourers*, reiterated in the Poor Laws, and reasserted in colonial practices, the notion of deserving and undeserving poor is a fundamental premise of income security in Canada today. The idea is that those physically able to work should be forced to work by law. Those persons who are not physically able to work are considered deserving poor.

Economic Security versus Disincentives to Work

The principle of less eligibility was debate with the rise of income security in Canada. The concept was based on the idea that the amount of assistance had to be less than that of the lowest-paying job. It stipulated that the "able-bodied pauper's" condition be less eligible (that is, less desirable or favourable) than the condition of the independent labourer. Less eligibility meant that the pauper received less by way of relief than the labourer did from wages, and the pauper received it in such a way (in the workhouse, for example) as to make pauperism less respectable than work. The intention was to stigmatize relief.

Bare Subsistence versus Adequate Standard of Living

To determine which applicants should receive bare subsistence levels of income, income security programs use either a means test or a needs test. A means test looks at the income and assets of applicants — the applicants' means of supporting themselves. It is sometimes called an *income test* when only income (not assets) is considered. A needs test involves an assessment of the person's resources and budgetary needs. When this idea was implemented in the Unemployment Insurance program in 1956, it was thought that the new test would provide assistance that would allow for a social minimum or an adequate standard of living.

Fact of Need versus Cause of Need

Early programs assumed that the unemployed were somehow personally defective. This came from the mindset of the early settlers — rugged individualists with a frontier mentality. Receiving relief had the stigma of failure attached to it, and it involved humiliating inquiries into the personal affairs of the receiver. Although it was generally assumed that the person had a defect, the cause of need was important in determining eligibility. The fact-of-need approach establishes that the person is indeed experiencing risk; the person is therefore assumed to be in need and benefits are paid without personal inquiry.

The Rise of Income Security in Canada

We can divide the rise of income security in Canada into four periods. These coincided with major political, social, and economic changes. In each period, certain characteristics predominated and particular programs emerged:

- the colonial period, 1840–67
- the industrialization period, 1868–1940
- the welfare state period, 1941–74
- the era of erosion, 1975–present

Phase 1: The Colonial Period, 1840–67

This period spans from the arrival of settlers from France and England to Confederation and the proclamation of the *British North America Act* of 1867. In this era, social welfare was local and private, and economic security was a matter for the family, not the government. Social welfare consisted of regulations about family, economy, charities, and Aboriginal peoples. Public income security provisions were extremely limited and consisted of poor relief, prisons, and care for neglected children, the insane, and the handicapped. The French settlers introduced quite different responsibilities, assigning the care of the elderly, sick, and orphaned to the Catholic Church.

This period is characterized by:

- local and limited relief for the poor
- social welfare as a private service (little role for government)
- an aversion to taxes
- a reserve system and *Indian Act* imposed on the First Nations

As we have seen, the Poor Laws approached poverty by regulating the poor rather than by addressing the causes of poverty. British Poor Law–style relief was implemented in Nova Scotia (1758) and in New Brunswick (1786). Upper Canada (now Ontario) did not enact a Poor law, but encouraged private charities to assist the poor and destitute. The first statute of Upper Canada in 1792 stated that all British laws would apply, except the Poor Law.

Lower Canada (now Quebec), with its French traditions, relied on charity through the church. Despite these varied laws, the underlying ideas of the Poor Law greatly influenced the basis for relief.

In colonies such as Canada, the pioneering character left the problem of poverty to a "help-thy-neighbour" principle. Vagabonds were often "warned-out" or ordered to leave a community, whipped and confined to jail, or publicly auctioned to the lowest bidder. The townsperson who offered to take care of the person for the lowest amount — to cover food, clothing, and shelter — would win the person's labour (Blyth 1972, 10)

Care of the poor was generally assigned to the smallest unit of government or the parish, and the principles of indoor and outdoor relief persisted in Canada. Indoor relief in Canada involved providing food and shelter in a poorhouse, where poor people would work for assistance. Examples of this include the Toronto-based House of Industry, formed in 1837, and the Halifax workhouse known as Bridewell. To make relief less appealing, applicants underwent a workhouse test; doing unpleasant work was a mandatory step in getting assistance, and it was a way to judge whether or not need was genuine. Outdoor relief was provided by private charities or local governments in the residence of the person requesting aid. This type of assistance became more popular at the end of the 1800s, as it became difficult to find enough unpleasant jobs for people to do in poorhouses. There was also uneasiness about building too many large institutions filled with poor people. With this turn of events, the workhouse test became known as a work test, for which a person would stay at home but would be required to perform jobs such as cutting wood or breaking rock.

As this homeless family indicates (Toronto, 1903), not everyone succeeded in Canada's colonial economy.

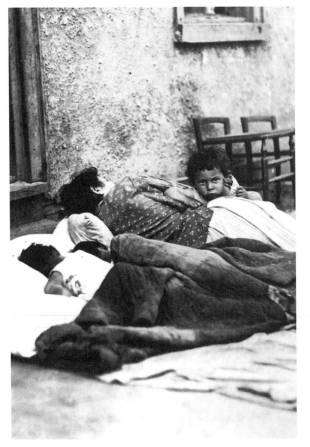

Although income security in Canada was supposedly available to every citizen who met the conditions of the particular program, there has been a double standard when it comes to Aboriginal peoples. What we now know as Canada, of course, was not a vacant place during this period — the ancestors of First Nations, Inuit, and Métis peoples had lived on the continent for thousands of years before the settlers came. Vibrant and diverse communities existed, with developed methods of social and communal caring.

Social welfare was different for Aboriginal peoples, being based more on notions of assimilation and domination (see Chapter 7 for more discussion of this). In this context, a separate system of monetary assistance was established for Aboriginal people, which remained in place until the early 1900s. Any kind of monetary relief for Status Indians was taken from the trust accounts of Indian bands. Relief was granted at the discretion of the local Indian Agent, who was appointed by the federal government. Non-registered Indians, Métis, and Inuit were on the margin of the Indian relief system, although their economic circumstances were similar to, or worse than, those of the "Indians" (Moscovitch and Webster 1995, 212).

Phase 2: The Industrialization Period, 1868–1940

This phase covers the post-Confederation period up until World War II. After 1867, Canada industrialized rapidly. This drew people from small, self-sufficient rural communities into towns and cities. Many people left the security of the family to look for greater economic opportunity, sometimes ending up with an insecure factory job. In terms of government aid for the poor, the pioneer values of independence and individualism still predominated. Poverty was still seen as an individual failure, and relief was minimal and carried a stigma.

This period is characterized by:

- a transition from private to public social welfare
- World War I
- significant protest and social unrest
- rapid industrialization and urbanization
- the economic hardship of the Great Depression
- the emergence of Keynesian economic ideas

Until World War I, income security was minimal and slow to develop. As the country grew and the process of industrialization took hold, new ideas and initiatives were introduced. This generated significant protest and social unrest. Rapid industrialization, the economic hardship of the Great Depression, and the internal migration of Canadians from rural to urban centres not only increased the magnitude of social and economic needs, but transformed these problems from local issues into regional and national issues. At the same time, the cost of income security was becoming too burdensome for local governments and parishes. These factors instigated a shift in responsibility for income security provision and funding from local governments and parishes to provincial and federal governments.

During this phase, the transition from private to public social welfare was important. Social welfare was no longer seen as the private domain of families. A new vision of public social welfare emerged. The perception was that the state had the potential to improve the economy and the lives of people. State policies and programs were used to promote economic stability and even family stability.

The calamity of World War I produced intense changes in Canadian society. Relative to its population, Canada suffered huge losses, and as men returned from the war, they faced poverty and misery. People assumed that, if the government had the resources to finance the Great War, it also had the funds to alleviate suffering. It was also a time of spreading social unrest. The Russian Revolution occurred in 1917 and the European labour movement and their Social Democratic and Communist parties were growing rapidly. Fearing socialism, governments reacted to this unrest by enacting social security programs. The early programs were seen as security for the government against a revolution by men trained in the use of arms (Blyth 1972, 27).

The important provisions passed in this period were:

- *Government Annuities Act*, 1908
- *Workmen's Compensation Act*, Ontario, 1914
- Mothers' Allowances, Manitoba, 1916; Ontario, 1920
- *Old Age Pensions Act*, 1927
- *Unemployment Insurance Act*, 1940

The *Government Annuities Act* of 1908 made it possible for those who had the private funds to prepare for their old age; this was done by making periodical or occasional payments into a government-operated scheme. After retirement, the individual would receive regular payments representing the return of the original funds, plus accumulated interest. Government annuities were offered to the public in order to avoid the institution of a public pension, which was considered unnecessary in Canada by the politicians of the time. Between 1908 and the passage of the federal *Old Age Pensions Act* in 1927, about 7,713 annuities were issued (Guest 1999, 36).

A modern income security system in Canada began to emerge when the Ontario Workmen's Compensation Act was introduced in 1914. Around this time, the size and number of industrial accidents were beginning to increase, and so were the lawsuits against employers. Employers pressed the government for protection from such lawsuits, and the government responded with a Royal Commission and federal legislation in 1914.

The act eliminated workers' rights to sue employers, and instead provided compensation according to a formula. This was the first state social insurance scheme in Canada. The *Workmen's Compensation Act* of Manitoba, enacted in 1916, quickly followed suit. The passage of British Columbia's *Workmen's Compensation Act* happened in 1902, but it did not come into force until 1917, when the Workmen's Compensation Board was created. Legislation eventually followed in all other provinces and territories. The Yukon did not pass legislation until the 1958 Workmen's Compensation Ordinance. Saskatchewan passed legislation in 1930, Prince Edward Island followed in 1949, and Newfoundland in 1950.

Programs of assistance for mothers appeared first in Manitoba in 1916, followed by Saskatchewan in 1917, Alberta in 1919, and British Columbia and Ontario in 1920. The eastern provinces did not follow suit until later: Nova Scotia enacted its relevant legislation in 1930, followed by Quebec in 1937. In New Brunswick, legislation was enacted in 1930, but not implemented until 1944. These early Mothers' Allowance programs were developed in response to pressure from the emerging women's movement, led by the suffragette Nellie McClung. Canadian women obtained the right to vote in federal elections in 1918, and between 1916 (Alberta) and 1940 (Quebec), the provinces extended voting rights to women.

It is not surprising, therefore, that benefit programs for women quickly followed. Mothers' Allowance programs were partly a response to protests by women's organizations against the poverty of families left fatherless by the war, and were also a way of encouraging women to leave the workforce and return to the home after the war. The informal social security system of rural Canada had been disrupted by industrialization, as was the family unit, and this increased the needs of one-parent families for assistance. During World War I, the federal government extended pensions to the widows and children of soldiers who gave their lives. There was an obvious difference in the treatment of war widows and of single-parent women who were left alone for other reasons.

After the war, there was an increased concern for children. The large loss of life in the war, the loss of life during the postwar influenza epidemic, and the extension of the vote to women increased support for Mothers' Allowance programs elsewhere in the country. By 1920, five provinces had instituted Mothers' Allowance.

The *Old Age Pensions Act* of 1927 was the first major intervention by the federal government in the area of income security. Recommendations for old age pensions were contained in several postwar reports on labour unrest in Canada. In the 1921 federal election, the first three labour members of Parliament (MPs) were elected to the House of Commons. These MPs, who became known as the "Ginger Group," included J.S. Woodsworth, a former Methodist minister and social worker. Later, Woodsworth was one of the founders and the first leader of the Co-operative Commonwealth Federation (CCF), the forerunner of today's New Democratic Party. In a 1926 electoral deadlock, Woodsworth traded the support of the CCF to Mackenzie King and the Liberal Party in return for the passage of the Old Age Pensions legislation. The Liberal Party under King was elected to government and fulfilled its promise, passing the act.

The *Old Age Pensions Act* of 1927 was the first foray by the federal government into the provision of a minimum income program, but it depended on the participation of the individual provinces. The act provided federal funds to those provinces that were prepared to institute a public pension for Canadian citizens over the age of 70,

Pre-Depression Programs

■ **Government annuities**: an early example of a government retirement savings program

■ **Workmen's Compensation acts**: provided standardized compensation for injured workers, while taking away their right to sue employers

■ **Mothers' Allowances**: the first allowances were developed to deal with war widows and to encourage women to leave the workforce after World War I

■ *Old Age Pensions Act*: the first major income security program in Canada

WOMEN'S RIGHT TO VOTE

Canadian women's suffrage, or the right to vote, is less than one hundred years old, although the late 1800s saw many extensions of suffrage to women in various colonies, states, and territories in the western world. Women in Canada first gained the right to vote during World War I; those women with male family members fighting in Europe were extended the right to vote, to help pass the *Conscription Act*. But after the war, Canada, extended the right to all women.

Despite being able to vote, women in Canada were still not considered persons under the law until the "Famous Five" — Emily Murphy, Nellie McClung, Irene Parlby, Louise McKinney, and Henrietta Muir Edwards — challenged the status quo. Several of these prominent women held powerful positions in Canadian society — magistrates and members of legislative assemblies — but their authority was challenged because they were not considered persons. The Supreme Court of Canada decided that the word "person" in the *British North America Act* did not include women. But the Famous Five took their fight to the Privy Council in England, which at the time, was Canada's highest court. They won their case at the Privy Council, and they won the right for women to serve in the Senate and other public offices.

When Could Women Vote?

1916	Manitoba
1916	Saskatchewan
1916	Alberta
1917	British Columbia
1917	Ontario
1918	Nova Scotia
1918	**Canada**
1919	New Brunswick
1919	Yukon
1922	Prince Edward Island
1925	Newfoundland and Labrador
1940	Quebec
1951	Northwest Territories

and the provinces were obligated to introduce means testing to limit the availability of the pension to the poorest of the elderly. By the 1930s, only a few provinces were using the new federal pension plan. In 1937, the Old Age Pensions were extended to blind persons aged 40 and over. The 1927 act excluded Indians and Inuit, "but was available to the Métis" (Scott 1994, 18). The first Unemployment Insurance Act, passed in 1940, also excluded most Aboriginal peoples from eligibility from its benefits (Scott 1994, 20). The *Old Age Pensions Act* remained in place until 1952.

In 1929, the American stock market crashed, and this, along with other economic problems, led to a complete collapse of economies across the world, including in Canada. The Great Depression was a time of economic stagnation, and many people in this country lived in great poverty. The Western provinces were also affected by a wide-spread drought on the Prairies, which destroyed the wheat crop.

In 1932, the Conservative government of R.B. Bennett introduced a *Relief Act* to assist the provinces with relief funding. On the advice of the military, unemployment relief camps were introduced to provide work and shelter for single, unemployed, and homeless men. The mandatory work of clearing bush, building roads, planting trees, and building government buildings was done for 20 cents a day under the supervision of the Department of National Defence. The camps were formed in lieu of a job creation program. The Depression peaked, and Bennett's government was seen as indecisive and ineffectual.

The government resisted doing anything else, and fully expected that natural forces would correct the market. Meanwhile, in the United States, Roosevelt's New Deal was putting people to work in public works projects. Taking a cue from this and the Canadian social unrest, Prime Minister Bennett went on the radio in January of 1935 and told Canadians he would bring in his own New Deal, which would include Unemployment Insurance.

Social unrest and political action precipitated the government's increased openness to social programs. Two related events of social unrest, the "On to Ottawa Trek" and the "Regina Riot," motivated Bennett to act. In 1935 thousands of angry relief camp workers in Vancouver went on strike and decided to ride freight trains from British Columbia to Ottawa to peacefully protest their treatment.

The trek was prompted by the poverty, dismal working conditions, and poor benefits in the unemployment relief camps — and by the federal government's inaction in getting people back to work. Believing that the men should be grateful for any assistance at all, the government did not react to their demands. Bennett ordered the RCMP to stop the trekkers in Regina, claiming that they were a threat

Unemployed workers in the west joined the "On to Ottawa Trek" in June 1935; the trains were stopped in Regina.

THE NEW DEAL IN THE UNITED STATES

Just like in Canada, the United States underwent major demographic changes in the late 1800s and early 1900s: industrialization, urbanization, the disappearance of the extended family network, and a marked increase in life expectancy. When the stock market crashed in 1929, leading to the Great Depression of the 1930s, Americans lost faith in their newly elected president, Herbert Hoover.

Franklin D. Roosevelt was elected president in 1932. Roosevelt's response to the Depression was called the New Deal: a series of programs between 1933 and 1937 with the goal of relief, recovery, and reform of the United States economy. The programs were extensive and were often called "alphabet soup" because of the acronyms by which they were known. The programs included the Federal Emergency Relief Administration (FERA), which provided funds to depleting local relief agencies; the Civil Works Administration (CWA), which employed men to build or repair roads and airports; the Civilian Conservation Corps (CCC), which put 2.5 million unmarried men to work maintaining and restoring forests, beaches, and parks; and the Works Progress Administration (WPA), which put 8 million Americans to work in several different areas, including an arts program designed to employ entertainers and provide inexpensive entertainment to the public. The emphasis of Roosevelt's New Deal was to put Americans back to work, and it had the added side effect of developing infrastructure across the country.

In 1935 Roosevelt introduced the *Social Security Act*, which in addition to several provisions for general welfare, created a social insurance program designed to pay retired workers aged 65 or older a continuing income after retirement in the form of a single, lump-sum payment. Social Security continues today in the United States.

to the government, and several people were arrested. This prompted the Regina Riot of July 1, 1935. One man was killed and hundreds were injured. Eventually, the RCMP took control of the situation and trekkers were provided with transportation back west. The camps were turned over to provincial control, and conditions improved significantly.

The culmination of all of these factors led Prime Minister Bennett to introduce the 1935 *Employment and Social Insurance Act*. Canadian federalism and the division of powers specified in the *British North America Act* hampered its passing — it was struck down by the courts, which found that only the provinces could enact such legislation according to the rules of the *British North America Act*. Therefore, at the end of the 1930s, the new Liberal government formed the Royal Commission of Dominion-Provincial Relations to establish the roles of the federal and provincial governments. The commission concluded that the provincial government should retain responsibility for unemployed people who were unemployable – the "deserving poor" – such as seniors, single parents, and the disabled, and that the federal government should take responsibility for the employable or "non-deserving poor." The commission established the agenda for postwar discussions on social reform.

Under Mackenzie King, the Liberals reintroduced an amendment to the *British North America Act* that allowed the passage of a new federal Unemployment Insurance bill with a national scope. By 1940, Unemployment Insurance was finally legislated. With the *Unemployment Insurance Act* Canada became the last industrialized country to adopt a contributory-based unemployment insurance program.

In 1945, the federal government made a series of proposals to the provinces for a more comprehensive approach to social welfare, based on federally funded social programs. However, one condition stipulated that the federal government would have exclusive use of the income tax and the corporate tax. The provinces refused, and social welfare change came to a halt for a few years. Federal-provincial debates about jurisdiction continued to hamper social welfare progress, and these still persist today.

Reinforcing these changes was the emergence of Keynesian economic ideas. The British economist John Maynard Keynes provided an economic rationale to the government's intervention in the economy. As outlined in Chapter 3, Keynes's theory provided the foundation for demand-management through government spending and other fiscal policies. Fiscal policy continues to play a major role in the government's efforts to manage the ups and downs of the Canadian economy.

The Great Depression was an important event in the rise of income security and social services in Canada. It was so financially devastating that people were shocked into changing long-held beliefs about why people are poor and what the state should do to help. People began to see that poverty and unemployment were not the result of individual inadequacy or laziness, but were common and insurable threats to everyone's livelihood. Public perception of the poor began to shift. Massive numbers of people were unemployed, and Canadians began to see that this could not possibly be due to individual fault, but had more to do with the operation of the economy. People started to recognize that social forces and government policy affected unemployment and impoverishment. The notion that help for the poor should be a local or family responsibility was replaced with the idea that the government should be responsible for providing relief to the unemployed.

Depression-Era Programs

■ *Relief Act,* **1932**: provided assistance to the provinces for relief funding

■ *Employment and Social Insurance Act,* **1935**: introduced by Bennett, but struck down for constitutional reasons

■ *Unemployment Insurance Act,* **1940**: introduced by Mackenzie King, after his government passed an amendment to the *British North America Act*

Canada and World Events	Social Welfare
1940s War-related state controls Crown corporations End of World War II High labour unrest International revolutions Emergence of Keynesian economic ideas Beginning of transition to public social welfare Economic hardship of Great Depression remembered Urbanization and rapid industrialization	Universal social legislation *Unemployment Insurance Act* (1940) Marsh Report (1943) Family Allowance (1944) Veterans benefits (1944) White paper on employment (1945) Hospital construction Organization of provincial departments of social services End of federal grants for relief
1950s Prosperity High employment Cold War purges of left Low level of unrest Liberal government Acceptance of government intervention	Expanded social programs Old Age Pension for all at age 70 (1952) Means-tested pension at age 65 (1952) *Disabled Persons Act* (1955) *Unemployment Assistance Act* (1956) Allowances for blind disabled Hospital care coverage (1957)

Figure 2.1: Key Events and the Implications for Social Welfare in the 1940s and 1950s

Phase 3: The Welfare State Period, 1941–74

This was a period of rapid development of social welfare in Canada. Dennis Guest, author of *The Emergence of Social Security in Canada*, believes that World War II was the catalyst for social security advancement (1999, 103). The role of government in society had changed as a result of the Depression and the war, and Keynesian economic ideas had been firmly established. In terms of protecting the security of citizens, the government was seen as playing an important role in society and the economy. The urgencies of war had placed large responsibilities and fiscal powers with the federal government, and this was carried into the area of income security.

This period was characterized by:

- a post-World War II desire for security
- rapid industrialization and urbanization
- a remembrance of the lessons of the Depression
- an acceptance of government intervention
- an acceptance of Keynesian economics
- a variety of landmark income security programs and legislation
- the 1966 Canada Assistance Plan (CAP)
- a growth of the socialist and reform movement (CCF)

Most importantly, World War II had a profound impact on the role of the federal government and the Canadian acceptance of deep government involvement in economic and social affairs. During the war, the government oversaw labour activities and gained far-reaching economic powers. It became the largest employer of labour and used significant taxation and spending powers to aid the war effort. Most

Canadians viewed the government in a positive way — as an efficient and positive force in society. This perception, in association with the Keynesian theory of government intervention in regulating markets and social spending, provided the foundation for the welfare state. In fact, the term *welfare state* was coined to denote the shift from a "warfare state," concerned primarily with World War II, to a welfare state, concerned with advancing the welfare of its citizens. Canadians saw the government's deep involvement in economic and social affairs merely as a shift in government priorities.

By 1971, social programs had reached a point where they were touching the lives of most Canadians. Between 1930 and 1970, the change was nothing less than revolutionary. Unfortunately, by the mid-1970s many changes affected Canada — inflation and unemployment grew, oil prices went up, and the global economy changed. This began a downward spiral in terms of government revenues and expenditures. As more people became unemployed, more people turned to Unemployment Insurance. This drove up the cost of insurance, yet fewer employed people were supporting the program. This was a very active period of social welfare legislation and reform. The following is a brief summary of some of the major events during the period and the important social services and income security programs that were legislated.

The Beverage Report came out of Britain in 1943, the same year as the subsequent Canadian Marsh Report. These reports established the baseline for the rapid expansion of social welfare. Sir William Beverage wrote a comprehensive report on postwar social security for Britain. It included comprehensive health insurance and income security. This crucial report was followed by a Canadian equivalent written by Dr. Leonard Marsh. The *Report on Social Security for Canada* became commonly known as the Marsh Report and received extensive media attention. In it, Marsh detailed the need for comprehensive and universal social welfare programs. His report sparked debate over universal income security benefits versus targeted income security benefits.

Many consider the Marsh Report to be the most important report in the history of the Canadian welfare state. Marsh suggested that the country should establish a "social minimum" — a standard aimed at protecting the disadvantaged through policies such as social insurance and children's allowances. At first, the study did not attract much attention from policy-makers, but, by 1966, most of Marsh's recommendations had become law. His work served as the blueprint for the modern Canadian social security system. Marsh himself viewed his report as the natural outgrowth of the decade of social studies he had directed at McGill University.

In the report, Marsh established the concept of a desirable living minimum income. He went on to outline proposals that meet the principal types of contingencies that characterize industrial society,

Social Security Reports

■ **Beverage Report, 1943**: British report on social security, named for its author, Sir William Beverage

■ **Marsh Report, 1943**: Canadian equivalent to the Beverage Report, named for author Dr. Leonard Marsh

Even in the prosperous post-war economy, many Canadians, like these children in Montreal (c. 1949), required social assistance.

coining the three categories of contingencies, which are still used today to describe social welfare. He proposed a two-pronged system of social insurance to cover both employment risks and universal risks: the first covered wage-earners and the second covered all persons for old age, disability, and death. He also proposed children's allowances and health insurance. Finally, he emphasized the importance of training and placement programs to help people, especially youth, prepare for employment.

The report made headline news as the media spoke about the proposed social spending of billions of dollars. People sensed the beginning of a new era in which they would have medical insurance coverage and protection from unemployment. These were new ideas to most people, and these ideas sparked debate about what this would mean for Canadian society. While some stressed the positive impacts on citizenship and responsibility for one another, others spoke of the onset of communism. (Some social workers at the time, such as Charlotte Whitton, spoke negatively about the idea of social insurance. She advocated for social assistance, in which trained social workers supervised and counselled people needing assistance.)

By 1966 the Indian relief system had collapsed and was replaced with access to mainstream social welfare programs (Moscovitch and Webster 1995). This turnaround was the result of a recognition by the government that it was failing in attempts to assimilate or to eradicate the Métis, the Inuit, and the First Nations. To facilitate this change, several federal acts related to income security were changed, and the Canada Assistance Plan was established.

This era marked the arrival and development of many of Canada's social welfare programs. These programs include:

- the *Family Allowance Act*, 1944
- the *Old Age Security Act*, 1951
- the *Old Age Assistance Act*, 1951
- the *Unemployment Assistance Act*, 1956
- the Canada/Quebec Pension Plan, 1965
- the Canada Assistance Plan, 1966
- the *Unemployment Insurance Act*, 1971

We will discuss the form and content of these programs in later chapters, but from simply looking through this list of social welfare programs, you can see how important this period was in establishing the essentials of the Canadian welfare state. Total expenditures on social welfare, health, and education grew from 4 percent of gross domestic product (GDP) in 1946 to 15 percent of GDP by 1976 (Moscovitch and Albert 1987, 31).

The first piece of government legislation for this period was the *Family Allowance Act* of 1944. It was the first universal income security program in Canada, and when it was introduced, considerable debate took place over the feasibility of a universal program. The goals of this important piece of legislation were to protect the up-and-coming generation and to maintain purchasing power. By giving money to mothers of children, it was thought that the money would be spent, and this would subsequently stimulate the postwar economy.

Following an amendment to the British North America Act to permit the federal government to operate a pension plan, the *Old Age Security Act* (OAS) of 1951 provided a universal pension, or demogrant of $40 per month to everyone, beginning at the age of 70. Pension payments began in 1952 and were taxable.

At the same time, the *Old Age Assistance Act* of 1951 provided a means-tested amount of $50 per month for those aged 65 to 69. This program was cost-shared 50-50 by the federal and provincial governments but was administered by provincial welfare departments who used a needs test to determine eligibility. It was viewed by the elderly as a personally invasive and stigmatizing program. The *Unemployment Insurance Act* of 1955 reformed the previous Unemployment Insurance program.

The Canada/Quebec Pension Plan of 1965 provided a wage-related supplement to OAS and was the first program to be indexed to inflation, or the cost of living allowance (COLA). It provided wide coverage and advanced the concept of a social minimum.

In 1966 the Canada Assistance Plan (CAP) was introduced (see Appendix B). CAP was instrumental in standardizing and funding Social Assistance nationwide, and was in effect between 1966 and 1996. This program was the consolidation of federal-provincial programs based on means tests or needs tests. Half the costs of all shareable items were assumed by the federal government, provided a needs test was given. Assistance was possible for the working poor, and the public was given the right to appeal decisions. It also forbade the use of workfare in Social Assistance.

The historic debate concerning "fact of need" versus "cause of need" peaked when CAP was introduced. The Canada Assistance Plan was intended to meet needs regardless of the cause for need. This was a strong effort to reverse the long-held belief that those in need were somehow defective. Others debated this notion, stating that cause of need was necessary to prevent the undeserving from obtaining assistance. This fact-of-need concept, combined with a needs-assessment procedure, was first introduced with the *Unemployment Assistance Act* in 1956.

Canada and World Events	Social Welfare
1960s Grassroots unrest — growth of anti-poverty, Indian, labour, student, and peace organizations Founding of NDP Quebec separatism Economic growth and employment	*General Welfare Assistance Act* (Ontario) (1960) *National Housing Act* (1964) Canada/Quebec Pension Plan (1965) Canada Assistance Plan (1966) *Medicare Act* (1968)
1970s Fiscal crisis of state Conservative business ideas prominent Shift to residual concept of social welfare Rise of U.S. influence in Canada Rise of women's movement Rise in women's employment	Cutbacks begin in health, education, and welfare programs More law and order Rise of contracting out NGOs funding militant groups *Unemployment Insurance Act* (1971) Established Program Financing (EPF) legislation to finance education and health

Figure 2.2: Key Events and the Implications for Social Welfare in the 1960s and 1970s

CAP was the basis for cost-sharing, not only for income security programs, but also for a range of social services and programs including health services, children's services, Social Assistance, disability allowances, old-age assistance, services for the elderly, and institutional care. This program was the cornerstone of Canada's social service funding until 1996, when it was replaced with the Canada Health and Social Transfer (CHST). The CHST is discussed in the next section.

The 1969 Senate Committee on Poverty discovered high poverty levels and recommended an income supplementation scheme for the working poor, but the plan was rejected by the provinces as being too costly. In 1970 the federal government undertook a major review of income security programs, which resulted in two important reports: the White Paper entitled *Income Security for Canadians,* and the White Paper on Unemployment Insurance. The former report called for greater emphasis on anti-poverty measures and stated that resources should be concentrated on those with the lowest incomes. In other words, it recommended that selective benefits replace universal programs. The debate between universal and targeted programs was re-ignited. The reports also advocated for benefits that provide an adequate standard of living, rather than poverty- or subsistence-level benefits. For the first time, significant government reports recommended benefit levels that addressed poverty and provided adequate standards of living. This ignited heated debate about the role of income security programs in Canadian society.

These reports were followed by program expansions and increases in old age benefits and Unemployment Insurance. The *Unemployment Insurance Act* of 1971 extended Unemployment Insurance to cover more people and eased qualifying conditions. Benefits were raised to two-thirds of wages. These income security program changes created benefits that neared the level of an adequate standard of living.

Phase 4: The Era of Erosion, 1975–Present

The current period has seen a great decrease in the scope and influence of social welfare legislation. Many of the income security programs implemented in the previous phases have been eroded or terminated altogether. Expenditures on income security programs have been cut, and greater restrictions have been placed on eligibility. Unemployment has been placed lower on the list of priorities, and old debates about issues such as fraud and workfare have been resurrected.

This period is characterized by:

- a shift away from the institutional conception of social welfare
- increases in economic integration or globalization
- cuts to income security expenditures
- greater restrictions built into the design of social welfare programs
- an emphasis on work incentives
- the Canada Health and Social Transfer (CHST)
- an expansion of corporate tax deductions
- the growth of public debt
- the implementation of monetarist policies

Monetarist economics, representing a major move away from post-war Keynesian economic policies, took hold during this period. The 1980s began with double-digit inflation and the most severe economic recession (1981–83) since the Depression. Rising oil prices and growing unemployment created a situation where the economy experienced both high rates of unemployment and inflation. This led to a questioning of Keynesian economic principles and put substantial pressure on government expenditures. In order to return to economic prosperity, the preferred solutions included decreasing government expenditures and controlling inflation. The debate between universal and targeted benefits re-emerged, and targeting benefits was seen as a way of cutting costs.

This period also began with rapid increases in international economic integration, also known as *economic globalization*. Large corporations expanded their access to global markets, and new international institutions and agreements were forged to facilitate the expansion, such as the World Trade Organization (WTO) and the North American Free Trade Agreement (NAFTA). Each new agreement limited the Canadian government's ability to address the income security needs of Canadians, and some have referred to this as an era of the post-sovereign state. The focus of the era has been on free trade and expanding market forces, and on a retrenchment of public spending and programs. Debates about income security shifted from helping people face insecurities in a market economy, to debating the effects on the

Canada and World Events	Social Welfare
1980s Monetarist economics Deepening poverty Globalization on the rise Conservative policies U.S. dominance in Canada Cold War tensions Third World unrest Waves of refugees Rise in militancy and popular coalitions	Major contracting out, cutbacks, workfare Period of cost control for social programs with significant spending cutbacks Increases in punitive programs Women's issues (daycare, reproductive choice, pay equity, violence) discussed but little concrete progress Rise of food banks, role of charities increases Rise of free trade (NAFTA) *Young Offenders Act* (1984)
1990s Economic stabilization Rising militancy of First Nations, women, visible minorities, disabled, etc. *Agenda: Jobs and Growth* report (1994) Environmental movement strong Polarization of rich and poor Popular demands for real social justice Rising labour militancy at grassroots Rise of information and communications technology (ICT) and knowledge-based economy Labour market restructuring	Attempts to dismantle welfare state, and to transfer costs to provinces, cities CHST and Social Union Framework Agreement (SUFA) Canada Child Tax Benefit and National Child Benefit (1998) Regressive taxes The new *Employment Insurance Act* (1995) Cuts in corporate taxes Free trade Privatization of universal programs Cuts to women's, immigrants', and Native rights and programs Move to workfare and privatization (residual model)

Figure 2.3: Key Events and the Implications for Social Welfare in the 1980s and 1990s

economy and international competitiveness. This era saw the beginning of a harmonization of welfare states around the world, and the Canadian government quickly cut back on social programs in what its opponents referred to as a "race to the bottom."

After the election of Brain Mulroney's Progressive Conservative government in 1984, the way was paved for deep cuts to income security programs in Canada. This government was committed to reducing the deficit, shrinking the public sector, and expanding the private sector. Several reports were commissioned, including the Royal Commission on Economic Development, the Forget Commission on Unemployment Insurance, and the Neilson Task Force Report on the Canada Assistance Plan. The government identified four key problems with the income security system: (1) spending was too high, (2) programs were not targeted to those most in need, (3) public social benefits were becoming a disincentive to work, and (4) public benefits were becoming a substitute for earned income.

The federal Liberals under Jean Chrétien were expected to expand the social agenda. They began by commissioning Lloyd Axworthy to examine social security. His 1994 Green Paper entitled *Improving Social Security in Canada* provided recommendations in a variety of areas, but resulted in the termination of the Canada Assistance Plan and a cut of over $6 billion in annual transfers to the provinces for social programs.

A key piece of federal legislation introduced during this period was the Canada Health and Social Transfer (CHST). The CHST, which is provided to provinces and territories through both cash and tax transfers, is a block fund providing support for health care, post-secondary education, Social Assistance, and social services, including early childhood development. In the last year of the CHST (2003), the CHST provided $35.7 billion. The CHST was created by rolling together the former federal transfers under the Established Programs Financing (EPF) and the Canada Assistance Plan (CAP). The CHST had far-reaching effects on income security in Canada – it fundamentally changed the social safety net and the role of the federal government in the social policy field. Some believe that the CHST diminished the power of the federal government in order to ensure that social programs continued, while others believed it was necessary to put the financial house in order.

The most recent government legislation affecting income security is the Social Union Framework Agreement (SUFA) of 1999. The agreement was based upon mutual respect between different orders of government and their willingness to work more closely together. The agreement aimed to smooth out relations after the fallout from the unilateral discontinuation of CAP and the implementation of the CHST. The SUFA refers to a range of programs such as medicare, social services, and education. It also addresses how these programs are funded, administered, and delivered. It remains to be seen how this new agreement will affect Social Assistance.

In 2004 the CHST was restructured to create a separate Canada Health Transfer (CHT) and a Canada Social Transfer (CST) (see Appendix A). The objective of the change, as stated by the federal government, was to increase transparency and accountability. Critics believed that the move would enable the federal government to take credit for increases in funding to popular health care programs while allowing social programs such as welfare to remain underfunded. The CHT and CST are made up of both cash transfers and tax transfers. In 2006/07 the CHT cash and tax transfers were $32.9 billion, of which $20.1 billion in cash and $12.7 billion in tax transfers and CST cash and tax transfers were $16.3 billion, of which $8.5 billion in cash and $7.8 billion in tax transfers.

The particular shape and character of Canada's welfare state stems from an important shift in the concept of social welfare (see Chapter 1, p. 2). The residual view or concept, which shaped policy until the 1940s, upheld the Protestant work ethic and relied on private relief agencies. The residual concept gave way to the institutional view or concept, which followed the Keynesian means of integrating income security into the fabric of the economy. The era of erosion

Social Welfare Legislation

■ **Canada Social Transfer and Canada Health Transfer (CST/CHT)**: CST is a $16.3 billion (2006/07) federal block transfer to provinces and territories in support of post-secondary education, social assistance and social services, including early childhood development and early learning and childcare; CHT is a $33 billion (2006/07) transfer for healthcare

■ **Social Union Framework Agreement (SUFA)**: intended to smooth out relations between levels of government, this agreement determines how programs such as medicare, social services, and education are to be funded, administered, and delivered

A BRIEF HISTORY OF THE HEALTH AND SOCIAL TRANSFERS

1966	The Canada Assistance Plan (CAP) was introduced by the federal government, creating a cost-sharing arrangement with the provinces for Social Assistance programs. Conditions were attached to federal funding.
1977	The federal government introduced Established Programs Financing (EPF) to fund provincial educational programs.
1982	It was announced that a GNP per capita escalator would be applied to the total EPF, including both cash transfers and transfer tax points, rather than to just EPF cash.
1983	The post-secondary education portion of EPF was limited to 6 percent and 5 percent growth for 1983/84 and 1984/85 under the "6&5" anti-inflation program.
1984	The federal government enacted the *Canada Health Act* (CHA). Funding to provinces was conditional on respecting the five criteria of the CHA (universality, accessibility, portability, comprehensiveness, and public administration), and provisions for withholding were introduced.
1995	Effective in 1996, EPF and CAP programs were to be replaced by a Canada Health and Social Transfer (CHST) block fund. For 1995/96, EPF growth was set at GNP — 3 percent, and CAP was frozen at 1994/95 levels for all provinces. CHST was set at $26.9 billion for 1996/97 and $25.1 billion for 1997/98. CHST for 1996/97 was to be allocated among provinces in the same proportion as combined EPF and CAP entitlements for 1995/96.
1996	The federal government announced a five-year CHST funding arrangement (1998/99 to 2002/03) and provided a cash floor of $11 billion per year. For 1996/97 and 1997/98, total CHST funding was maintained at $26.9 billion and $25.1 billion respectively. Thereafter the transfer was set to grow at GDP — 2 percent, GDP — 1.5 percent, and GDP — 1 percent for the next three years.
1998	CHST legislation put in place a $12.5 billion cash floor beginning in 1997/98 and extending to 2002/03, meaning that federal funding could not go below that amount.
1999	The federal government announced increased CHST funding of $11.5 billion over five years, targeted only for health care.
2000	Provincial first ministers agreed on a plan for renewing health care and investing in early childhood development. The federal government committed to invest $21.1 billion of additional CHST cash, including $2.2 billion for early childhood development over five years.
2003	Early learning and child care (ELCC) was a priority, with $900 million over five years in increased federal support announced.
2004	The CHST was separated into the Canada Health Transfer (CHT) and the Canadian Social Transfer (CST)

Source: Based on Department of Finance Canada. 2006. A brief history of the health and social transfers. Federal Transfers to Provinces and Territories. www.fin.gc.ca/FEDPROV/hise.html (accessed Jan. 8, 2007).

began when social policy discussions became dominated by the notion that governments must cut back spending and rein in the debt.
Income security programs were seen as being too generous and therefore affecting people's incentive to take employment, especially at the
low end of the pay scale.

Conclusion

The ideas underlying Canada's income security programs have their
roots in the Poor Laws and the colonial period. The Elizabethan Poor
Laws were enacted to address the large numbers of desperately poor,
and to control workers entering the wage-based labour market. The
laws also gave rise to the conceptions of the deserving and undeserving poor. Those considered deserving were people who were very old,
sick, or severely disabled. Able-bodied poor were thought to be capable of working and therefore undeserving of assistance. Canadian
poor relief and subsequent income security programs were strongly
influenced by the Poor Laws.

The emergence of our current system breaks down into four periods:
the colonial period, 1840–67; the industrialization period, 1868–1940;
the welfare state period, 1941–74; and the era of erosion, 1975–present.
The colonial period is characterized by limited and local charity, and
the provision of outdoor and indoor relief to those seen as deserving.
The industrial period saw a gradual shift from private to public social
welfare, the emergence of Keynesian ideas, and a shift from blame-
oriented beliefs to socially oriented beliefs (in order to explain post-
Depression poverty). After World War II, Canada saw the development
of the welfare state, as we have come to know it. In this period, the
role of the government changed dramatically. Following the war effort, there was general acceptance of government intervention in the
economy and society, and Keynesian economic ideas took hold. The
era of erosion, from the mid-1970s to the present, brought this to an
abrupt end. Monetarism and globalization fuelled deep cuts to income
security programs and caused changes that emphasized work incentives and restricted eligibility.

A new vision of social welfare now needs to assert itself — a vision
that balances economic production and social equity. The creation of
such a vision and social movement underlies the current debates over
the future of the welfare system in this country, and it is the subject of
the next chapter.

Chapter Summary

Key Concepts

- Beverage Report
- Canada Assistance Plan (CAP)
- Canada Health and Social Transfer (CHST)
- Capitalism
- Deserving and undeserving poor
- Elizabethan Poor Law of 1601
- Feudalism
- Great Depression
- Indoor Relief
- Marsh Report
- Outdoor Relief
- Poor Law of 1834
- Principle of less eligibility
- Social Union Framework Agreement (SUFA)
- *Statute of Labourers*
- Workhouses

Review Questions

1. What factors led to the emergence of income security in conjunction with the economic system of capitalism?
2. How do our current conceptions of social welfare remain linked to the ideas of early British society?
3. What are the five principles of the English Poor Laws, and how do they compare with the ideas underlying income security for the poor today?
4. What are the key historical debates in the rise of income security, and how do they continue today?
5. What are the four phases in the rise of income security in Canada, and what ideas and programs characterize each phase?
6. What factors have contributed to the decrease in scope and size of income security since 1975?
7. What are the three pieces of broad federal legislation that affected all income security programs in Canada, and what were the specific impacts?

Exploring Social Welfare

1. How has history affected the social policies that we have today? Pick an income security program and trace back the history of the program, using a variety of sources.
2. Throughout Canada's history, negotiations regarding federal funding contributions to income security have been ongoing and at times intense. Research the Canada Assistance Plan, the Canada Health and Social Transfer and the current Canada Social Transfer and Canada Health Transfer. Write a five-page report that discusses the major differences between these transfer methods.

Websites

A State of the Art Review of Income Security Reform in Canada, 1998
http://idrinfo.idrc.ca/archive/corpdocs/110126/contents.html#0
The entire report by Jane Pulkingham and Gordon Ternowetsky of the International Development Research Centre is online and presents an excellent overview of the major issues confronting our welfare state.

The Canada Assistance Plan: A Twenty Year Assessment, 1966–1986
www.canadiansocialresearch.net/allanm.htm
This article by Allan Moscovitch originally appeared in the 1988–89 edition of *How Ottawa Spends* (Carleton University) and provides an excellent critical analysis of CAP's history.

Canada's Unique Social History
www.socialpolicy.ca/cush
Canada's Unique Social History is an interactive online course which provides an overview of different aspects of the history of social welfare in Canada, including a glossary, photos and additional resources.

References

Blyth, Jack. 1972. *The Canadian Social Inheritance.* Toronto: The Copp Clark Publishing Company.

Graham, John, Karen Swift, and Roger Delaney. 2003. *Canadian Social Policy: An Introduction.* 2nd ed. Toronto: Pearson Education Canada Inc.

Guest, Denis. 1999. *The Emergence of Social Security in Canada.* 3rd ed. Vancouver: UBC Press.

Moscovitch, Allan, and Jim Albert, eds. 1987. *The Benevolent State: The Growth of Welfare in Canada.* Toronto: Garamond Press.

Moscovitch, Allan, and Andrew Webster. 1995. Aboriginal social assistance expenditures. In *How Ottawa Spends: 1995–96: Mid-Life Crisis*, ed. Susan Philips. Ottawa: Carleton University Press.

Scott, Kimberly A. 1994. Aboriginal health and social history: A brief Canadian history. Unpublished. Author's personal collection.

Webb, Sidney, and Beatrice Webb. 1927. *English Local Government: English Poor Law History.* New York: Longmans.

3 Social Welfare Theory

Why People Differ on What to Do

Canadians disagree about the nature and importance of social welfare programs. Some of this divergence of views is based on common myths about the programs and the people these programs are designed to help. However, much of the disagreement rests in differing political ideologies, basic values, and theoretical understandings that people hold, either implicitly or explicitly. This chapter unravels some of these ideologies and theories.

Government officials, academics, and social welfare activists differ widely on their views about social welfare and the role it should play in our society. Commonly, introductory textbooks examine such differences in terms of political ideologies (George and Wilding 1993; Djao 1983) or in terms of sets of ideals and beliefs (Mullaly 1993). Reducing differences in the overall approach to social welfare to people's values and beliefs does not address the day-to-day complexities of

"A free and open society is an ongoing conflict, interrupted periodically by compromises."

— Saul Alinsky (1909–72), U.S. community activist and author of Rules for Radicals, *which stressed "the difference between being a realistic radical and being a rhetorical one"*

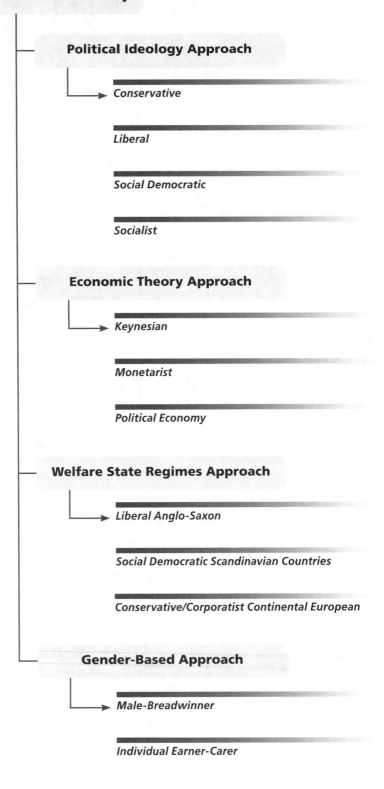

Figure 3.1:
Four approaches to social welfare theory: (1) the political ideology approach, (2) the economic theory approach, (3) the welfare state regimes approach, and (4) the gender-based approach. There is considerable overlap between these broad orientations.

implementing social welfare policy in a capitalist economy such as our own. Nevertheless, it is important for students of social welfare to understand the ideas that lie behind the debates about how the social welfare system works. Here, before getting into the more descriptive chapters, we will examine the differing ideologies and theories about social welfare.

In this chapter, we will examine four approaches to social welfare: (1) the political ideology approach, (2) the economic theory approach, (3) the welfare state regimes approach, and (4) the gender-based approach. In most cases, there is considerable overlap between these orientations. All are discussed in detail later in the chapter.

1. The political ideology approach situates social welfare in the context of economic, social, and political theory — in Canada, this is normally distinguished according to conservative, liberal, social democratic, and socialist beliefs.
2. The economic theory approach, as its name implies, focuses on the influence of economic theories. Economists have differing theories about the root causes of unemployment and poverty that generally derive from the three economic theories: Keynesian economics, monetarism, and political economy. Each body of economic theory has a different view of the role of government and the effects of social spending on the economy.
3. The welfare state regimes approach classifies welfare states according to how social welfare is provided in a given society.
4. The gender-based approach to social welfare identifies two regime types based on an analysis of the family and unpaid labour: the male-breadwinner regime and the individual earner-carer regime.

Further to these four approaches, social welfare can be examined within a social inclusion framework — an approach that is particularly popular in the European Union. Social inclusion emphasizes a wider perspective on income security, taking into consideration non-monetary issues, such as education, community life, health care access, and political participation. The concept is often referred to as being about "removing the bar" rather than "raising the bar" or, in other words, the need to remove barriers and sources of exclusion.

Political Ideology Approach

One way to look at the different approaches to social welfare is to examine the political ideologies underlying the approaches. These are normally divided according to conservative, liberal, social democratic, and socialist belief systems. Most people present these ideologies in terms of "right wing" or "left wing," with the former referring to the conservative ideology and the latter referring to social democratic or socialist beliefs. Liberals are often referred to as "centrists," that is, somewhere between the right and left.

The Conservative Party of Canada

For most of the 1980s, the Progressive Conservative (PC) Party ran a majority government in Canada, but in 1993 it lost all but two of its seats. While many conservatives voted with the Liberal Party in that election, much of the conservative vote went to a new party from Western Canada, the Reform Party, which later became the Canadian Alliance. The Conservative Party of Canada began in 2003 with the merging of the Canadian Alliance and Progressive Conservative parties. While the two parties often disagreed on key policy issues, especially social issues, with the Canadian Alliance Party having a more socially conservative ideology, the two parties recognized that the right would never win an election if they continued to split the conservative vote. In 2005 the Conservative Party of Canada won a minority government under Prime Minster Stephen Harper.

Conservative Ideology (Anti-Collectivists)

Conservative ideology places its emphasis squarely on individual freedom; it holds that each person knows best what he or she wants, and therefore the individual should have the maximum opportunity to pursue his or her own interests. Adherents to this view accept that this may lead to inequality in terms of wealth and power, but see this as a necessary aspect of society.

The basic values of conservative ideology are:

■ freedom
■ individualism
■ inevitability of inequality

According to this approach, the role of government (including interference in the free market economy) should be limited, and the role of private property and private enterprise should be paramount. Conservatives believe that the best government is the one that governs the least. In other words, governments should establish the rules of the game (e.g., the pursuit of self-interest) but not be a primary actor — there should be a limited number of laws and regulations, and political institutions should not be involved in economic activity. Instead, conservatives say, the best system is a private system in which everything is bought and sold through the market. In short, free enterprise and all that follows is the most efficient way to organize society.

In accordance with this underlying philosophy, conservatives believe that social welfare interferes with the labour market and creates a dependency on government. They believe that much of social welfare is misguided and creates the opposite of freedom and individualism. They believe that many social programs hinder the operation of the market, and thereby limit efficiency and wealth creation. In their view, social welfare expenditures are often too generous, which results in inflated demands on the public purse. Insofar as welfare is necessary, they argue that private social welfare is better — it reduces social services and targets social program benefits to only the very needy.

George and Wilding refer to these people as "anti-collectivists" (1993, 19) due to their adherence to individualism and inequality. Individualism, as a belief system, is composed of two things. First is the belief that social phenomena can only be understood through an analysis of the actions of individuals. Secondly, individualism sees people as irrational, self-centred, and fallible. According to this "anti-collectivist" ideology, competition is at the root of modifying the behaviour of irrational and imperfect citizens, and is the surer road to progress.

Liberal Ideology (Reluctant Collectivists)

This group is more difficult to define. The liberals endorse the private (free) enterprise system, but at the same time they believe that the market needs a degree of government regulation.

The primary values of a liberal ideology are:

- pragmatism
- liberty
- individualism
- inevitability of inequality
- humanism

Pragmatism means that, as a government or an individual, you do what needs to be done. Liberals have often been described as less ideological, which means they are willing to do things that suit the circumstances, but that may not exactly follow "liberal" principles. With liberalism, there is an acceptance of the basic tenets of conservatism – such as liberty, individualism, and social inequality – but the inclusion of two other values, pragmatism and humanism, differentiate liberalism. Liberty, individualism, and social inequality are tempered by a bottom line of social justice for the poor. So, competition and markets are tempered by a concern for people and the need for a certain basic level of social security.

The liberal view is that the government should regulate the free market to a degree and provide a minimum of income security benefits. George and Wilding refer to this group as the "reluctant collectivists" (1993, 44). The key idea here is that, despite the value of free enterprise and private markets, liberals believe that there is a tendency for economic power to concentrate in the hands of a few people, and a tendency for markets to break down without government intervention. Liberals firmly believe that governments should intervene to ensure that the economy and the society remain stable and grow over time – private markets require regulation, and it is legitimate to restrict the freedom of the market in order to establish a social minimum and to preserve society by avoiding unrest.

Liberals are strong proponents of the insurance principle, particularly the idea of social insurance. They believe that the risk of unemployment and other interruptions in earnings – social contingencies – should be spread evenly across society. Everybody pays, and everyone benefits if and when they need to. This is not the same as a targeted program, insofar as it creates entitlements in the sense that if you pay in, you have a right to take money out. In contrast, targeted programs are based on the principles of charity. At the same time, liberals advocate a social minimum program, such as basic welfare, to provide benefits for those who may not be covered by social insurance.

Liberals believe in a mix of targeted programs for those in need as well as universal programs, such as medicare, that are available to all Canadians. They believe in "taking the middle ground" and "resisting extremes." In many ways, the famous interwar economist John Maynard Keynes epitomized the liberal ideology. He believed in the free market economy, but also that there must be a way to

The Liberal Party of Canada

The Liberal Party of Canada embraces the values of the liberal ideology. Its philosophy is that the dignity of each individual man and woman is the cardinal principle of democratic society. The Liberals led majority governments throughout the 1990s under Jean Chrétien, but after his retirement, the party was only able to secure a minority government under Paul Martin in 2004 and was forced to call another election in 2005, losing to the Conservative Party. In 2006 the Liberal Party elected a new leader, Stéphane Dion.

organize it in order to avoid unemployment and poverty. Writing in the depths of the 1930s recession, concern about unemployment was at the root of Keynes's work, and it had a lasting effect on postwar economic and social policies in the West. (Keynes's ideas are described more fully later in this chapter.)

Social Democratic (or New Democratic) Ideology

The ideology of the social democrat (or, in Canada, the new democrat) is a middle ground between liberalism and full-fledged socialism. It is characterized by belief in the democratic process and adamant support for public social welfare programs.

The key values of social democratic ideology are:

■ social equality
■ social justice
■ economic freedom
■ fellowship and cooperation

To the social democrat, social inequality wastes human ability and is inefficient in its distribution of resources. In an unequal society, issues of class, gender, and race determine opportunities in the labour market. Social democrats argue for social justice on the basis that in "natural law" everybody has an equal claim to the wealth of society, and no one has a claim to immense wealth. Freedom for social democrats is not only political, it is economic – the kind of freedom that results from government intervention in maintaining a stable economy and stable employment.

Finally, social democrats believe in cooperation and the common good. This is a very different understanding of what governments should be doing, particularly in the area of social welfare. Markets must be regulated, and government enterprise has a substantial role. The economy itself, they believe, should be a mixture of public and private companies; hence their notion of the "mixed economy."

The income security provisions of a social democratic government would highlight universal programs, full employment, and citizenship. Full employment, the social democrats believe, should be a matter of government policy. Social democrats also support the use of national income for social programs. They feel that this kind of development represents a positive expansion of the idea of citizenship, encompassing not only voting, freedom of expression, and access to the court system, but a range of universally provided social services. For this reason, they de-emphasize income testing and income targeting, and use these only when necessary. They believe that unemployment is a waste of the talents and capacities of citizens, and a socially and economically destructive drain on our productive potential.

The New Democratic Party

The New Democratic Party is Canada's social democratic party, and its origin is in several labour and agrarian organizations formed before and during the Great Depression. According to their official mission statement, the New Democratic Party seeks fundamental change, and seeks to focus government efforts on equality and social justice. The NDP has never won a federal election, but uses its position as the "balance of power" to influence the actions of the governing party. The NDP believes that it is part of a greater national and international movement that seeks to challenge the dominant political agenda of market globalization and the resulting environmental, social, and economic problems.

Socialist Ideology

Socialists believe that the means of production and distribution in a society should be owned by that society. Modern socialist ideology has its roots in the influential writings of Karl Marx. Marx believed that socialism was a transitional state between capitalism and communism — a transition to a new society would come about by means of a social and political revolution.

The socialist ideology could be described as emphasizing:

- freedom
- collectivism
- equality

Socialists believe in equality and a society that operates to meet people's needs. Marx's saying, "From each according to their abilities, to each according to their needs," summarizes this view. In short, production should be organized according to social criteria and distributed according to need. Here, equality means the absence of special privilege.

Socialists believe that people cannot truly be free unless they are free from poverty and have the opportunity to develop as human beings — in other words, political and civil rights cannot be separate from economic and social rights. Socialists believe that individuals are social beings and have the potential to act cooperatively and harmoniously with each other if society is organized in such a way that this is encouraged. Competition and consumerism in a capitalist economy, they argue, creates an unfavourable environment for collective action. Socialism has evolved and adapted to the changing times — even countries such as Cuba and China, which maintain a socialist approach, are moving more towards a mixed economy with elements of state and private ownership of production.

Social democrats, or New Democrats, differ from the socialists in that they believe in the idea of a social welfare state. Socialists promote a view of society where the proletariat, or the workers, own the means of production (productive enterprises) through their own state. In other words, social democrats work within the bounds of capitalism in developing their social welfare programs, whereas socialists view state-instituted social welfare programs as mechanisms of social control — mechanisms that serve capitalism and foster inequality by regulating and controlling the subordinate classes.

Canada's political parties represent a variety of ideologies. Here, Stephen Harper, Conservative leader and prime minister, speaks in the House of Commons in 2007 as Stéphane Dion, leader of the Liberals, looks on.

SOCIALISM AND KARL MARX (1818–83)

Karl Marx is, without a doubt, the most influential socialist thinker in history. He is most widely known for authoring the *Communist Manifesto* with Friedrich Engles in 1848, which argued that class struggle was the basis of all history, and which ends with the famous adage: "workers of the world, unite." However, Marx wrote several other works of political economy, including *Theory of Surplus Value* (1862) and *Capital* (1867–94), a work published in several volumes, examining the capitalist process of production.

Marx is often misrepresented by both Marxists and anti-Marxists, who focus solely on the revolutionary ideas in the *Communist Manifesto*. Marx's work predicted an end to capitalism; because the industrial revolution turned the worker into a commodity, Marx argued that the workers would rise up against the industrialists, and that the process of production could not continue. While this never happened to the extent Marx predicted, his arguments have inspired generations of workers to fight for reforms from industry and government, and generations of politicians, theorists, and activists to fight for social equality.

Economic Theory Approach

Another way to look at social welfare and social welfare systems is from the point of view of the economic theory that underlies them. As John Maynard Keynes wryly remarked: "Practical men, who believe themselves to be quite exempt from any intellectual influences, are usually the slaves of some defunct economist."

Certainly, economic theory has had a profound impact on the development of social welfare programs in all capitalist countries. In fact, social policy analysts would generally agree that without the theory of Keynes himself, we would not have developed a welfare state in the postwar period. Some even refer to this period as the "Keynesian Welfare State."

The Keynesians, the monetarists, and the political economy theorists have fundamentally different views on the role of government in the social and economic sphere. They also have contrasting views on unemployment, the causes of poverty, and the impact of social spending on society. The Keynesians believe that governments should use policies to combat unemployment and to maintain the income of consumers. The monetarists believe that governments should keep inflation in check and not discourage unemployment. Political economists believe that private ownership creates two classes that are structurally antagonistic, and that unemployment results when unions are weakened and cannot protect the jobs of the working people. Let us look at each in more detail.

The Keynesians

Keynesian is the adjective used to describe a follower of the economic theory of the British economist John Maynard Keynes (1883–1946). Much of Keynes's important work took place during the Great Depression in the 1930s, and his best-known work is *The General Theory of Employment, Interest and Money*, published in 1936. His theories, culminating in the publication of *The General Theory*, precipitated the "Keynesian Revolution," as it came to be known. His economic theories provided the intellectual rationale for the intervention of governments in economies and the transformation of social policy. Keynes's ideas were considered radical at the time, and some mistakenly called Keynes a socialist in disguise.

Aggregate demand is the total spending of consumers, business investors, and public agencies. Keynes believed that any increase in aggregate demand in the economy would result in an even bigger increase in national income. Any increase in aggregate demand leads to more people being employed; if more people are employed, more people are spending their income; and more spending leads to even more employment. With more income there is even more spending, and so forth. Keynes referred to this as the multiplier effect.

Keynes argued that markets would not automatically lead to full-employment equilibrium, but that the economy could settle into equilibrium at any level of unemployment. In other words, the economy could reach equilibrium even with high unemployment and impoverishment. Unemployment, according to Keynes, is a result of the overproduction of goods — that is, the previous output of products cannot be sold because those who would buy them are now unemployed and impoverished. This results in a general economic depression. According to Keynes, classical economic policies of government non-intervention in the economy would not work. Economies need prodding, and this means active intervention by the government to manage the level of aggregate demand.

Keynes's theory appealed to economists and governments of the day because it provided an alternative to the traditional view that unemployment can and should be eliminated by a drop in wage rates. Keynes's theory was much more politically palatable. According to Keynes, the solution to unemployment was a growth in government spending, with the government purposely taking on budget deficits. Government spending to stimulate the economy was part of what Keynes called *fiscal policy*. Fiscal policy takes place when the government gets actively involved in the economy through spending in order to manage the level of demand.

Demand management means adjusting the level of demand to ensure that the economy arrives at full-employment equilibrium. If there is a shortfall in demand, such as in a recession (a deflationary gap),

John Maynard Keynes (1883–1946)

Keynes was a British economist who revolutionized economics with his classic work, *The General Theory of Employment, Interest and Money* (1936), which is regarded as one of the most influential pieces of writing in the twentieth century. Heavily influenced by the Great Depression, Keynes argued for government intervention to help mitigate the effects of economic recessions and booms. His theory quickly and permanently changed the way the world looked at the economy and the role of government in society. No other single book, before or since, has had such an impact.

Monetary versus Fiscal

■ **Fiscal policy**: the use of government expenditure to manage the economy

■ **Monetary policy**: the process of controlling interest rates and the money supply to manage the economy

the government will need to reflate the economy. If there is an excess of demand, such as in a boom, the government will need to deflate the economy.

Keynes also believed that unemployment decreases savings, as the general population withdraws money from savings in the struggle to survive. Without savings, Keynes said, there is no investment; without investment, no employment; without employment, there is no spending; without spending, there is an overproduction of goods that cannot be sold.

Reflationary policies to boost economic activity may include:

- increasing the level of government expenditure
- cutting taxation to encourage spending
- cutting interest rates to discourage saving and encourage spending
- allowing some money supply growth

Deflationary policies to dampen the level of economic activity may include:

- reducing the level of government expenditure
- increasing taxation to discourage spending
- increasing interest rates to encourage saving and discourage spending
- reducing money supply growth

Keynesian economics had a direct and major influence on the policies of most governments, including Canada's, in the period after World War II. Governments accepted the maintenance of a high and stable level of employment as one of their primary aims and responsibilities after the war to promote maximum production and purchasing power.

The Monetarists

The monetarists advocate the use of monetary policy to stimulate the economy. Monetarist theory asserts that managing the money supply and the cost and availability of credit or interest rates (monetary policy), rather than focusing on government expenditure (fiscal policy), is the key to managing the economy. According to monetarism, the government should not stimulate the economy through government spending, but should maintain a steady money supply. Market forces will then adjust inflation, unemployment, and production automatically and efficiently.

For example, if money is readily available because interest rates are low, people can afford to borrow and spend. But production must keep pace, so that there will be enough goods and services to meet the demand created by this borrowing and spending. In the face of excessive demand, producers and suppliers have incentives to raise their prices. As time goes by, prices spiral upward, leading to uncontrolled inflation, during which dollars lose their value. Thus, the key to keeping inflation in check is to maintain stable interest rates and not to let the money supply grow too rapidly.

The term *monetarism* was coined in 1968 by Karl Brunner, and it refers to the macroeconomic theories and doctrines most closely associated with University of Chicago economist Milton Friedman. Although "born" in 1956, monetarism only became a powerful intellectual force in the late 1960s and early 1970s, and had to wait until the late 1970s and early 1980s to be channelled into economic policy. By the mid-1980s, however, monetarism was largely a spent force and, today, one would have to search very far indeed to find an old-fashioned "monetarist," although governments still use the principles of monetary policy to manage their economies.

Modern monetarist theory was developed to try to explain a new economic phenomenon during this period – stagflation. *Stagflation* was an expression coined to try to explain two simultaneous economic problems: stagnation and inflation. Much of the monetarists' work revolved around the role of expectations in determining inflation, and a key part of their theory was the development of the expectations-augmented Phillips curve. The Phillips curve showed a trade-off between unemployment and inflation (more of one led to less of the other). Friedman argued that there were a series of different Phillips curves for each level of expected inflation, hence the theory of the expectations-augmented Phillips curve. The theory asserts that full employment is bad for the economy because it leads to inflation. If workers see other unemployed workers as ready and willing to take their jobs, they are less likely to seek wage increases. Therefore, according to monetarist theory, some unemployment is good for the economy because it helps to control inflation caused by wage demands.

Monetarist economists formulated the idea of natural unemployment or NAIRU (non-accelerating inflation rate of unemployment). They believe that there is a natural, acceptable, and beneficial level of unemployment. Attempts to lower unemployment below NAIRU will result in the risk of accelerating or increasing inflation. This is in sharp contrast to the Keynesian idea of full employment.

Two kinds of unemployment make up the idea of NAIRU: structural and frictional. With structural unemployment, the number of vacant jobs exceeds the number of persons unemployed, because the available jobs do not match the skills of the unemployed persons. Frictional unemployment is caused by workers moving between jobs to look for work that is more suitable.

The other aspect of the theory is control of the money supply. Money refers to anything that serves as a generally accepted medium of exchange, a standard of value, and a means of saving or storing purchasing power. The money supply is the total quantity of money in

Milton Friedman (1912–2006)

Milton Friedman, widely regarded as the leader of the "Chicago School" of monetary economics, which stresses the importance of the quantity of money as an instrument of government policy and as a determinant of business cycles and inflation, is the twentieth century's most prominent economist advocate of free markets. In his 1962 book, *Capitalism and Freedom*, Friedman argued that the role of government in a free market should be minimal. Friedman was also a supporter of many libertarian policies, such as the decriminalization of drugs and the end of the American military draft.

"SORRY YOU'RE LOSING YOUR JOB BUT IT'S FOR THE GOOD OF THE COUNTRY...."

The monetarist's goal of controlling inflation can often lead to increases in unemployment.

the economy. Governments can directly affect the money supply by printing or destroying currency, bills, and coins, or indirectly by adjusting interest rates.

The key to monetarist policy is to control consumer and business spending by raising and lowering interest rates. The Bank of Canada (a government agency) controls prime interest rates. Lowering interest rates can stimulate the economy and slow money supply growth. Lower interest rates, for example, tend to increase spending (aggregate demand) and reduce savings. Conversely, higher interest rates tend to curb domestic spending. Strong demand for Canadian goods and services puts upward pressure on prices if the demand is larger than the economy's capacity.

Since the work of monetarists is mainly limited to their view of inflation, their policy recommendations emphasize fighting inflation. They believe that if inflation control is the main priority, the economy will be more stable and be able to grow at its optimum rate. The key policy is controlling the money supply to control inflation. The government should not intervene to try to reduce unemployment because the economy will automatically tend to the natural rate of unemployment. The only way to change the natural rate is through supply-side economics.

Supply-side economics is the view that the best way to change the economy is to work on changing supply rather than demand. Rather than spending money to stimulate the economy, the government should not intervene except to reduce taxes, to maintain a steady money supply and rate of inflation, and to provide financial incentives to businesses. The end result, according to monetarism, is more business activity, and therefore more employment.

Supply-side economic policies may include:

- reducing taxes (which leads to more business profits, creates more businesses, or creates more personal incentive to work)
- lowering interest rates (which encourages more consumer spending and business expansion)
- privatizing government-owned companies (which removes unfair competition in the marketplace)
- deregulating the economy (which creates more cash flow in businesses and a more flexible business environment)
- providing financial incentives to businesses, such as direct grants of money, low interest loans, or deferred taxes (which encour-

ages businesses to maintain or expand production and increase employment)

■ improving education and training (which makes the workforce more occupationally mobile)
■ making people more geographically mobile by scrapping rent controls or simplifying house buying
■ reducing the power of trade unions

For the past two decades, Canadian governments have largely adhered to monetarist economics. Monetary policy has been emphasized over fiscal policy, taxes have been cut, and government social spending has decreased. Rather than viewing income security spending as part of demand management policy, Canadian governments have increasingly viewed it as a negative influence on work incentives. Governments at all levels have abandoned the notion of increasing spending during recessions in order to stimulate the economy.

Political Economy Theorists

Among the economic theories, the third variant has wide-ranging economic, political, and cultural components. Political economy theorists believe that the operation of economic markets is tied to private concentrations of ownership and is essentially exploitative.

Most adherents to the political economy perspective would argue that social spending serves to prop up and justify an unjust economic system. The welfare state, in their view, is one of the contradictions of capitalism: it increases well-being, particularly for the rich countries of the world, but it also frustrates the pursuit of a truly just society. It reinforces the very institutions and values that the welfare state was established to do away with.

Many advocates of a political economy orientation go beyond a strictly Marxist analysis. They recognize that society is divided into social classes, the predominant division being between workers and owners, but they also emphasize other sources of inequality and oppression, such as gender relations and ethnicity.

Political economy policies attempt to decrease the inequality in society by transferring the ownership of main sectors of production to ordinary workers and by expanding and developing high-quality and accessible health, education, and social services. Such policies may include:

■ improving education and health services for all sectors of society
■ decreasing private ownership of productive resources
■ increasing the power of trade unions
■ encouraging community economic development initiatives to make capital available
■ increasing the provision of public goods

The political economy perspective has never been a central tenet of government social policy in Western societies, but it has nevertheless shaped many of the critiques of the present-day welfare state. Political economy theorists would opt for nationalizing the major economic sectors and for pursuing community economic development and worker-owned and state-owned enterprises. A well-developed social infrastructure – including free education, health care, and other services – would also be central to this vision.

Welfare State Regimes Approach

To this point, we have examined social welfare systems from the point of view of ideologies and economic theories. A third classification is based on how welfare is actually practised in different countries. The "welfare state regimes" approach classifies nations or welfare state regimes according to established patterns of income security provision.

Building on the work of Richard Titmuss (1958), Gøsta Esping-Anderson (1999) identified three world regimes of social welfare state types: (1) liberal Anglo-Saxon welfare states, (2) social democratic Scandinavian countries, and (3) conservative/corporatist continental European welfare states. It is important to point out that these were conceived as ideal types and that no welfare state exists in this pure sense. This categorization is meant to distinguish nations only according to their commonalities.

Welfare states are classified according to three criteria: public/private sector mix, extent of decommodification of citizens, and extent of inequality reduction or reinforcement. Decommodification occurs when a social program is delivered as a matter of right, and when a person can maintain a livelihood without reliance on the market. People are decommodified, so to speak, when, due to the existence of income security programs, they do not need to rely on selling their labour as a commodity to survive.

Many social welfare theoreticians have added to or changed the Esping-Anderson dimensions. Others have rigorously critiqued the approach. In particular, many feminist scholars have focused on gender-relevant dimensions and others have examined racial dimensions. Fiona Williams, a British social welfare scholar, for example, has pointed out how the discipline of social welfare as a whole has marginalized gender and race. She developed a framework that accounts for patriarchy, imperialism, and the international division of labour (Williams 1989).

Liberal Anglo-Saxon Welfare States

Esping-Anderson's liberal welfare regimes include countries such as Canada, the United States, Australia, the United Kingdom, and Ireland. He used the term *liberal* to refer to the classical liberalism that is concerned with laissez-faire economics and minimal government interference (which is different from the use of the term *liberal* as a political ideology). Linked to many of the ideas of the early Poor Laws, welfare regimes of this type emphasize minimal benefits in order to discourage people from choosing public assistance instead of work. Overall, benefits are residual, available only as a last resort and only to those in need. Income security programs have low benefit levels and are limited, needs-based, and selective. As a percent of GDP, total expenditures are low, and private sector delivery of programs is encouraged.

The overriding principles of the liberal model are privatization and targeting of benefits. In many of the countries within this model, the desire to reduce taxation and expenditures is paramount. Over the past decade, these aspects of this model have taken increased hold in many countries. Middle classes have opted for an increased level of private welfare, and the government has sought to distribute benefits to the most needy. In addition, there has been increased concern with ensuring that work incentives are strong.

Social Democratic Scandinavian Countries

During much of the twentieth century, many people have associated social democracy with Scandinavia, and Esping-Anderson's social democratic welfare regimes include countries such as Sweden, Finland, and Norway. This model emphasizes citizenship rights and the creation of a universal and comprehensive system of social benefits. The model is focused on optimum conditions for the citizen — as a right. This model resembles an institutional approach to social welfare. Full employment, the elimination of poverty, access to high-quality and well-paying jobs, comprehensive health care, a safe working environment, and a decent retirement are among the basic rights that are guaranteed (Olsen 2002, 75).

The Swedish Social Democratic Party has been the most successful labour party in the world, and social democracy is the foundation of the Scandinavian welfare state. Despite some significant economic problems in the 1990s in Sweden and Finland, Scandinavian countries have fundamentally maintained, and even strengthened, their welfare states during the last decade. They largely escaped the shift to monetarism and were able to preserve social welfare protections.

Scandinavian social democracy emphasizes universal income guarantees, maximum employment levels, and highly developed programs for children, people with disabilities, and the elderly. The principle underlying this model is that benefits should be provided to all citizens, regardless of their employment or family situation. Government authorities provide most of the income security benefits, and churches or charities fulfill a limited role. Intertwined with these comprehensive and universal income security benefits is a wide range of health and social services. These are either free or subsidized. Education services and health services are free in Scandinavian countries.

Such programs, however, are expensive and require a high level of personal and corporate taxation to function. This calls for broad support from the middle classes. The combination of high taxes and generous benefits results in the redistribution of income from high-income earners (who pay more taxes) to low-income earners (who receive more income security benefits). Because of these programs, citizens of these countries are more "decommodified" than citizens in other advanced capitalist nations. In other words, they do not need to rely on income from the labour market to survive.

Conservative/Corporatist Continental European Welfare States

Germany, Austria, and France typify the conservative/corporatist continental welfare states model. Esping-Anderson referred to these welfare states as "conservative" or "corporatist" at different times in his writing. Both terms refer to the basic principles of authority, tradition, and resistance to change. Welfare states following this model provide income maintenance to uphold the status quo and maintain income difference between classes. They are not concerned with eradicating poverty or creating a more egalitarian society. Employment-linked social insurance programs financed through employee contributions are directed at income maintenance and do not seek to redistribute income between the classes.

Germany provided the ideas behind the first laws on social insurance. Underlying this approach, social benefits are given only to those who have been in the labour market. This evolved into the conservative or corporatist model, which emphasizes the protection of people with stable, lifelong employment. But people with a tenuous connection to the labour market, such as workers with irregular careers, face difficulties in being eligible for benefits. Continental welfare states have developed a variety of family support and ad hoc income security programs to build some kind of social minimum into the system. This provides little support for women. Northern European countries are inclined to address the concerns of poor families, but lack the necessary tax base for programs that redistribute wealth. These countries provide more generous benefits and a limited role for the private sector.

Gender-Based Approach to Welfare State Regimes

Gender-Based Approach to Welfare State Regimes

■ Male-breadwinner regimes
■ Individual earner-carer regimes

Patricia Evans and Gerda Wekerle, two Canadian social work scholars, view Esping-Anderson's "welfare state regimes" framework as flawed because it only considers the state-market dimension in meeting needs, and subsumes women within the family. According to Evans and Wekerle, this ignores the distribution of labour within the household and between the family and state (1997, 11). Many other feminist scholars have sought to address such weaknesses and have developed their own theories or models that take into account the very specific and unique contexts in which women, children, and families find themselves in society.

Many aspects of social welfare policy and programming can and certainly should be examined in conjunction with gender concerns. In particular, there should be a recognition that the needs of the family and the unpaid work by women produces stratification along gender lines. The definition of decommodification can be refashioned to include the capacity of women to maintain an autonomous household, free from the dictates of the market.

All social welfare theoreticians can also appreciate Sheila Neysmith's discussion of how the separation of family life, the labour market, and state responsibilities in separate domains has hampered social welfare advancement. Her analysis demonstrates that public and private labour – or production and reproduction – need to be connected to achieve a complete theoretical understanding of the social welfare system (Neysmith 1991). In this view, it is crucial that our theoretical ideas do not separate the world into boxes that are different from the true experience of people.

Diane Sainsbury of the University of Stockholm, a prominent author in the field of gender and welfare studies, has outlined a gender approach to welfare state regimes. Her model is different from Esping-Anderson's in that it distinguishes regimes based on ideologies that describe actual or preferred relations between men and women, principles of entitlement, and notions of caring. She distinguishes between the male-breadwinner regime and the individual earner-carer regime (her most recent work added the separate gender roles regime).

In the traditional patriarchal family, women were responsible for child care. Within the individual earner-carer regime, men are just as likely to be caregivers and therefore have access to social welfare programs previously reserved for women.

Male-Breadwinner Regimes

Male-breadwinner regimes are characterized by an ideology of male privilege based on a division of labour between the sexes that results in unequal benefit entitlements (Sainsbury 1999, 77). Men are seen as the family providers and thereby are entitled to benefits based on their labour force participation or their position as "head of the household." In such regimes, marriage is the preferred family form. Women are viewed primarily as wives and mothers and receive their entitlements as such – their primary role is to care for their husbands and children in the form of unpaid work. There is little state involvement in caregiving. Unmarried mothers and divorced women fall outside the confines of the "normal" policies of this type of regime.

Individual Earner-Carer Regimes

In sharp contrast, individual earner-carer regimes are based on shared roles between men and women leading to equal rights (Sainsbury 1999, 79). In this model, both sexes have equal rights to social entitlements as earners and caregivers. Paid work in the labour market and unpaid caregiving work have the same benefit entitlements, thereby neutralizing gender differentiation with respect to social rights. Both men and women are seen as equals. The state plays a central role in the provision of services and payments, whether it be caring for children, elderly relatives, the sick, or people with disabilities.

The gender-based approach to welfare state regimes provides a useful lens for analyzing social welfare. With this approach, we can see how entitlements are awarded and how this is often based on an ideology that supports a gendered division of labour, with men as breadwinners and women as caregivers. This approach goes beyond looking at relations in the market and takes into account relations within the family and relations between men and women.

SOCIAL CITIZENSHIP: RIGHT OR INVESTMENT?

Underpinning social welfare is the idea of social citizenship, first espoused by T.H. Marshall, which is based on a guarantee of rights partly realized through state intervention. It involves granting citizens civil, political, and social rights. T.H. Marshall's lecture, "Citizenship and Social Class," has influenced social welfare thinking for decades. In it, he outlines the history of social rights, beginning first with the rights and obligations in feudal society.

In feudal society, each person had a status (noble, commoner, or serf) that accorded certain rights and duties. With the transition to capitalism, these rights were dissolved and this started a series of conflicts. Struggles over rights resulted in the acquisition of civil rights in the eighteenth century, political rights in the nineteenth century, and social rights in the twentieth century. This culminated in the notion of citizenship rights and the postwar mindset that underlies the welfare state.

According to Marshall, citizenship rights are best fulfilled through a welfare state and through that state's involvement in economic and social affairs. A key component of Marshall's citizenship rights are social rights, which include the right to economic welfare and security, the right to share in social heritage, and the right to live according to the standards prevailing in society. Social rights underpinned the development of post-World War II welfare states in Western industrialized countries, including Canada. The period was typified by a shift from a residual approach (seeing social welfare as a form of stigmatizing charity) to an institutional approach to social welfare (seeing social welfare as a right or entitlement). Social rights were placed on the agenda beside civil and political rights. But as time went on, some have argued that civil and political rights, including property rights, have tended to receive an enhanced importance while social and economic rights have declined.

Social Inclusion

Before ending this chapter, it is necessary to touch on the idea of social inclusion as another way of looking at social welfare delivery. The concept of social inclusion emerged in Europe during the 1980s as a means of addressing growing social divides, and it is now a central topic in Canadian social policy discussions. The concept challenges social welfare scholars to consider the non-economic aspects of society that lead to social disadvantages or social exclusion, such as education, community life, health care access, and political participation. The concept is often referred to as being about "removing the bar" rather than "raising the bar." This idea refers to the need to remove barriers and sources of exclusion.

Mitchell and Shillington, two Canadian social policy researchers, define *social inclusion* as a process of investments and actions that will ensure that all children and families are able to participate as valued, respected, and contributing members of society by closing the physical, social, and economic distances that separate people (2002, 6).

In the past few years, social policy analysts have begun to outline social welfare within a "social investment" framework — the "third way," or "removing the bar." The goal of social investment is social inclusion. It therefore requires change at multiple levels — change that goes beyond meeting basic needs. One example of how a social investment approach would differ from a social rights approach is the provision of education for the homeless. Within a social rights model, the government might assign teachers for children located in a shelter for the homeless. The social investment approach would emphasize and respect the need for children to attend and participate in community school life.

The new approach has merit because it uncovers the multiple aspects of social welfare. Others critique it for its "softness" on the need for structural change. They argue that the introduction of social investment and social inclusion may obscure the difficult issues of poverty, racism, and other forms of inequality and powerlessness.

Table 3.1: Comparison of Social Rights and Social Investment Frameworks

	Social Rights Framework	Social Investment framework
Vision	Social welfare is a right of citizenship	Social welfare is achieved by giving people equal opportunity
Time Horizon	Meeting social welfare needs in the present	Improving the present to prepare for the future
Strategy	Provide income protection	Provide equal opportunity
Problem Identification	Lack of income	Multi-dimensional nature of problems
Target	Raising the bar	Removing the bar

Figure 3.2: The European Union's View of Policy Interactions

Source: Canadian Policy Research Networks. Redesigning the "Welfare Mix" for Families: Policy Challenges by Jane Jenson. Published February 2003. Reprinted with permission.

Social welfare programs organized according to this perspective would go beyond providing material or income benefits. They would also include (1) developing the capacities of people to earn their own income, (2) the direct participation of people in the decisions that affect them, (3) respecting and valuing of differences, and (4) reducing the social and physical distance between people (i.e., mixed-income neighbourhoods and integrated classrooms).

In a market-based economy, income and other material resources are key to facilitating opportunities or capacities. The social inclusion perspective challenges us to move beyond income and material resources to consider other items that affect well-being and human development. For example, the United Nations' well-known Human Development Index (HDI), on which Canada has consistently scored high, measures more than income. The index also includes life expectancy, adult literacy, and the gross enrolment ratio. It measures items that shape future opportunities, such as basic and advanced education and health, taking a social inclusion viewpoint on inequality. Amartya Sen, an influential scholar in this area, states that deprivation is determined by what people possess and by what it enables them to do. Therefore, when examining social welfare, it is important to consider access to housing, health, education, community life, and political life.

Overall, the concept of social inclusion as a solid framework for social welfare is still a work in progress. Some scholars and social welfare activists have cautioned that it is soft on the need for structural change, that it can be too general (thereby letting governments off the hook concerning issues such as poverty and racism), that it does not adequately confront historical exclusionary practices (such as the colonization of First Nations peoples), and that the looseness of the concept allows governments to equate inclusion with employment (thereby ignoring the multiple dimensions of social exclusion). This book focuses on welfare programs that further income security, one of the pillars of social inclusion. But this is not meant to minimize other aspects of social inclusion. These other aspects are the basic building blocks for survival, and they develop opportunities and the capacities of individual members of society. All of these work together to form social inclusion.

Conclusion

There are different ways to categorize the diverse ideas that underpin income security provision in Canada. This chapter provides a brief overview of some of the more prominent approaches. It is essential to understand that there is a range of theories and that no theory captures all the aspects of the welfare state — all have merit, and together they help us understand how welfare provision works. While general theories and models can provide a context for understanding and critiquing social welfare policy, it is also important to keep sight of the useful contribution, at any given time, of particular policies targeted to individuals, who are within the welfare system through no fault of their own.

The next six chapters examine income security programs in Canada from differing perspectives: the labour market, globalization and human rights, women and the family, minority groups, Aboriginal peoples, and poverty. When reading these chapters, bear in mind that behind these programs may well be, to repeat Keynes's words, "some dead economist." Try wherever possible to identify the social welfare theory that stands in the background. After that, Chapters 10 to 14 describe specific income security programs. As you move through these chapters, you can draw upon some of the material presented in this chapter to see where the ideas and debates that guide these programs may have originated.

Canadian Centre for Policy Alternative (CCPA)

http://www.policyalternatives.ca/

The CCPA is a non-profit research organization founded in 1980 to promote research on economic and social policy issues from a progressive point of view. Under the heading research and publications' the CCPA has a wide variety of reports on relevant social welfare issues, such as the report entitled *The Rich and the Rest of Us*.

Chapter Summary

Key Concepts

- ☐ Conservative ideology (anti-collectivist)
- ☐ Conservative/corporatist continental welfare states
- ☐ Economic theory approach
- ☐ Gender-based approach
- ☐ Individual earner-carer regimes
- ☐ Keynesians
- ☐ Liberal ideology (reluctant collectivist)
- ☐ Liberal welfare regimes
- ☐ Male-breadwinner regimes
- ☐ Monetarists
- ☐ Political economy theorists
- ☐ Political ideology approach
- ☐ Social democratic ideology
- ☐ Social democratic welfare regimes
- ☐ Social inclusion
- ☐ Socialist ideology
- ☐ Welfare state regimes approach

Review Questions

1. What are the four approaches to social welfare, and how do they differ?
2. What is an ideology? What political ideologies exist in Canada, and how do they differ in their views of social welfare?
3. Keynesianism and monetarism are two different approaches to economic management. Define each approach and discuss two ways in which the two approaches differ.
4. Explain the political economy perspective, and discuss how its policies would differ from the other two economic approaches.
5. What are the welfare state regime types? Discuss two differences between them.

6. What dimensions are added by the gender-based approach to welfare state regimes? Based on this, what two types of welfare state regimes emerge?

7. Why do you think there are so many different ways to conceptualize social welfare?

Exploring Social Welfare

1. Each political party in Canada has a unique platform in relation to social welfare and income security programs. Pick one federal or provincial political party, and on its website locate its views on social welfare in its platform. How does the platform with regard to social welfare relate to the political ideologies discussed in this chapter?

2. Social welfare debates are greatly influenced by economic theory. Research the issue of "minimum wage" and discuss the economic arguments for and against raising it. To get started, you could visit the website of the National Union of Public and General Employees (NUPGE) or the Canadian Union of Public Employees (CUPE), do a search for "minimum wage," and compare the results to the economic theory presented by the government at the Federal Labour Standards Review Commission.

Websites

Social Policy Research Centre (SPRC)
    www.sprc.unsw.edu.au/dp/index.htm
This is the discussion paper section of the SPRC, an independent research centre of the University of New South Wales, Australia, with some Canadian content.

National Anti-Poverty Organization
    www.napo-onap.ca
The NAPO, "the voice of the poor," considers its mission to be the "eradication of poverty in Canada." The website offers resources onsocial assistance, social housing, human rights, minimum wage, unemployment and Federal budget priorities. NAPO is a non-profit, non-partisan organization.

National Council of Welfare
    www.ncwcnbes.net
This is one of the most extensive collections of online reports on social welfare and other social issues. The NCW is a citizens' advisory body to the Minister of Human Resources and Development Canada on matters of concern to low-income Canadians.

References

Djao, A.W. 1983. *Inequality and Social Policy.* Toronto: John Wiley & Sons.

Esping-Anderson, Gøsta. 1999. *The Three Worlds of Welfare Capitalism.* Princeton, NJ: Princeton University Press.

Evans, Patricia, and Gerda Wekerle, eds. 1997. *Women and the Canadian Welfare State.* Toronto: University of Toronto Press.

George, Vic, and Paul Wilding. 1993. *Ideology and Social Welfare.* London: Routledge.

Mitchell, Andrew, and Richard Shillington. 2002. *Poverty, Inequality and Social Inclusion.* Perspectives on Social Inclusion Working Paper Series. Laidlaw Foundation.

Mullaly, Robert. 1993. *Structural Social Work: Ideology, Theory, and Practice.* Toronto: McClelland & Stewart Ltd.

Neysmith, Sheila. 1991. From community care to a social model of care. In *Women's Caring: Feminist Perspectives on Social Welfare,* ed. Carol Baines, Patricia Evans, and Sheila Neysmith. Toronto: McClelland & Stewart Ltd.

Olsen, Gregg M. 2002. *The Politics of the Welfare State: Canada, Sweden, and the United States.* Don Mills, ON: Oxford University Press.

Sainsbury, Diane, ed. 1999. *Gender and Welfare State Regimes.* Oxford: Oxford University Press.

Titmuss, Richard M. 1958. *Essays on the Welfare State.* London: Allen and Unwin.

Williams, Fiona. 1989. *Social Policy: A Critical Introduction.* Cambridge: Polity Press.

4 Labour Market and Employment

Economic and Social Perspectives

Social welfare and the labour market are inextricably linked. In our capitalist economy, one's social welfare is largely determined by attachment to the labour force. If all members of a society were able to consistently meet their needs through wages from employment, investment income, or inheritance, the need for income security programs would be drastically reduced or eliminated.

Together, Employment Insurance (EI) and Social Assistance (SA) are the pillars of income support for those of working age in Canada. Employment Insurance provides a level of income replacement to those workers who are temporarily out of work and meet strict eligibility conditions. Social Assistance provides minimal income support to those who do not qualify for EI. A variety of factors can result in someone becoming unemployed. Demand for one's occupation may fall, one's training may become outdated, there might not be enough

> **"** Annual income twenty pounds, annual expenditure nineteen nineteen six, result happiness. Annual income twenty pounds, annual expenditure twenty pounds ought and six, result misery."
>
> *— Charles Dickens,* **David Copperfield,** *ch. xii*

jobs to go around, the overall economy might dip, or perhaps a life event results in a personal crisis. Regardless of the cause, an unemployed person in a market economy requires money to survive.

EI and SA help people who are unemployed, yet many Canadians living in poverty are underemployed and part-time employed. Income support is often not available in these cases unless earnings are extremely low, and even then it is a minimum amount. Underemployment occurs when the education and training required for the job obtained are less than the education and training of the worker that is doing the job. Part-time employment is also a growing sector of the labour market. Many people are working part-time involuntarily, and would prefer full-time work.

There is debate about the merit of income security programs such as EI and SA. Some people believe that these programs hurt the labour market and hinder economic growth, while others believe that the programs benefit both individual citizens and the economy. Still others, along with countries in the European Union, believe that social welfare programs are productive, rather than a drain on the economy. In this chapter, we will look at this debate by examining employment and unemployment and their relation to income security. Finally, we will look at the relationship between economic efficiency and social equity, and the role that income security can play in managing an efficient and fair economy.

Employment and Unemployment

In the nineteenth century, the concept of unemployment did not exist. People who were physically able to work, but did not work, were assumed to be lazy. In modern times, we define *unemployment* as the involuntary loss of wage income. In our economy, the possibility of losing wage income is a frightening prospect for individuals and their families.

Employment includes any legal activity carried out for pay or profit. It also includes unpaid family work, when it is a direct contribution to the operation of a farm, business, or professional practice owned or operated by a related member of the household.

Some employed people are self-employed. Self-employment is becoming prevalent as people provide services on contract, produce products, or sell someone else's product. Self-employed people rely on their own initiative and skills to generate income, and undertake the risks and uncertainties of starting and operating their own businesses. Official unemployment (as it is counted in the unemployment statistics) is made up of people in the labour force who do not have paid employment, are available to take work, and are actively looking for a job.

If an unemployed person has given up searching for a job, he or she is not considered to be part of the labour force and is not included in the unemployment statistics. As noted earlier, many Canadians also face **underemployment** – when the education and training required for the job is less than the education and training of the worker who is doing the job. Underemployment is generally not measured in Canada. Evidence indicates that underemployment increases as higher quality jobs become relatively fewer in number.

Anyone can lose his or her job, often when it is least expected. The notion of the unemployed being lazy has been replaced with a more realistic view as more people experience job loss or have a relative or friend experiencing it. Prior to the economic downturn from 2000 to 2003, many high technology workers and managers thought that their jobs were secure and that they were in a booming sector of the economy. Many suddenly found themselves without a job, and did not find employment for a number of years. According to Statistics Canada data (2004), 47.7 percent of those who became unemployed in 2002 did so through layoffs; 23 percent had been unemployed in the previous year, and only 1.7 percent left their job for personal or family reasons (2.6 percent for women and 1 percent for men).

Some unemployment is unavoidable, due to people moving between jobs and mismatches between the skills of the unemployed and the requirements for available jobs. Employees who move between jobs cause what is known as **frictional unemployment**. This includes new labour force entrants, such as those returning to the labour force after completing school or raising children. **Cyclical unemployment** occurs due to a temporary downturn in the job market. The most common form of cyclical unemployment occurs when workers are temporarily laid off.

If, on the other hand, unemployed people do not have the skills for available jobs, do not live where jobs are available, or are unwilling to work at the wage rate offered in the market, this form of unemployment is known as **structural unemployment**. The extent of structural unemployment will depend on various things:

- **MOBILITY OF LABOUR.** If people quickly switch jobs from a declining industry to a rapidly growing one, there will be less structural unemployment.

- **THE PACE OF CHANGE IN THE ECONOMY.** If demand, supply, and people's tastes change at a fast rate, industry has to adapt quickly to change. This leads to more structural unemployment.

- **THE REGIONAL STRUCTURE OF INDUSTRY.** If declining industries are heavily concentrated in one area, this may make it much more difficult for people to find new jobs. For example, both the shipbuilding and mining industries were heavily concentrated. Some areas have taken many years to adapt to and reduce the level of structural unemployment.

Underemployment

■ when the education and training of the worker exceeds the requrements for the job

Unemployment

■ **Frictional unemployment:** when employees move between jobs, or return to the workforce
■ **Cyclical unemployment:** results from a temporary downturn in the job market
■ **Structural unemployment:** when workers do not possess the required skills for the jobs, do not live where jobs are available, or are unwilling to work at the offered wage

The Great Depression

As was explained in Chapter 2, the Great Depression caused hardship in Canada and around the world, mostly by destroying the labour market. There was massive unemployment in Canada — 27 percent at the height of the Depression in 1933 — and a reduction in wages. The Depression ended in 1939, when the outbreak of World War II created a demand for war materials.

The Great Depression was a turning point for Canada. Before 1930, the government intervened as little as possible, believing that the free market would take care of the economy, and that churches and charities would take care of society. But in the 1930s, a growing demand arose for the government to step in and create a social safety net with a minimum hourly wage, a standard work week, and programs such as medicare and Unemployment Insurance.

A combination of frictional and structural unemployment results in what is referred to as natural unemployment or NAIRU (non-accelerating inflation rate of unemployment). According to monetarist economists, attempts to lower unemployment below NAIRU will risk the acceleration or increase of inflation. This is discussed in more detail in Chapter 3.

A 1997 study entitled *The Future of Work in Canada* explored the "pervasive public anxiety" that exists regarding jobs, the economy, and our ability to cope with change (Betcherman and Lowe 1997). This anxiety is caused by the individualization of the risk associated with trends of high unemployment, downsizing, and restructuring. According to the study, individual Canadians are increasingly bearing the risks of unemployment at the same time that the social safety net — in the form of Employment Insurance and stable employment relations — disintegrates.

Some believe that we should completely reorganize our economic system so as to ensure that everyone who wants to work has a job. In 1945 the Canadian government issued a statement committing itself to full employment in the *White Paper on Employment and Income*, acknowledging that unemployment results from the unregulated operation of markets. The government committed to intervening in the economy to create jobs and control job losses. This was a recognition that the government could reduce unemployment by directly generating economic activity and assisting the private sector. At the time, this social policy commitment represented a strong break from the past, when individuals had been solely responsible for their own employment.

However, the notion of full employment as a government policy objective has slowly been abandoned. The *Unemployment Insurance Act* of 1971 addressed the concept of full employment and established that 4 percent unemployment was considered full employment. Subsequent to this, the idea of full employment had been rarely mentioned, and never directly applied in social policy.

Underemployment and Part-Time Employment

People who have paid jobs are considered employed. However, not all employed people are employed full-time. Full-time employment refers to people who usually work 30 or more hours per week, or to people who work fewer than 30 hours per week but consider themselves to be employed full-time. Part-time employment refers to people who usually work fewer than 30 hours each week. The voluntary part-time worker chooses to work fewer than 30 hours a week because he or she is a student, has personal or family responsibilities, wants to spend time in other pursuits, or may not need the income of a full-time job. The involuntary part-time worker prefers full-time work but can only find part-time employment.

Checking for jobs at a Human Resources Centre in Vancouver in 2002: Statistics Canada reported that day that unemployment had jumped from 7.5 to 8 percent, the highest level in almost three years.

Women are much more likely than men to work part-time. In 2004, 27 percent of employed Canadian women (over 2 million) worked part-time. This compared to just 11 percent of employed men. Women account for 70 percent of all part-time employees, a figure which has not changed appreciably since the mid-1970s (Statistics Canada 2006b, 109).

Dave Broad, director of the Social Policy Research Unit at the University of Regina, found that one of the most pronounced recent labour force trends has been the increase in the number of part-time workers. He found that part-time employment, as a percentage of total employment, has grown steadily from 3.8 percent in 1953, to 12 percent in 1973, to 16.9 percent in 1983, to 18.5 percent in 1999 (Broad 2000, 13). Part-time workers generally experience substandard living and working conditions, and a range of social problems resulting from holding several jobs while trying to balance paid work and family responsibilities. Many commentators believe that this shift to part-time work has resulted from the desire of employers to lower operating costs by substituting high-paying jobs with non-unionized, lower-cost, flexible labour.

Many people who take part-time work do so involuntarily – they would prefer a full-time job if one were available. Involuntary part-time work is defined as a job involving fewer than 30 hours a week that is held by a worker who has been unable to find full-time employment. These workers are dealing with an underemployment problem. According to Grant Schellenberg, author of *The Changing Nature of Part-Time Work* (1997), half of all part-time workers would prefer to work more hours for more pay, and about 35 percent want to work full-time. This trend has increased significantly among mothers with children, indicating that part-time employment is more the result of

Case Study:

Ginette and Uri

Ginette Leduc is a 32-year-old Canadian. After graduating with a communications degree from the Université de Montréal, Ginette worked for eight years with a major telecommunications company as a communications officer. She was responsible, among other things, for the publication of a company newsletter.

Four years into her job, Ginette met Uri. The two decided to get married and had a daughter, Patricia. Ginette took six months of topped-up maternity leave as provided under the collective agreement and Unemployment Insurance (as it was called in 1991).

Shortly after Ginette went on leave, Uri was laid off, and rather than look for another job, he started his own business. He and Ginette had often spoken about the advantages of a home-based business that would allow them the flexibility and autonomy to meet family needs and put their professional skills to profitable use. So, although he pursued some leads for jobs in other businesses, Uri devoted himself to getting his business started while Ginette devoted herself to Patricia.

When she went back to work, Ginette asked if she could work a four-day week in order to spend more time with Patricia. This request was granted, and as Patricia grew, the part-time arrangement provided Ginette with time to volunteer in Patricia's preschool. It also gave Ginette one day a week to devote to her sick mother.

Then, in 1994, Ginette received word that her employment was being terminated. Her supervisor explained that the company was facing stiff international competition, and all non-essential operations were being reduced or shut down. The news could not have come at a more difficult time. Ginette was three months pregnant with their second child, her mother was seriously ill, and although Uri's business was beginning to make money, he was working 50 to 60 hours a week.

The silver lining, if there was one, was that Ginette's supervisor informed her she would be offered a contract to continue to produce the newsletter she had been writing. The supervisor could not guarantee how long this would last, but it looked reasonably secure for another year or two. Ginette could work from home. In essence, she would be doing most of the tasks she had been doing while employed, but she would have more flexibility with respect to work hours.

Ginette estimated that the work would take about 15 hours a week and thought this would be ideal, as it might give her more time to care for her mother and attend to the demands of a three-year-old and a newborn. **continued>**

Case Study:

Ginette and Uri (continued)

The difficulty, of course, was that all the benefits and advantages of paid employment were now gone. Those benefits had been crucial to the well-being of the family, because Uri, as a self-employed worker, did not have a benefits package. As an independent contractor, Ginette knew she would not have access to the maternity leave provisions of Unemployment Insurance, and she knew the extended health care plan, disability and life insurance, dental care, and employer contributions to her pension plan were gone. However, given her circumstances, Ginette felt she had no choice but to accept the contract.

The couple's combined income was about $35,000 per year when their second daughter was born. In spite of their difficult financial circumstances, Ginette felt fortunate to have the time to spend with her children and mother. In fact, she felt that were it not for the financial difficulties they were having, their lifestyle would be quite good. ■

Source: Excerpt from Law Commission of Canada. 2004. Is Work Working? Work Laws that Do a Better Job*. Ottawa: Law Commission of Canada, 6–7.*

a lack of employment options for this group, rather than a voluntary choice to balance paid and unpaid work.

In Canada, one quarter of all workers are low-paid, earning less than two-thirds of the national median hourly wage (under $11). In a recently published book, Andrew Jackson, the national director of social and economic policy with the Canadian Labour Congress, found that the frequency of low pay is higher for women (one in three) than men (one in five) (Jackson 2005, 20). His comparative analysis found that the United States has a similar rate, but other countries such as Sweden (one in twenty) and Germany (one in eight) have a much lower incidence of low pay (215). According to Ron Saunders, the work network director with Canadian Policy Research Networks, the proportion of low-paid workers in Canada has remained the same since 1980 (Saunders 2006b, 18).

The polarization of the workforce — with one group receiving good wages, benefits, and job security, and another (including most part-time workers) receiving poor wages, no benefits, and little security — is worsening. Since 68 percent of involuntary part-time workers are women, this labour market issue is a gender issue. Analyzing this data according to family characteristics produces disturbing results. The involuntary part-time rates of single mothers (18 percent) far exceeds those of the other groups (Statistics Canada 2002, 12). Comparing full-time, full-year employment also finds women at a disadvantage, earning 71.7 percent of what men earn, on average.

Recent immigrants are more likely to be in low-paying jobs, and the problem is compounded if one is also a visible minority. Twenty-five percent of recent immigrants (defined as those who arrived in Canada during the five preceding years) earned less than $10 per hour in 2000, compared to 17 percent for Canadian-born workers. Visible minorities are most likely to earn less than $10 per hour — almost 33 percent, compared to less than 20 percent of recent immigrants who were not visible minorities (Saunders 2006a, 2–3).

Rate of Unemployment

Unemployment rate

■ the percentage of the labour force that is unemployed

The unemployment rate is the percentage of the labour force that is unemployed. The rate of unemployment can be determined by the following calculation:

$$Unemployment\ Rate = \frac{Number\ of\ Unemployed\ People}{Number\ of\ People\ in\ the\ Labour\ Force} \times 100$$

However, not all unemployed people are counted as unemployed. If you are unemployed, but have given up your search for a job, you are no longer counted as unemployed. In other words, many people including those who have given up the search for a job are not considered part of the labour force — they therefore are not included in the preceding equation.

Labour force

■ the number of people in the country 15 years of age or over who have jobs or are looking for jobs

The official definition of the labour force is the number of people in the country 15 years of age or over who either have a job or are actively looking for one. This excludes people living on reservations, full-time members of the armed forces, and institutional residents (for example, prison inmates and patients in hospitals or in nursing homes who have resided there for more than six months). Retired people, students, people not actively seeking work, and people not available for work for other reasons are also not considered part of the labour force, although they may be part of the working-age population. Discouraged workers is the term used to refer to those individuals who are no longer looking for a job because they believe they will not find one. Discouraged workers are classified as not being in the labour force.

The rate of unemployment in Canada has varied over the years. During the Depression, the rate was around 25 percent. In the 1960s, the rate was as low as 3.4 percent. Since the mid-1970s, unemployment has risen to 10 percent and has stayed just above or below this level most of the time. Unemployment rates are higher for youth, women, persons with disabilities, and Aboriginal persons. Unemployment rates also differ widely between provinces.

The unemployment rate in February 2006 was 6.4 percent. This means that, of those who were officially counted as being part of the labour force and actively looking for work, 6.4 percent could not find a job. The labour force consists of 17.7 million Canadians, or

67.6 percent of the adult population. Of this 17.7 million, 1.1 million could not find paid employment. The total number of employed Canadians was therefore 16.6 million. Of these, almost 3 million worked part-time (Statistics Canada 2006a, 43).

Canada's unemployment rate is generally higher than that of the United States, Japan, Australia, and New Zealand. It is also almost double for young people aged 15–24 (16.6 percent for men and 13.7 percent for women). As well, increasing numbers of Canadians are working part-time, many involuntarily. This is a form of partial unemployment that is not measured by unemployment statistics. For example, 27 percent of women and 11 percent of men work part-time (Statistics Canada, 2006b, 109).

Two alternative measures of labour force activity (in addition to the unemployment rate) are the labour force participation rate and the employment population ratio. The ratio of the labour force to the working-age population (age 15 or over) is referred to as the labour force participation rate.

Labour force participation rate

■ the percentage of the working-age population included in the labour force

$$Labour\ Force\ Participation\ Rate = \frac{Labour\ Force}{Working\text{-}Age\ Population} \times 100$$

In 2006, the labour force participation rate was just over 67 percent (Statistics Canada 2006a, 43). This means that 67 out of every 100 persons aged 15 years and over were part of the labour force. The rate varies widely between provinces, with Newfoundland at roughly 60 percent and Alberta in the low 70s. Even if both provinces had the same unemployment rate, Alberta would be considered to be better off because a greater part of its population was employed. A high participation rate means that a large proportion of the working-age population is either employed or actively looking for work. A high participation rate can reflect optimism about the availability of jobs. The employment population ratio is the ratio of employed to the working-age population.

Employment population ratio

■ the percentage of the working-age population that is employed

$$Employment\ Population\ Ratio = \frac{Employed}{Working\text{-}Age\ Population} \times 100$$

Unionization

The rise of industrialization in Canada spawned the development of the trade union movement. One in three employees in Canada belongs to a union. Trade unions are organizations that represent those individuals working in particular industries or industrial sectors, and they work to defend and advance the interests of these workers in terms of wages and working conditions, as well as broader welfare concerns.

Workers first organized against the threat of mechanization and later to improve working conditions. In 1886, the Trades and Labour

The Knights of Labour, seen here in Hamilton, Ontario, c. 1885, organized mass unionism in the main Ontario centres during this period in Canadian history.

Congress was formed. In 1902 this was changed to the Canadian Federation of Labour, as Canadian unionists sought to become more independent from the American union movement. These early union efforts appear to have had little impact on work conditions or wages. It was not until the 1920s that unions began to have an impact on the economy, but this was forestalled by the Great Depression of the 1930s. After the Depression, between 1940 and 1956, union membership quadrupled. After 1956, union membership grew more slowly due to the increase in white-collar workers, who were less inclined to organize. The period from 1967 to 1997 saw a renewed growth in union organization, as women increasingly entered the workforce. The percentage of working women who are members of unions has increased dramatically in the last three decades; the unionization rate for women went from 16 percent in 1966 to 32 percent in 2004. In contrast, the rate for men fell from 40 percent to 32 percent in the same period. The rise in women's union membership is due, in large part, to the unionization of the teaching and health professions where women predominate. The shift away from manufacturing jobs to more service industry jobs accounts for the decrease of union membership among men.

Unionization has had an important impact on Canadian social welfare. Unionized jobs generally provide higher wages, greater non-wage benefits, and better work arrangements. The role of unions also extends beyond the workplace setting. Unions often promote public income security provisions and other social and health services.

In more recent years, with globalization and greater economic instability, the organized labour movement has faced new challenges. Among these are the transfer of manufacturing jobs to Third World countries, where labour is cheap and working conditions are unregulated, as well as a shift to low-paying, part-time and temporary jobs. All these have made union organizing more difficult and more urgent.

The Economic and Social Costs of Unemployment

There are social and economic costs associated with unemployment. Unemployment represents a loss of revenue for society and, more important, it has a negative impact on individual citizens.

First, let us examine the economic costs. Using human resources for work produces goods and services and allows the employed to earn a salary. Unemployment, on the other hand, leads to a reduction

INFLATION AND UNEMPLOYMENT

Inflation is defined by the federal Department of Finance as the average rate of increase in prices. Inflation is usually measured as a percentage increase in the Consumer Price Index (CPI). Canada's inflation target, as set out by the federal government and the Bank of Canada, aims to keep inflation within a range of 1 to 3 percent. If the rate of inflation is 10 percent a year, $100 worth of purchases last year will, on average, cost $110 this year.

According to monetarist theory, inflation and unemployment have an inverse relationship under ordinary conditions. However, recent history has shown that the Canadian government has chosen to fight inflation, rather than unemployment. Canadians wonder why this is so.

People who have an abundance of money tend to store that money in the form of assets such as stocks and bonds, which pay a rate of return. They tend to benefit more when the rate of inflation is low because their return after inflation is higher. On the flip side, average income earners do not own much in the way of assets, so they are less concerned with inflation. Keeping their job is crucial, so a low unemployment rate is desirable.

Some social policy analysts argue that the government's monetary policy is more concerned with protecting the interests of people with an abundance of money, rather than the average working person.

of the output of goods and services and a loss of income for employees. However, this is only a fraction of society's loss. For example, Human Resources Development Canada (HRDC) analysis points out that the 1994 total production loss associated with cyclical and structural unemployment was estimated by various studies to have ranged from 3.8 percent to 10.2 percent of the $748 billion GDP. That adds up to a loss of $29–$77 billion.

In addition to production losses, governments suffer revenue losses from personal and corporate taxes as well as increased expenditures on EI and SA. For all governments, the budget costs of Canada's unemployment rate of 10.4 percent in 1994, compared to an unemployment rate of 8.5 percent, might range from $8 to $12 billion (Human Resources Development Canada 1996, 1).

To summarize, the economic costs of unemployment include:

- **LOSS OF OUTPUT TO THE ECONOMY.** The unemployed could be producing goods and services. If they are not, the GDP is lower than it could be.
- **LOSS OF TAX REVENUE.** Unemployed people are not earning wages, and therefore they aren't paying taxes. The government loses a potential source of tax revenue.

UNDERSTANDING GROSS NATIONAL/DOMESTIC PRODUCT

What is valuable?

Growth in the economy is usually referred to as a growth in gross national product (GNP) or gross domestic product (GDP).

The GNP includes all economic activity or the monetary value of all goods and services produced in the world by Canadian-based firms. The GNP can be expressed including inflation (nominal GNP) and excluding inflation (real GNP). For example, if the GNP grew by 10 percent but the inflation rate was 8 percent, the real growth would be 2 percent. In this example, most of the growth is due to increases in prices, and only 2 percent of the growth is in real production. On the other hand, if the GNP grew by 5 percent and the inflation rate was still 8 percent, the economy contracted by 3 percent. Data on GNP is available in constant or current dollars. To compare GNP over a number of years, it is better to use constant dollars, because this accounts for inflation. The dollar value of the current year is known as the "current dollar." Since the GNP includes products and services produced by Canadians outside Canada, it is not necessarily a good measure of the Canadian economy.

The GDP includes all economic activity (the monetary value of all goods and services produced) taking place within Canada or a province. This indicator is available for both Canada and the provinces. The same rationale as for the GNP is used to compare the growth rates for GDP (in real terms and using constant dollars).

Many people throw around the terms GNP and GDP, but few of us know where this system of quantification originated. In her book, *Counting for Nothing: What Men Value and What Women Are Worth*, economist Marilyn Waring tells us that GDP and GNP come from a small calculation in the UN System of National Accounts (UNSNA). She believes that UNSNA has allowed women's work and much of the rest of life to be made invisible, and subsequently to be deemed unimportant in measures of economic progress. The UNSNA is described by its proponents as a coherent, consistent, and integrated set of macroeconomic accounts, balance sheets, and tables based on

■ **INCREASE IN GOVERNMENT EXPENDITURES.** The government has to pay out benefits to support the unemployed.

■ **LOSS OF PROFITS.** With higher unemployment, firms are unlikely to perform better and make higher profits.

Perhaps the main costs of unemployment are those incurred by the unemployed themselves. Individuals lose their self-esteem and confidence. If they are unemployed for a long time, they may also lose their skills. In addition to these effects, unemployment often leads to poor health as well as a range of social and family problems not calculated in official statistics.

Economic Theories on Unemployment

Economists do not agree on the causes or solutions to unemployment. Debate generally revolves around explanations derived from the three economic theories: Keynesian economics, monetarist eco-a set of internationally agreed concepts, definitions, classifications, and accounting rules. The UNSNA presents economic data in a format that is designed for economic analysis, decision making, and policy making. It is commonly used as a way of comparing the supposed economic well-being of countries. However, the UNSNA ensures that certain factors of economic life appear far more important than others. Waring says that when the economy includes only activities that involve monetary transactions, much of women's productive and reproductive work is excluded. Bearing children, mothering, tending a garden, feeding one's family, milking a family cow, and raising sheep for wool you use yourself are all excluded as economic activities and do not find their way into any country's System of National Accounts. In other words, through a traditional understanding of the economy, much of the work of half of the population becomes invisible.

Here is how the UNSNA divides life, according to Waring:

Things with economic value:

- trees when they are cut down
- the tobacco industry
- arms and missile production
- the weight-loss industry
- crime, the court system, and imprisonment
- prostitution
- illness, clinics, and hospitals
- death and the funeral business
- rebuilding countries after natural disasters or terrorist attacks
- war
- oil spills
- women's bodies used in media advertising

Things without economic value:

- rivers and forests (when they are not being harnessed for economic gain)
- health
- caring for your own children
- vegetables grown in your own garden and eaten by your family
- caring for the Earth
- a mother's contribution to the birthing process
- beauty (except if it is for sale in an art piece)
- doing your own dishes and laundry
- hunting, fishing, and trapping your own food

nomics, and political economy. Each has a completely different view of the role of government in the economy and the effects of social spending on the economy, as was discussed in detail in Chapter 3. The Keynesian approach is based on the concepts of demand and labour. The premise is that unemployment results from a lack of demand for commodities, because people have less money to spend. This creates a vicious circle. Economists of this persuasion believe that the government should spend when unemployment is high to maintain consumer demand. The Keynesian approach was widely implemented after World War II, and provided the impetus and foundation for the development of modern social welfare programs.

In the last decade or so, the monetarist approach has dominated government policies in Canada and other industrialized countries. In this approach, inflation is considered to be the primary problem. Low inflation is seen as a condition that is necessary to attract investment,

Theories on
Unemployment

■ **Keynesian approach:**
unemployment is caused
by decreased demand for
goods and services.

■ **Monetarist approach:**
unemployment is caused
by high inflation, which
decreases investment.

because people will not invest their money in countries that have high inflation. Monetarists tend to see unemployment as not necessarily a bad thing; they believe that the government can use unemployment as a tool to keep inflation in check — it cools inflation by keeping wage demands lower, and less income means that people are buying fewer commodities.

The political economy approach concentrates on the relationship between politics and economics and is generally critical of government employment policy. In this approach, the economic power belongs to the corporate elite, which influences the political powers to pursue the corporate elite's interests, rather than those of the unemployed. The political economy approach focuses on the large concentration of ownership of major corporations and the large spread and great inequality between employers at the top and workers at the bottom.

Minimum Wage and Social Welfare

Canada's provinces all set a standard minimum wage. This is the lowest wage rate, by law, that an employer can pay employees to perform their work.

Wage laws were originally created to protect women and children from uncontrolled exploitation. Minimum wage laws were first instituted in Canada in 1918 in the provinces of British Columbia and Manitoba, but only women were covered. By 1920, four other provinces followed: Nova Scotia, Quebec, Ontario, and Saskatchewan. British Columbia was the first province to include men, with the *Men's Minimum Wage Act* (1925). The act set a higher minimum wage for men, reflecting the belief that the man should be the family's breadwinner and therefore should be paid more.

In 2006, about 5.5 percent of Canadians earned minimum wage. Many people believe that only struggling students or people without higher education make the minimum wage, but this is not the case: 61 percent of minimum wage workers are adults, 64 percent are women, and 48 percent have some post-secondary education (Goldberg and Green 1999, 4).

Table 4.1: Who Earns Minimum Wage?		
	2004 Male	**2004 Female**
Young (15–24)	12.9%	21.9%
Old (over 24)	1.3%	2.5%
	2004 Male and Female	
Dropout	13.2%	
High School Grad	4.6%	
College or Trade	2.1%	
Univ. Grad	1.3%	

Source: Based on data from Statistics Canada (2005). Fact sheet on minimum wage. *Perspectives on Labour and Income.* September.

The minimum wage varies by province and territory. The general minimum wage in Ontario was $7.75 in 2006, and $8.00 per hour in 2007. The 2007 provincial budget called for a rise to $8.75 in 2008, $9.50 in 2009 and $10.25 in 2010. The Ontario government views these increases as a key mechanism for addressing child poverty.

The rates are raised periodically to account for a portion of inflation, but the general purchasing power of the minimum wage has decreased over the past few decades. The real value of the minimum wage (after inflation) has fallen dramatically from its peak in the mid-1970s.

A recent study by the Canadian Union of Public Employees (CUPE 2006, 2) found that the real value of the minimum wage is 20 percent less in real dollars than 30 years ago. For example, the average minimum wage in 1976 was $2.71, equivalent to $9.14 in today's dollars after adjusting for inflation. This is well below the minimum wage in every province.

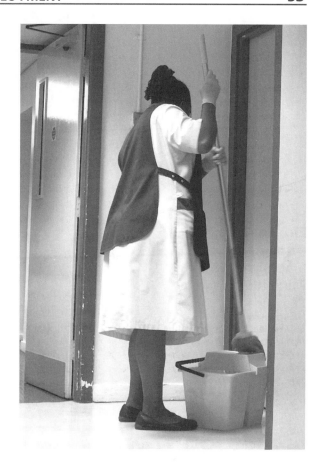

Killer of Jobs?

The level of minimum wages has been the subject of considerable public debate. Some view the minimum wage as a "killer of jobs"— hurting those it intends to help by pricing low-wage earners out of the job market. Others, specifically labour unions and anti-poverty groups, view it as a policy instrument for promoting greater wage equity and anti-poverty goals.

The impact of increasing the minimum wage on employment levels appears to be minimal. Analysis shows that large increases in the minimum wage have been followed by both increases and decreases in employment, demonstrating that other trends in the economy have greater influence on employment levels than do minimum wages. Thus, minimum wages are not a "killer of jobs," as some would have us believe (Goldberg and Green 1999, 17). Studies looking at the employment effects of minimum wage changes typically find that a 10 percent increase in the minimum wage produces declines in the range of 0 to 2 percent in the employment-to-population ratio. No negative effect on employment would be preferable, but the benefits, including the social benefits of increasing low-income wages by 10 percent, must be weighed against the costs of slightly higher unemployment.

Some social policy advocates state that minimum wages should be set at the poverty line. They believe that, in a just society, people

Many people living in poverty are participating in the workforce. In most places in Canada, people working full-time in minimum wage jobs would be below Low Income Cut-off for their area.

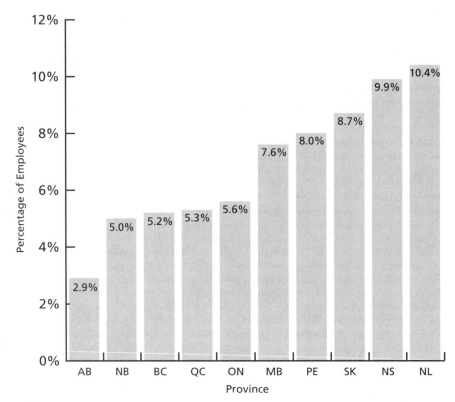

**Figure 4.1:
Percentage of
Employees Earning
Minimum Wage by
Province**

*Source: Alberta Employment,
Immigration and Industry.
2006. Alberta minimum wage
profile (12 month average:
July 2005–June 2006).
Reprinted with permission.*

working full-time should not find themselves living in poverty. Setting a higher minimum wage would raise the floor for low-income earners and reduce the costs for many of our income security programs. People would be getting their income from the labour market, rather than having to turn to government transfers. However, governments must also consider possible negative impacts on the overall economy.

Factors Influencing Unemployment

Unemployment occurs when the supply and demand for human resources or labour are out of synch. Supply and demand, in turn, are influenced by a range of forces created by the interaction of economic, structural, and policy factors.

Economic Factors

There is a range of more strictly economic factors that influence employment and unemployment levels. These affect the supply and demand equation for jobs. Consider the following:

■ **BUSINESS CYCLES.** Agreement among economists is rare, but they do agree that market-driven economies move in cycles, and it is during the dips that unemployment may result. The cause of cycles is not as clear, but it is generally agreed that it is a function of supply and demand throughout the economy.

- **INDUSTRIAL ADJUSTMENT.** Production may move from high-wage countries to low-wage countries, from inefficient facilities to newer ones, and these moves can leave a trail of unemployed workers.

- **COST OF PRODUCTION AND PRODUCTIVITY.** Low productivity may result from obsolete plants and equipment, high cost of labour per unit, high transportation costs, bad management, and high taxes. The value of the Canadian dollar relative to other currencies, particularly the U.S. dollar, also has a major impact on the business costs and competitiveness.

- **TECHNOLOGICAL CHANGES.** Increased automation may result in a decreased demand for labour. It can also result in skills redundancies – situations in which the original workers do not have the technological skills necessary for the new types of occupations. (On the positive side, technological change can also result in new products, new markets, or increased productivity.)

Structural Factors

Unemployment levels are also affected by a number of quasi-economic factors, which we will refer to as "structural." These include the following:

- **GROWING LABOUR SUPPLY.** Since 1981, Canada's labour supply has grown more than at any time in its history. Women, persons with disabilities, and Aboriginal peoples have entered the labour force in growing numbers.

- **IMBALANCE BETWEEN SKILLS SUPPLY AND DEMAND.** People may not be able to take advantage of job opportunities because they lack the skills needed for the jobs available in their area. The mismatching of skills in demand with those available is a common and persistent cause of unemployment. As Canada shifts to a more knowledge-based economy, the availability of jobs for those without high levels of education will shrink.

- **MOVEMENT BETWEEN JOBS.** Called *frictional unemployment*, this phenomenon refers to people who switch jobs. While they are between jobs, they are considered unemployed.

- **SEASONAL LAYOFFS.** People get laid off in seasonal occupations such as the resource industries, construction, and tourism. Canada is particularly affected by seasonal layoffs.

- **INTERNAL MIGRATION.** Rural-to-urban migration can increase unemployment until the migrating people find jobs.

Policy Factors

Government economic and social policies continue to be used as tools in effecting certain outcomes, such as the rate of inflation, deficit levels, and international trade. The following affect employment:

- **INTEREST RATES.** The use of high interest rates to combat inflation increases the cost of doing business and the cost of financing government deficits. This may lead to unemployment.
- **EXCHANGE RATE POLICIES.** The exchange rate policy of keeping the dollar artificially high may make Canadian products less competitive.
- **EDUCATION AND JOB TRAINING.** Government job-training initiatives can influence employment levels. These include job-specific training and support to schools, colleges, and universities, as well as apprenticeship programs.

The Efficiency/Equity Debate

Debates about economic efficiency and social equity are at the heart of many mainstream social policy discussions. Economic efficiency generally refers to economic growth with a flexible and increasingly productive labour market. Social equity, on the other hand, refers to the existence of adequate levels of health and security for all people, and a reasonably equal distribution of income and wealth. For example, a society may consider the objective of redistribution to the poor a valued objective, but if such a redistribution comes at a substantial cost in terms of misallocated resources and income losses, it may not be politically or economically sustainable.

Statements such as "Canada cannot afford generous social programs" or "more taxes will just kill the economy" contain ideas about trade-offs between economic efficiency and social equity. On one side of the debate are organizations, such as the Fraser Institute, who believe that economic freedom is the key to prosperity. They quote monetarist theorist Milton Friedman, "Freeing people economically unleashes individual drive and initiative and puts a nation on the road to economic growth," to back their claim (Gwartney and Lawson 2003). Key to economic freedom, according to the Institute, are low taxes and minimal social spending. At the other end of the debate are organizations such as the Canadian Council on Social Development (CCSD). They believe that Canada must "knock down the barriers to social exclusion by investing in well-designed social policies that can contribute to a healthy, productive and safe Canadian population – from cradle to grave" (CCSD 2003). The Fraser Institute has developed the Economic Freedom Index (see www.fraserinstitute.ca) to measure economic efficiency; the CCSD has developed the Personal Security Index (see www.ccsd.ca/pubs/2003/psi/) to measure social equity.

Social policy analysts are often confronted with the argument that social welfare programs cause inefficiencies in the economy, and that economic efficiency and social equity are incompatible goals. Some argue that social spending undermines the competitiveness of Canadian business by channelling valuable resources away from making business firms more competitive. Others counter that social spending helps improve employee skill levels, employee health and confidence, as well as family security, thereby making Canada more competitive. So what is the relationship between economic efficiency and social equity? Is there a direct trade-off, as many would have us believe?

Income security and social services increase the health and security of people. Whether or not this negatively or positively affects Canada's competitiveness is a scientific question. Many European countries have found that social spending has more beneficial impacts on economic growth than do tax cuts for upper-income earners.

In the end, the efficiency/equity trade-off debate is a question that can only be answered by examining the relevant empirical data. The largest collection of research on the issue is the Luxembourg Income Study (LIS) project, a database of household income surveys. These surveys provide demographic, income, and expenditure information on three different levels (household, person, and child), from twenty-five countries on four continents (Europe, America, Asia, and Oceania). The LIS data generally shows that the "efficiency-equality trade-off associated with welfare state economies does not hold" (Bohácek 2002, 1). Many of the reports arising from LIS can be downloaded from www.lisproject.org/publications/wpapers.htm.

Perhaps there is no real inverse relationship (if one goes up, the other goes down) between economic growth and social equity. Well-designed social and economic policies should reinforce each other, building both a strong economy and a just society.

From Welfare State to Social Investment State

New ideas have emerged about how to provide social welfare, and scholars worldwide are examining new approaches. For example, sociologist Anthony Giddens proposes a social investment state that

What Is the Personal Security Index?

Developed by the Canadian Council on Social Development, the Personal Security Index (PSI) is a tool to measure annual changes in the security of Canadians according to three key elements:

■ economic security in the broad sense of job and financial security

■ health security in the sense of protection against the threats of disease and injury

■ physical safety in the sense of feeling safe from violent crime and theft

The PSI measures changes in both empirical data and in people's perceptions of their personal security.

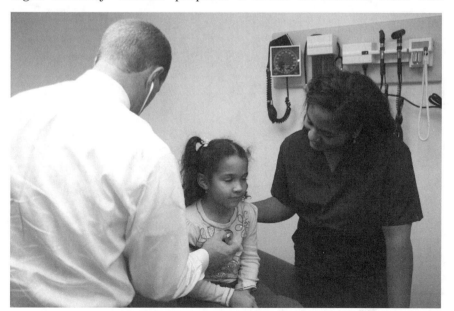

Social equity calls for adequate levels of health care for all; however, many argue that universal health care is not economically efficient.

focuses on social inclusion by strengthening civil society and providing equality of opportunity rather than equality of outcomes (1998). Giddens believes that jobs that are not low-paying and dead-end are essential to attacking involuntary social exclusion. Nevertheless, an inclusive society must also provide for the basic needs of those who cannot work, and must recognize the wider diversity of goals that life has to offer (1998, 31).

Giddens rejects the ideologies of liberalism and socialism as workable options (see Chapter 3 for further explanation of these ideologies). The social investment state, according to Giddens, is a mixed economy with an interaction of state, family, work, and community, with each area reinforcing one another. Giddens emphasizes investment in human capital to cultivate human potential wherever possible, rather than directly providing income support. He calls this a positive welfare society. In such a state, the government would focus on providing employment-training opportunities for working-age adults and a positive educational and nurturing environment for children.

In the last decade, governments worldwide have started to recognize that a new policy mix is required to respond to changing labour markets, an aging population, worsening inequality, poverty, and a knowledge-based economy. Governments in the European Union are now considering social policy, economic policy, and employment policy in a new way — as being interrelated. Rather than seeing an inverse trade-off, they see each area reinforcing one another. With this in mind, they put forward a social welfare policy mix that addresses employment support, income support (especially for families with children), and service support (such as housing and child care). They call this an "activation for social inclusion strategy."

"You're all on the wrong floor, try the basement."

The social investment state and its variations focus on:

■ partnership investments in lifelong learning and training

■ encouragement for family-friendly workplaces

■ support for innovation, entrepreneurship, and expansion of existing enterprises

Labour Market Experiences and Incomes of Recent Immigrants

Canada has always been a nation of immigrants (other than the original inhabitants of this land – the Aboriginal peoples). Since 1967, there has been a major shift in the source countries from which immigrants have come to Canada. Fewer now come from Western Europe; most now come from the countries of Asia, Africa, and Central and South America. In addition, today, three in four recent immigrants to Canada belong to visible minority groups, making them more vulnerable to racial discrimination and social exclusion. Visible minorities are defined as being neither Caucasian nor Aboriginal. Members of visible minority groups now make up about 13 percent of the total Canadian population, compared to just 6 percent as recently as 1986.

Chapter 9 details the broader aspects of poverty in Canada, but clearly employment and the labour market are crucial aspects of inclusion for recent immigrants. Poverty among recent immigrants stands at 27 percent, and their annual wages and salaries are one-third less than those of other Canadians. Many recent visible minority immigrants perceive themselves as having been discriminated against in the job market.

Ekuma Smith, senior research associate with the Canadian Council on Social Development (CCSD) and Andrew Jackson, then CCSD research director, studied levels of employment, earnings, family incomes, and poverty rates of recent immigrants, and compared them to the rest of the Canadian population over the economic recovery period from 1995 to 1998. Their key findings indicate that the "rising tide" of economic recovery in the mid- to late 1990s had a positive impact on the employment opportunities and incomes of recent immigrants. This indicates that a healthy labour market can provide a major impetus towards equality and the inclusion of recent immigrants into the economic and social mainstream. However, they also found that the gap between recent immigrants and the rest of Canadians remains large.

The non-recognition or the undervaluing of foreign education, skills, and credentials are emerging as key factors that help explain why recent immigrants do not do as well in the job market. A variety of policies is required to assist the process of inclusion and confront discrimination. These policies include employment equity, credentials recognition, promotion of the "hidden skills" of new immigrants to

Visible minorities

■ peoples who are neither Caucasian nor Aboriginal; in the 2001 Canadian census, 13 percent of the population identified itself as a visible minority

■ the United Nations Committee on the Elimination of Racial Discrimination released a report in 2007 stating that Canada should reconsider using the term "visible minorities" to define people facing discrimination, suggesting the phrase itself is discriminatory

Centre for
Social Justice

www.socialjustice.org

The Centre for Social
Justice is a non-partisan
organization that conducts
research, provides
education and advocacy
to help narrow the gap in
income, wealth, and power,
and to enhance peace
and human security, and
brings together people
from universities and
unions, faith groups, and
community organizations
in the pursuit of greater
equality and democracy.

prospective employers, and provision of language and skills training to new immigrants.

A recent study by Statistics Canada (Frenette and Morissette 2003) discovered that recent immigrant men employed on a full-year, full-time basis saw their real earnings fall 7 percent on average from 1980 to 2000, even though they had a substantial increase in their educational attainment. During the same period, however, real earnings of Canadian-born men went up 7 percent. Earnings of recent immigrant women rose over the period, but not as quickly as among Canadian-born women.

The rapid integration of immigrants into the Canadian labour market is key to the country's future prosperity. To achieve successful integration, we must recognize that racism is a factor. Racism can be a subtle phenomenon. It may be less about excluding candidates from consideration for a job because of their skin colour than about fearing that they will not "fit in." And it may be about seeing foreign credentials and experience as "obviously inferior," rather than assessing skills and abilities on an individual basis according to Ekuwa Smith in a presentation to Carleton University first year students in 2003. Other crucial factors are language-skills training opportunities, overall economic growth, and well-designed and accessible settlement services.

A Statistics Canada study (Li, Gervais, and Duval 2006) on overqualification and underemployment of recent immigrants found that immigrants who had been in Canada for ten years or less had a higher incidence of overqualification than their Canadian-born counterparts. For example, more than one-half (52 percent) of recent immigrants with a university degree worked in a job requiring only high school education at some point during the six-year period under study. This was almost twice the proportion of 28 percent among their Canadian-born counterparts. They also found that their period of overqualification lasted longer. They concluded that much of this problem relates to the recognition of their foreign educational credentials and a lack of Canadian workplace experience.

Another Statistics Canada study (Galarneau and Morissette 2004) found that recent immigrants were twice as likely to be in jobs requiring low education as their Canadian-born counterparts. It pointed to contributing factors such as institutional and language barriers, difficulties related to recognition of foreign credentials and experience, and a variety of incidental factors such as discrimination encountered by some immigrants. For more on this topic, see Chapter 8.

Youth Unemployment

While they are working, young people gain valuable experience and life skills. In fact, young people who are employed part-time generally have better school performance and a lower dropout rate. By the same token, teens who lack skills and job experience are at a disadvantage when competing for jobs. Research confirms that teens who have dropped out of school are having much greater difficulty finding full-time jobs than even a decade ago, and many of those working earn minimum wage. Youth unemployment – the difficulty many young people have in finding meaningful work that will enable them to make a smooth transition to adulthood – is a major problem in Canada, and it is one that is unlikely to go away without conscious policy intervention.

Youth at Work, an extended study of the labour market experiences of teenagers (aged 15–19 years), found that the employment rate of teens fell sharply from 1989 to 1997. The lack of jobs during the recession and recovery sharply limited the opportunities for teenagers to find work. Overall, the teen employment rate in 2004 was 45 percent, up from the low of 37.1 percent in 1997, but not near the rate of 51.6 percent in 1989. Employment rates were typically lower for teens from lower-income and immigrant families, and (not surprisingly) high-unemployment regions and communities.

A key problem for teens (and young adults to a lesser degree) was that the recession and cuts to Employment Insurance forced many middle-aged and older workers with more skills and experience to accept low-income jobs. This effectively shut many employable teens and young adults out of the job market. Even after the recovery began, teens were still stuck behind 20- to 24-year-olds in the job queue. It is possible that welfare reforms in various provinces, such as making young adults ineligible for benefits, also heightened competition for relatively low-wage jobs.

A series of policy initiatives directed towards youth employment seems particularly urgent. The importance of young people having an opportunity to acquire work experience and skills, as well as to develop the personal confidence that accompanies employment, cannot be overemphasized if they and their families are subsequently to participate fully in the Canadian economy and society.

Conclusion

While Canada has sustained impressive economic growth over the past decade or so, it still does not generate or distribute enough employment to sustain all Canadians, and secure employment is key to reducing the incidence of poverty. Increasingly, those with jobs are in uncertain situations, are working part-time, or are in temporary jobs. The "just-in-time" economy of the 1990s has resulted in less secure employment and fewer benefits.

There are social and economic costs to unemployment – costs often overlooked in the thrust to compete globally. Unfortunately, arguments for economic efficiency often preclude an intelligent debate about social equity, and many assume that a direct trade-off between economic efficiency and social equity exists. However, unstable work, low wages, and the decreasing purchasing power of the minimum wage have been obstacles to reducing and preventing poverty in Canada. Economic prosperity in Canada is increasingly polarized — corporate executive salaries and the use of food banks and shelters for the homeless are both hitting all-time highs.

Advanced capitalist economies such as Canada's are changing, and changes in social welfare policy need to keep pace. Rather than viewing social programs as a drain on the economy, there is a need to look more closely at the interactions between the economy, employment, and social policy. There is a need for more government involvement in the economy to ensure that people actively participate in all aspects of community life.

Many social welfare analysts are now calling for a change in the direction of our economic and social policies, a change that is premised on the idea of social inclusion. The belief underlying this premise is that social inclusion will lead to social cohesion, economic growth, and, in the long run, a reduction in the number of individuals who require social welfare assistance.

Chapter Summary

Key Concepts

- ■ **Cyclical unemployment**
- ■ **Discouraged workers**
- ■ **Economic efficiency**
- ■ **Employment**
- ■ **Employment Insurance**
- ■ **Employment population ratio**
- ■ **Frictional unemployment**
- ■ **Full-time employment**
- ■ **Labour force**
- ■ **Labour force participation rate**
- ■ **Minimum wage**
- ■ **Natural unemployment**
- ■ **Part-time employment**
- ■ **Self-employment**
- ■ **Social Assistance**
- ■ **Social equity**
- ■ **Social investment state**
- ■ **Structural unemployment**
- ■ **Trade unions**
- ■ **Underemployment**
- ■ **Unemployment rate**
- ■ **Visible minorities**
- ■ **Youth unemployment**

Review Questions

1. What are some of the recent trends that are affecting the income and job security of Canadians?

2. Why are people who are discouraged, or, in other words, have stopped looking for a job, not counted in the official unemployment statistics?

3. What is the relevance of the social costs of unemployment to future government expenditures?

4. List and explain the three theories on unemployment. How would each theory differ in its approach to solving unemployment?

5. List the economic, structural, and policy factors that influence unemployment.

6. Define what is meant by the concepts of "economic efficiency" and "social equity," and explain why some might regard the two as being in a trade-off relationship.

7. Describe the labour market experiences of recent immigrants, and explain two possible reasons for these experiences.

Exploring Social Welfare

1. Statistics Canada publishes *Perspectives on Labour and Income,* available at www.statcan.ca. Check the chronological index for a complete listing, and find an article about a topic that interests you and read it. Find one other article on your topic, and write a brief report with proper references to each of your articles. Use the APA style for citing articles (APA is short for American Psychological Association). You can find APA citation guides online, such as at http://library.osu.edu/sites/guides/apagd.php.

2. Go online to the Statistics Canada website and Search for "reasons for part-time work by sex and age group." List the reasons men and women are working part-time. Is there one reason that stands out for you that is different for men and women? Given your analysis, what possible policies might the government adopt to address the part-time work problem?

Websites

Just Labour: A Canadian Journal of Work and Society
www.justlabour.yorku.ca
York University's Centre for Research on Work and Society publishes an online journal with extensive coverage of labour market issues in Canada.

Canadian Labour Congress
www.clc-ctc.ca
The CLC conducts research and publishes employment- and labour-related reports, many of which are available online.

Canadian Centre for Policy Alternatives
www.policyalternatives.ca
The CCPA is a non-profit research organization founded in 1980 to promote research on economic and social policy issues from a progressive point of view.

References

Betcherman, G., and G. Lowe. 1997. *The Future of Work in Canada: A Synthesis Report*. Ottawa: CPRN.

Bohácek, Radim. 2002. The efficiency-equality tradeoff in welfare state economies" (February 5). CERGE-EI Working Paper No. 193. http://ssrn.com/abstract=317862.

Broad, D. 2000. Living a half life? Part-time work, labour standards and social welfare. *Canadian Social Work Review* 17 (1).

Canadian Council on Social Development (CCSD). 2003. *Imagining a Future of Inclusion: CCSD's Submission to the House of Commons Standing Committee on Finance*. Ottawa: CCSD.

Canadian Union of Public Employees (CUPE). 2006. *Thirty Years of Dwindling Minimum Wages in Canada*. Ottawa: CUPE. http://cupe.ca/publications/Thirty_Years_of_Dwin.

Frenette, Marc, and René Morissette. 2003. *Will They Ever Converge? Earnings of Immigrants and Canadian-Born Workers over the Last Two Decades*. Ottawa: Statistics Canada.

Galarneau, Diane, and René Morissette. 2004. Immigrants: settling for less? *Perspectives on Labour and Income* 16 (3). www.statcan.ca/english/studies/75-001/archive/e-pdf/e-0431.pdf.

Giddens, Anthony. 1998. Equality and the social investment state. In *Tomorrow's Politics: The Third Way and Beyond*, ed. I. Hargreaves and I. Christie. London, U.K.: Demos.

Goldberg, Michael, and David Green. 1999. *Raising the Floor: The Social and Economic Benefits of Minimum Wages in Canada*. BC: Canadian Centre for Policy Alternatives. www.policyalternatives.ca/documents/BC_Office_Pubs/raising_floor.pdf.

Gwartney, James D., and Robert A. Lawson. 2003. *Economic Freedom of the World: 2003 Annual Report*. Vancouver: Fraser Institute.

Human Resources Development Canada. 1996. Tallying the economic and social costs of unemployment. *Applied Research Bulletin* 2 (2).

Jackson, A. 2005. *Work and Labour in Canada: Critical Issues*. Toronto: Canadian Scholars' Press.

Li, Chris, Ginette Gervais, and Aurélie Duval. 2006. *The Dynamics of Overqualification: Canada's Underemployed University Graduates*. Ottawa: Statistics Canada. www.statcan.ca/english/research/11-621-MIE/11-621-MIE2006039.pdf.

Saunders, R. 2006a. Making work pay. *CPRN Policy Brief* 2. Ottawa: Canadian Policy Research Networks. www.cprn.com/en/doc.cfm?doc=1579.

Saunders, R. 2006b. *Risk and Opportunity: Creating Options for Vulnerable Workers*. Ottawa: Canadian Policy Research Networks. www.cprn.com/en/doc.cfm?doc=1339#.

Schellenberg, Grant. 1997. *The Changing Nature of Part-Time Work*. Social Research Series Report no. 4. Ottawa: Canadian Council on Social Development.

Statistics Canada. 2002. *Longitudinal Aspect of Involuntary Part-Time Employment.* Ottawa: Statistics Canada. www.statcan.ca/english/research/ 75F0002MIE/75F0002MIE2000003.pdf.

Statistics Canada. 2004. *Women in Canada: Work Chapter Updates.* Ottawa: Statistics Canada. www.statcan.ca/english/freepub/89F0133XIE/ 89F0133XIE2003000.pdf.

Statistics Canada. 2005. Fact sheet on minimum wage. *Perspectives on Labour and Income, September 2005.* www.statcan.ca/english/studies/75-001/comm/2005_09.pdf.

Statistics Canada. 2006a. *Labour Force Information for Week ending February 18, 2006.* Ottawa: Statistics Canada. www.statcan.ca/english/ freepub/71-001-XIE/0020671-001-XIE.htm.

Statistics Canada. 2006b. *Women in Canada: A Gender-Based Statistical Report,* 5th ed. Ottawa: Statistics Canada. www.statcan.ca/english/ freepub/89-503-XIE/0010589-503-XIE.pdf.

5

Globalization and Human Rights

The Social Welfare Context

We have entered a period of tremendous economic transition. The world is being transformed into a vast global marketplace by complex financial systems and revolutionary information technologies. As global corporations gain more power and influence, they are preparing regulations to protect their interests, and they are relying on institutions such as the World Trade Organization to enforce them. In the face of this vast concentration of resources and power in fewer and fewer hands, human beings need new mechanisms to protect their rights and their welfare.

Major corporations that operate around the globe are growing larger and more powerful. This growth in power and influence is affecting social welfare in countries throughout the world, and Canada is no exception. Globalization is creating new patterns of interaction

" Civil and political rights — the right to vote — is meaningless in the absence of having your basic needs met. An adequate standard of living is a right."

— *Josephine Grey, founding director of Low Income Families Together (LIFT)*

International Forum on Globalization

www.ifg.org

The International Forum on Globalization is an organization representing over sixty organizations that seek to explore the implications of economic globalization and promote alternative policies for equity, diversity, and sustainability.

among people, states, and private companies, but it is also threatening to compound many existing challenges, and it is deepening the economic marginalization of those most vulnerable. As globalization progresses, social protections are being eroded. In this chapter, we will see how the concept of human rights has become a key response — global-based standards of human rights can provide the structures for global social welfare, equality, and justice.

Human rights became an international priority for the United Nations fifty years ago, and were addressed formally in the December 1948 *Universal Declaration of Human Rights*. In today's complex world, these rights have gained prominence as a universally recognized set of norms and standards that increasingly shape our relations as individuals and as collective members of groups, within communities and among nations. Human rights include:

- the rights of political choice and association, of opinion and expression, and of culture
- the freedom from fear and from all forms of discrimination and prejudice
- the freedom from want and the right to employment and well-being and, collectively, to development

Today, there is near-universal recognition that respect for human rights is essential to achieving the three agreed-upon global priorities of peace, development, and democracy. But achieving these priorities is proving to be difficult. As nations compete to become more "investor friendly," social welfare is eroded in favour of tax cuts and government debt payment. Globalization has also provided capital with an exit option — if corporations do not like what they see in the policy of a particular country, they leave. This gives corporations more control over working conditions and civil society. In the global age, Keynesian policies of demand management, progressive social policy, and full employment are no longer priorities.

The social welfare of people, whether it be in a country or worldwide, can be based on the idea of human rights or social standards. In this chapter, we will explore how a human rights–based approach to social welfare can act as a counterbalance to globalization. It provides a framework and mechanism for pursuing global social welfare within increasingly limited confines. Corporations have globalized and protected their interests through free trade agreements and institutions. Social welfare must take a similar course, and at the same time it must hold corporations accountable to human rights standards.

As the international community becomes increasingly integrated, how can cultural diversity and integrity be respected? Is a global culture inevitable? If so, is the world ready for it? Can we respect cultural differences and have universal, worldwide human rights? These are some of the issues, concerns, and questions underlying the debate over universal human rights.

Canada in the World

To this point, we have focused on economic disparity and social welfare in Canada, but it is also important to understand how Canada fits into the larger global picture. We have seen how in Canada a relatively small number of people own a large share of the resources and obtain a large share of total income. At the international level, the same phenomenon occurs. Canada is a wealthy country, possessing more than its share of wealth per capita. Canada's rank in North America in 2006 is illustrated in Table 5.1 on p. 112.

These disparities of wealth among countries are not simply a matter of entitlement. It does not mean that as Canadians we work harder than our Mexican neighbours; in fact, the reverse may be true. Our consumer-driven lifestyle depends directly upon the production of cheap goods by our poorer neighbours. Bananas, coffee, clothing, electronics, and sugar are among the many products that are produced outside of Canada, and Canadians routinely purchase them at a price that does not represent a fair trade.

Unless one is directly involved in international social work, it is a little difficult to grasp how what we do in Canada affects people in other countries. Knowledge about how the international economy operates — what is commonly referred to as economic globalization — is the first key to developing a deeper understanding.

Human Development Indicators

One way of understanding and measuring the effects of economic globalization is to examine human development indicators; the United Nations is one of the best sources for such indicators; produced by the United Nations Development Programme (UNDP), the Human Development Report (HDR) was first launched in 1990 when it began reporting on the Human Development Index. Since the first report, three additional indexes have been developed: the Gender-related Development Index, the Gender Empowerment Measure, and the Human Poverty Index.

The most well-known index — the Human Development Index (HDI) — measures more than income. Amartya Sen, an influential scholar in this area, states that deprivation should not be measured only by what people possess but also by what they are able to do. Therefore, when examining social welfare, it is important to consider access to housing, health, education, community life, and political life.

Following Sen's analysis, the index includes life expectancy, adult literacy, and the gross enrolment ratio. It measures items that shape future opportunities, such as basic and advanced education and health, taking a social inclusion viewpoint on inequality. The HDI compares the countries of the world according to their average achievements in three basic dimensions of human development:

Canadian Policy Research Networks

www.cprn.com

This organization is a network of people conducting research on public policy. It has an extensive list of free publications available for downloading from its site.

Table 5.1: Human Development Indicators, 2006 (measured in USD)			
	Canada	**U.S.**	**Mexico**
Life Expectancy	79.9 yrs	77.3 yrs	74.9 yrs
GDP per Capita	$32,263	$39,676	$9,803
Under 5 Mortality Rate (per 1,000 Live Births)	6%	8%	28%
Inequality Measure (Ratio of Richest 10% to Poorest 10%)	9.4%	15.9%	24.6%
Proportion below 50% of Median Income	11.4%	17%	20.2%
Per Capita Health Expenditures	$2,989	$5,711	$582

Source: Based on data from United Nations Development Programme. 2006. *Human Development Report 2006*. New York: Palgrave Macmillian. (also available at http://hdr.undp.org/hdr2006)

a long and healthy life, knowledge, and a decent standard of living. It is calculated for 177 countries and areas for which data is available.

The HDI takes what is called a *human development approach*. This approach values capacities such as health and education as ends in themselves, rather than as a means to increasing income. This can be contrasted to the human capital approach, which views increases in capabilities such as education and health only in terms of the potential increase in productive capacity or income.

What Is Globalization?

Economic globalization is the growing integration of international markets for goods, services, and finance. There are three main characteristics of economic globalization:

- **FREE TRADE AND INVESTMENT EXPANSION.** Globalization allows for expansion in the trade of goods and services between countries, and transnational corporations (TNCs) are expanding the geographical extent of their investments.

- **CONCENTRATED TNC POWER.** Economic power is concentrated in the hands of large TNCs.

- **ENFORCEMENT AND TNC RIGHTS PROTECTION.** International bodies, such as the World Trade Organization (WTO), are devising policies and enforcement practices to protect the rights of TNCs and their capital worldwide.

Globalization is essentially a new stage in the global expansion of the economic system of capitalism. Globalization means that products and services are increasingly flowing between countries and that territorial units such as the nation state are decreasing in importance. For example, while a car may be made in a factory in Canada, the various parts for an automobile may be produced in different countries, assembled in another country, and sold to the automobile maker. This shift from national production and trade between nations to global commerce reflects the power of transnational corporations. When this is combined with corporate control of media (film, television, and even news), these transnational corporations are able to exert considerable influence over our lives in what is known as "economic fundamentalism." This influence, which used to be held by governments for the advancement of a people or their nation, is now held by businesses, for the advancement of their profits.

Free Trade and Corporate Power

Free trade refers to the lowering and dismantling of the barriers and regulations that might impede the international flow of capital and products, or restrict marketplace demand. Globalization opens domestic markets through the removal of international trade barriers. Free trade is embodied in the growing collection of free trade agreements and international trade organizations, including the General Agreement on Tariffs and Trade (GATT), the Asia-Pacific Economic Cooperation (APEC), and the North American Free Trade Agreement (NAFTA). Powerful lobbying by big corporations is behind these developments. Globalization is also encouraging the trend towards the privatization and marketization of social services and health services.

As the economies of individual countries become increasingly interdependent, the political sovereignty of countries is slowly diminishing. New telecommunication technologies have enabled large corporations to move capital and productive capacity quickly to anywhere in the world. They have enabled TNCs to open new operations in countries around the world, as opportunities present themselves, and to execute "lean production" to ensure maximum profitability.

Transnational corporations (TNCs) are organizations that possess and control the means of production or services outside of the country in which they were established. Two hundred corporations, most of them larger than many national economies, now control one-quarter of the world's economic activity and have a combined revenue of $7.1 trillion (Rice and Prince 2000, 21). One-third of the world's trade consists of transactions among various units of the same corporation (Clarke 1996). The power of TNCs is increasing, as is the influence of the most powerful Western nations, and this power is increasingly being used to dictate how less powerful countries should be run.

Calculations by the Institute for Policy Studies (IPS) indicate that the top 200 global firms account for an alarming and growing share of the world's economic activity. Based on a comparison of corporate sales and country GDPs, of the 100 largest economies in the world, 51 are corporations; only 49 are countries (Anderson and Cavanagh 2000).

CorpWatch: Holding Corporations Accountable

www.corpwatch.org

CorpWatch investigates corporations for human rights abuses, environmental misdeeds, fraud, and corruption around the world. The goal of CorpWatch is to encourage global justice, independent media activism, and democratic control over corporations.

The Philip Morris corporation is, economically speaking, larger than New Zealand, and it operates in 170 countries. Instead of creating an integrated global village, these firms are weaving webs of production, consumption, and finance that bring economic benefits to, at the most, only a third of the world's people. Two-thirds of the world (the bottom 20 percent of the rich countries and the bottom 80 percent of the poor countries) is left out, marginalized, or hurt by these webs of activity.

Enforcement and Rights Protection for the Transnational Corporations

In this new era of globalization, the rules for the global economy that were once made by national governments are increasingly being made by international organizations that are not accountable to anyone. International bodies such as the World Trade Organization (WTO), the International Monetary Fund (IMF), the World Bank, and the G8 are devising policies and enforcement practices to protect the rights of TNCs and capital. The traditional concerns of social welfare practitioners about addressing the basic needs of people are the last thing on the agenda.

These international institutions, along with the free trade agreements that they enforce, increasingly are shaping the policy-making and budgetary decisions of governments around the world. Social policy professors James Rice and Michael Prince (2000, 21) maintain that these institutions and agreements limit the ability of local and national governments to solve social problems. In effect, they shift economic thinking, placing free trade and narrow economic concerns ahead of social policy (moving from the Keynesian to the monetarist approach) and thereby provide direct limits on what local governments can do. Some have called this a *post-sovereign state*, meaning that the state or government is no longer free to make its own decisions.

One of the primary vehicles for advancements in free trade is the World Trade Organization (WTO), created in 1995. According to the WTO's website, "The World Trade Organization (WTO) is the only international organization dealing with the global rules of trade between nations. Its main function is to ensure that trade flows as smoothly, predictably and freely as possible." The WTO, for example, can rule that various environmental or social policies of countries are in violation of the WTO agreement, and can mandate elimination of what would then be deemed a trade barrier.

According to critics, the WTO has ruled that every environmental policy it has reviewed is an illegal trade barrier that must be eliminated or changed. With one exception, the WTO has also ruled against every health or food safety law it has reviewed. An organization with this type of far-reaching power certainly affects Canadian social welfare.

With this much global power and influence, the regulation of TNCs is clearly necessary for the promotion of human rights. The UN bodies currently responsible for regulating TNCs are the United Nations Conference on Trade and Development (UNCTAD) and the Division on Transnational Corporations and Investment (DTCI). Until 1993, the United Nations Centre on Transnational Corporations (UNCTC) held this responsibility, and in 1998, after twenty years of discussion and redrafting, the UNCTC published the *Draft Code of Conduct on Transnational Corporations*. It was never adopted, due to extreme pressure from corporate lobby groups and Western governments.

One of the last attempts to introduce international corporate regulation via the UN was at the 1992 UN Conference on Environment and Development (UNCED) – the "Earth Summit" – held in Rio de Janeiro. The UNCTC drafted recommendations to be included in Agenda 21 (UNCED's global plan of action) for the environmental regulation of TNCs. Again, pressure from a coalition of Western governments and corporate lobbies resulted in the removal of the recommendations.

At the present time, there is a TNC regulatory vacuum at the UN. The Bangkok Declaration and Plan of Action, adopted in 2000 at the 10th session of UNCTAD, provides the main thrust for the work of the current UNCTAD. The retooled UNCTAD has moved away from TNC regulation towards trade and investment policy. Its work now centres on analyses of economic trends and major policy issues of international concern, rather than dealing with the human rights violations of TNCs (as revealed on its new website at www.unctad.org).

Given this new era of globalization, the traditional concerns of social welfare will need to be broadened to include a concern with the issue of global human rights. As noted earlier, global social welfare (a concern with justice, social regulation, social provision, and redistribution between nations) is already a part of the activities of various supranational organizations or international governmental organizations of the United Nations.

Within this new world context, several new political strategies have emerged for regulating global competition. These involve making international institutions such as the World Trade Organization and G8 more accountable, as well as empowering the United Nations and its international organizations to effect changes that enhance the welfare of individuals and communities around the world.

Globalization in Operation

Advocates of globalization would have us believe that freer trade will automatically benefit all countries of the world. The economic theory is that poorer countries would be able to specialize their production in areas where they have a competitive advantage, and they could export those products to richer countries. This theory may work in some cases, but in practice, it tends to enrich some countries and impoverish others.

The G8

The G8, or Group of Eight, has existed for over thirty years. Since 1975, the leaders of the major industrial democracies have met annually to discuss the major economic and political issues facing their domestic societies and the international community as a whole.

France, the United States, Britain, Germany, Japan, and Italy, attended the first G6 summit; Canada joined the group at the 1976 G7 summit. In 2006, Russia hosted the summit, completing its process of becoming a full member. The group is now known as the G8.

Each year the G8 selects major priorities, as set by the hosting country. When Canada hosted the summit in 2002, the major priorities included global terrorism and a new aid plan for Africa. The 2006 summit in St. Petersburg, Russia, was dedicated to energy, security, infectious diseases, and education.

Structural Adjustment

Have you ever noticed that bananas are often cheaper than apples, even though apples could have been grown in your Canadian backyard? The process of structural adjustment, which is commonly forced upon countries that are seeking loans, helps to explain this phenomenon. The process operates as follows:

1. A country needs a loan due to a currency crisis, crumbling infrastructure, or a variety of other reasons.

2. The country approaches monetary organizations such as the International Monetary Fund (IMF) and the World Bank (WB).

3. The IMF and WB agree to lend money if the borrowing country agrees to undertake what is called *structural adjustment*. The new economic policies focus on reducing social spending and other government expenditures, increasing GDP by decreasing labour and environmental regulations, lowering any trade barriers, specializing production, allowing currency to freely trade, and encouraging foreign investment.

4. As part of the structural adjustment, the country may agree to change from subsistence agriculture to monocropping. Monocropping or monoculture occurs when agricultural land is used to grow a great deal of one product instead of a variety. So the country converts a large percentage of its agricultural production from rice to bananas. The country becomes dependent on one or two crops.

5. Foreign corporations purchase large tracts of land and hire former farmers to work as agricultural workers. (The new mega-farms are known as *agribusiness*.)

Many object to the role and subsequent power of the World Trade Organization; wherever the organization meets, there are extensive protests, like this one in the Philippines in 1999.

6. Labourers work long days, for very low wages, under poor conditions. The very best produce is shipped for sale to foreign markets, leaving the local market with bruised bananas or no local produce.

7. Environmental deregulation leads to increased use of pesticides and health risks for labourers. Soil is rapidly spent as a consequence of monocropping and overuse. As a result, the country turns to deforestation to expose rich, unused soil.

8. Western nations are able to import cheap bananas, and the profits benefit the shareholders of the foreign agribusiness.

Export Processing Zones

Globalization encourages people to do business wherever the conditions are most favourable. For large corporations, this means they can do business where their costs are minimized and profits are maximized. The deregulation of capital and freeing of trade barriers allow corporations to rapidly move their capital across international borders, making it easy for a company to set up a mobile factory in a place where labour regulations are relaxed, environmental legislation is weak, and tax laws are favourable. In fact, a country can set up in an export processing zone designed specifically for this purpose.

An export processing zone (EPZ) is a particular area in a country from which benefits come in the form of preferential financial regulations and special investment incentives. There are export processing zones all over the world. Have a look at the tags on the clothing you are wearing and imagine what the working conditions, environmental standards, and wages were for the person who made your garment.

Naomi Klein, activist and author of *No Logo: Taking Aim at the Brand Bullies*, examines how TNCs use migrant factories to move around to different EPZs in order to follow the tax breaks and incentives. She calls it "zero-risk globalization" (2000, 287).

According to Klein, corporations primarily produce brands, rather than products. Corporate brands are ideas, values, experiences, and even cultures. Nike, Gap, Disney, Levi's, and Starbucks are as much about branding as they are about products. Through the advertising and sponsorship of athletes and music stars, the TNCs create demand for their vision. In many cases, companies spend more on advertising and branding than on actually producing the product.

Most export processing zones employ a high proportion of women with minimal education. These women are subjected to pregnancy tests, locked out of washrooms, expected to work in conditions that strain their eyesight, forced to work overtime, paid low wages, and fired for pregnancy or joining a union (Ehrenreich and Fuentes 1992).

Problems with the World Trade Organization

There are many people and organizations that object to the role and power of the WTO. The main criticisms are that

■ it operates in secret
■ it promotes free trade over social and human rights
■ it places priority on commercial interests
■ it makes poverty and inequality worse
■ it benefits large corporations and rich countries
■ it dictates the ideal path to development (in conjunction with the World Bank and International Monetary Fund)
■ it transforms citizens into consumers

International
Development
Research Centre
(IDRC)

www.idrc.ca

Created in 1970, IDRC is
a Canadian organization
that helps developing
countries find long-
term solutions for the
social, economic, and
environmental problems
they face. IDRC funds
the work of researchers
working in universities,
private enterprise,
government, and non-
profit organizations in
developing countries.

The Debt Crisis

Debt continues to prevent poor countries from developing their economies — debt that was often accumulated by prior rulers and dicta-
tors, many of which were supported by Western nations or by colonial governments. For example, South Africa is still paying off
debts from the apartheid regime. The scale of the debt continues
to rise, despite ever-increasing payments, while aid is falling. For
example, the developing world now spends $13 on debt repayment
for every $1 it receives in grants. For countries classified as low in-
come by the World Bank, outstanding external debt has risen 430
percent since 1980 and now amounts to US$523 billion. For the
heavily indebted poor countries, external debt has risen 320 percent
since 1980 to US$189 billion (Kapoor 2005, 5).

Many have called for 100 percent cancellation of multilateral debt
for all countries where debt repayments are seriously hindering the
country's efforts towards attaining the Millennium Development Goals
(MDGs). This would entail a 100 percent debt cancellation for most
low-income countries, plus significant additional resources if they are
to have any hope of reaching the MDGs by 2015.

What Are Human Rights?

Before discussing how the human rights–based approach to social
welfare can counterbalance and challenge the process of globalization, we need to understand what human rights are and how human
rights protection operates in the world today.

Human rights are a common standard of achievement for human
dignity, for all peoples and all nations. They are those inherent rights
without which we cannot truly live as human beings. A *right* is a
justified claim or entitlement by someone or some institution in
society. A person or community claiming a right must offer the rest
of society sufficient reason why the claim should be met. Rights
are not a property of a person, but rather are a reason to treat a person in a certain respectful way. Many human rights advocates and
writers would agree with Ronald Dworkin's famous declaration that
"rights are trumps" — a rights claim "beats" all other competing
social values.

Human rights are commonly considered as being universal,
indivisible, inalienable, and inabrogable (Ife 2001, 12). *Universality*
means that human rights apply to all human beings. *Indivisibility* refers to the conception that all human rights must be pursued and
realized — we cannot pick and choose which rights are enforced and
which are abandoned. The *inalienability* of human rights means that
human rights, as a general rule, cannot be taken away. Of course,
there are emergencies that may necessitate the suspension of some
human rights. For example, in a medical epidemic, a quarantine in-
fected person may find that his or her rights to freedom of movement

> ## The UN Millennium Development Goals (MDGs)
>
> In 2000, at the United Nations Millennium Summit, the international community adopted the Millennium Development Goals (MDGs), an expanded vision that promotes human development as the key to sustaining social and economic progress. It is the most significant and accepted commitment to the development of poor countries in history. The MDGs recognize the importance of creating a global partnership for development and have been commonly accepted as a framework for measuring development progress. The eight goals are to:
>
> 1. eradicate extreme poverty and hunger
> 2. achieve universal primary education
> 3. promote gender equality and empower women
> 4. reduce child mortality
> 5. improve maternal health
> 6. combat HIV/AIDS, malaria, and other diseases
> 7. ensure environmental sustainability
> 8. develop a global partnership for development
>
> The UN Secretary-General reports yearly on progress towards implementation of the Millennium Declaration, including the MDGs. The first comprehensive review was conducted in 2005. Subsequent yearly reports are available at www.un.org/millenniumgoals.

have been suspended. Finally, the *inabrogable* nature of human rights refers to the idea that one cannot voluntarily give up one's human rights or trade them for special privileges.

The belief that humanity has a duty to protect the universal and inalienable rights of all people is now a recognized part of the heritage of humankind. This recognition has led to international cognizance, declarations, legislative laws, and regulations.

International Human Rights Instruments

The *International Bill of Human Rights* is the primary basis of United Nations activities to promote, protect, and monitor human rights and fundamental freedoms. The bill comprises three texts: the *Universal Declaration of Human Rights* (1948); the *International Covenant on Economic, Social, and Cultural Rights* (1966); and the *International Covenant on Civil and Political Rights* (1966) and its two optional protocols.

These instruments enshrine global human rights standards and have been the inspiration for more than fifty supplemental United Nations human rights conventions, declarations, bodies of international minimum rules, and other universally recognized principles. These additional standards have further refined international legal norms

Human Rights

■ **Negative rights**: civil and political rights that must be protected

■ **Positive rights**: economic, social, and cultural rights that governments must ensure are realized by their citizens

■ **Collective rights**: the rights held by groups of people, the most common being the right to self-determination of a cultural or ethnic group

relating to a very wide range of issues, including women's rights, protection against racial discrimination, protection of migrant workers, and the rights of children.

The 1948 *Universal Declaration of Human Rights (UDHR)* defined the fundamental expectations for freedom and dignity in a free and just society. It stated that "disregard and contempt for human rights have resulted in barbarous acts which have outraged the conscience of mankind, and the advent of a world in which beings shall enjoy freedom of speech and belief and freedom from fear and want has been proclaimed as the highest aspiration of the common people." Accepted human rights include freedom of expression, freedom of association, freedom from fear and persecution, and freedom of religion, as well as the right to shelter, education, health, and work, among others.

The 1966 *International Covenant on Economic, Social, and Cultural Rights* and *International Covenant on Civil and Political Rights* are international legal instruments. Thus, when member and non-member states of the United Nations ratify a covenant and become a "state party" to it, they are wilfully accepting a series of legal obligations to uphold the rights and provisions established under the text in question. Various committees of the United Nations investigate and report on states that have ratified each covenant. For example, the Committee on Economic, Social, and Cultural Rights recently examined and reported on Canada's compliance with the *International Covenant on Economic, Social, and Cultural Rights* (see Appendix B), which it has signed. The report is contained in Appendix C, and it outlines important areas where Canada is not in compliance with the covenant. A few items outlined in the report include:

- the low proportion of unemployed workers eligible for receiving insurance benefits
- the impact of the National Child Benefit "clawback system" on the poorest families in Canada, especially single-mother families
- the lack of affordable housing and inadequate assistance for women in abusive relationships
- the fact that Canada did not supply sufficient information regarding the standard of living possible under social assistance rates
- the 11.2 percent of our population that still lived in poverty in 2004
- the poverty rates that are still very high among groups such as Aboriginal peoples, African Canadians, immigrants, persons with disabilities, and single mothers

The report made numerous recommendations that are of interest for social welfare purposes.

THE CANADIAN MUSEUM FOR HUMAN RIGHTS

If the rights of a single human are dimmed, does all humanity fall under a shadow? Can a gesture by one nation stir change oceans away? Will we ever be able to promise all human rights for all, once and for all? When it comes to the simple matter of humankind's basic rights, there are no simple questions, no wrong ones, and never enough. And soon, we will have a place to ask them. The Canadian Museum for Human Rights. It will be the largest human rights centre in the world. An international forum for learning and reflection, dialogue and debate. An unprecedented showcase of our social triumphs and human tragedies. A call to action for a new generation of human rights leaders. A national landmark, a global meeting place, a spark of hope. For Canada. For the world.

— *Canadian Museum for Human Rights advertisement*, **Ottawa Citizen, October 6, 2006, A14.**

The Canadian Museum for Human Rights is a new project underway in Winnipeg, Manitoba — the crossroads of Canada — scheduled to be open to the public in 2010. With funding from several groups, including the Government of Canada, this museum is intended to be a national and international destination and will provide education on the history and current state of human rights, with a special emphasis on teaching young people to become human rights leaders and advocates. For more information on the Canadian Museum for Human Rights, visit www.canadianmuseumforhumanrights.com.

Negative, Positive, and Collective Rights

Some people distinguish between different human rights according to whether they are negative, positive, or collective rights. Others refer to these dimensions as "generations" of human rights. The way human rights are viewed and analyzed is a topic of considerable debate, but let us consider the following three categories of human rights:

1. Negative rights: civil and political rights (Articles 2–21 of the *UDHR*)
2. Positive rights: economic, social, and cultural rights (Articles 22–27 of the *UDHR*)
3. Collective rights: social and international order rights (Article 28 of the *UDHR*)

Negative Rights

The first category of human rights refers to civil and political rights. These are individually based and include the right to life, the right to liberty and security of person, the right to vote, the right to freedom of assembly, the right to equality before the law, the right to presumption of innocence until proven guilty, the right to freedom of movement, and the right to own property, to name a few (Ife 2001, 25). These rights are detailed in Articles 2–21 of the *Universal Declaration of Human Rights*. They are further expounded in the *International Covenant of Civil and Political Rights*, the *Optional Protocol to the International Covenant on Civil and Political Rights,* and a wide range of other covenants that add more detail to specific rights. They address protection from torture, ill-treatment, and disappearance; the rights of women, indigenous peoples, and visible minorities; the rights of prisoners and detainees; the rights of children and juvenile offenders; the

Armed conflicts are one of the common causes of human rights crises. War Child Canada is helping children in war-torn regions all over the world, like these children in Bosnia.

rights of employment and forced labour; and the rights of disabled persons, to name a few of the broad areas.

These are referred to as negative rights because their emphasis is on protection. They are rights that need to be protected rather than realized through social security or provision. They are rights that call for inaction on the part of the person or institution fulfilling the rights. The right is met by merely refraining from acting in a way that would violate the right. When Canadians hear the phrase "human rights," it is generally these rights that spring to mind. This category of human rights has roots in the intellectual tradition of the eighteenth-century Enlightenment and the political philosophy of liberalism. Enlightenment thinkers such as Voltaire, John Locke, and David Hume believed that human reason could be used to combat ignorance, superstition, and tyranny, and to build a better world. Their principal target was the domination of society by a hereditary aristocracy. The liberal tradition has centred on religious toleration, government by consent, personal freedom, and, especially, economic freedom. Based on these traditions, negative rights have emphasized individual liberties and freedom.

Positive Rights

The second category of human rights concerns economic, social, and cultural rights. These rights are outlined in Articles 22–27 of the *Universal Declaration of Human Rights*. They are detailed further in the *International Covenant on Economic, Social, and Cultural Rights*. These rights refer to the various forms of social provision, such as health, education, social services, food, housing, employment, adequate wages, and the right to form trade unions. Article 25 directly addresses economic rights, stating that "everyone has the right to a standard of living adequate for the health and well-being of himself and of his family, including food, clothing, housing and medical care and necessary social services, and the right to security in the event of unemployment, sickness, disability, widowhood, old age or other lack of livelihood in circumstances beyond his control."

These rights are referred to as positive rights because they imply that the state plays a more positive and active role in ensuring that these rights are realized. A positive right requires action, rather than inaction, on the part of the duty-bearer or the person or institution fulfilling the right. For instance, for the right to an adequate income to be realized, the state must act to provide that income to those who do not have it. These rights are pursued by means of welfare state provision: universal health care, education, social housing, and employment and labour legislation, among others. They require the state to play an active role in providing income security and services.

These rights generally have their roots in social democracy, socialism, and social movements. There is less consensus in Western capitalist democracies about such rights. At times, the rights themselves seem to run contrary to models that emphasize the rule of market forces.

Collective Rights

The third category of human rights are rights held by a group of people, such as a cultural group, and are referred to as collective rights. They are briefly mentioned in the *Universal Declaration of Human Rights*, Article 28: "Everyone is entitled to a social and international order in which the rights and freedoms set forth in this declaration can be fully realized." These types of rights generally have their roots in anti-colonial struggles, environmental activism, and the efforts for self-determination of indigenous peoples.

There is a risk in equating human rights with only negative rights. Pervasive poverty and lack of access to basic survival necessities are ignored within such a framework. However, it is not always easy to get social, economic, and cultural rights on the agenda of national governments and international organizations. Civil liberties, property rights, and political rights are generally consistent with the demands of the marketplace, but often economic and social rights are at odds with these demands. Indeed, many governments are embracing the market as the solution to all of society's ills, and leaving economic and social rights to the private sector.

Canada's Parliament passed the *Canadian Human Rights Act* in 1977. The purpose of the act is to ensure equality of opportunity, and freedom from discrimination in federal jurisdiction. In 1982 the *Canadian Charter of Rights and Freedoms* was enacted as part of the *Constitution Act*. It has sections pertaining to legal rights, democratic rights, and equality rights, but it makes no mention of social and economic rights. Each province and territory also has a human rights act that applies to businesses and organizations within its jurisdiction. For example, discrimination in housing would be brought to the provincial or territorial human rights commission.

More recently, the *Modernization of Benefits and Obligations Act*, 2000, was brought about due to human rights challenges under the *Canadian Charter of Rights and Freedoms*. In its May 1999 ruling in *M. v. H.*, the Supreme Court of Canada made it clear that governments cannot limit benefits or obligations by discriminating against same-sex

War Child Canada

www.warchild.ca

Founded in 1999 by Samantha Nutt, Steven Hick, and Frank O'Dea, War Child Canada is assisting thousands of children and youth in some of the most devastated areas on earth. They work with youth in North America to promote the awareness of human rights issues and the cause of war-affected children. War Child Canada also works closely with the music industry to help raise funds and build awareness for the cause of war-affected children and youth worldwide.

Human Rights Internet (HRI)

www.hri.ca

This website lists human rights educational resources, subject-oriented rights forums, urgent human rights alerts, and educational resource sites. It also includes publications and articles on children's rights. The World Calendar includes an international snapshot of human rights events each month.

common-law relationships. Denying equal treatment before the law to same-sex common-law partners is contrary to the principles of equality enshrined in the *Canadian Charter of Rights and Freedoms*, as well as the *Canadian Human Rights Act*. Sixty-eight statutes involving some twenty departments were affected. Amendments were made to statutes such as the *Income Tax Act*, the Canada Pension Plan, the Criminal Code, and the *Old Age Security Act*. For example, under the Canada Pension Plan, the surviving spouse in a married relationship or the surviving partner in an opposite-sex common-law relationship may qualify for survivor's benefits. Now this applies to same-sex couples.

However, the *Canadian Human Rights Act* does not protect the poor from discrimination. In 1998, the Senate Bill S-11 attempted to add the grounds of social condition to the *Canadian Human Rights Act*, but the House of Commons defeated it. The 1998 UN Committee on Economic, Social, and Cultural Rights stated in its concluding remarks that Canada should "expand protection in human rights legislation to protect poor people from discrimination because of social or economic condition."

Social Welfare, Globalization, and Human Rights

In this era of globalization, social welfare policies aimed at protecting the poor and disadvantaged members of society seem to be in retreat. Whereas capital is now freer to move across borders to seek higher and higher rates of return, local governments are no longer the main sites for social and economic activity. Although the post-World War II consensus was to maintain high levels of employment and a welfare state based on a sense of social citizenship in a nation, the era of globalization has severely eroded this belief.

Overall, the future of the welfare state has become a central issue of contention between the forces of globalization and civil society in nations worldwide. In his 1999 book, *Globalization and the Welfare State*, Ramesh Mishra refers to this as "decentring the nation state." He sees the following globalization impacts on social welfare:

- Globalization undermines the ability of national governments to pursue (Keynesian) policies of full employment and demand management.
- Globalization is increasing inequality in wages and work conditions, and high-paying unionized jobs are shrinking as non-standard and part-time work grows.
- Globalization prioritizes deficit reduction and tax cuts over systems of social security.
- Globalization shifts power to capital or corporations and away from labour and civil society, thereby weakening the support for social welfare programs.

- Globalization constrains the social policy option of national governments, due to the threat of capital flight if one nation is not as "investor friendly" as another.

The logic of globalization conflicts with the logic of community and democratic politics; it is eroding not only the welfare state, but also democratic politics.

The post-World War II welfare state was based on general consensus between labour, civil society, and capital. It was believed that the welfare state was necessary to ensure steady economic growth and social stability. In this new era of globalization, governments and the owners of business have taken the position that labour should be subjected to market forces as much as possible, like any other commodity. TNCs generally resist policies that limit the reach of the market, such as minimum wages, employment insurance, and health and safety legislation – policies that protect people from the negative impacts of the market.

To meet this challenge head-on, a new approach is called for, one that involves taking a human rights approach to social welfare. A human rights–based approach to social welfare would differ from traditional conceptualizations in several ways:

1. Programs and policies would be conceptualized as rights or entitlements rather than as needs or problems.
2. Collective rights to participation in community life would see social welfare as an investment in people.
3. The state-centric model of viewing the state or government as the exclusive provider of social welfare would have to be changed.
4. International bodies would be required to provide for global social welfare and to ensure that TNCs uphold human rights.

The traditional needs-based model of welfare puts emphasis on the assessment of needs, and then on the process of addressing those needs. By framing the issue as a person's right to an "adequate standard of living for his or her health and well-being," it shifts income security away from a charity model, whereby only the deserving receive charity, for which they should be extremely grateful, towards the idea of social entitlements as a right of citizenship.

Some social welfare activists go further, arguing that social inclusion must be addressed through a model of social investment. The social investment approach emphasizes the need for change in a variety of institutions, policies, and practices that deal directly with social inequality in the present and in the future (see Chapter 3 for more information on social investment). Many social welfare advocates see this as a means of going beyond the provision of income

The Council of Europe Social Charter

www.coe.int/T/E/ Human_Rights/Esc/

The countries comprising the European Community (EC) have instituted the European Social Charter. It protects the social rights of people in the nations comprising the EC in seven areas, including housing, health, education, employment, social protection, movement, and non-discrimination. A key element is the entrenchment of social protection and the elimination of poverty and exclusion.

An anti-globalization protest in the Philippines; many aspects of a person's life can be affected by globalization, including income security.

security to a more dynamic improvement a well as the participation of traditionally marginalized individuals in community life.

Social activists such as bell hooks and Stephen Lewis speak about mutual respect, dignity and compassion for each other. Their model of meeting human rights is based both on a shift in consciousness or how we view the people of the world visa vi ourselves and on a shared responsibility to attaining certain normative standards. As bell hooks has famously stated: "If we want a beloved community, we must stand for justice, have recognition for difference without attaching difference to privilege."

With globalization working to limit the state's ability to meet basic needs, the transition from a needs orientation to a rights affirmation will be required. Whatever the language or relations involved, the notion of concern for members in one's community can be universalized across cultures and societies. In many non-Western countries, for example, the notion of individual rights is non-existent. In such countries, people are viewed in relation to one another, as a community, and social welfare entails interdependence and solidarity. In such countries, community standards, rather than individual rights, may be more relevant.

New trade discussions at the WTO are ringing alarm bells for many social policy analysts. Since February 2000, negotiations have been underway in the WTO to expand and "fine-tune" the General Agreement on Trade in Services (GATS). GATS is an international trade agreement that came into effect in 1995. It aims to gradually remove all barriers to trade in services, such as banking, education, health care, rubbish collection, tourism, and transport. These negotiations have aroused unease worldwide. Many believe that GATS will threaten the ability of governments to provide social security and protection to citizens. It may mean the privatization of education, health care, and social insurance. It may also limit the capacity of governments to regulate health and environmental standards.

Discussions on freer trade between rich and poor nations began in 2001 in Doha, Qatar. The negotiation became known as the Doha Development Agenda by the WTO. In 2006, the Doha Development Agenda negotiations were suspended because gaps between the rich developed nations and underdeveloped nations were too wide. Developing nations blamed the failure of the talks on wealthy nations. Instead of tackling the distortions of their own subsidies, the industrialized nations demanded improved market access that would have put subsistence farmers in poor countries at risk.

Conclusion

In a recent speech, Professor John Polanyi stated that we shall never have peace as long as large segments of humankind are voiceless. Much of the world's population, being poor, is at the mercy of the rich. According to Polanyi, for the half of the world's population that lives on less than $2 per day, it would be better to be a European cow that receives $2.20 daily in subsidies from the European Community taxpayer. He concludes that change will come from the clamour of the poor made effective through international agreements and law.

The trend towards economic globalization has crucial implications for social welfare activists throughout the world. Globalization means that national borders become less relevant to every aspect of our lives, including social welfare. Given this new era, the traditional concerns of social welfare practitioners in addressing the immediate needs of their clients will need to be broadened to include concern for the issue of global human rights.

TNCs are increasing in size and power to the point that they threaten the sovereignty of nation states. Freer trade adds to their power. Some question whether or not nation states will be able to maintain the tax base necessary for adequate social welfare programs, especially in the face of pressures to lower taxes to appease transnational corporations.

There is an epic struggle between the forces of economic globalization and the forces of human rights and civil society. Its resolution may determine the fate of humanity for many generations to come. Human rights are inseparable from social welfare theory, values, ethics, and practice. Rights corresponding to human needs have to be fostered and upheld, and advocacy for such rights should be an integral part of social welfare.

Chapter Summary

Key Concepts

- ☐ **Collective rights**
- ☐ **Economic globalization**
- ☐ **Export processing zone (EPZ)**
- ☐ **Free trade**
- ☐ **G8**
- ☐ **Global social welfare**
- ☐ **Human rights**
- ☐ *International Bill of Human Rights*
- ☐ **International Monetary Fund (IMF)**
- ☐ **Negative rights**
- ☐ **Positive rights**
- ☐ **Structural adjustment**
- ☐ **Transnational corporations (TNCs)**
- ☐ *Universal Declaration of Human Rights*
- ☐ **World Bank**
- ☐ **World Trade Organization (WTO)**

Review Questions

1. What are human rights? What are the three categories of human rights?
2. What is globalization, and how does it compare to economic globalization?
3. Why do some commentators see economic globalization as a problem for the social welfare of the citizens of the world?
4. How do developing nations become impoverished by structural adjustment programs?
5. How can a human rights–based approach to social welfare act as a counterbalance to economic globalization?
6. What critical challenges result from a human rights–based approach?
7. What impacts of globalization on the welfare state have been observed? Are they negative or positive? Can you think of any positive impacts of economic globalization?

Exploring Social Welfare

1. Read the report (Appendix C) by the Committee on Economic, Social, and Cultural Rights on Canada's compliance with the *International Covenant on Economic, Social, and Cultural Rights.* Pick one of the major areas where the committee has concerns about Canada's performance. Visit the website of the Office of the United Nations High Commissioner for Human Rights (www.ohchr.org/english/bodies/cescr/cescrs36.htm) to explore your chosen issue. Write a letter to your MP, a Cabinet minister, or the prime minister to outline your concerns about Canada's lack of compliance.

2. Some critics have argued that the world needs "fair trade" and not "free trade" to address global poverty. Research this issue for yourself. Does free trade contribute to global income inequalities? If so, how does this happen? If not, why do you think global poverty remains with us? Write a two-page report with full APA citations.

Websites

International Forum on Globalization (IFG)
www.ifg.org/
The goal of the IFG is twofold: to expose the multiple effects of economic globalization in order to stimulate debate, and to seek to reverse the globalization process by encouraging ideas and activities that revitalize local economies and communities and ensure long-term ecological stability.

The Council of Canadians
www.canadians.org
Founded in 1985, The Council of Canadians conducts research and runs national campaigns aimed at putting some of the country's most important issues in the spotlight. Look at their trade campaign for information on globalization and its effects on Canada and the world.

Human Rights Research and Education Centre
www.cdp-hrc.uottawa.ca/index_e.html
This website has an extensive collection of resources. Check out their virtual library, publications, and links.

International Council on Social Welfare (ICSW)
www.icsw.org
Founded in Paris in 1928, the ICSW is a non-governmental organization that now represents organizations in more than fifty countries. ICSW and its members are active in the areas of social development, social welfare, and social justice.

References

Anderson, Sarah, and John Cavanagh. 2000. *Top 200: The Rise of Corporate Global Power.* San Francisco: Institute for Policy Studies. www.corpwatch.org/article.php?id=377.

Clarke, Tony. 1996. Mechanisms of corporate rule. In *The Case Against the Global Economy*, ed. Jerry Mander and Edward Goldsmith. Sierra Club Books.

Ehrenreich, Barbara, and Annette Fuentes. 1992. *Women in the Global Factory.* Boston: South End Press.

Ife, Jim. 2001. *Human Rights and Social Work: Towards Rights-Based Practice.* Cambridge, U.K.: Cambridge University Press.

Kapoor, Sony. 2005. *Paying for 100% Multilateral Debt Cancellation: Current Proposals Explained.* www.globalpolicy.org/socecon/develop/debt/2005/01payingforrelief.pdf.

Klein, Naomi. 2000. *No Logo: Taking Aim at the Brand Bullies.* Toronto: Vintage Canada.

Mishra, Ramesh. 1999. *Globalization and the Welfare State.* Cheltenham, U.K.: Edward Elgar Publishing.

Rice, James, and Michael Prince. 2000. *Changing Politics of Canadian Social Policy.* Toronto: University of Toronto Press.

6

Women and the Family

Changing Roles and Emerging Trends

Over the decades, social policy analysts have examined income security, paying special attention to women and families — and for good reason. A gendered division of labour exists in Canadian society that has resulted in women earning less than men, and in addition, many women bear the primary responsibility of caregiving for dependent family members. While there are income security programs in place to assist women and families, they are often based on outdated conceptions and can help perpetuate women's disadvantaged position.

One of the defining social characteristics of the second half of the twentieth century has been the increasing labour force participation of women. Indeed, the participation rate for Canadian women more than doubled in a thirty-year period, from 29 percent in 1961 to almost 60 percent in 1991. The social implications of this remarkable economic

> *"Most people do not understand sexism or if they do they think it is not a problem...Their misunderstanding of feminist politics reflects the reality that most folks learn about feminism from patriarchal mass media."*
>
> *— bell hooks, African-American scholar, writer and social activist*

shift were phenomenal (Gunderson 1998). Among other things, it gave rise to the dominance of the two-earner family, increased the demand for child care, increased the need for part-time work and flexible work arrangements, and heightened the pressure for legislation that would foster and ensure equality between men and women.

Nevertheless, by virtue of the primary role they are expected to play in caregiving, and their disadvantaged position in the labour market, more women than men live in poverty. In the case of lone-parent families, the burden is even greater. Despite all the legislative changes in the area of pay equity and employment equity, there is a continuing need for social policymakers and social work practitioners to be aware of the economic problems women still face as women. This chapter examines the role that income security programs play in perpetuating or alleviating the challenging conditions that Canadian women and families face.

The Feminization of Poverty

Even with advances in labour force participation, women dominate the ranks of those living in poverty. An examination of the situation reveals persistent problems for women in many areas of economic life.

Feminization of poverty

■ the social phenomenon of the growing numbers of women living in poverty

POVERTY. Women constitute a substantial segment of the working poor. High poverty rates are concentrated in three family types: unattached women under age 65 (41 percent, compared to 34.3 percent for men), unattached women 65 and older (38.1 percent, compared with 29.1 percent for men), and single mothers with children under 18 (52.1 percent, compared to 10.8 percent for men) using before tax Low Income Cut-offs (LICOs) (Statistics Canada 2004a).

PART-TIME WORK. Women still constitute a large proportion of part-time workers in Canada and, as such, are usually underpaid and therefore are particularly vulnerable to economic downturns. As we discussed in Chapter 4, part-time employment as a percentage of total employment has grown steadily from 3.8 percent in 1953, to 12 percent in 1973, to 16.9 percent in 1983, to 18.5 percent in 1999 (Broad 2000, 13). In 2004, 27 percent of the total female workforce were part-time employees, compared with 11 percent of employed men. Seventy percent of these part-time workers were women (Statistics Canada 2006, 109).

MINIMUM WAGE LEGISLATION. Because women hold 64 percent of minimum wage jobs, they are the group most in need of minimum wage legislation. Although Ontario's minimum wage was recently increased, it had been fixed since 1995. Providing a living wage for women can be a policy instrument for promoting greater wage equity and anti-poverty policy goals.

MATERNITY AND PARENTAL LEAVE. Women still perform a double duty — even if they work outside the home, women are most often the primary caregivers for dependent relatives and therefore have to work another "full shift" with the family. Employment Insurance (EI) benefits can play a significant role in addressing this issue, if women are eligible for the benefits. As is discussed in Chapter 10, EI was expanded in 2000, allowing parents to receive benefits for up to one year while caring for a child, but many women find that they are not eligible.

DEPENDENT CARE. Because women are most often the primary caregivers of dependent relatives, Canada's lack of universal daycare (child care) programs is a significant barrier to women's full participation in the labour force. Daycare is a necessity for many employed mothers. In 2004, 65 percent of all women with children under age 3 were employed. This is more than double the figure in 1976, when just 28 percent were employed (Statistics Canada 2006, 105).

FREE TRADE AND GLOBALIZATION. These global trends, involving competition from low-wage countries, particularly affect women who find themselves in low-wage jobs.

PENSION PROGRAMS. These programs are of special significance to women, because fewer women have access to other sources of retirement income. Of the income of women aged 65 and over, 70 percent is from government transfers (compared to 52 percent for men). Of persons collecting C/QPP retirement benefits in June 2005, women averaged $333.76 per month while men averaged $527.04 per month (Social Development Canada 2005).

RECESSIONS. Economic downturns affect women disproportionately — they are typically the last employees to be hired and the first employees to be fired.

Table 6.1: Average Annual Earnings of Women and Men Employed Full-Time, Full-Year, by Educational Attainment, 2003

Educational Attainment	Women	Men	Women's Income as Percentage of Men's
	$	$	%
Less than grade 9	21,700	31,200	69.4
Some secondary school	22,900	40,000	57.3
Secondary school graduate	30,500	43,000	71.0
Some postsecondary	31,500	41,600	75.6
Postsecondary certificate or diploma	34,200	49,800	68.6
University degree	53,400	77,500	68.9
Total	36,500	51,700	70.5

Source: Statistics Canada. 2006. *Women in Canada: A Gender-based Statistical Report.* Fifth Edition. Catalogue 89-503. Ottawa, p. 153. http://www.statcan.ca/english/freepub/89-503-XIE/0010589-503-XIE.pdf

Feminization of Homelessness

If the feminization of poverty means that more women than men are poor, why are the majority of the homeless people we see on the streets men?

The answer is that only a fraction of homeless people are seen on the streets during the day. Many of the homeless, women in particular, are not visible. Of the 26,000 people using emergency shelters in Toronto in 1996, half were in families and 5,000 were children (Faith Partners 1999). Young homeless women are particularly vulnerable to being recruited as prostitutes in order to make ends meet. You may not see them on the streets during the day, but you see some of them at night. Most homeless people you never see at all.

Case Study:

Women's Work

Safa is a 26-year-old single mother of two children. A severe learning disability made it a struggle for her to complete her education. She dropped out of school after Grade 10 and moved to Winnipeg where she worked at a series of waitress, sales, and cleaning jobs. She married Roger when she was 20 and had two children. Safa was looking forward to staying at home with the two children until they were in school. However, when she and Roger split up, Safa had to rethink her plan. After a month of unsuccessful efforts to find better work, Safa returned to her job as a waitress at a local restaurant and bar. There she earned minimum wage, but even with tips, the money was not enough to support herself and her two children.

Just as she was considering turning to social assistance, Safa met an old high school friend named Pascale. Pascale and her 2-year-old daughter needed a place to live and so, to reduce the cost of her rent, Safa agreed to let Pascale and her daughter share her townhouse. Pascale worked as an exotic dancer at an upscale club in Winnipeg. She offered to help Safa get started dancing at the same club. Although initially reluctant to do a job she was sure her parents would disapprove of, Safa was surprised to find that it was not so bad. In fact, she really enjoyed some aspects of the work, and the extra money really helped to make ends meet. Safa and Pascale worked out an arrangement so one was always available to be with the three children while the other was working at the club. The two women were pleased with the arrangement and trusted each other's ability to deal with their children.

Then, one day, Safa slipped on some water while on stage and broke her leg. It required surgery and a long recovery. That was when the wheels fell off the smoothly running operation Safa and Pascale had created. Safa was no longer able to dance and required a lot of help to look after the children, take care of the house, and get to and from appointments with the lawyer, doctors, teachers, etc. She was in a great deal of pain, and she was short-tempered and irritable. She resented looking after Pascale's daughter while Pascale worked, and she found it extremely difficult to cope with all three children. Finally, Pascale and her daughter moved out. As Safa struggled to deal with the financial stress of not having a roommate or partner, the words of the emergency-room nurse dragged her down even further: "Well, if you hadn't decided to go prancing around on a wet stage with only your high heels on, you wouldn't be in this kind of pain, would you!" ■

Source: Excerpt from Law Commission of Canada. 2004. Is Work Working? Work Laws that Do a Better Job. Ottawa: Law Commission of Canada, 27–28.

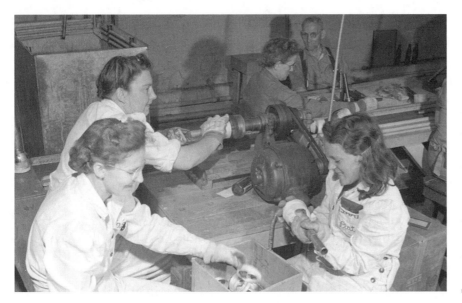

Women first entered the male-dominated labour force to help with the war effort during the First and Second World Wars; today women make-up close to half of the Canadian labour force.

EMPLOYMENT INSURANCE PROGRAMS. Even those programs that are designed to assist workers can place women at a disadvantage. Increases in the required eligibility periods make it more difficult for women than men to collect Employment Insurance. Only 30 percent of unemployed women received EI in 2000 compared to 42 percent for men (Canadian Labour Congress 2000, 1).

Over 16 percent of adult women live below the Statistics Canada Before Tax LICO (Statistics Canada 2004b). Women are falling further and further into poverty. The term now commonly used to capture this social phenomenon is the feminization of poverty.

In 2003, there was a total of 208,000 single-parent mothers. The average income of these families was $6,300 below the poverty line (Statistics Canada 2005, 148). The after-tax low-income rate for female one-parent families was 38 percent in 2003 (Statistics Canada 2005, 120).

Lack of access to affordable child care limits women's abilities to participate in paid work. In 2003, about 38 percent of women aged 25 to 44 who were employed part-time said they were working part-time because they were caring for children or had other personal or family responsibilities. This immediate need for child care should be part of a comprehensive family policy that would address the needs of mothers and children (Statistics Canada 2004b, Table 9).

Women in the Labour Force

Women's poverty is caused by different factors than men's poverty. Many studies (Gunderson, Muszynski, and Keck 1990; Townson 2000) found that men's poverty can be more directly related to low-wage employment, whereas women's poverty also arises from factors such as divorce and separation, and from women's responsibilities as mothers, homemakers, caregivers, and nurturers.

Since the 1970s, rapidly increasing numbers of women have entered the labour force. As a result, there has been a shift in the policy representation of women from "stay-at-home mothers" to "worker-mothers." This shift has changed the idea of the economic dependency of women, but it has not significantly altered the disadvantages that women face. There are six main reasons for this:

- Women are overrepresented in part-time, temporary, low-paying jobs.
- Women still earn less than men for doing the same jobs. This is an inequality that pay equity legislation was supposed to address.
- Women still face discrimination in employment practices. This is an inequality that employment equity legislation was supposed to address.
- Women still tend to hold primary responsibility for child and family care and household chores in the family.
- Child care provisions are deteriorating across Canada.
- Child support payments from absent fathers are often inadequate or are not paid at all.

Statistics reveal that an increasing number of women are active in the labour force, except for short periods while they are on parental

EMPLOYMENT EARNINGS FOR MEN AND WOMEN

While women have entered many high-paying professions previously reserved for men, women as a group still earn much less than men. The following table compares the average annual earnings of men and women.

In 2003, the average wage earned by women was 64 percent of that of men. Even when we remove part-time employment (a higher percentage of women work part-time, and this pulls down their average), women earn less.

Of those employed full-time and full-year, women earn less than three-quarters of the wage for men. Women earn less than men even when they have the same education (see Table 6.1 on p. 131). Even with a university degree, the average earnings of women working full-time and full-year was only 69 percent of comparable male counterparts in 2003.

Table 6.2: Average Earnings of Men and Women in 2003, and the Ratio of Women's Earnings to Men's

	All Earners, Including Part-Time	Full-Time, Full-Year Only
Women	$24,800	$36,500
Men	$39,100	$51,700
Earnings Ratio	63.6%	70.5%

Source: Based on data from Statistics Canada. 2006. *Women in Canada: A Gender-based Statistical Report.* Fifth Edition. Catalogue 89-503. Ottawa, pp. 133–158. http://www.statcan.ca/english/freepub/89-503-XIE/0010589-503-XIE.pdf

leave. Women accounted for 47 percent of the employed 2004 workforce; or, seen another way, 58 percent of all women aged 15 and over are working, compared with 68 percent for men (Statistics Canada 2006, 103). The problem, then, is not that women are not working; the problem is in the pay that women receive. Statistics Canada found that the average annual pre-tax income of women aged 16 and over from all sources, including employment earnings, government transfer payments, investment income, and other money income was $24,400 in 2003. This was 62 percent of male average income, which was $39,300 (Statistics Canada 2006, 133).

Even when women do take responsibility for earning a living, they and their families remain economically vulnerable. Not surprisingly, lone-parent families headed by women run the greatest risk of poverty among all groups. In 2003, 38 percent of all families headed by lone-parent mothers had incomes that fell below the after-tax Low Income Cut-off (Statistics Canada 2006, 144).

Of those who are employed full-time, women are more than twice as likely as men (34.3 percent as opposed to 16.1 percent) to be earning low pay (which is defined as less than two-thirds of the median wage). Over 70 percent of Canadian part-time workers are women earning much less than men. Women working full-time, full-year in 2003 had average earnings of $36,500, or 71 percent of what men made (Statistics Canada 2006, 139).

Women and Pay Equity

In the economic sphere, there were many legislative changes in the post-World War II period, and especially in the 1970s and beyond, aimed at fostering greater gender equality at work. In particular, important policy initiatives were taken that were intended to create a more equitable playing field for working women.

Among these policy initiatives were the following:

- equal pay policies (including pay equity or equal pay for work of equal value) designed to improve women's pay
- equal employment policies (including employment equity) designed to help women's employment and promotion opportunities
- other facilitating policies (such as child care and parental leave) designed to put women on an equal footing with men in the labour market

One of the fundamental issues facing women in the labour force is pay inequities – women being paid less than men for work of the same value. We have had pay equity legislation in Canada since the 1970s. An equal value provision was first legislated in 1976 in Quebec in its *Charter of Human Rights and Freedoms*. The federal government passed its equal value provision (section 11) under the *Canadian*

Canadian Human Rights Commission

www.chrc-ccdp.ca

The Canadian Human Rights Commission administers the *Canadian Human Rights Act* and enforces the *Employment Equity Act*.

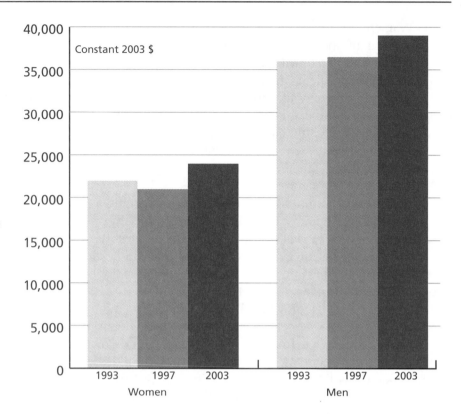

Figure 6.1: Average Income of Women and Men, 1993, 1997, and 2003

Source: Statistics Canada. 2006. Women in Canada: A Gender-based Statistical Report. *Fifth Edition. Catalogue 89-503. Ottawa, p. 133. http://www.statcan. ca/english/freepub/89-503-XIE/0010589-503-XIE.pdf*

Human Rights Act in 1978. Subsequently, all provinces, except Alberta, have enacted pay equity law or policy. Of these, six provinces have passed proactive legislation that mandates employers to comply with procedures to redress gender-based wage inequities. The policies of the other three provinces are complaint-driven – employees must file a complaint to address a pay inequity. These laws apply only to the public sector, and only Ontario, Quebec, and the federal government extend pay equity into the private sector (Gunderson 1998).

Nevertheless, although more and more Canadian women entered the labour force in this period, they seldom did so on equal terms with men. The industries and occupations initially open to women were the less-prestigious ones. Women's incomes were far inferior to those of men in the same occupations, and all sorts of sexist justifications for this fundamental inequality were readily available. In addition to economic inequality, the patriarchal family model and social relations were still in full force, and in many households, women were expected to tend to children, husband, and family affairs, as well as earn an income outside the home.

Defining the Modern Family

This text uses the term *family* with some caution. Many definitions of families exclude common-law couples, most exclude lone-parent families, and pretty well all still exclude same-sex relationships.

MARGINALIZED WOMEN IN CANADA

Aboriginal Women

The percentage of Aboriginal women living in poverty is more than double the percentage of non-Aboriginal women who are poor. At the time of the 2001 Census, based on before-tax incomes, more than 36 percent of Aboriginal women, compared with 17 percent of non-Aboriginal women were living in poverty.[1] Like many other women living in poverty, Aboriginal women are particularly affected by the social assistance policies of provincial and territorial governments. Aboriginal women employed on reserves may not be covered by the Canada Pension Plan.

High rates of poverty among Aboriginal people are having disastrous consequences. Their life expectancy is seven years less than that of the overall Canadian population. As well, there are almost twice as many infant deaths among Aboriginal peoples — a higher rate than the poorest neighbourhoods in Canada.[2]

Visible Minority Women and Immigrant Women

Data from the 2001 Census, based on before-tax incomes in 2000, indicated 29 percent of visible minority women were living in poverty. While the poverty rate for all foreign-born women was 23 percent, women who immigrated to Canada between 1991 and 2000 had a poverty rate of 35 percent. It is perhaps significant that the majority of these women were also from visible minority groups.[3]

Racism and discrimination almost certainly contribute to high rates of poverty among racialized women. Immigrant women may also face difficulties in finding paid employment because credentials from their countries of origin are not recognized in Canada. Access to language training may also be a problem. Many immigrant seniors do not receive Old Age Security benefits because they have not been in Canada long enough to qualify for a benefit.[4]

Women with Disabilities

Data from the 2001 Census, based on before-tax incomes in 2000, showed 26 percent of women with disabilities were living in poverty.[5] Provincial social assistance programs may provide income support for these women, but rates are abysmally low. Welfare incomes for single people with disabilities were the lowest in Alberta and New Brunswick at 39 percent of the poverty line and highest in Ontario at 59 percent of the poverty line (based on before-tax LICOs).[6]

1 Census data supplied by Statistics Canada refer to 2000 income.
2 Monica Townson, *Health and Wealth: How Social and Economic Factors Affect Our Well Being* (Ottawa: Canadian Centre for Policy Alternatives and James Lorimer and Co. Ltd., 1999), 39.
3 Census data supplied by Statistics Canada.
4 National Council of Welfare, *Poverty Profile 2001* (Ottawa: National Council of Welfare, 2004), 83.
5 Census data supplied by Statistics Canada.
6 National Council of Welfare, *Welfare Incomes 2004* (Ottawa: National Council of Welfare, 2005), 28.

Source: Townson, Monica. **Poverty Issues for Canadian Women.** *Prepared for Status of Wome Canada. (Ottawa, August 2005), 2–3. Portions reproduced with the permission of the Minister of Public Works and Government Services Canada, 2007. Portions also adapted from Statistics Canada. 2006.* **Women in Canada: A Gender-based Statistical Report.** *Fifth Edition. Catalogue 89-503. Ottawa http://www.statcan.ca/english/ freepub/89-503-XIE/0010589-503-XIE.pdf.*

In Canada today, the term family is defined according to either structural criteria (what they look like) or functional criteria (what they do).

Statistics Canada, for example, uses a structural definition of the family to count the number of families for census purposes. Statistics Canada defines a "census family" as a now-married couple (with or without never-married sons and/or daughters of either or both spouses), a couple living common-law (again with or without never-married sons and/or daughters of either or both partners), or a lone parent of any marital status, with at least one never-married son or daughter living in the same dwelling.

The definition focuses on what can be objectively measured – who lives with whom and under what circumstances. Previous definitions of the family included specific reference to marriage and ignored common-law living.

The reality of Canada today tells us that the old definition of family simply isn't sufficient. Traditional households consisting of four or more people – typically a mother, father, and their children – accounted for only a quarter of all Canadian households in 2001. Two decades earlier, they accounted for a third.

The Vanier Institute of the Family (2000), a national, charitable organization dedicated to promoting the well-being of Canadian families, uses a functional definition of the family that emphasizes the activities of family members. It defines families as any combination of two or more persons who are bound together over time by ties of mutual consent, birth and/or adoption or placement, and who, together, assume responsibilities for variant combinations of some of the following:

- physical maintenance and care of group members
- addition of new members through procreation or adoption
- socialization of children
- social control of members
- production, consumption, and distribution of goods and services
- affective nurturance – love

This definition emphasizes the work and accomplishments of people who commit themselves to one another over time. It avoids many of the biases that have crept into definitions of the family. It acknowledges heterosexual and same-sex couples, lone-parent families, extended patterns of kinship, blended families (step-families), couples with children and those without, the commitments of siblings to one another, and the obligations and affection that unite the young and the old as their lives weave together. Canadian federal law, however, defines same-sex couples as common-law relationships – different from marriage.

Same-sex marriage was legalized across Canada by the *Civil Marriage Act* (Bill C-38) enacted in 2005. Canada joins the

---

The Vanier Institute of the Family

www.vifamily.ca

Founded after the 1965 Canadian Conference on the Family, convened by Governor General Georges Vanier, this organization advocates for the role of the family in Canadian society.

The nature of the Canadian family is changing along with our views on the definition of marriage. Here, same-sex marriage supporters rally in Fredericton, N.B. in 2003. Same-sex marriage was recognized under federal law in 2005.

Netherlands and Belgium as the only countries in the world that recognize same-sex marriage. Earlier provincial court decisions in eight out of ten provinces and one of three territories had already legalized same-sex marriage; before the federal act, only Alberta and Prince Edward Island and the territories of Nunavut and the Northwest Territories had not recognized same-sex marriage. In 2006 the Conservative government brought in a motion to the House of Commons attempting to reopen the issue and reinstate the traditional definition of marriage. The motion was defeated by a vote of 175 to 123.

Seven Biases

Discussions about families are loaded with value judgements. These can be based on religious beliefs, moral beliefs, popular culture, advertising or media representations, as well as many other social and cultural forces. According to Margrit Eichler (1997, 7), there are seven types of biases that have crept into society's analysis of the family and have prevented social programs from keeping up with the changing nature of today's family.

1. **MONOLITHIC BIAS.** The monolithic bias suggests that there is one basic, uniform type of household — the nuclear, breadwinner-dependent family with one or more children and a woman who maintains the home: the "Cleaver"-type family. As we will see later in this chapter, this is more of a myth than a reality.
2. **CONSERVATIVE BIAS.** The conservative bias ignores changes taking place in family structures and relationships — for example, the blended family and the same-sex family.
3. **SEXIST BIAS.** The sexist bias assumes a functional differentiation of work between men and women. Women taking care of children

at home would be viewed as a natural role, rather than a role that is socially constructed.

4. **MICRO-STRUCTURAL BIAS.** The micro-structural bias leads to a refusal to look outside the family in order to understand what is influencing it. Individual or family conduct is explained by looking only within the family unit, without considering extraneous factors. An example of this occurs when people express a concern for building "self-reliance" among welfare recipients without considering the availability of jobs, daycare, and other supports.

5. **AGEIST BIAS.** This bias shows up in discussions about families when only the perspective of middle-aged adults is considered. Here, the perspectives of children and the elderly are ignored.

6. **RACIST BIAS.** The racist bias concerns a devaluing or discounting of culturally or ethnically different families. The treatment of First Nations families in Canada — where children were placed in residential schools — is a tragic example of this bias.

7. **HETEROSEXIST BIAS.** The heterosexist bias treats the heterosexual family as "natural" and, therefore, the only legitimate form of family. Denying family status to lesbian and gay families typifies this bias.

Being aware of these societal biases helps policy-makers design social welfare programs that reflect real, existing families, not just "ideal" families. Problems can occur when practitioners bring their biases into counselling or referral, because people must have access to services based on the family they live in, as opposed to the family the practitioner thinks they should live in. Families exist outside of these biases (whether we like it or not); acknowledging this enables practitioners to practise in a more reflective and appropriate manner.

In order to obtain an accurate and realistic definition of what a family is, these biases need to be challenged. The changing nature of families that define themselves as families, but are not recognized as such in social policy or government legislation, requires us to rethink our outdated and restricted notions of "family."

Changing Families

In many ways, our income security programs are based on outdated, traditional notions of women and family. Although the vast majority of Canadians live in some kind of family setting, the contemporary Canadian family bears little or no resemblance to families of Canada's past. The "Cleaver" family ideal, based on the sitcom *Leave it to Beaver*, consists of two parents — a working father and a supportive non-working wife — and a couple of children. This ideal has remained dominant for many decades despite the fact that it has not really been reflective of reality.

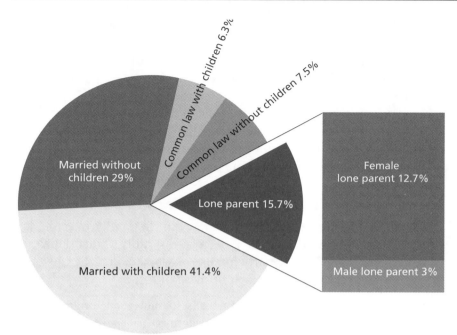

Common law with children 6.3%

Common law without children 7.5%

Married without children 29%

Married with children 41.4%

Lone parent 15.7%

Female lone parent 12.7%

Male lone parent 3%

Figure 6.2: Families in Canada

Source: Vanier Institute of the Family. 2000. Profiling Canada's Families II. Ottawa. Reprinted with permission.

Certainly, today's family is better protected than it was thirty years ago. For example, if a family member gets sick, our health care programs provide government-supported medical help. A myriad of government social programs are also available to provide external services to assist the family. Yet, family structures have changed dramatically.

Over the past thirty years, the proportion of **male-breadwinner families** has decreased drastically, and is now well below 25 percent of the total of all Canadian families. Currently, it is **dual-earner families** that predominate. This change has led to a complete revision of family obligations in a very short time and, hence, a great deal of uncertainty. For example, there are no clear societal expectations with regards to an individual's responsibility to care for a step-uncle who gets sick. At the same time, fewer children are taking responsibility for the care of their aging parents; this has made the question of government support to the elderly an issue where it once was not. Modern families take many different forms. The number of single-parent families is rising (up to 15 percent of the total), and many new entities are emerging, such as same-sex couples with children, and blended families who bring with them other-family obligations.

According to Statistics Canada's 2001 census, there are 8.4 million "census families" in Canada, up from 7.8 million in 1996. Of these:

- 41.4 percent are married couples with children
- 29 percent are married couples without children
- 6.3 percent are common-law couples with children
- 7.5 percent are common-law couples without children
- 15.7 percent are lone-parent led (81 percent of which are female)

The 2001 census showed that an increasing proportion of couples are living common-law. Married couples accounted for 70 percent of all families in 2001, down from 83 percent in 1981. At the same time, the proportion of common-law couples rose from 6 percent to 14 percent.

The 2001 census is the first to provide data on same-sex partnerships. A total of 34,200 couples identified themselves as same-sex common-law couples, accounting for 0.5 percent of all families, with 55 percent of these being male couples.

One barrier to full participation of women in the workforce is the lack of universal daycare. Without access to child care, some women who may otherwise be able to work are forced to go on Social Assistance.

Some Factors Changing the Modern Family

The main factors that have led to changes in the family over the last fifty years are increased longevity, decreased fertility, industrialization of housework, labour force participation of women, and the increased rate of divorce. Let us look at each of these in turn.

LONGEVITY. Improved public health leads to increased longevity, and this has had implications for family structure. The percentage of the population over age 65 has increased by 60 percent over the past five decades. As well, women usually live longer than men, which has implications for pension and medical systems, as well as for relationships.

FERTILITY. Birth rates have fallen by more than half over the past five decades. Decreased fertility in all age categories is a worldwide trend. In 1968 the Criminal Code legalized access to birth control. This has meant that women are involved in childbearing for fewer years and therefore have time for other activities.

HOUSEHOLD TECHNOLOGY. Especially since World War I, advances in technology have led to the automation of certain types of housework. This has drastically changed the family of the twentieth century. Electrification, hot water, central heating, air conditioning, refrigeration, vacuum cleaners, and mass production of clothing and automobiles are all aspects of the industrialization of housework.

WOMEN IN THE WORKFORCE. The proportion of women in the labour force has tripled over the past five decades. In 2000, 73 percent of women who were married to men worked and, of those, most contributed a significant share of total family income.

18% — Wife's earnings make up 50%+ of family income

32% — Wife's earnings make up 10% to 29% of family income

37% — Wife's earnings make up 30% to 49% of family income

13% — Wife's earnings make up less than 10% of family income

DIVORCE. The increase in the proportion of women who are working outside the home has led to women, in general, becoming less economically dependent on their spouse or partner. In 1968 the grounds for divorce were expanded beyond adultery to include separation and incompatibility. The divorce rate has increased sixfold over the past five decades. This increased divorce rate has, in turn, contributed to changes in family structures.

Figure 6.3: Contribution of Wives' Earnings to Overall Family Income

Source: Vanier Institute of the Family. 2000. Profiling Canada's Families II. Ottawa. Reprinted with permission.

The Women's Liberation Movement and Other Factors

There are additional factors that have caused changes in family composition. Consider the women's liberation movement.

The first wave of the women's movement occurred in the last thirty years of the nineteenth century, and the first twenty years of the twentieth century. During this time, the movement was mainly political, and was primarily concerned with the acquisition of women's right to vote. The second wave occurred in the 1960s, partly as a reaction to the rigidity of the male-dominated family structure with its fixed gender roles, and also as a result of the isolation of suburban life. The impact of this movement on improving women's lives has been phenomenal and far-reaching.

Consider also the decline of the extended family — the family "ideal" now consists of nuclear family units that by and large live in their own homes. Thus, housing has expanded rapidly, especially the suburban single-family home. There is also the decline of religious influence. This has meant that barriers to divorce have come down, and there has been a widespread acceptance of birth control (and a corresponding reduction in unwanted pregnancies, particularly among young women). Finally, increased cultural diversity in the Canadian population has caused us to become more familiar with different family types.

Pressing Problems Today

All these changes to the Canadian family obviously have a direct bearing on how social programs operate and how income security programs are delivered. In devising programs that work for women and families, social analysts and policy-makers now urgently need to take into account the following:

- growth in the number of single-parent families, mostly led by women (single-parent families now account for approximately 25 percent of Canadian families with children)
- growth in the number of blended families
- growth in the number of same-sex families, some of which include children, now comprising 34,200 families
- growth in the number of mothers in the labour force, including women with children under the age of five
- decline in the number of extended family members who live in one family
- growth in the number of single-person households

Three Models of the Family

Women are now participating in the labour force in ever-larger numbers, and many families could not survive if this were not the case. At the same time, however, government income security policy has continued to be based on the outdated assumption that women are available to care for family members and undertake domestic chores (as if they were at home all day).

Sociologist Margrit Eichler (1997) presents three conceptual models of the family upon which new policies directed at the work-family relationship can be based. In devising income security policy and programs, governments tend to use one of these three approaches or models. At present, the patriarchal family model perspective is losing popularity, and the individual responsibility model is gaining in influence. The following sections describe the characteristics of each model.

Patriarchal Model of the Family

The patriarchal model of the family is based on perceptions that were dominant at the turn of the last century. Under this paradigm, the husband was considered the undisputed master of the family, and the wife was economically and socially beneath her husband. Children were also treated as dependants of the husband/father. Within income security programs, this belief was reflected in the rule that a woman could not receive public assistance if her husband was alive. The wife/mother was seen as responsible for providing care and services to family members without pay. Finally, divorce did not exist (although there were separations not recognized by law), and because homosexuality was seen as an illness, same-sex couples were not recognized in any way.

Three Models of the Family

■ **Patriarchal:** features the husband and father as the "master" of the family

■ **Individual responsibility:** features gender equality, gender-neutral policies, and equalized caregiving

■ **Social responsibility:** features the individual as the societal unit and views domestic tasks as socially useful service; the public shares the responsibility with both parents

Individual Responsibility Model of the Family

The individual responsibility model of the family consists of three main elements: formal gender equality, gender-neutral policies, and equalized caregiving. The *Canadian Charter of Rights and Freedoms* introduced gender equality and enshrined it in law, necessitating numerous changes in family policy. Some analysts point out that these legal gains constitute only "formal gender equality" – in other words, in the ideal world of policy, all people are treated "equally" despite continuing real-world inequalities.

Within this model, the family unit is still treated as the normal unit of administration, but the husband and wife are seen as equally responsible for the economic well-being of themselves, each other, and any children. Fathers and mothers are seen as equally responsible for caregiving. This model reflects the idea of gender neutrality or gender "blindness." In formulating social policy, gender neutrality ignores the differences in life experiences and caring responsibilities between men and women. The emergence of this model within provincial Social Assistance programs means that women can no longer make claims on the state as mothers. Either parent is assumed to be capable of fulfilling the care and provider functions in the family. The lack of recognition that one parent cannot care for dependent children and work full-time has led to an erosion of entitlements for lone-parent families, which are predominantly led by women.

Social Responsibility Model of the Family

As an alternative, the social responsibility model of the family directly addresses gender inequality, gender-sensitive policies, and the social dimension of caregiving. This model sees the individual, rather than the family, as the societal unit of administration. Examples of this are our health care system, which treats every citizen as an individual, and our tax system, which is based on individual taxation. Within this model, familial caring and housework – which usually become the responsibility of women – are seen as socially useful services (rather than privately useful services). In this context, the public shares the responsibility with both parents for the care of dependent children. Similarly, the costs of care for dependent adults (such as elderly family members or individuals with disabilities) are a public responsibility, although family members may also provide the care.

According to Eichler (1997, 16), this model contains minimal gender inequality or stratification. It is important to note that this is different from the assumption of absolute gender equality. Eichler (1997, 124) believes that differentiation is a necessary aspect of our complex society, which in turn leads to stratification. The goal, therefore, should shift from moving towards a society based on equality to one where inequality is minimized.

The Harper Government on Child Care

In the 2007 federal budget $1 billion of previously committed early learning and child care funding was cut and replaced with tax credits to businesses for the creation of workplace child care spaces. The budget also included a new flat child tax credit paid to parents for each child. The Code Blue for Child Care Campaign (www.buildchildcare.ca) argues that this money, combined with the UCCB, would be enough to federally fund universal child care for three to five year olds.

Daycare in Canada

There has been a substantial increase in the number of licensed child care spaces available to families in the past several decades. By 2003, there were almost 750,000 licensed child care spaces in Canada, 59% more than in 1998. The current figure is also twice that in the early 1990s and close to seven times greater than that in 1980 . . .

The majority of licensed day-care spaces in Canada are in regular day-care centres . . . Between 2001 and 2003, the number of family day-care spaces increased by 54%, while the number of regular day-care spaces rose by only 21% . . .

Most regular day-care centre spaces were in non-profit centres. In 2003, 79% of all day-care centre spaces were in non-profit centres, while 21% were in commercial centres.

Source: Excerpts from Statistics Canada. 2006. Women in Canada: A Gender-based Statistical Report. Fifth Edition. Catalogue 89-503. Ottawa, p. 108. http://www.statcan. ca/english/freepub/89-503-XIE/0010589-503-XIE.pdf

The idea of "family making" was developed by Leslie Bella, a professor of social work at Memorial University of Newfoundland. According to Bella (2003), we can identify and value family, regardless of the living arrangements of family members. *Family making* is defined as the processes through which we develop relationships that are enduring, caring, and intimate, that in turn nurture and support us. According to this definition, a family relationship exists to the extent that the relationship between two or more individuals is characterized by endurance, caring, and shared domestic space. Family making is the process through which individuals create, maintain, and strengthen relationships that constitute "family" as thus defined (Bella 2003).

The idea of defining a family by identifying relationships and processes rather than family composition is useful for social welfare policy-makers. Existing social policies have a tendency to disregard or invalidate non-traditional family forms and approaches to care. Conversely, policies based on family making include the wide range of family relationships. It enables social policy-makers to address the concerns of those in diverse family forms and different cultural settings. It allows us to break away from policy based on limited or patriarchal definitions of the family. Such policies are more responsive to the diversity of family forms that actually exist in Canadian society.

Women and Caring

Currently, the individual responsibility model underpins Canada's social welfare programs. However, to tackle women's poverty, governments need to develop strategies to deal with the unique problems faced by women – women's employment, child care, Social Assistance rates, and general income security.

Patricia Evans, a professor of social work at Carleton University, has written extensively on this topic, and details several reasons why it is important to examine income security programs from the perspective and experience of women. First, she maintains that many programs are based on outdated assumptions about the roles and responsibilities of women and simply do not work. Second, it is women who dominate both sides of the social welfare encounter – as primary users of services and as service providers (Evans and Wekerle 1997, 4).

The exact relationship between social welfare and women's daily experiences is neither straightforward nor simple. Understanding women's responsibility for caring, and how income security programs play into it, is vital to the study of the Canadian social safety net. It is important to note that women and men benefit differently from the income security system. Men tend to obtain their income security benefits from social insurance-type programs such as Employment Insurance or Workers' Compensation – programs that are less stigmatizing and more generous. Women, on the other hand, tend to draw benefits as citizens from minimum-income programs such as Social Assistance and Old Age Security. These programs provide bare minimums, are either needs tested or means tested, and are more stigmatizing. If our society, and our income security programs, rewarded caring as highly as labour force participation, a key aspect of women's inequality could be surmounted.

Not only are women the main recipients of minimum-income Social Assistance programs, but the programs themselves perpetuate certain biased models of the family. For example, what was once known as the "man-in-the-house" rule (now known as the "spouse-in-the-house" rule), stipulates that a woman who is living with a man is immediately not eligible for Social Assistance. The policy assumes that a man who lives with a woman should be financially responsible for her and her family, even when he is not the father of her children and has no other legal responsibility to support her or her children. Under the *Family Law Act*, people are not considered spouses until after three years of living together, but the Ontario government deems that there is economic interdependence as soon as there is evidence of cohabitation – no matter the time period. This policy was widely criticized and changed for several years in some provinces (the rule was declared unconstitutional by the Ontario Supreme Court in 2002). The Ontario government appealed the decision and lost, but has yet to change its policy.

Other policies, many of which are presented as being gender-neutral, actually ignore the special circumstances of women. For example, workfare (viewing lone mothers as workers, rather than as mothers) ignores the circumstances that single mothers face. Lack of child support, lack of child care opportunities, and a lack of jobs that will pay sufficiently to support a family on one income are ignored by this policy. When combined with the low levels of income support through Social Assistance, it is no wonder that the majority of single mothers and their children live below most definitions of poverty.

Women's poverty is often related to their family obligations. Many policies do not account for the complex relationship between social welfare and women's traditional responsibility for caring in our society.

Theorization of Women's Work and Caring

According to Statistics Canada, women comprise three-quarters of the adults who spend more than 30 hours per week caring for children in the home. Status of Women Canada, a federal government agency, has gone as far as to say that the unequal sharing of dependant care in the family may be the most persistent barrier to gender equality.

Womyn's Voices

http://womynsvoices.ca/

This website provides a forum for online activism for women's rights and civic participation, through the medium of information and communication technologies.

Mothers Are Women

www.mothersarewomen. com

Mothers Are Women (MAW) is a feminist organization that advocates for mothers as primary caregivers; it argues that until the unpaid work of women in the home is recognized as a valuable and necessary contribution, women will never achieve equality in our society.

Beginning in the 1960s and throughout the following decades, a variety of theories were developed in an attempt to explain the nature and conditions of women's work and caring. Theorists disagreed about the extent to which gender-based work division was determined by ideas, biology, culture, material conditions, or patriarchal family structures. Early debates were directed at rejecting the idea that women's work divisions, in both the workplace and the home, were determined by biological factors, such as physical size or shape, "natural" skills or aptitudes, maternal instincts, or emotional makeup. Canadian feminist writers, such as Helen Levine, Pat Armstrong, Patricia Evans, Sheila Neysmith, and Dorothy Smith, undertook extensive research to show that gender-based work and caring divisions were socially constructed or socially organized. In fact, today's feminist theorists use the term *gender* as opposed to *sex* to highlight the socially constructed differences, rather than the biological dichotomy.

To examine social welfare, it is necessary to appreciate the dimension of gender. This text has drawn attention to the circumstances that contribute to the inequality of women, but more work remains to be done if we are to fully understand this relationship and be able to act on it. Sheila Neysmith, a leading social work scholar at the University of Toronto, shows how social welfare progress has been hampered by the separation of family life, the labour market, and state responsibilities into separate domains. She believes that the public and private need to be connected in our theoretical understandings (Neysmith 1991).

Many feminist social policy experts and women in community-based organizations believe that caregiving by mothers should be recognized as work comparable in value to the work performed in the marketplace. In the same vein, Mothers Are Women (MAW), an Ottawa-based grassroots group, advocates for a more equal sharing of the work between men and women, and of responsibilities and rewards for paid and unpaid labour within families and within society. They believe that a fundamental recognition of the unpaid caregiving work of mothers is necessary to break the feminization of poverty.

Another unresolved issue is the dilemma of professional child care versus caregiving. Many believe that the current emphasis on supporting professional child care devalues caregiving and the women who do it, and prioritizes professionalization and the development specialist over the caregiver. These and other issues are the subjects of ongoing debates and research. What remains undisputed is that the current welfare system is not adequately addressing the range of problems faced by women, and that action is urgently required to establish basic equality between the sexes.

Conclusion

The term *feminization of poverty* depicts the phenomenon of women and families who are living in poverty in increasing numbers. Almost 12 percent of adult women, and around 38 percent of single mothers, live below Statistics Canada's after-tax LICO measure. According to 2004 LICO before-tax measures, 16.6 percent of women and 52.1 percent of single mothers live below LICO (Statistics Canada 2004a). Income security programs have not adequately anticipated and adjusted to the changing nature of the family, and this has resulted in poverty issues for women.

Many social programs assume the existence of the traditional model of the family but, in reality, this model is not the norm. Currently, the individual responsibility model of the family governs social policy. For example, social welfare programs put in place in 1966, just two years before the *Divorce Act* of 1968, did not anticipate the rapid growth in the numbers of single-parent families resulting from the act. Since then, the question has been asked: should single parents, who are mainly women, be considered employable and obligated to seek work, or should they be considered unemployable and, therefore, in effect be granted a pension during their child-bearing years?

Beyond the income security issues facing families, women are also disadvantaged in the labour market. Women generally receive lower pay than men, and other issues — such as divorce and separation, and women's responsibilities as mothers, homemakers, caregivers, and nurturers — lower the earning potential of women. The shifting of women from "stay-at-home mothers" to "worker-mothers" has decreased the economic dependency of women, but it has not significantly altered the disadvantages they face. The problem is not that women are not working — the problem is the pay that women are receiving. In many respects, the legislative changes of the postwar period that were meant to foster greater equality at work have not improved the economic situation of women.

Women and Human Rights

Canada has been a signatory to the United Nations *Convention on the Elimination of All Forms of Discrimination Against Women (CEDAW)* since 1981. In a single treaty, CEDAW brings together human rights standards for women and girls in public and in private life. The 2000 Optional Protocol to CEDAW (the "Optional Protocol") is a human rights instrument that creates new procedures to enhance oversight of compliance with CEDAW. It is hoped that the Optional Protocol will contribute to the recognition and protection of women's human rights and the promotion of gender equality in Canada and around the world.

Chapter Summary

Key Concepts

- ☐ **Dual-earner families**
- ☐ **Family**
- ☐ **Feminization of poverty**
- ☐ **Individual responsibility model of the family**
- ☐ **Male-breadwinner families**
- ☐ **Patriarchal model of the family**
- ☐ **Pay equity legislation**
- ☐ **Social responsibility model of the family**
- ☐ **Vanier Institute of the Family**

Review Questions

1. What factors contribute to the disadvantaged economic status of women in Canadian society? What are some of the solutions being proposed?
2. Define and describe the concept of "feminization of poverty."
3. List and describe the structural and functional definitions of the family.
4. Define the concept of "family," and describe how families have changed over the past decades. What factors have led to these changes?
5. What are the three models of the family, and how would adhering to a social responsibility model change the way we provide income security programs in Canada?
6. Why is it important to understand income security in relation to women?
7. The shift from "stay-at-home-mothers" to "worker-mothers" has not dramatically changed the disadvantaged status of women. Explain why this is so.

Exploring Social Welfare

1. Identify and discuss the key factors contributing to women's lower pay situation. To begin, read the Status of Women Canada publication *Women and Employment: Removing Fiscal Barriers to Women's Labour Force Participation* by Kathleen A. Lahey, available online at the Status of Women Canada website (www. swc-cfc.gc.ca).

2. According to Status of Women Canada (2004), gender-based analysis (GBA) is a "tool to assist in systematically integrating gender considerations into the policy, planning and decision-making processes." Read about the GBA on the Status of Women Canada website (www.swc-cfc.gc.ca): documents such as *Gender-Based Analysis: A Guide for Policy-Making* and *An Integrated Approach to Gender-Based Analysis* are available. Then pick one income security program and complete a basic GBA of it: examine the differential impact on men and women (and adverse impacts on women) of the program; compare how and why women and men are affected by the program; and make three basic recommendations.

Websites

Status of Women Canada
  www.swc-cfc.gc.ca
This federal government agency, which promotes gender equality and the full participation of women in economic, social, cultural, and political life, has a publications section with a large selection of online documents.

DisAbled Women's Network Ontario
  http://dawn.thot.net
DAWN Ontario (DisAbled Women's Network Ontario) is a progressive, feminist, and cross-disability organization dedicated to social and economic justice. The network is active in many areas of social welfare advocacy.

Canadian Women's Foundation
  http://www.cdnwomen.org/
The foundation raises money and makes grants to help stop violence against women and build economic independence for women and their children. The web site contain links to numerous publications particularly dealing with violence against women and girls and poverty.

References

Baker, Maureen. 2002. *Families, Labour and Love: Family Diversity in a Changing World*. Vancouver: UBC Press.

Baker, Michael, and Nicole Fortin. 2000. *Does Comparable Worth Work in a Decentralized Labor Market?* Montreal: CIRANO.

Bella, Leslie. 2003. Family making: A framework for anti-oppressive practice. Conference paper presented at the University of Regina.

Broad, D. 2000. Living a half life? Part-time work, labour standards and social welfare. *Canadian Social Work Review* 17 (1).

Canadian Labour Congress. 2000. *Analysis of UI Coverage for Women*. Ottawa: Canadian Labour Congress. http://action.web.ca/clcpolcy/attach/wom-ui-00e.pdf.

Eichler, Margrit. 1997. *Family Shifts: Families, Policies and Gender Equality*. Toronto: Oxford University Press.

Evans, Patricia M., and G. Wekerle, eds. 1997. *Women and the Canadian Welfare State*. Toronto: University of Toronto Press.

Faith Partners. 1999. *Poverty Hurts Series*. Ottawa: Faith Partners.

Gunderson, Morley. 1998. *Women and the Canadian Labour Market: Transitions Towards the Future*. Ottawa/Toronto: Statistics Canada/ITP Nelson.

Gunderson, Morley, Leon Muszynski, and Jennifer Keck. 1990. *Women and Labour Market Poverty*. Ottawa: Canadian Advisory Council on the Status of Women.

Hay, David. 1997. Campaign 2000: Child and family poverty in Canada. In *Child and Family Policies: Struggles, Strategies and Options*, ed. J. Pulkingham and G. Ternowetsky. Halifax: Fernwood. Neysmith, Sheila. 1991. From community care to a social model of care. In *Women's Caring: Feminist Perspectives on Social Welfare*, ed. Carol Baines, Patricia Evans, and Sheila Neysmith. Toronto: McClelland & Stewart.

Social Development Canada. 2005. *Statistical Bulletin: Canada Pension Plan, Old Age Security*. June 2005, Table 36.

Statistics Canada. 2001. *Income Distribution by Size in Canada*. Ottawa: Statistics Canada. CANSIM Table 202-0802.

Statistics Canada. 2004a. *Persons in Low Income Before Tax, by Prevalence in Percent (2000 to 2004)*. CANSIM Table 202-0802.

Statistics Canada. 2004b. *Women in Canada: Work chapter updates: 2003*. Ottawa: Statistics Canada. www.statcan.ca/english/freepub/89F0133XIE/89F0133XIE2003000.pdf.

Statistics Canada. 2005. *Income in Canada 2003*. Ottawa: Statistics Canada. www.statcan.ca/english/freepub/75-202-XIE/75-202-XIE2003000.pdf.

Statistics Canada. 2006. *Women in Canada: A Gender-Based Statistical Report*, 5th ed. Ottawa: Statistics Canada. www.statcan.ca/english/freepub/89-503-XIE/0010589-503-XIE.pdf.

Status of Women Canada. 2004. *An Integrated Approach to Gender-Based Analysis*, 2004 ed. Status of Women Canada. www.swc-cfc.gc.ca/pubs/gbainfokit/gbainfokit_pdf_e.html.

Townson, M. 2000. *A Report Card on Women and Poverty*. Ottawa: Canadian Centre for Policy Alternative.

Vanier Institute of the Family. 2000. *Profiling Canada's Families II*. Ottawa: Vanier Institute of the Family.

7 Aboriginal Social Welfare

From Oppression to Self-Government

The social and economic conditions of many Aboriginal peoples in Canada is dismal — many call it Canada's disgrace. An oppressive history of colonial government policies, broken government promises, and basic foot-dragging has resulted in the situation we have today. To move forward we must understand the current situation and what got us here. Aboriginal people believe that healing and respect are central to the process.

The Aboriginal peoples of Canada are the descendants of the original inhabitants of North America. Three groups of Aboriginal people are recognized by the Canadian *Constitution Act*, 1982: Indians, Métis, and Inuit. We now generally use the term First Nations in place of *Indian*. The term *Indian* is used in a legal capacity, as government policies such as the *Indian Act* apply to Status or Registered Indians (persons who are listed in the federal government's Indian Register).

" Our people are dying earlier and more often than anyone else in [this] country. We have a Third World in our front yard and our back alleys."

— Assembly of First Nations National Chief Phil Fontaine

Aboriginal Statistics (2001 Census)

Total population of Canada: 29,639,035

Total people of Aboriginal origin or ancestry: 1,319,890

Total people of Aboriginal identity: 976,310

North American Indian identity: 608,855

Métis identity: 292,310

Inuit identity: 45,075

Multiple Aboriginal identities: 6,665

Aboriginal identity not included elsewhere: 23,415

Source: Based on data from Statistics Canada. 2003. Aboriginal Peoples of Canada: A Demographic Profile. 2001 Census: Analysis Series. Ottawa: Statistics Canada. Cat no. 96F0030XIE2001007.

The notion of a Status Indian also has little bearing on the reality of Aboriginal peoples, and these general demarcations are made by non-Aboriginal Canadian politicians for the purposes of governing. The reality is that Aboriginal peoples are a diverse population of distinct peoples with unique heritages, languages, cultural practices, and spiritual beliefs.

In the past twenty years, successive federal governments have established policy goals of working in consultation with Aboriginal communities to improve their overall well-being or social welfare. Nevertheless, at the same time they have limited funding increases in important departments such as **Indian and Northern Affairs Canada (INAC)** to 2 percent per year. INAC is the federal government department responsible for policy and administration of programs and relations with Aboriginal peoples.

Aboriginal people live in what many have described as Third World conditions; remedying this situation will require extensive resources, but current government funding (on a per person basis) spent on providing Aboriginal services is less the average going to other Canadians.

To understand the debates about Aboriginal social welfare, we must begin by examining issues such as treaties, the reserve system, and the *Indian Act*. This chapter will also provide an overview of the social and economic conditions within which Aboriginal people live, including specific social welfare issues such as poverty, health care, housing, and unemployment, relating them to the history of colonialism and government policy objectives. The chapter will also look at the relationship between self-government and social welfare, as identified by the 1996 Royal Commission on Aboriginal Peoples (RCAP).

Deciphering the Issues

Before discussing social welfare, income security, and Aboriginal peoples, it is necessary to decipher some issues that are often unnecessarily complicated by legal debates. Five key issues are treaties, the reserve system, the *Indian Act*, residential schools, and how these four tools of colonialism relate to the growing call by Aboriginal peoples for self-government.

Treaties

The British government signed various treaties with native groups before Confederation, such as the *Peace and Friendship Treaty* (1752) and the *Robinson Treaties* (1850). After Confederation, the administration of Rupert's Land (which included much of what is now Manitoba, Saskatchewan, and Alberta) went to the Canadian government. The development plan for Canada included the building of the railway and the settlement of Rupert's Land; however, because Canadian law recognized that Aboriginal people held title on that land, the government had to form agreements with Aboriginal leaders.

The treaties signed by the newly formed Canadian government are known as the numbered treaties and began with Treaty No. 1 in 1871 with the Ojibway and Swampy Cree of Manitoba. The final treaty was signed in 1921. While the treaties were quite different in their terms and complexity, they generally served to establish peaceful relations, institute payments, and gain the surrender of land. The treaties generally stipulated the relinquishment of the Indian right and title to specific land and provided for the annual payment of five dollars per person (this amount has not changed and was never indexed to inflation). These treaties also led to the creation of the reserve system; in exchange for title on the larger tract of land, the people were given smaller parcels or reserves.

However, almost half of the land in Canada is not under a treaty. No treaties were signed between the Aboriginal peoples of Quebec, the Maritimes, and most of British Columbia. In fact, almost half of the population of Registered Indians did not sign land treaties. These land treaties (or in many cases, the lack of them) are currently in dispute across the country. First Nations' leaders believe the notion of surrendering land was alien to their ancestors, as there was no traditional notion of land ownership in Aboriginal culture. The lands were seen as part of creation and people merely the stewards of it.

The Reserve System

As the main vehicle for regulating and controlling Aboriginal movement and ways of living, the federal government established the Department of Indian Affairs, which administered the reserve system. Indian reserves are parcels of land that have been set aside for exclusive occupation and use by Aboriginal communities. An Indian reserve refers specifically to a parcel of land, and is not synonymous with nation, community, or band; the community that occupies a reserve will often have a different name than the reserve itself. There are over 2,000 reserves in Canada with over 600 bands.

The reserve system is a by-product of the treaties. Once land was ceded and Canadian settlements were established, Aboriginal peoples were moved onto small parcels of land largely devoid of any economic potential and which could not be used as collateral to develop business ventures (given that Indian land was held in trust). The Government of Canada also created reserves in regions not surrendered through treaty, such as the Wikwemikong Unceded Indian Reserve on Manitoulin Island, Lake Superior, in Ontario.

The Indian Act of 1876

The Department of Indian Affairs gained its authority through the *Indian Act* of 1876, which provided for the government's guardianship over

Indian lands. The *Indian Act* was, and still is, a piece of social legislation of very broad scope that regulates and controls virtually every aspect of Aboriginal life. The *Indian Act* was administered in Aboriginal communities by government officials known as "Indian Agents." The act has been amended throughout the years, but remained largely intact until major changes were made in 1996.

The *Indian Act* strictly defines the requirements for determining who is a Status Indian. For the last century, this has fragmented the Aboriginal population into legally distinct groups with different rights, restrictions, and obligations. Canada is one of the few countries to have a legislative act that has separate laws for a specific group based on race or ethnicity.

The social control aspects of the *Indian Act* placed Aboriginal peoples in the position of a colonized people with limited rights. Prior to 1960, Registered Indians could not vote in federal elections, but the act spelled out a process of enfranchisement whereby Indians could acquire full Canadian citizenship (and the right to vote), but only by relinquishing their ties to their community – giving up their culture and traditions, and any rights to land. People could also lose their status for a variety of reasons, such as marrying non–Status Indians or non-Aboriginal individuals or by living outside the country for too long. The passing of Bill C-31 in 1985 allowed over 100,000 individuals to regain Registered Indian status.

In the 2001 census, 1.3 million people identified themselves as Aboriginal, including First Nations, Inuit, and Métis. According to the 2001 census, there are just over 500,000 Registered Indians, and more than 100,000 individuals who identify as non-Registered Indians. Status or Registered Indians have access to benefits such as tax exemptions and land rights not afforded to unregistered Indians. Métis and Inuit people have different administrative relationships with the government, and are not considered Indians under the *Indian Act*; according to the 2001 census, only a very small number of Registered Indians identify as Métis or Inuit, but there are close to 300,000 self-identified Métis people in Canada, and over 45,000 Inuit.

Residential Schools

The 1867 *Constitution Act* brought about the policy of Aboriginal assimilation, and residential schools were to play a significant role in this policy. Laws were developed that forced Aboriginal parents, under threat of prosecution, to send their children to these schools. Residential schools is a term used to refer to a range of historical institutions including industrial schools, boarding schools, student residences, hostels, billets, and residential schools tasked with educating Aboriginal children. The hundred or so schools were operated by various religious organizations in partnership with the Government of Canada. In 1969 the government took over the operation of the

Residential schools took Aboriginal children, like these girls, away from their communities and forced them to assimilate to the dominant European culture. The last residential school closed in 1996.

schools; most were closed by the mid-1970s, but seven were left open throughout the 1980s with the last closing in 1996. Over 100,000 Aboriginal children were forced into the schools, and probably 80,000 of those children are still alive today.

The residential schools prohibited the use of Aboriginal languages, traditions, and customs, and many were abusive. During the hearings of the Royal Commission on Aboriginal Peoples, people came forward with personal and painful stories of physical and sexual abuse at residential schools. Many resorted to legal litigation to obtain compensation, forcing the federal government to negotiate and ultimately announce the Residential Schools Settlement Agreement in 2006. The $1.9 billion agreement involves the paying of compensation and the intention to move forward with a healing process.

Part of the settlement agreement is an initiative called the Truth and Reconciliation Commission (TRC). The TRC bears the same name as the commission that heard the stories of violence and racism in South Africa after apartheid. The purpose of Canada's exercise is to give former residential school students a formal opportunity to tell their stories and to create a report that will be part of Canada's official historical record. The $60 million commission is a key healing component of the residential school settlement.

Continuing Colonialism

Treaties, the reserve system, the *Indian Act*, residential schools, and subsequent government actions are the method by which Aboriginal people were colonized, subjugated, and created as second-class citizens in their own land. We often think of countries in Africa or South America when we discuss colonialism, but in many ways the Aboriginal people of Canada have suffered much like indigenous people in

**Figure 7.1:
Population
Reporting Aboriginal
Ancestry (Origin),
1901–2001**

*Source: Statistics Canada.
2003. Aboriginal peoples
of Canada: A demographic
profile. Catalogue
96F0030XIE2001007. Ottawa.
2001 Census: analysis series.
http://www12.statcan.ca/
english/census01/Products/
Analytic/companion/abor/
canada.cfm*

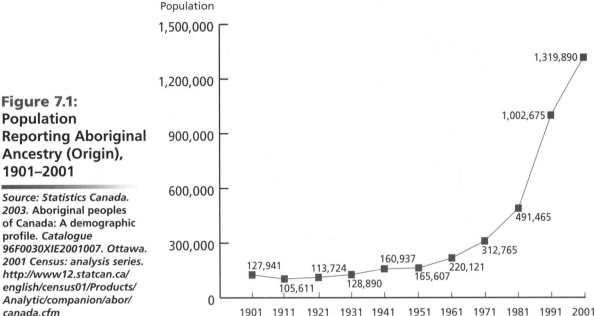

other parts of the world. Many Aboriginal people in Canada live in so-called Third World conditions, with limited access to water, health care, education, or even a healthy diet.

There are also political similarities. The anti-imperialist movements in Third World countries resulted in the overthrow of colonial empires. The European powers were rapidly pushed out of Africa, Asia, and elsewhere as occupying colonial powers. Internal indigenous people within settler societies are now pushing more than ever for the removal of the institutions of domestic colonialism. This is a global phenomenon and not specific to Canadian history. The First Nations, Métis, and Inuit of Canada recognize that they are not alone, but often it appears that the Canadian government refuses to admit or does not understand that the political challenges they face are intertwined with global history. The call for self-government is the natural response to hundreds of years of colonial oppression.

A Demographic Profile

The Aboriginal population of Canada is increasing at a significant rate, as shown in Figure 7.1, and has increased tenfold in the last century. Across Canada, the Aboriginal population is younger and has been growing more quickly than the non-Aboriginal population. For example, in 2001, half of the total Registered Indian population was under the age of 24, while half of the total population of Canada was under the age of 37. For Registered Indians living on reserve, the median age was even younger at 22 (Statistics Canada 2003a, 7).

As well, the Aboriginal population is growing more rapidly than the Canadian population as a whole. In 2001 the average number of children per family for the Registered Indian population living on reserve was approximately twice that of the Canadian average. According to the 2001 census, one-third of the Aboriginal population consists of children under the age of 14. This is far higher than the corresponding share of 19 percent in the non-Aboriginal population (Statistics Canada 2003a, 7).

According to the 2001 census, the total population of people of Aboriginal origin in Canada is 1.3 million or 4.4 percent of the total population. Aboriginal people comprise 85 percent of the population of Nunavut, 51 percent of the population of the Northwest Territories, 23 percent of the Yukon, and about 14 percent of the populations of Manitoba and Saskatchewan. Slightly less than 20 percent of Aboriginal people live in Ontario, although this comprises only 2 percent of the total population of Ontario (Statistics Canada 2003a, 10). The 2001 census reported that 69 percent of the total Aboriginal population in Canada lives off reserve, with almost three-quarters of these individuals living in urban areas.

A 2005 INAC report compared the socio-economic conditions of Registered Indians both on and off reserve with the general Canadian population. This comparison shows that in 2001, the high school completion rate for Registered Indians was 48.6 percent as compared to 68.7 percent for the total Canadian population. Also, only 39.9 percent of Registered Indians 15 years of age and over report having any post-secondary education, compared to 54.6 percent for the Canadian population. Also, among Registered Indians in the labour force, the unemployment rate was 23.3 percent in 2001, compared to 7.4 percent for the total Canadian population. INAC's comparison report also showed that between 1995 and 2000, the average individual income of the total Canadian population increased from $27,445 to $29,769, whereas the average income for Registered Indians rose from $15,558 to $16,935 (INAC 2005b, 3).

The Socio-Economic Situation and the Royal Commission

The gap between Aboriginal peoples and the general population is not limited to low educational attainment and high unemployment. In 1991 the Canadian government set up a commission on the state of Aboriginal people in Canada; after five years of study, the commission, which included jurists, researchers, and Aboriginal leaders, released its five-volume report, shocking many Canadians. Aboriginal peoples were found to suffer physical and mental ill-health, to live in poor housing, and to have few economic opportunities. The report concluded that this is due, in large measure, to a long history of "false promises" and government policies based on domination, displacement, and assimilation. The goal of the commission was to make significant changes in the lives of Aboriginal peoples in twenty years' time. However, in 2006 the Assembly of First Nations (AFN) published a ten-year report card, examining the commission's recommendation and the government's actions (2006b). The report outlines a general failure by the government to implement the necessary programs, legislation, and funding that would improve the lives of Aboriginal peoples. The following list identifies some of the key issues supporting the argument that many Aboriginal people in Canada live in Third World conditions.

- **LIFE EXPECTANCY.** Life expectancy is the number of years a person can be expected to live at birth on the basis of the mortality statistics for a given observation period. According to 2001 census data, the gap in life expectancy between Aboriginal peoples and the Canadian population is 6.7 years (70.4 for Aboriginal men compared to 77.1 for men overall, and 75.5 for Aboriginal women compared to 82.2 overall).

- **SUICIDE.** The suicide rate of Registered Indian youth (ages 15 to 24) is eight times higher than the national rate for females and five times higher for males (Health Canada 2003). Another way to gauge the impact of suicide is to measure the potential years of life lost (PYLL). Used by Health Canada, the PYLL is calculated by subtracting the age at death from 75 (the age before which a person is considered to have died prematurely). For example, a suicide at age 25 has lost 50 potential years of life. In 2000, suicide accounted for approximately 1,079.91 potential years of life lost (PYLL) per 100,000 First Nations persons. According to Health Canada, this is nearly three times the 2001 Canadian rate (2005).

- **INFANT MORTALITY RATE (IMR).** Infant mortality is the number of deaths per 1,000 live births. For First Nations on reserve, it fell from 28 to 11 per 1,000 live births between 1979 and 1993. In 2000 it stood at 7.2. This is a dramatic improvement, but still worse than the rate of 5.2 for other Canadians (INAC 2005a, 3). For the overall Aboriginal population in 2000, the infant mortality rate was 6.4 deaths per 1,000 live births – 22 percent higher than the rate of 5.2 for other Canadians (Health Canada 2003). In Nunavut, the infant mortality rate was 16.1 in 2004 (Statistics Canada 2006b).

- **CHILD POVERTY.** According to the AFN report, one in four First Nations children live in poverty, compared to one in six for Canadian children. They have double the rates of disability, and over one-third of their homes are overcrowded (AFN 2006b, 2).

- **CHILDREN IN CARE.** In 2004, 8,846 on-reserve Registered Indian children were in care, accounting for 5.7 percent of on-reserve children (INAC 2005a). According to the AFN report, 0.67 percent of non-Aboriginal children were in child welfare care as of

May 2005, compared to 10.23 percent of Status Indian children (AFN 2006b, 2).

■ **SUBSTANCE ABUSE.** The rate of death due to alcohol use and abuse by the general population is 23.6 per 100,000 people, just over half the rate for Aboriginal peoples, which is 43.7 per 100,000 people (NNAPF 2000). Alcohol remains the primary substance being abused among the Aboriginal peoples at 58.4 percent compared to 20 percent for narcotics/hallucinogens (NNAPF 2000). Among the Aboriginal youth, solvent abuse is a major health concern. A 1993 survey found that 43 percent of the Aboriginal youth have tried sniffing solvents at least once, 38 percent are social users, and 19 percent are chronic users (Public Health Agency of Canada 2005a).

■ **HIV/AIDS.** HIV/AIDS is on the rise among Aboriginal peoples, and they are contracting HIV at a younger age than non-Aboriginal peoples. The Aboriginal populations are becoming increasingly vulnerable to HIV infection and are overrepresented in the Canadian HIV/AIDS epidemic. The number of positive HIV tests among Aboriginal peoples rose from 18.8 percent in 1998 to 25.3 percent in 2003, and the number of reported AIDS cases among Aboriginal peoples rose from 1.2 percent before 1993 to 13.4 percent in 2003 (Public Health Agency of Canada 2005b).

■ **VIOLENCE IN THE HOME.** Aboriginal people are three times more likely to be victims of spousal violence than non-Aboriginal people (Statistics Canada 2006a). Overall, 24 percent of Aboriginal women and 18 percent of Aboriginal men said that they had suffered violence from a current or previous spouse or common-law partner in the five-year period ending in 2004. This was the case for 7 percent of non-Aboriginal people (Statistics Canada 2006a).

■ **INCARCERATION RATES.** Adult Aboriginal peoples are incarcerated at more than six times the national rate, and are 6.5 percent more likely to be incarcerated than non-Aboriginal people. Furthermore, the number of Aboriginal offenders rose from 11 percent (in 1991/92) to roughly 17 percent (in 1998/99) of all admissions to federal institutions. The number of Aboriginal offenders is expected to increase as the Aboriginal youth population ages (Correctional Service Canada 1999).

Aboriginal Peoples and the Human Development Index

As discussed earlier, some social policy analysts charge that the social conditions of Aboriginal peoples in Canada resemble those of developing countries. AFN National Chief Phil Fontaine has stated, "our people are dying earlier and more often than anyone else in [this] country. We have a Third World in our front yard and our back alleys" (AFN 2006c, 3). Internationally, the measure used to determine Third World

Public Health Agency of Canada

www.phac-aspc.gc.ca/publicat/epiu-aepi/epi-note/index.html

The Public Health Agency of Canada website offers additional information about HIV and AIDS and Aboriginal peoples.

conditions is the Human Development Index (HDI), published annually by the United Nations Development Programme (see Chapter 5 for more on the HDI). Specifically, the HDI measures life expectancy, literacy, education, and standards of living. It is a standard means of measuring well-being, and whether a country is developed, developing, or underdeveloped. HDI scores are calculated for 177 countries for which data is available.

In 2006 Canada ranked twelfth overall (in 1992 Canada ranked first). A 2004 INAC-sponsored study calculated the HDI score for Registered Indians to be 0.765 (Cooke, Beavon, and McHardy 2004, 8). Ecuador received the same score and ranked eighty-third in the world. China, the Philippines, and Peru, all considered developing countries, received similar scores. The HDI score for Inuit in Canada was calculated at 0.738 by Sach Senécal (2006, 4). The country with the closest score to this value is the Occupied Palestinian Territory.

ABORIGINAL YOUTH AND FAMILIES

As in the rest of Canada, Aboriginal family life has changed drastically over the last few decades. "The Aboriginal family in traditional, land-based societies was, until recently, the principal institution mediating the participation of individuals in social, economic and political life" (Castellano 2002, 16). But with the shift away from their traditional land-based societies, Aboriginal families have had to adapt to many pressures.

Aboriginal family life is also affected by urbanization; in 2001, 28 percent of Aboriginal people lived in large urban centres, and 30 to 40 percent of urban Aboriginal people in the West are under the age of 15. In large centres, 46 percent of Aboriginal children live in lone-parent families, and in smaller centres the number is 40 percent. That is significantly higher than the percentage of lone-parent families among non-Aboriginal people (15 percent). The proportion of lone-parent Aboriginal families decreases in rural areas, both on and off reserve; however, it is still higher than the national rate. Anecdotal evidence also suggests that many Aboriginal households are multifamily households — as many as 1 in 10 on reserve (Castellano, 2002).

While the social and economic circumstances have changed for Aboriginal people, Castellano notes that "the notion of the caring, effective, extended family, co-extensive with community, continues to be a powerful ideal etched deep in the psyche of Aboriginal people" (2002, 16).

Source: Adapted from Canadian Council on Social Development. 2006. The Progress of Canada's Children and Youth. Ottawa: CCSD, 12. www.ccsd.ca/pccy/2006/labour. htm; and Mary Brant Castellano. 2006. Aboriginal Family Trends: Extended Families, Nuclear Families, Families of the Heart. Ottawa: Vanier Institute of the Family.

Colonialism and Government Policy Objectives

As we have established, it is important to understand Aboriginal social welfare within the context of colonialism. It has played a crucial role in shaping government policy towards Aboriginal peoples now and historically, and it explains the situation of Aboriginal peoples today. In settler nations such as Canada, colonists take administrative control from the colonizing nation, thereby instituting a particular type of colonialism known as *internal colonialism*, which creates political and economic inequalities between regions or peoples. This approach in Canada created a system of incursion, cultural destruction, racist domination, foreign rule, and social and economic dependency, and shaped subsequent Canadian government policy.

In two works on the subject, Roger Gibbins and Rick Ponting outline the major goals or policy themes of national government public policy towards Aboriginal peoples, which are summarized in the following list (Ponting 1997).

- **PROTECTION.** The officials developing early Aboriginal policy were very aware of the problems of alcoholism, greed, and prostitution that flourished on the frontier of Canada in the 1800s. Some had humanitarian goals and sought to protect Indians until they could be assimilated into white society. This led to laws prohibiting the private sale of Indian land, the use of alcohol by Indians, and the prostitution of Indian women. These officials saw the reservation system as a way to isolate and protect Indians. It can also be argued that these goals of protection were mostly illusory, glossing over the underlying goal of exploitation. For example, by isolating Indians on reserves, the government was free to exploit other vast Indian lands.

- **ASSIMILATION.** The central pillar or thrust of federal government Indian policy was the goal of assimilation or the absorption of Aboriginal peoples into Canadian society. It was desired and expected that eventually all Indians would give up their traditional customs, culture, and beliefs and become like those of the dominant society. The failure of this assimilation process can largely be attributed to barriers posed by systemic and societal discrimination. In short, the racism that facilitated the attitude of assimilation at the same time erected barriers to actual assimilation.

- **CHRISTIANIZATION.** The core assimilation policy was supported by a variety of other policies, such as the process of Christianization. To the colonial government, the civilizing of the Indians was synonymous with their Christianization. Aboriginal ceremonies and cultural practices were officially discouraged or outlawed. Education through church residential schools was seen as a way to destroy the social, spiritual, and cultural systems and relations of the Indians and replace them with the

Assembly of First Nations

The Assembly of First Nations (AFN) was founded in 1982 from other political organizations. It is the national organization representing First Nations citizens in Canada. There are over 630 First Nations communities in Canada, and the AFN provides them with a national voice through their leaders, advocating for issues such as Aboriginal and treaty rights, economic development, education, languages and literacy, health, housing, social development, justice, taxation, land claims, and the environment. The Assembly is made up of chiefs who meet annually, and they elect a national chief every three years. The AFN also includes regular meetings of the Confederacy of Nations, made up of the chiefs and regional leaders, whose number is determined by population. The Assembly of First Nations is funded mainly by Indian and Northern Affairs Canada.

Canada has a long history of attempting to convert Aboriginal peoples, as seen in this photo from the late 1800s.

beliefs of mainstream Canadian society. However, because the residential schools isolated Indians from the mainstream, they worked at cross-purposes to the goal of assimilation. They were the source of great antagonism in Aboriginal communities and continue to be so to this day.

- **ENFRANCHISEMENT.** As mentioned previously, this was the method envisioned for Indians to obtain citizenship and thus be fully recognized as Canadians. By enfranchising, Aboriginal people lost their status and band membership, renounced their native identity, and merged with the non-Aboriginal society. The most common reason for choosing enfranchisement was to pursue the right to vote in a federal election. Relinquishing their Indian status was the only way that Aboriginal peoples were permitted to vote in a federal election until March 1960, when the House of Commons finally gave Aboriginal people the right to vote.

- **LAND SURRENDER.** For the government, obtaining land held by Aboriginal peoples for the settlement of non-Aboriginal people was a primary goal. Reserves were seen as a way to move Indians into agriculturally based communities, both to assimilate them and to free vast tracts of land for non-Aboriginal settlement. As immigration increased, the government moved to make more and more Aboriginal land available for non-Aboriginal settlement.

- **GOVERNMENT AUTHORITY.** The *Indian Act* of 1876 gave sweeping power and authority to the colonial administrators, taking away Aboriginal peoples' right to self-determination. This external political control is a fundamental aspect of colonization.

The Historical Context of Income Security for Aboriginal Peoples

During the sixteenth and seventeenth centuries, before extensive settlement began, the relationship between Aboriginal peoples and Europeans in Canada was relatively harmonious and mutually advantageous. At first, Aboriginal peoples served as partners in exploration and trading. As the English and French became locked in an imperialistic struggle for control over the North American continent, the relationship with the Aboriginal peoples evolved into military alliances. Then, the presence of Aboriginal peoples on lands needed for settlement became the "Indian problem," and an impediment to "civilization." This problem was addressed by land-cession treaties and assimilation policies, such as residential schools, the Indian Registry, and the reserve system. These issues continue to shape contemporary relations between Aboriginal peoples and Canadian governments.

With the *Indian Act* and reserve system in place, as well as the goals of Christianization and assimilation, the colonial powers, and later the Government of Canada, were faced with the need to "take care" of the Aboriginal population — settlement interfered with traditional ways of living and effectively created a colonial underclass that persists today.

Early Relief Programs

The introduction of the reserve system was similar in many ways to the poorhouse (see Chapter 2), which was a designated place for the deserving poor. The difference, of course, is that the Aboriginal peoples' own income security had been taken away by settlement and European methods of commerce. Early relief efforts were seen as a means of easing the Aboriginal peoples' distress (often caused by starvation) and to maintain order and peace (Shewell 2004).

The first system of income security for First Nations was a ration system based on confiscated Indian monies that were placed in a band trust account. Annuity trusts were created with the land sales, and monetary relief was taken from the trust accounts and was granted at the discretion of the local Indian Agent. These monies were grossly inadequate and were used as much as a means to sanction behaviour or reward assimilation as for relief (Moscovitch and Webster 1995, 211). The decision to grant relief was based on the old practice of distinguishing between the "deserving" and the "undeserving" poor, and Indians were generally considered undeserving. This system applied British Poor Law principles until the mid-1960s. "Non-registered Indians, Métis and Inuit were on the periphery of the Indian relief system although their economic circumstances were similar to, or worse than, those of the Indians" (212).

An Overview of Aboriginal History in Canada

www.collectionscanada. ca/02/0201200110_e.html

Library and Archives Canada provides numerous resources on Canada, and an extensive collection on Aboriginal peoples, including this Overview of Aboriginal History in Canada.

Inclusion in National Programs

The first Old Age Pension of 1927 excluded Indians and Inuit, but was available to the Métis. (Scott 1994, 18). The *Old Age Pensions Act* was explicit in stating that an Old Age Pension would not be available to Aboriginal peoples with the exception of Métis (Guest 1999, 77). The first *Unemployment Insurance Act*, passed in 1940, also excluded most Aboriginal people from eligibility. The *Family Allowance Act* of 1944 did apply to Aboriginal peoples, but only provided "in kind" rations.

The Old Age Pension program remained in place until 1951; however, in 1948 a law was passed that allowed Registered Indians over 70 years of age to apply for a monthly allowance known as the *Allowance to Aged Indians*. In 1951 the *Old Age Security Act* and *Old Age Assistance Act* were passed to supersede the *Old Age Pensions Act* of 1927; these provisions did include all Aboriginal peoples, making it the first income security program to apply to all Aboriginal peoples.

The *Unemployment Assistance Act* of 1956 was supposed to be a cost-shared program available to Aboriginal people, but the provinces refused to pay any part of what they saw as a federal government responsibility. With the *Unemployment Assistance Act* of 1956, the federal government attempted to mirror the standards and procedures of the provincial systems. In most cases, however, they had lower benefit rates. This was the beginning of a process of parallel income security systems: one for mainstream society and one for Aboriginal people. The provinces remain unwilling to fund on-reserve Social Assistance.

Social Assistance, or welfare, for First Nations in Canada is rife with struggle between federal and provincial governments over who should pay. Although welfare in Canada is supposedly available to any citizen who meets the conditions of a particular program, a double standard has existed for Aboriginal peoples dating back to the 1800s. The *Indian Act* gave the federal government total control over Indian or First Nations monies and the government exercised this power. Between 1951 and the early 1960s, the Indian relief system collapsed and was replaced by access to the mainstream welfare state (Moscovitch and Webster 1995). This occurred after the development of several federal acts related to income security, the amendments to the *Indian Act* in 1951, and the establishment of the Canada Assistance Plan. After the collapse of the Indian relief system, the Treasury Board implemented a policy (Treasury Board Minute Number 627879) in July 1964 establishing the provincial regulations and standards for Social Assistance programs. Authorization to administer Social Assistance on reserves was given to the Department of Indian Affairs and Northern Development (now known as INAC) upon its creation in October 1966.

Social Assistance Today

The majority of First Nations now administer Social Assistance to members under various provincial guidelines, but under the direct supervision of INAC. In 2000/01, 534 First Nations administered their own programs (this does not include those First Nations functioning under self-government arrangements). The federal government continues to fund on-reserve Social Assistance, but the benefits are tied to provincial rates. Some off-reserve Aboriginal communities also deliver their own programs according to provincial standards. Urban Aboriginal people receive Social Assistance through the mainstream system.

First Nations' Social Assistance usage rates vary widely across the country, from 20 to 30 percent in Quebec, Ontario, and the Yukon, to 48 to 58 percent in the four western provinces, to a high of almost 75 percent in the Atlantic provinces (INAC 1997, 74). These rates, on a national basis, have been increasing each year, from an average of 35 percent in 1982, to 45 percent in 1994, to 50 percent in 2002, and they are expected to reach 57 percent by 2010 (INAC 2000). According to INAC figures, 45 percent of on-reserve residents receive Social Assistance (INAC 2000).

INAC itself has acknowledged that the current welfare system for First Nations people living on reserves must be replaced with a more dynamic and progressive system. The Royal Commission on Aboriginal Peoples (RCAP) proposed several recommendations to that effect. Canada's 1998 response to the recommendations made in the RCAP report, called *Gathering Strength: Canada's Aboriginal Action Plan*, outlined a commitment by the government to take a "bottom-up" approach with First Nations to reform on-reserve Social Assistance programs.

Past "made-in-Ottawa" solutions have resulted in programs that have failed. Therefore, INAC undertook the Income Security Reform (ISR) initiative, which ended in 2003. The objective of the ISR initiative was to transform the passive on-reserve welfare system to a dynamic system that promotes opportunities and self-sufficiency. The overall goal of the initiative was to develop a new social policy framework for Social Assistance delivery with First Nations on reserve.

In 2003 INAC completed an evaluation of the ISR, finding that the results were promising in many First Nations communities, but that a new framework was still forthcoming. Many Aboriginal leaders have expressed frustration that consultations regarding income security reform have largely stopped. Some First Nations communities believe that the ISR was focused more on lowering Social Assistance case loads, rather than providing opportunities.

Evaluation of the Income Security Reform Initiative

www.ainc-inac.gc.ca/
pr/pub/ae/ev/2003/01-
20/index_e.html

The INAC website provides the complete evaluation of the Income Security Reform initiative completed in 2003.

Poverty and Aboriginal Peoples

The Royal Commission on Aboriginal Peoples concluded that Aboriginal people are more reliant on various forms of Social Assistance as a major source of income than the rest of the Canadian population (RCAP 1996, 168). Low income rates (below Low Income Cut-off [LICO]) for First Nations households — even after taking into

NEEDED: A COLLABORATIVE URBAN ABORIGINAL STRATEGY THAT WORKS

There is one aspect of Canadian society, one aspect of our history, that casts a shadow over all that we have achieved. The continuing gap in life conditions between aboriginal and other Canadians is intolerable. It offends our values and we cannot remain on our current path. With our partners, we will tackle head-on the particular problems faced by the increasing number of urban aboriginals and Métis. We will not allow ourselves to be caught up in jurisdictional wrangling, passing the buck and bypassing their needs.

— *Prime Minister Paul Martin,* Hansard, *February 4, 2004*

Responding to the specific needs of urban Aboriginal communities, now the majority of the Aboriginal population, is critical if Aboriginal children and youth are to thrive not merely survive. With an increasing Aboriginal population that is urban, young, and living in lone parent families, Canada must address the extremes of poverty that are their daily reality.

Aboriginal peoples have one of the highest rates of poverty among social groups in Canada. Sixty-nine percent of Aboriginal peoples live off reserve, and 50% of all Aboriginal peoples now live in urban areas.

- Children (0-14 years) make up 33% of Canada's Aboriginal population, compared to 19% of the non- Aboriginal population.[1]
- Almost half (46%) of Aboriginal children under 15 years old live with a lone parent.[2]
- Forty percent of off-reserve Aboriginal children live in poverty. [3]
- One in every four off-reserve Aboriginal children lives in poor housing conditions, compared to 13% of all children in Canada.[4]
- Urban Aboriginal peoples are a high risk group for food insecurity.[5]

Throughout the 1990s federal and provincial governments cut funding for programs dedicated to urban Aboriginal children aged 6-12, funding for Friendship Centres, and funding for Aboriginal language programs.[6] Without investment and partnership between all levels of government and Aboriginal organizations we risk seeing the growth of high poverty urban Aboriginal neighbourhoods in Canada's major cities.

Important progress in higher educational attainment and participation in the labour market has been achieved, yet Aboriginal peoples in 2001 had an unemployment rate that is over twice as high as the general rate.[7] Aboriginal workers earned only two-thirds of an average worker's wages.[8] The Aboriginal workforce is a critical resource for Canada, particularly to maintain the labour force as the baby boom retires. Manitoba and Saskatchewan, where Aboriginal participation will increase to 17% of the total workforce over the next 15 years, stand to benefit significantly.[9]

consideration tax breaks and income transfers from governments – are more than double the national rate. For example, among Aboriginal people in metropolitan areas, 41.6 percent lived below after-tax LICO, which is more than double the national average for metropolitan areas (Statistics Canada 2004). According to the 2001 census, the incidence of low income for all households was 31.2 percent compared with

---

Now is the time for governments at all levels to collaborate with Aboriginal organizations to ramp up social investments that enable young Aboriginals to succeed. Culturally appropriate child care programs and schools are the essential foundation. Aboriginal applicants must be ensured access to universities, apprenticeship, trade and upgrading programs.[10]

More specifically, the Federal Government must ensure that all Aboriginal programs and services are accessible to the 50% of Aboriginal peoples who live in urban areas. Federal investment is needed in programs and services directed at urban Aboriginal children who live in poverty. The Urban Aboriginal Strategy must be redesigned to ensure that urban Aboriginal peoples across Canada have access to programs and services addressing education, employment, housing and health needs. Similarly, the Aboriginal Human Resources Strategy should be redesigned with Aboriginal communities to ensure that urban Aboriginal peoples have equitable access to this labour market program. Renewed investment to enhance and expand the Aboriginal Friendship Centre Program is needed so that urban Aboriginal peoples across Canada have access to a well resourced and stable safety net.

It is clear that children and families in First Nations, rural Métis, remote and northern Inuit communities experience high rates of poverty, even though adequate data are not available. This poverty is systemic and long-standing and requires concerted attention from all levels.

---

1. Anderson, J. (June, 2003). *Aboriginal Children in Poverty in Urban Communities: Social Exclusion and the Growing Racialization of Poverty in Canada.* Ottawa: Canadian Council on Social Development.
2. Ibid.
3. Ibid.
4. Statistics Canada (2003). *Aboriginal peoples Survey 2001: Initial Findings.* Ottawa: Ministry of Industry.
5. Ontario Federation of Indian Friendship Centres (June, 2003). *Child Hunger and Food Insecurity Among Urban Aboriginal Families.* Toronto: Ontario Federation of Indian Friendship Centres.
6. National Association of Friendship Centres (October, 2005). *The Impact of Aboriginal Friendship Centres Program on Increasing Canada's Productivity, Brief to the Standing Committee on Finance.*
7. Mendelson, M. (April, 2004). *Aboriginal peoples in Canada's Labour Market: Work and Unemployment, Today and Tomorrow.* Ottawa: Caledon Institute.
8. Prepared by Campaign 2000 from Statistics Canada, 2001Census 97F0019XCB01048.
9. Mendelson, M. ibid.
10. Ibid.

With permission from Campaign 2000, quoting its annual report card on child poverty (2005, p. 5). www.campaign2000.ca.

Aboriginal People and Unemployment

A primary reason for the high rates of poverty among Aboriginal people is unemployment. In 1995 only 25.3 percent of Aboriginal people had full-time, year-round employment, and 38.4 percent of working-age Aboriginal people were unemployed (Lee 1999, 11). The average annual income of Aboriginal women is about $16,500 (as of 2000), compared to $23,000 for non-Aboriginal women. In 2000, 40 percent of Registered Indian families on reserve had incomes lower than $20,000 (INAC 2000).

an overall national rate of 12.4 percent (Statistics Canada 2003b). In 2000 the median income of Aboriginal individuals was $13,593 compared with a median income for the non-Aboriginal population of $22,431. The Métis had the highest median income of Aboriginal groups ($16,347), followed by Indians off reserve ($13,838) and the Inuit ($13,700). On-reserve Indians ($10,471) and on-reserve Aboriginal people ($10,502) had the lowest median incomes (Statistics Canada 2004).

Figure 7.2 illustrates the gendered dynamic of poverty among Aboriginal peoples versus non-Aboriginal people. Non-Aboriginal men have the highest average income at all age levels, whereas women, both Aboriginal and non-Aboriginal, experience low incomes. Aboriginal women are hit doubly hard. They experience the highest rates of low income, earning an average of less than half that of non-Aboriginal men in many age groups.

The overall poverty of Aboriginal peoples can be seen in a host of social concerns. Aboriginal people are incarcerated in correctional centres and penitentiaries more than other groups. Aboriginal people are twice as likely to be imprisoned and are more likely to receive a full prison sentence than non-Aboriginal people. The rate of suicide and suicide attempts is at least three to four times higher among Aboriginal peoples, especially among those 15–20 years old, than the rest of Canadians (RCAP, 1996).

These poor social conditions, in combination with a lack of economic development and high unemployment rates, have caused many Aboriginal people to leave their own communities for urban centres, particularly within the last thirty years. However, poverty does not disappear in cities. In 1996, 47 percent of Aboriginal people lived in metropolitan areas of Canada. According to the 2001 census, this percentage now stands at 49 percent (Statistics Canada 2003a, p.10) Half of these lived in the Prairie provinces. Winnipeg has by far the largest Aboriginal population at 43,200 or almost 20 percent of the total Canadian urban Aboriginal population (Lee 1999, 9). Of the total Aboriginal urban population, 50.4 percent live below Statistics Canada's LICO as compared to 21.2 percent of the non-Aboriginal population. Perhaps the most shocking statistic is that 77 percent of Aboriginal single-parent families live below this line. The cities with very high percentages of Aboriginal peoples living below LICO are Saskatoon (63.7 percent), Regina (62.2 percent), and Winnipeg (60.5 percent) (Lee 1999, 10).

Health Care

A community's overall health and access to health care serve as excellent litmus tests for well-being and standards of living. Aboriginal peoples in Canada are no exception. According to Health Canada, heart attack rates for First Nations populations are about

Average Income

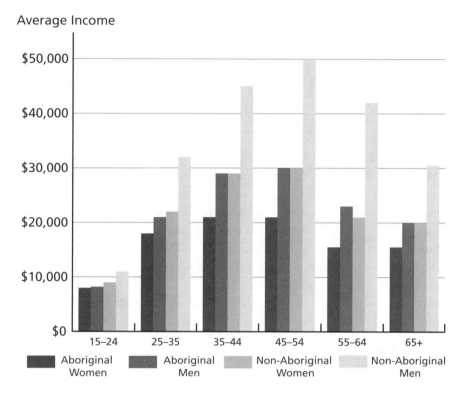

Figure 7.2: Average Income by Age Group, Gender, and Aboriginal Identity, 2001

Source: Aboriginal women: a profile from the 2001 Census. *Ottawa: Indian and Northern Affairs Canada, 2006. http://www. ainc-inac.gc.ca/pr/pub/abw/ abw_e.pdf. Reproduced with the permission of the Minister of Public Works and Government Services Canada, 2007.*

20 percent higher than the national rate, and the rate of stroke is almost double (Health Canada 2005). Tuberculosis is also a major concern in Aboriginal communities. Throughout the 1990s, TB rates in the First Nations population were six to eleven times higher than the national rate (Health Canada 2001), and according to the Medical Services Branch of Health Canada, First Nations people experience a 6.6 times greater incidence of tuberculosis. First Nations individuals are also three times as likely to be diabetic and twice as likely to report a long-term disability than the general Canadian population (INAC 2004). According to the Statistics Canada Aboriginal Peoples Survey conducted in 2001, 45 percent of Aboriginal adults had one or more chronic medical conditions. Arthritis or rheumatism was the top chronic condition among those aged 15 and over, with nearly one in five (19 percent) Aboriginal adults reporting this diagnosis (Statistics Canada 2003c).

The health status of non-reserve Aboriginal people seems to be improving, particularly among young people. The majority, or 56 percent, of non-reserve Aboriginal people reported that their health was excellent or very good. This compares with 65 percent for the total Canadian population (Statistics Canada 2003c). This similarity disappears for older non-reserve Aboriginal people, particularly for women. Older Aboriginal women self-report their health as being poor or very poor at a much higher rate than non-Aboriginal women.

Housing

Many Aboriginal people live in substandard housing. Housing conditions have improved over the last few decades, but much still needs to be done. Data from the 2001 census shows that throughout Canada 1 percent of houses are considered to be overcrowded, but in First Nations communities 12 percent of houses are overcrowded. More recent data also indicates that about 22 percent of homes in First Nations communities are in need of major repairs, and close to 6 percent need to be replaced outright (INAC 2005c).

Housing in northern communities is heavily dependant on public sector funding, as market-based development is hampered by climate, environment, resource availability, and the lack of road and train access (Inuit Tapiriit Kanatami 2004). According to the Inuit Tapiriit Kanatami, an Inuit advocacy group, in 1993 the federal government cut public social housing spending for off-reserve Aboriginal peoples; because the majority of Inuit live in social housing, this measure led to serious overcrowding. Roughly half of all Inuit in Canada live in overcrowded conditions.

Federal Government Expenditures on Aboriginal Social Welfare

According to the federal government, it spends $8.2 billion on First Nations programs and services. While this is delivered via fourteen different federal departments, 67 percent is provided by Indian and Northern Affairs Canada, whose mandate is focused on Status Indians on reserve and Inuit. Health Canada delivers programs directed primarily to First Nations on reserve, accounting for 20 percent of total expenditures on First Nations.

Of the $8.2 billion, $5.36 billion (65 percent) is transferred to First Nations' control, although that control is severely restricted through a variety of funding mechanisms, such as contribution agreements. The Assembly of First Nations sees this approach as inequitable, calculating that this $5.36 billion amounts to $7,200 per person. By way of contrast, the federal government spent approximately $6,000 on each of Canada's 31 million people, and other levels of government upwards of $8,000 (AFN 2006a, 6). As an example, the AFN says that when the federal, provincial, and municipal budgets are measured against population, the average citizen of the City of Ottawa receives services costing approximately $14,900.

In all areas except income transfers (income security programs such as SA, EI, CPP, OAS), First Nations are getting a smaller expenditure per person than the average Canadian. In the area of income transfer, the ratio of expenditure is equal. First Nations people draw much more from SA programs, whereas other Canadians draw more often from EI, CPP, OAS, and other programs.

Inuit Tapiriit Kanatami

www.itk.ca

The Inuit Tapiriit Kanatami is a national Inuit Organization that represents the four Inuit regions in Canada: Nunatsiavut (Labrador), Nunavik (northern Quebec), Nunavut, and the Inuvialuit Settlement Region in the Northwest Territories. Founded in the 1970s from earlier organizations, the ITK advocates for Aboriginal rights, land claims, and resource development, and it fights against global warming and climate change as public health and human rights issues.

WHO'S RESPONSIBLE FOR ABORIGINAL HOUSING?

Native Leaders Blame Ottawa for Aboriginal Homeless Problem

Native leaders say there are more homeless aboriginal people in Winnipeg than there were a decade ago and they're blaming the federal government.

Ten years ago, Ottawa stopped investing in a program that built low-income rental homes for urban aboriginals. Since then, waiting lists for the existing properties have grown and so have the number of native people living in motels, shelters and on the streets.

Aboriginal housing advocates from across Canada met in Winnipeg on Friday [April 16, 2004] to find ways to deal with the problem.

Larry Wercherer, who runs the Neeginan emergency shelter, says there are hundreds of homeless aboriginal people in Winnipeg who should have a better life. "Because of the lack of housing in Canada, the lack of social housing, the lack of affordable housing, it's very frustrating for them."

Wayne Helgason, with the Social Planning Council of Winnipeg and the former head of the Aboriginal Council, says it is impossible to know exactly how many people are living on the streets or in shelters.

"We did a homeless count, a random sample of about 350 people who were homeless a year ago. We found that over 75 per cent of the people in shelters, requiring intervention or on the street, were aboriginal people."

Helgason believes that number will continue to rise because of a lack of affordable housing.

But Manitoba's Housing Minister, Christine Melnyk, says the issue is not that simple.

"A trend that we're seeing is that the housing situation on reserves is really in quite a serious state, so we're seeing a lot of in-migration into the city of Winnipeg.

"So on-reserve housing plays a big piece in the whole housing issue here, not only in Manitoba but across Canada. So again we need [Ottawa] to co-ordinate and to be in for the long-term."

Claudette Bradshaw, the federal minister responsible for homelessness, says Ottawa has already committed $1 billion to tackle the problem of housing and homelessness.

Bradshaw says much of the money hasn't been spent, in part, because the provinces haven't contributed their share of the funding.

Wercherer says it's time people stop passing the buck and look in the right places for help.

"They've really got to include the housing groups in the solutions because they're on the frontline here, they know what needs to be done and they've been doing it cost-effectively for 20 years in some cases, and who better to guide government with their policies?"

Source: "Native leaders blame Ottawa for aboriginal homeless problem." CBC. ca. April 16, 2004. Available http://www.cbc.ca/canada/story/2004/04/16/ homeless040416.html. Reprinted with permission.

Towards Aboriginal Self-Government

Movement towards self-government for Aboriginal peoples has occurred in several stages. One of the most important developments was the introduction in 1969 of the White Paper (Statement of the Government of Canada on Indian Policy) written by the then Minister of Indian Affairs, Jean Chrétien. In an effort to modernize the government's relationship with Aboriginal people, the White Paper argued that Aboriginal peoples should be treated as regular citizens, that they should take control of their lands, and that the Indian affairs department should be disbanded. But the report galvanized the First Nations in united opposition, arguing that ending "the special status of the Indians," was not a solution to the problem. Harold Cardinal of the Indian Association of Alberta wrote a response titled "Citizens Plus," which came to be known as the *Red Paper*. The report mapped out an alternative view whereby Aboriginal peoples would contribute to Canadian society while concurrently exercising rights and power at the community level. With this and other protests, the First Nations successfully forced the federal government to abandon the recommendations of the White Paper in the 1970s.

Under sections 25, 35, and 37 of the *Constitution Act*, 1982, the Government of Canada has recognized the inherent right of self-government as an existing Aboriginal right. Building on this in the late 1990s, the Royal Commission on Aboriginal Peoples (RCAP) and *Gathering Strength: Canada's Aboriginal Action Plan* (the government's response), the approach to self-government has evolved to include a framework for new government-to-government relationships and structures for negotiating self-government agreements. According to INAC, the new policy is based on "the view that Aboriginal peoples of Canada have the right to govern themselves in relation to matters that are internal to their communities, integral to their unique cultures, identities, traditions, languages and institutions, and with respect to their special relationship to their land and their Resources" (INAC 2005a, 78). The objective of the policy, according to INAC, is the negotiation of concrete self-government agreements. In 2005 INAC was engaged in seventy-two negotiations for self-government, representing 445 Aboriginal communities (INAC 2005a, 78).

Perhaps the most prominent example of Aboriginal self-government is in the territory of Nunavut, one of the traditional homes of the Inuit in Canada. After an almost twenty-year process of legal and political negotiation, the eastern half of the Northwest Territories officially became the territory of Nunavut in 1999. While Nunavut operates a democratic parliamentary system like the rest of Canada, it combines it with the practices of consensus government: all of the elected members of the legislative assembly select the premiere and ministers together, and decide as a group the priorities for the

The Congress of Aboriginal Peoples

www.abo-peoples.org

The **Congress of Aboriginal Peoples (CAP)** is an organization that represents off-reserve and Métis people. Founded in the 1970s, the organization's mission is to represent the interests of Aboriginal people who are not legally recognized under the *Indian Act*, including non-Status Indians and Métis peoples.

Two Inuit junior rangers unveil the territorial flag of Nunavut at the April 1, 1999, inaugural event for the new territory. The creation of an autonomous territory is one expression of Aboriginal self-government, as encouraged in the Royal Commission.

government. The Government of Nunavut also uses Inuit traditional knowledge and values to guide decision making and to create policies and laws that represent the territory's Inuit majority (www.gov.nu.ca).

The Royal Commission Today

As has been explained, the Royal Commission on Aboriginal Peoples in 1996 was an extensive study of the situation of Aboriginal people in Canada, and it was followed by the 1998 government response, *Gathering Strength: Canada's Aboriginal Action Plan*. In 1991, when the commission was called, Aboriginal peoples were in the forefront of national awareness due to land protests across the country and nation-wide debate over the Meech Lake Accord, which proposed amendments to the *Constitution Act* of 1982. A central conclusion of the report was that "the main policy direction, pursued for over 150 years, first by colonial then by Canadian governments, has been wrong" (AFN 2006b, 1). The dominant theme presented in the recommendations was that "Aboriginal peoples must have room to exercise their autonomy and structure their solutions" (AFN 2006b, 1).

The commission's report included hundreds of recommendations, including specific socio-economic targets, namely to improve the gap between Aboriginal and non-Aboriginal people by half and to improve general social conditions in twenty years. It has been over ten years since the report was released, and we, as a nation, have failed to make progress in this area. In its ten-year report on progress towards meeting the specific goals in RCAP, the AFN summary analysis found "a clear lack of action on the key foundational recommendations of RCAP and a resultant lack of progress on key socio-economic indicators. Based on our assessment, Canada has failed in terms of its action to date" (AFN 2006b, 2).

According to volume 5 of the RCAP Report — *Renewal: A Twenty-Year Commitment* — the foundation for a renewed relationship involves recognition of Aboriginal nations as political entities. At the core of the 440 recommendations contained in the report is a rebalancing of political and economic power between Aboriginal nations and other Canadian governments. The report points to five key themes:

1. Aboriginal nations have to be reconstituted.
2. A process must be established for the assumption of powers by Aboriginal nations.
3. There must be a fundamental reallocation of lands and resources.
4. Aboriginal people need education and crucial skills for governance and economic self-reliance.
5. Economic development must be addressed if the poverty and despondency of lives defined by unemployment and welfare are to change.

In addition, there must also be a sincere acknowledgement by non-Aboriginal people of the injustices of the past (RCAP 1996, Chap. 1).

Conclusion

There are 1.3 million Aboriginal peoples in Canada, according to the 2001 census. Since the time of the *Indian Act* in 1876, the Aboriginal peoples of Canada have been subjected to colonial government polices concerned with obtaining and keeping their land, first for settlers and more recently for the economic gains of resource extraction. As part of this, government policies that have been labelled assimilation policies attempted to absorb Aboriginal peoples and break their cultural and language ties. Residential schools are perhaps the most well-known aspect of this policy. In the end, it is the Aboriginal people that suffer, experiencing social conditions similar to those in Third World countries.

Successive federal governments have stated that addressing the social welfare of Aboriginal people in Canada is a major priority. Ultimately, little is done and measures are only half taken. Some analysts argue that top-down solutions from Ottawa are doomed to fail. Others blame the failure on jurisdictional squabbling between the provinces and the federal government over who should pay. Often, in the end, no one pays.

Social justice initiatives such as the Residential Schools Settlement Agreement and the Truth and Reconciliation Commission are steps in the right direction. They provide opportunities for both compensation and healing. As well, increased efforts by governments at sincere self-determination negotiations may pave the way for increased social welfare for Aboriginal peoples. Much needs to be done to reverse the damage done to the Aboriginal peoples of Canada.

Chapter Summary

Key Concepts

- ■ **Aboriginal peoples**
- ■ **Assembly of First Nations (AFN)**
- ■ **Assimilation**
- ■ **Christianization**
- ■ **Congress of Aboriginal Peoples (CAP)**
- ■ **Department of Indian Affairs**
- ■ **Enfranchisement**
- ■ **First Nations**
- ■ **Income Security Reform (ISR)**
- ■ *Indian Act* **of 1876**
- ■ **Indian and Northern Affairs Canada (INAC)**
- ■ **Inuit Tapiriit Kanatami (ITK)**
- ■ **Land surrender**
- ■ **Reserve system**
- ■ **Residential schools**
- ■ **Royal Commission on Aboriginal Peoples (RCAP)**
- ■ **Status or Registered Indians**
- ■ **Treaties**

Review Questions

1. How do the social and economic conditions of Aboriginal people differ from that of other Canadians?
2. What are the specific factors in the history of the relationship between Aboriginal peoples and the governments of Canada that have impacted the social welfare of Aboriginal peoples?
3. What were the six major policy goals of public policy in relation to Aboriginal peoples as identified by Ponting?
4. What would be the main characteristics of a social policy approach that might be effective with Aboriginal peoples?
5. Why is Aboriginal self-government such an important idea for promoting the social welfare of Aboriginal peoples?

6. Do governments in Canada spend more or less on Aboriginal services as compared to services for the average Canadian? Are the facts regarding this question consistent with public perception? If not, why do you think this is the case?

Exploring Social Welfare

1. Pick one of the social and economic conditions outlined in this chapter (such as unemployment, infant mortality, etc.). Research the issue further and write a brief report describing the situation of Aboriginal peoples as compared to other Canadians. Outline the polices that the government has recently undertaken to address this issue, and discuss their effectiveness or your views on its potential effectiveness.

2. In 2006 the federal government announced the $1.9 billion Residential Schools Settlement Agreement to compensate former residential school students. The settlement agreement proposes a Common Experience Payment for all eligible former students of Indian Residential Schools, an Independent Assessment Process for claims of sexual or serious physical abuse, as well as measures to support healing, commemorative activities, and the establishment of a Truth and Reconciliation Commission. Conduct further research and further describe this agreement. Two good sources are government websites at www.iacobucci.gc.ca and www.irsr-rqpi.gc.ca/english/index.html. It would also be useful to obtain information from the AFN and other Aboriginal organizations.

Websites

Aboriginal Canada Portal
www.aboriginalcanada.gc.ca

This federal government site is a window to Canadian Aboriginal online resources, contacts, information, and government programs and services.

Aboriginal Policy Research Conference
http://sociology.uwo.ca/aprc/crmpa/

The second Aboriginal Policy Research Conference was held in 2006, and showcased a wide range of presentations on Aboriginal issues, with the goal of providing evidence-based research to influence social policy. The website has links to several of the papers presented at the conference.

Aboriginal Photograph Database, Saskatoon Archives
http://library2.usask.ca/native/nphotoh.html

The Aboriginal Photograph Database is part of the Saskatoon Archives and hosted by the University of Saskatoon. It provides a thematic index of photographs relevant to aboriginal studies.

References

Assembly of First Nations (AFN). 2006a. *Federal Government Funding to First Nations: The Facts, the Myths, and the Way Forward*. Ottawa: Assembly of First Nations.

Assembly of First Nations (AFN). 2006b. *Royal Commission on Aboriginal People at 10 Years: A Report Card*. Ottawa: Assembly of First Nations.

Assembly of First Nations (AFN). 2006c. *Submission to the Committee on Economic, Social and Cultural Rights Regarding the 5th Periodic Report of Canada*. Ottawa: Assembly of First Nations.

Castellano, Mary Brant. 2002. *Aboriginal Family Trends: Extended Families, Nuclear Families, Families of the Heart*. Ottawa: Vanier Institute of the Family.

Cooke, Martin, Daniel Beavon, and Mindy McHardy. 2004. *Measuring the Well-Being of Aboriginal People: An Application of the United Nations' Human Development Index to Registered Indians in Canada, 1981–2001*. www.ainc-inac.gc.ca/pr/ra/mwb/index_e.html.

Correctional Service Canada. 1999. *Demographic Overview of Aboriginal Peoples in Canada and Aboriginal Offenders in Federal Corrections*. Ottawa: Correctional Service Canada. www.csc-scc.gc.ca/text/prgrm/correctional/abissues/know/10_e.shtml.

Guest, Denis. 1999. *The Emergence of Social Security in Canada*, 3rd ed. Vancouver: UBC Press.

Health Canada. 2001. *Tuberculosis in First Nations Communities, 1999*. Ottawa: Health Canada.

Health Canada. 2003. *A Statistical Profile on the Health of First Nations in Canada for the Year 2000*. Ottawa: Health Canada. www.hc-sc.gc.ca/fnih-spni/pubs/gen/stats_profil_e.html.

Health Canada. 2005. *First Nations Comparable Health Indicators*. Ottawa: Health Canada. www.hc-sc.gc.ca/fnih-spni/pubs/gen/2005-01_health-sante_indicat/index_e.html.

Indian and Northern Affairs Canada (INAC). 1997. *Implications of First Nations Demography*. www.ainc-inac.gc.ca/pr/ra/execs/index_e.html.

Indian and Northern Affairs Canada (INAC). 2000. *Backgrounder: Income Security Reform Demonstration Projects*. www.ainc-inac.gc.ca/nr/prs/j-a2000/99175bk_e.html.

Indian and Northern Affairs Canada (INAC). 2004. *Social Development: Health and Social Indicators*. www.ainc-inac.gc.ca/gs/soci_e.html.

Indian and Northern Affairs Canada (INAC). 2005a. *Basic Departmental Data 2004*. Cat No. R12-7/2003E. Ottawa: Department of Indian Affairs and Northern Development. www.ainc-inac.gc.ca/pr/sts/bdd04/bdd04_e.pdf.

Indian and Northern Affairs Canada (INAC). 2005b. *Comparison of Socio-economic Conditions, 1996 and 2001 Registered Indians, Registered Indians Living on Reserve and the Total Population of Canada*. Ottawa: Department of Indian Affairs and Northern Development. Cat. no. R32-163/2001E-PDF. www.ainc-inac.gc.ca/pr/sts/csc/csc_e.pdf.

Indian and Northern Affairs Canada (INAC). 2005c. *First Nations Housing*. Ottawa: Indian and Northern Affairs Canada. www.ainc-inac.gc.ca/pr/info/info104_e.html.

Inuit Tapiriit Kanatami. 2004. *Backgrounder on Inuit and Housing: For Discussion at Housing Sectoral Meeting November 24 and 25 in Ottawa*. Ottawa: Inuit Tapiriit Kanatami. www.itk.ca/roundtable/sectoral-housing-backgrounder.php.

Lee, K. 1999. Measuring poverty among Canada's Aboriginal people. *Insight* 23 (2).

Moscovitch, Allan, and Andrew Webster. 1995. Aboriginal social assistance expenditures. In *How Ottawa Spends 1995–96: Mid-Life Crisis*, ed. Susan Philips. Ottawa: Carleton University Press.

National Native Addictions Partnership Foundation Inc. (NNAPF). 2000. *NNADAP Renewal Framework for Implementing the Strategic Recommendations of the 1998 General Review of the National Native Alcohol and Drug Abuse Program*. Muskoday, Sask: National Native Addictions Partnership Foundation Inc. www.nnapf.org/english/pdf/publications/NNAPF_nnadap_renewal_framework.pdf.

Native leaders blame Ottawa for Aboriginal homeless problem. *CBC News online*, April 16, 2004, www.cbc.ca/canada/story/2004/04/16/homeless040416.html.

Ponting, J.R. 1997. *First Nations in Canada: Perspectives on Opportunity, Empowerment, and Self-Determination*. Toronto: McGraw-Hill Ryerson.

Public Health Agency of Canada. 2005a. Parents be aware: sniffing kills! *Canadian Health Network*. www.canadian-health-network.ca/servlet/ContentServer?cid=113 0518313213&pagename=CHN-RCS/CHNResource/CHNResourcePageTemplate&tc=C HNResource.

Public Health Agency of Canada. 2005b. *HIV/AIDS Epi Notes, Understanding the HIV/ AIDS Epidemic among Aboriginal Peoples in Canada: The Community at a Glance*. www.phac-aspc.gc.ca/publicat/epiu-aepi/epi-note/index.html.

Royal Commission on Aboriginal Peoples (RCAP). 1996. *Report of the Royal Commission on Aboriginal Peoples*. Ottawa: Indian and Northern Affairs Canada.

Scott, Kimberly A. 1994. Aboriginal health and social history: A brief Canadian history. Unpublished. Author's personal collection.

Senécal, Sach. 2006. *The Well-Being of Inuit Communities 1991–2001*. Ottawa: Indian and Northern Affairs Canada. www.ssc.uwo.ca/sociology/aprc-crmpa/ 100-%20Sacha%20Senecal-%20Inuit_HdI_CWB_PreConf.swf.

Shewell, Hugh E.Q. 2004. *Enough to Keep Them Alive: Indian Welfare in Canada, 1873–1965*. Toronto: University of Toronto Press.

Statistics Canada. 2003a. *2001 Census: Analysis Series, Aboriginal Peoples of Canada: A Demographic Profile*. Ottawa: Statistics Canada. Cat no. 96F0030XIE2001007. www12.statcan.ca/english/census01/Products/Analytic/ companion/abor/pdf/96F0030XIE2001007.pdf.

Statistics Canada. 2003b. *2001 Census: Selected Income Characteristics (35A), Aboriginal Identity (8), Age Groups (6), Sex (3) and Area of Residence (7) for Population, for Canada, Provinces and Territories, 2001 Census – 20% Sample Data*. Ottawa: Statistics Canada. Cat. no. 97F0011XCB2001046.

Statistics Canada. 2003c. *Aboriginal Peoples Survey 2001: Initial Release – Supporting Tables*. Ottawa: Statistics Canada. Cat. no. 89-592-XIE. www.eco.gov. yk.ca/stats/federal/aboriginal01.pdf.

Statistics Canada. 2004. Low income in census metropolitan areas. *The Daily*, April 7, 2004.

Statistics Canada. 2006a. *Family Violence in Canada: A Statistical Profile, 2006*. Ottawa: Statistics Canada. Cat. no. 85-224-XIE. www.statcan.ca/english/ freepub/85-224-XIE/85-224-XIE2006000.pdf.

Statistics Canada. 2006b. Infant Mortality Rates, by Province and Territory. Ottawa: Statistics Canada. CANSIM Table 102-0504. www40.statcan.ca/l01/cst01/ health21a.htm.

8 Immigration, Race, and Social Welfare

Employment Barriers and Income Security

by Purnima Sundar

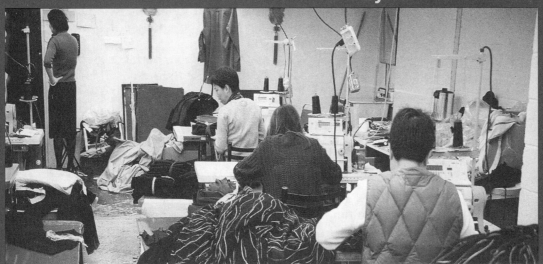

Canada is perhaps one of the most ethnically, racially, and culturally diverse countries in the world and has an international reputation for being friendly to diverse cultures — a place where one can live while retaining cultural traditions. Many call this *multiculturalism*. Canada is also regarded throughout the world as a welcoming destination for immigrants and a safe haven for refugees. However, Canada is also facing an increase in the percentage of newcomers who are unemployed or underemployed and live in poverty.

Canada was the first country to develop an explicit commitment to promoting ethnic and racial diversity, through the 1971 Multicultural Policy. From this, other policies (such as Employment Equity) and practices (such as, the implementation of social services designed with the goal of meeting the needs of all people, regardless of race, ethnicity,

> "We've always been a country of immigrants, waves of people from every other shore coming here to join with the Aboriginal peoples. In recent decades, we have undertaken a massive experiment in citizenship. We are learning to practice the ideals of unity in diversity, and the rich variety in our population astonishes the world."
>
> — *Former Governor General Adrienne Clarkson on the occasion of a Citizenship Ceremony, 2005*

RACE, ETHNICITY, AND CULTURE
What's in a Definition?

- **Race.** *Race* is defined as the observable, physical features that are shared among several people, but that distinguish them from members of other groups. For example, if we orient to skin colour and hair texture, people who are labelled "black" differ visibly from those identified as "white."
- **Ethnicity.** *Ethnicity* describes a group of people who share a common descent, language, religion, and traditions. Although people might be members of the same racial grouping, they can differ in terms of ethnicity. For example, people who identify themselves racially as "black" may identify themselves *ethnically* as African, Jamaican, or Caribbean. Each of these ethnic groupings is linked to particular values and behaviours that differ considerably from one another, despite the perceived commonality in race.
- **Culture.** *Culture* is the set of ideals, norms, beliefs, and values that are shared by a group of individuals. This shapes the way people interpret the world, and informs the way they live their day-to-day lives. It is important to remember that cultures shift and change over time, and that members of a particular cultural group might differ from one another in terms of their specific customs and traditions.

and culture), have emerged to support our growing diverse ethno-racial and cultural mosaic. Such initiatives are viewed as an intrinsic part of our social, political, and moral order. However, the reality of immigrating to Canada can be somewhat different from the idealized image. Immigrants confront significant challenges and often have to struggle to meet their income needs.

In its early colonial history, Canada became home to immigrants from the United Kingdom, France, and other mostly Northern European countries; in the postwar period, many immigrants from other parts of Europe came to Canada. Changes to immigration policies in the late 1960s and early 1970s, however, resulted in the arrival of newcomers from non-European countries like Asia, Africa, the Middle East, South and Central America, and the Caribbean in greater numbers than ever before. Indeed, according to Statistics Canada data from the 2001 census, between 1981 and 2001 the number of "visible minorities" in Canada increased from 1.1 million to 4 million individuals, with members of South Asian, Chinese, Black, and Filipino communities being the most numerous in this group. This caused a dramatic shift in the ethno-racial makeup of our society and laid the foundation for what we now commonly refer to as "Multicultural Canada."

There are several factors that play a part in the increase in the number of low-income earners among new immigrants. This chapter

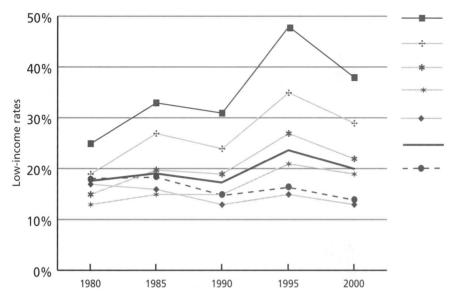

Figure 8.1: Low-Income Rates of Immigrants by Number of Years in Canada

Source: Picot, Garnett and Feng Hou. 2003. The rise in low-income rates among immigrants in Canada. Catalogue 11F0019MIE, No. 198. Ottawa: Statistics Canada, p. 36. Analytical Studies Branch research paper series. http://www.statcan.ca/english/research/11F0019MIE/11F0019MIE2003198.pdf

will explore one particular issue in some detail: the link between immigration and unemployment and underemployment among newcomers to Canada. Given the recent increase in the number of newcomers from visible minority (or non-white) groups, there will be a particular focus on obstacles that prevent these individuals from finding and keeping suitable work opportunities.

This chapter begins with an overview of some of the key challenges faced by new immigrants and then briefly reviews the history of Canadian immigration and our current, multicultural context. It looks at the various barriers immigrants face in finding and keeping work, and at the different ways we can understand the link between immigration and unemployment or underemployment. Finally, we'll look at some ways that we, as social workers, might respond to the income-related struggles newcomers often face.

Challenges Faced by New Immigrants

Challenges related to immigration and settlement can include any or all of the following:

- struggling with a new language and accessing educational programs
- experiencing difficulties finding suitable and affordable housing
- having to deal with racism, exclusion, and discrimination
- learning how to navigate complex health and social service systems

Added to these problems is the fact that many newcomers have had to leave family members and friends behind in their home countries, so they are also often dealing with concerns related to family reunification and a lack of extended kinship and social networks.

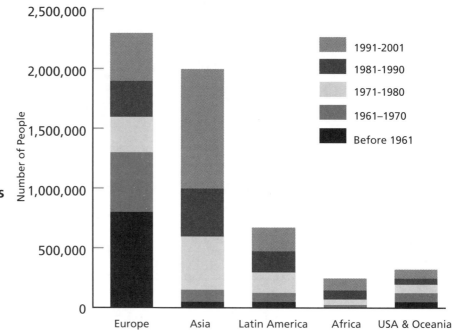

Figure 8.2: Canada's Immigrants by Region of Birth and Period of Arrival

Source: Steven Hick. 2006. Social Work in Canada, 2nd ed. Toronto: Thompson Educational Publishing, 230. Used with permission.

Perhaps the most pressing challenge experienced by newcomers today, however, is related to income security. In particular, many recent immigrants (those who have been in Canada for five years or less) are unemployed or underemployed, and are more likely to face low income than mainstream Canadians.

Unfortunately, this condition seems to be worsening over time. For example, recent immigrants in 1980 had a low-income rate 1.4 times greater than individuals born in Canada. By 1990, the low-income rate for newcomers had increased to 2.1 times greater, or more than twice that of their Canadian-born counterparts. In 2000 these individuals were 2.5 times more likely than non-immigrants to live below the Low Income Cut-off (LICO).

According to Garnett Picot and Feng Hou at Statistics Canada, one would not have expected this trend, considering that in 2000, some 42 percent of recent immigrants held university degrees compared with only 19 percent of those who arrived in 1980. Given this incongruence, these authors attempted to understand what factors might be contributing to this growing number of recent newcomers living on low incomes. Using a statistical procedure called a "regression analysis," Picot and Hou (2003) found that only half (48 percent) of the increase in the low-income rate among new immigrants could be explained by factors such as level of education, the newcomer's home country, her or his home language, the nature of her or his family structure (e.g., single- or dual-parent families), and her or his age. Based on this finding, we might pose the question "What *other* factors are contributing to the rise in low-income status for newcomers to Canada?"

A Brief History of Immigration to Canada

Canadian immigration policies have always been and continue to be shaped by the economic requirements of our country. Decisions about immigration are linked to our need for labour and the current level of population growth. When enacting these policies, however, politicians have been forced to take into account the general concerns and fears that mainstream Canadians have about the increased presence of newcomers.

In their book, *The Making of the Mosaic: A History of Canadian Immigration Policy*, Ninette Kelley a member of the Canadian Immigration and Refugee Board, and Michael Trebilcock, a professor of law and economics at the University of Toronto, chart the progression of immigration policy in Canada (Kelley and Trebilcock 1998). They believe that political and economic interests, and not an overall generosity and interest in "celebrating diversity," have been the primary forces in shaping important decisions about "who gets in." Their historical analysis finds that explicitly racist and discriminatory policies have been used to control the influx of people from certain ethno-racial and cultural groups into our country. Given our current commitment to diversity, equality, and freedom, many Canadians are surprised to learn that historically, racism and discrimination were quite common in this country.

Early in the 1900s, needs changed, and newcomers to Canada were sought after to help develop the country. During this time, official policies were designed to support the arrival of the "best" immigrants (for example, Germans, who were "solid and hardworking"), and exclude those who were less desirable (such as Asians, who were considered to be generally inferior to whites). For example, the Chinese Head Tax (which was levied on each member of a Chinese household), and the Continuous Journey Requirement (which prevented almost 400 South Asians from entering Canada), were deliberate attempts on the part of those in power to legally prevent individuals from particular ethno-racial groups (whom they found morally or socially unappealing) from entering the country.

During World War II (1939–45) and the years that followed, there was an increased demand for labour, which resulted in the redesign of immigration policies to meet the growing needs of business and industry. Intense economic growth created a favourable environment for immigration: professionals and skilled workers in different trades were sought after to populate urban environments. Finding the "right" kind of immigrant was still important, and there were continued efforts to keep Asians and others from diverse ethno-racial backgrounds (as well as homosexuals, drug addicts and traffickers, Nazi-sympathizers, and communists) out of Canada. Explicitly racist policies (like the Chinese Head Tax) were no longer tolerated, and various ethnic and racial

Structural Racism: Historical Canadian Immigration Policies

The Continuous Journey Requirement

In the late 1800s and early 1900s, over 2,000 individuals from the Indian subcontinent arrived to work in Canada with the hope of creating a better economic situation for their family. Fear and racism among mainstream Canadians, however, led to strict policies that discouraged South Asian immigration.

As members of the British Commonwealth, Indian citizens could not be explicitly denied entry, but those arriving in Canada were required to have $200 on their person; an outrageous amount given the standard wage in India of ten cents a day. Also, the *Continuous Journey Requirement* permitted entry to immigrants *only* if they arrived "from their country of birth or citizenship by a continuous journey on through tickets purchased before leaving the country" (Kelley and Trebilcock 1998, 146). On a continuous journey a ship could not stop in any port between departure and final destination — a condition that was impossible to meet, given the distance between Indian and Canadian ports.

In 1914, a businessman named Gurdit Singh attempted to overcome this restriction by commissioning a Japanese steamliner, the *Komagatu Maru*, to bring 376 prospective Punjabi immigrants to Canada. The vessel was denied entry, based on the Continuous Journey Requirement — while the ship had made a continuous journey from Japan the passengers had not arrived directly from their home country.

The Chinese Head Tax

The Canadian Pacific Railway was built in the late 1800s with mostly Chinese immigrant labour. The Canadian government sought immigrants from China to take on the difficult, physical labour of building the railway because domestic labour was simply not available. With the influx of labourers, many believed that the number of Chinese immigrants to Canada needed to be somehow "managed." However, because of the need for labourers and the necessity of trade with China, it was not possible to restrict immigration outright. Restricting immigration from China entirely would have seriously compromised trade with China and negatively affected economic growth within Canada.

To resolve the issue, Canada developed a series of policies aimed at discouraging Chinese immigration. The most famous policy was the *Chinese Immigration Act* (1885). Under the act, a "head tax" of $50 was imposed on all incoming persons of Chinese origin, with very few exceptions. This head tax was eventually increased to $100 in 1900, and then to $500 (the equivalent of two years of wages for a Chinese labourer) in 1903.

It is estimated that the federal government earned $23 million from the *Chinese Head Tax* policy, which resulted in family separation and poverty among members of the Chinese community in Canada. It was only in 2006 that financial restitution was made to the families of those who paid the Chinese Head Tax, and the government made a public apology for the explicitly racist and discriminatory policy.

groups were encouraged to work with the government to determine the best ways to manage and support immigration from non-European countries.

From the late 1960s to the mid-1990s, the decline in natural population growth and a rising need for skilled labour in technology and industry guided decisions about immigration policy. In response to widespread acknowledgement of the racist and discriminatory practices of the past, a new policy called the points system was introduced in 1967 to eliminate race as a determining factor in immigration decisions. The goal of this points system was to meet the economic and labour needs of Canada, while ensuring that justice and fairness characterized the immigration process.

Within the points system, individual qualities were accorded a certain number of "merit points." Higher numbers of "merit points" would increase one's chances of being granted entry into Canada. The qualities considered included level of education, personal attributes (such as adaptability, motivation, initiative), demand for the person's occupation in Canada, level of skill, the extent to which employment is already arranged, knowledge of English and/or French, the number of relatives already living in Canada, and the number of employment opportunities in their desired destination. In making the immigration process more transparent, less racist, and less subjective, the introduction of the points system prompted the arrival of the greatest number of non-white immigrants (from Asia, Africa, the Middle East, South and Central America, and the Caribbean) in Canada's history.

At the present time, the goals of the *Immigration Act* are threefold: to reunite families, to contribute to economic development, and to protect refugees. The three corresponding classes under which newcomers are admitted to Canada are *economic class* (including skilled workers or business immigrants), *family class*, and *refugee class*.

The points system continues to be used for evaluating those applying as economic class immigrants. Members of this class can be either skilled workers, business owners, or entrepreneurs. Citizens or permanent residents of Canada are able to sponsor relatives (spouse or common-law partner, parents, grandparents, dependent children, and other family members under 18 years of age who are orphaned) to immigrate to Canada in the family class. This requires that the citizen or permanent resident assume economic and personal responsibility for these family members for anywhere from three to ten years. Finally, in keeping with Canada's commitment to humanitarianism, thousands of individuals needing protection from persecution, torture, or cruelty in their home countries arrive in the refugee class each year. The criteria for entry into the country within this class are evidence of humanitarian need.

Citizenship and Immigration Canada

www.cic.gc.ca

The Citizenship and Immigration Canada website offers information about the process of immigration, relevant policies and regulations, and a range of research publications focused on how today's newcomers are faring socially and economically in Canada.

Immigration Classes

■ **Economic class:** includes skilled workers, business owners, or and entrepreneurs

■ **Family class:** requires a sponsor to provide economic and personal support for three to ten years

■ **Refugee class:** includes individuals who need protection from forces in their home country

The Current Context: Multicultural Canada

As described earlier, Canadian immigration policies are largely designed around our economic needs. Immigrants are essential for supporting Canadian trade and industry, and they contribute considerably to our financial and political health as a country. Throughout our history, it appears that when there is an economic need for labour, Canada welcomes newcomers. During times of economic hardship, however, immigrants are blamed for having taken the jobs of "real Canadians." This practice of scapegoating has a number of negative personal and social consequences for newcomers, including being denied housing and jobs, and experiencing racism and discrimination.

In an attempt to manage these and other mixed consequences of Canada's growing ethno-racial diversity, the Canadian Multicultural Policy was introduced in 1971. The overall goal of this policy was to try to defuse potential problems by reframing ethnic or racial difference as a national agenda of "unity within diversity." Its chief purposes, as described by Mahtani (2004) were first communicated by then Prime Minister Pierre Trudeau in the House of Commons, in October of 1971 as follows:

1. To assist all Canadian cultural groups that demonstrate a desire and effort to develop a capacity to grow and contribute to Canada
2. To assist members of all cultural groups to overcome cultural barriers to full participation in Canadian society
3. To promote creative encounters and interchange among all Canadian cultural groups in the interest of national unity
4. To continue to assist immigrants to acquire at least one of Canada's official languages, in order to become full participants in society

This official commitment to multiculturalism and the general acceptance of diversity are considered uniquely Canadian, setting us apart from other nations around the world. Indeed, according to Kelley and Trebilcock, a common sentiment among Canadians is that "racism and bigotry were European, or at least American, inventions that have little part in Canada's history, tradition, or psyche . . . Canada has a long history of welcoming refugees and dissidents" (1998, 441).

Canadian multiculturalism, however, is not perfect. In fact, there have been many debates about the benefits and limitations of this policy, and the values and beliefs that have shaped it.

Criticism of Canadian Multicultural Policy

Several Canadian scholars argue that multiculturalism has failed in reaching its intended goals, and that it may be detrimental to Canadian society. For example, George Dei, a professor at the Ontario Institute for Studies in Education, suggests that multiculturalism promotes "celebrations of diversity" that divert our attention away from the disturbing effects of racial inequality in society. This is referred to as the "saris, samosas, and steel band syndrome," and it involves displaying superficial aspects of a culture (such as ethnic trinkets, foods, and dance) to mainstream audiences at ethnic and cultural fairs and festivals. Dei argues that these celebrations do not encourage a deep and meaningful understanding of the customs and traditions of different ethnic or cultural groups. In addition, these events do not result in changes to the existing power structures that sustain inequalities between mainstream Canadians and ethno-racial minorities. Instead, these practices end up trivializing people's cultural practices and undermining the very ideology Canadians claim to protect and promote.

This view is shared by Canadian writer Neil Bissoondath, who elaborates by suggesting that this "celebratory" view of ethno-racial difference often ends up homogenizing people of colour. In other words, based on a limited look at certain cultural practices, all individuals who share a particular ethno-racial background are assumed to share stereotypical qualities that are different from (and less "normal" than) mainstream Canadians.

Further, Bissoondath argues that by stressing the differences between people with diverse ethno-racial backgrounds and mainstream Canadians, multiculturalism threatens the cohesiveness of Canadian society. The emphasis on preserving traditions and customs from "back home" encourages a lack of commitment to the "Canadian" way of life that should be the uniting force for all members of this society. This presents a barrier to the full integration of people from all ethno-racial groups into Canadian society, and instead results in their exclusion and marginalization from the mainstream. Bissoondath argues that rather than identifying ourselves as "hyphenated" Canadians (which would make him an East Indian-Trinidadian-Canadian), we should be proud to call ourselves simply "Canadian."

Despite these critiques, most average Canadians believe that over the last three decades, our experiment with multiculturalism has been relatively positive and productive. By engaging these critiques, however, we should challenge ourselves to reshape and improve the policy so that it addresses concerns that are raised, and so that it is responsive to the needs of all Canadians, including newcomers facing economic hardship.

Barriers to Finding and Keeping Work

Despite the critiques, Canadian multiculturalism has articulated an official commitment to the full integration and participation of all members of our society. So why do newcomers, especially those from visible minority groups, continue to experience barriers that prevent them from enjoying the benefits of appropriate employment?

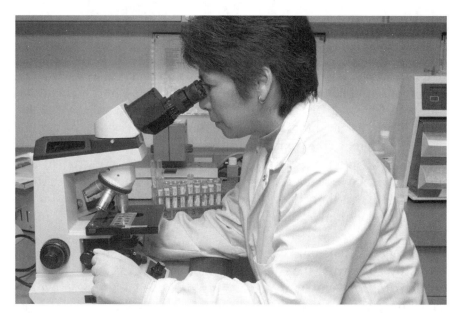

Many new immigrants find that their education and training is devalued in the Canadian job market, making it difficult for them to find jobs within their professions that make use of their skills and qualifications.

Work plays a critical role in people's lives, since it provides income, social recognition, a sense of efficacy and satisfaction, opportunities to socialize with others, and a sense of purpose and meaning. This is especially true for newcomers as they find a place in Canada.

In a report titled "Making Work Pay" published by the Canadian Policy Research Networks, Ron Saunders (2006) argues that recent immigrants are more likely than mainstream Canadians to be employed in low-paying jobs. A quarter of newcomers who arrived in Canada during the last five years earned less than $10/hour, compared to only one sixth of mainstream Canadians. This problem is further compounded when the immigrant is a member of a visible minority group, since people of colour earn less than newcomers who are white.

The barriers described in this section are grouped into five categories: factors related to skills and training, barriers linked to language and culture, personal characteristics and resources, factors related to migration, and racism and discrimination.

Factors Related to Skills and Training

Many newcomers to Canada arrive with impressive educational backgrounds and a wealth of professional skills and experiences. Despite holding advanced and professional degrees from their home countries, however, many newcomers experience unemployment or underemployment because of a devaluation of credentials. This means that Canadian organizations and institutions do not recognize, or undervalue, a person's qualifications.

Presumably, the criteria used in the points system should work as a safeguard to prevent people from experiencing unemployment or underemployment and its financial consequences. It does this by ensuring that there is a need for the skills and experiences the newcomer brings to this country. The problem, however, is that for many individuals, the advanced and professional degrees granted by their countries of origin, and their job skills and experiences gained prior to entry into Canada are not recognized or transferable in their current circumstances. These immigrants (referred to by those who work in this area as "foreign-trained professionals") are required, then, to spend a great deal of time and money to become "recredentialized." This involves going back to school or taking intensive exams in order to obtain local recognition of their credentials.

In cases where foreign-obtained credentials are recognized, the lack of "Canadian" experience can often prevent newcomers from getting the job they have been trained (and in some cases, retrained) to do. It is difficult, however, to gain local experience when not having it prevents people from acquiring appropriate employment in the first place.

Barriers Linked to Language and Culture

In cases where people are hired in suitable positions, other factors can make it difficult to keep those jobs. Problems with the language can interfere with how work is performed, and can make communicating with co-workers and managers difficult. In addition, not understanding the norms and conventions of the Canadian workplace can introduce social challenges that make it hard for newcomers to fit in with other employees. For example, in some cultures, it is not the custom to shake hands when meeting new people. In other groups, it is considered inappropriate to look superiors in the eye during a conversation. In mainstream North America, it is not only acceptable and appropriate to shake someone's hand or maintain eye contact while interacting, but it can be seen as rude or disrespectful to not do these things.

Personal Characteristics and Resources

People who study unemployment and underemployment among immigrants point to two important factors that can affect a person's success (or lack of success) in the job market: *age* and *gender*. The effects of age and gender, however, can in some cases be mediated or offset by the presence of various personal resources.

According to sociologist and University of Toronto professor Wsevolod Isajiw (1999), immigrants who are younger (in particular, those between the ages 20 and 34) often become employed more quickly than those who are older. This may reflect the general tendency in our society to value youth over age. It also may be the case, however, that younger newcomers are typically more comfortable with the dominant language, and may possess many of the personal resources described below. This likely enables younger immigrants to take risks and helps them to sell themselves in a potential job situation, thereby increasing their chances of gaining suitable employment.

Hire Immigrants

www.hireimmigrants.ca

Hireimmigrants.ca is a government-sponsored site that provides employers with information on hiring interns, mentoring, and community awareness programs to help skilled immigrants obtain jobs in their fields.

THE LIVE-IN CAREGIVER PROGRAM
Opportunity or Exploitation?

We are living in a time when more and more women are working outside the home, for reasons related to both personal fulfillment and financial need. There is a high demand for quality child care, with various options available to parents today. These include formal, licensed daycare settings, as well as various informal arrangements like child care settings in other people's homes, or child care provided by extended family members. An increasingly popular arrangement is in-home child care provision, with babysitters or nannies working and living within the family home. These individuals are provided with room and board in exchange for caring for the family's children.

In Canada, many applicants for in-home child care provision come from overseas (such as from the Caribbean, and more recently, the Philippines). The federal government's Live-In Caregiver Program is designed to fill a labour market demand that is difficult to fill locally. A placement agency brokers the relationship between families wishing to hire someone to provide in-home child care, and the potential live-in caregiver. These (mostly) women are offered full-time, live-in employment prior to entry into Canada and, upon arrival, have temporary status in the country. If a live-in caregiver's employment is terminated for some reason, she is subject to deportation. If all goes well, however, after two years she is permitted to apply for permanent, landed immigrant status. This would provide her with full citizenship rights, except for voting or working in jobs related to national security.

This program fills an important labour need, and provides women from other countries wishing to immigrate to Canada with the opportunity to do so. Live-in caregivers have legal rights that respect fair working conditions and treatment under employment standards legislation (such as the right to privacy, certain days off each week, vacation time with pay, minimum wage, and overtime pay).

This seems like an ideal situation: Canada has a particular labour shortage, and there are women from other countries who are available and ready to fill that need. The reality, however, is that these women typically come from Third World countries, and are seen as an inexpensive and captive source of labour. Despite the protections mentioned previously, these women can face a range of challenges and abuses. For example, the privacy that is provided is often questionable, and the boundaries between on-duty and off-duty times are unclear when a person lives and works in the same place. In addition, the tasks required by these women are typically not limited to child care, and can include everything from running errands and walking the family pet. Finally, these women are sometimes forced into domestic situations that can result in financial, physical, and even sexual abuse. The agencies that act as brokers between live-in caregivers and the families that hire them are not usually held accountable when these rights are violated, and if the woman goes to the authorities before the two years are up, she risks being deported.

Although well-intentioned and designed to meet a particular economic need, the Live-In Caregiver Program has several important limitations that threaten the basic human rights of some of the women who participate in this program. Significant policy changes that address these concerns (both here in Canada, as well as in the sending countries) are required, and education about how to create a respectful, productive, and caring work environment should be provided to potential employers and employees.

Canada's Live-In Caregiver Program provides child care workers from Places like the Philippines and the Caribbean; many believe the program's limitations lead to exploitation of workers.

A person's gender is also an important factor in determining how successful he or she will be in gaining suitable employment. According to the Canadian Research Institute for the Advancement of Women (2003), there has been a significant increase in foreign-born and visible minority women in Canada in recent years. While there are some women who arrive in Canada independently under the federal Live-In Caregiver Program, most come as family class immigrants, or as dependents of men entering under the economic class. Migrating without assurance that their skills are necessary in the Canadian labour market has a negative impact on these women's attempts to find suitable employment, and on their economic positions more generally.

While immigrant women deal with many of the same work-related barriers that immigrant men face, they also confront certain stressors that are unique to their gender. For example, many women must manage the added complexities of child care and family responsibilities, which can make it difficult to gain Canadian work experience. As well, immigrant women face a unique form of discrimination as a result of the combined effect of their ethno-racial background and gender.

The negative effects of age and gender on the ability to secure suitable employment can sometimes be counteracted by the presence of certain qualities in job-seekers. Aside from actual skills, a person's ability to know where to look for work, how to write a resume, how to prepare for an interview, and so on, are key in determining how successful she or he will be in finding the right job. These additional factors are personal resources that, when present, can help an individual to gain suitable employment. Those without these personal resources are often not able to effectively navigate the employment system, further disadvantaging them in the search for work.

Factors Related to Migration

The goals of migration can also play an important role in shaping newcomers' employment-related experiences. For those arriving as economic class immigrants, the goal of migration is to obtain suitable employment. For newcomers entering Canada under the family or refugee class, however, finding appropriate work opportunities is often a secondary goal to family reunification or general safety. Those in the former group are more likely to be equipped with the education, skills, and personal resources that can help them to move within the employment system with greater success, while those in the latter groups are unlikely to fare as well.

In addition, challenges related to the immigration process itself can interfere with newcomers' attempts to become employed in suitable work settings. People who move from one country to another must deal with various practical and emotional concerns. Practical issues can include finding a home, trying to locate appropriate schooling or child care if children are involved, adjusting to a new environment, and perhaps dealing with a different climate. Newcomers must also cope with stressful, emotional challenges such as missing family members and friends, and trying to learn about and understand a new culture. Together, having to manage these issues presents additional barriers to finding and keeping work.

Racism and Discrimination

Racism and discrimination related to employment can take on various forms. During the early stages of looking for work, culturally biased hiring practices that favour certain skills and behaviours can make it difficult for newcomers to find appropriate employment. For example, here in North America, "selling yourself" and your skills is not only desirable, but necessary when searching for a job. Members of some cultural groups, however, see this behaviour as rude and boastful, and find it uncomfortable to act with such assertiveness. Also during this stage, personal prejudices on the part of potential employers can prevent an immigrant from a visible minority group from being hired.

Once hired, racism within the workplace can make it difficult to stay in an employment setting. This can be overt, taking the form of discriminatory remarks or behaviours that are meant to set people of colour apart from mainstream Canadians. The expression of such personal prejudices not only creates a toxic work environment, but has serious negative psychological consequences for the victims of racism.

Racism in the workplace can also take on a more subtle appearance. For example, racism might be reflected in the gross earning differentials between immigrants and their mainstream counterparts. If hired, newcomers often make less money when compared to mainstream Canadians. This is especially true for people from visible

INCOME SECURITY AND ELIGIBILITY FOR PERMANENT RESIDENTS AND REFUGEES

As a social welfare state, Canada offers a range of income security benefits to individuals who live in this country. These benefits include those for raising children (Child Tax Benefits), retirement (Canada/Quebec Pension Plan, Old Age Security, and the Guaranteed Income Supplement), job-related injuries (Workers' Compensation), the loss of a job (Employment Insurance), and longer-term unemployment (Social Assistance).

Immigrants, or "non-Canadians," are considered **permanent residents** if they have lived in Canada for at least two consecutive years during any five-year period. These individuals enjoy the same rights and privileges as Canadian citizens, but are not allowed to vote or hold positions in public office until they are granted citizenship. Permanent residents are eligible for Child Tax Benefits, and, if they have had a history of employment in this country, the various unemployment and pension programs. Depending on their particular circumstances, immigrants are also eligible for longer-term Social Assistance.

Government-sponsored refugees are eligible to receive the Child Tax Benefit, and are also provided with financial resettlement assistance (for those without resources to meet their basic needs) under the Resettlement Assistance Program. This includes immediate support services (airport reception; temporary accommodations and help to find more permanent housing; help with registering for federal and provincial programs; orientation to emergency services, public transportation, education systems, and Canadian laws; support in setting up a bank account and help with budgeting; and referrals to other settlement programs), as well as a one-time, initial household start-up allowance. This is sometimes followed by monthly income support to help pay for food, shelter, fuel, clothing, prescription drugs, and other health services, with specific amounts being determined by provincial regulations.

Refugees are not, however, eligible to receive benefits for retirement, job-related injuries, or the loss of a job until such time as they gain paid employment. This is a challenge, given that refugees face many of the same barriers as immigrants in finding and keeping suitable employment (factors related to skills and training; barriers linked to language and culture; personal characteristics and resources; issues arising from the migration process; and racism and discrimination), but they also confront additional challenges related to the circumstances of their arrival (such as lost documentation related to education and work; problems with family reunification, etc.).

minority groups. According to Jeffrey Reitz at the University of Toronto, immigrants from non-European countries like Africa, the Caribbean, India, China, and the Philippines tend to earn 15–25 percent less than (white) immigrants from Europe (Reitz 2001). Consistent with this, researchers Ravi and Krishna Pendakur (1998) found that men from visible minority groups (both immigrants and those born in Canada) earn less than their white counterparts. While these earning differences might be explained with the argument that the skills and education acquired in European countries fit better with our employment needs here in Canada, race is a factor that is clearly at play.

Another example of subtle racism is the "glass ceiling effect." This involves allowing people of colour to advance only to a point in the organizational ranks, with top-level management positions reserved for those who are usually white and typically men. This phenomenon is referred to as the glass ceiling effect since the racial barrier is not apparent, and therefore not seen as a formal obstacle. Whether obvious or somewhat hidden, acts of racism and discrimination within the work environment threaten an immigrant's emotional and psychological well-being, and can result in her or him leaving the workplace.

Theoretical Approaches to Immigration, Income Security, and Employment

Labour market approach

■ argues that the labour market dictates employment levels among newcomers

There are several ways of thinking about the link between immigration, income security, and unemployment or underemployment. For example, a labour market approach would suggest that characteristics of the local job market, such as the demand for certain skills and other specific qualities of the geographic location, are key factors that determine the level of unemployment or underemployment experienced by newcomer groups. On the other hand, a human capital perspective might view an individual's attributes, specific skills, and personal resources as shaping her or his level of employment success. While the first approach emphasizes factors at the level of social systems, the second offers a more individual-level explanation for unemployment and underemployment among newcomers.

Human capital perspective

■ argues that newcomers' attributes, skills, and personal resources determine their employment levels

A third way of understanding the relationship between immigration, income security, and unemployment and underemployment among newcomers is using an anti-racist approach. This approach draws on a Marxist analysis of the economic system (see Chapter 3). In particular, it helps us understand the economic roots of racism and discrimination, and how these processes continue to be at play today.

An anti-racist perspective sees racism as an ideology that is used to justify a system in which the rights and experiences of those who are white are privileged socially, economically, and politically, at the expense of people of colour. According to this view, during the colonial period, white, European men used racial distinctions to make legitimate an economic system in which people of colour were viewed as property. People of colour were seen as "less human" than the Europeans, and therefore as incapable of managing themselves, their families, or their nations. Europeans, on the other hand, considered themselves to be enlightened and civilized, and therefore, to be the more advanced race. This meant that it was not only their right but their duty to "manage" the lives of people of colour. European men took ownership of these individuals, and turned them into slaves who were required to provide free labour. This general view of the white race as inherently superior to others was used to justify the exploitation of people of colour, and the seizing of their possessions and land. Racism, then, is more than just the problem of a small group of people holding negative beliefs about another group. Instead, racism is used to sustain a social, economic, and political system in which people of colour are marginalized and subjugated.

Today's problem of unemployment and underemployment among immigrants would, through this lens, be viewed as the result of a system in which the majority — mainstream Canadians — enjoys certain socio-economic and political benefits, while minority groups are over-represented in categories reflecting a lower socio-economic status and less political representation. Those who hold power in society (typically white men who tend to occupy positions in large corporations and government) need to maintain these inequalities between groups in order to protect their power. Since people in positions of power shape our economy and determine what our labour needs will look like, they determine who will be brought into the country, and what type of work they will do when they get here.

Since it is in the best interests of those in positions of power to protect that power, preventing those who are not "like us" from accessing powerful positions is not only desirable, but necessary. Newcomers, then, are either unemployed or relegated to working in jobs that Canadians either do not want to do, or will not do for the pay that is offered. Restrictions based on foreign-obtained credentials, racism and discrimination in the workplace, and the glass ceiling are effective ways of keeping people of colour out of positions of power, or kept to limited numbers. According to this perspective, people of colour constitute a cheap labour force that sustains the ruling class.

Immigrants, both legal and illegal, provide low-paid labour throughout the Canadian economy, often in jobs that established Canadians either do not want, or will not do for the pay that is offered.

Case Study:

Kuc and Samuel

Samuel and Kuc Yaul, aged 20 and 17, respectively, are from Sudan. In 1999, their father, mother, and sister were killed by government troops. Samuel, Kuc and their younger brother and sister fled to a refugee camp in Kenya. Samuel and Kuc were given the opportunity to come to Lethbridge, Alberta, as refugees in 2002, but their brother and sister remained in Kenya.

Because of the extent of the conflict and poverty in Sudan, neither had extensive formal education. However, the brothers are both hardworking and extremely interested in advancing their education. They would like to receive education and training in computer technology. They began by attending English as a second language classes.

At present, both Samuel and Kuc have two jobs. During the day, they work as shelf stockers at a major retail chain in Lethbridge. They earn $5.90/hour, the minimum wage. During the evening, they work as office cleaners where they earn $6.90/hour.

Although their jobs are demanding and physically exhausting, the men feel lucky to have employment. A year ago, Samuel was nearly fired for agreeing to meet with a union representative to discuss an organizing campaign. At the time, he thought it would be a good idea to have someone who could speak up for the workers. He knows in Canada it's illegal to work overtime and not be paid for it, yet the stock associates regularly stay late to compact boxes and work on special requests for management without being paid. So, when someone stopped him outside the store last year to talk about his work and the possibility of getting help, he agreed to talk. For that incident, he was called into his supervisor's office and told that if he took the matter any further both he and his brother would be fired. For several weeks after the encounter, Kuc and Samuel's shift hours were reduced.

After a year and a half of working all sorts of shifts and long hours, Samuel and Kuc finally managed to secure regular work hours during the day. This permitted them to take part-time jobs with an office-cleaning company. Although the jobs pay only a dollar per hour more than the retail jobs, Kuc and Samuel consider it a great stride forward to be able to accommodate the two jobs within their schedules, as now they are sometimes able to send money to their brother and sister in Kenya.

The cleaning work is sporadic. Kuc and Samuel only work when a regular worker is sick or can't make it to work for some reason. They receive very little notice and are expected to respond immediately to a call to come to work. **continued›**

Case Study:

Kuc and Samuel (continued)

As a result, Kuc and Samuel never plan to do anything in the evenings so they can be free to work if called.

Like the work at the store, cleaning is physically demanding. The two men work at a blistering pace for five hours, arriving home to their one-bedroom apartment after having put in a 13 to 15 hour day. Lately, the owner of the company has been making life more difficult for them and this has Kuc [and] Samuel worried. On several occasions, he has said their work is not good enough. Last month he docked $100 from each of their paycheques saying they didn't complete their work properly.

Samuel has been having trouble with his back and wonders if he can continue with the heavy physical work. He and Kuc have discussed the possibility of sharing one cleaning position so they can each have every other night off work. However, this would mean less money. So, for the time being, they continue to work both jobs, but are increasingly anxious to get an education and find alternative employment. ■

Source: Excerpt from Law Commission of Canada. 2004. Is Work Working? Work Laws that Do a Better Job. *Ottawa: Law Commission of Canada, 19–20.*

Responses to Income Security Barriers

There are a variety of ways to support newcomers who might be dealing with unemployment or underemployment, and issues related to income security more broadly. Social workers can play a key role by working with people at individual, family, group, and community levels. In addition, social workers can propose and develop policy changes as a way of addressing barriers within society's formal structures.

Many newcomers are faced with the challenges that arise from living on low incomes, as described in Chapters 4 and 9. For example, these people may be without appropriate or affordable housing, they may be experiencing difficulties with food security, and they could be dealing with health concerns related to the poverty they are experiencing. At the individual or family level, social workers can offer practical support to help people to cope with these income-related issues. For example, social workers can help newcomers to navigate the Social Assistance system, or connect them to other agencies who might offer more specific forms of support. Social workers can also provide job-search assistance in the form of advice on how to look for work, how to write a resume, how to prepare for an interview, and so on. In addition, social workers are particularly well-placed to provide emotional support to help people manage their emotions and feelings related to these challenges.

EMPLOYMENT EQUITY IN CANADA

In 1984, Canada's Royal Commission on Equality in Employment introduced new legislation designed to recognize and remove the barriers related to racism, classism, and sexism that have historically characterized the Canadian employment system. The purpose of this *Employment Equity Act* is to "achieve equality in the workplace so that no person shall be denied employment opportunities or benefits for reasons unrelated to ability and, in the fulfillment of that goal, to correct the conditions of disadvantage in employment experienced by women, Aboriginal peoples, persons with disabilities, and members of visible minorities by giving effect to the principle that employment equity means more than treating persons in the same way but also requires special measures and the accommodation of differences" (Department of Justice Canada 1995).

Studies have shown that members of particular groups — women, Aboriginal people, persons with disabilities, and people of colour — face greater challenges in finding work (for example, see Jackson 2002 in James 2003). Once employed, these individuals are typically paid less, have less job stability, and are more vulnerable to experiencing poverty. The goal of this act, then, is to eliminate the structural barriers faced by members of these groups, and to help to repair some of the damage that has resulted from this prolonged inequality, such as chronic unemployment, poverty, etc.

In principle, most mainstream Canadians support this act. They acknowledge that the history of discriminating practices that favoured white men over others has had damaging consequences both for the individuals who experienced them, and for the country as a whole. They feel that such an act is a good way of attempting to redress previous inequities. At the same time, however, these individuals feel disadvantaged by the act. Some people who are white feel that this is "reverse discrimination" and that *they* are now being disadvantaged because of their race or gender. Some people of colour resent this policy, feeling that it minimizes their skills and experience, and suggests that they are successful in employment not because of merit, but because of their race or gender.

Responses to the policy, then, are mixed. According to York University professor Carl James, it is important to understand these inequalities not as individual attitudes and actions rooted in ignorance, but as inherent in society's structures and institutions. Racist, sexist, and ableist policies and practices were put into place historically to favour those who constructed our institutions in the first place (i.e., white men) and to protect their privileged positions in society. Racism (and sexism, ableism, and so on) "must be constructed in terms of historical and structural factors if current equity programs are to be seen as valid and appropriate" (James 2003, 187). Today's equity policies, then, are designed to remove these obstacles, undo some of the negative effects of these inequalities, and ensure that history does not repeat itself.

At the group or community level, social workers can encourage networking within the client's social circle, including her or his ethnoracial community. For example, organizing support groups for newcomers experiencing unemployment or underemployment is often an effective way of helping clients to share information about jobs that are available, and to exchange strategies for moving through the employment system. As well, this can be a great opportunity for clients to socialize and receive support from one another. Social workers can also work with business owners and potential employers to find out what barriers might be preventing them from hiring and sustaining newcomers in positions within their organizations, and to brainstorm various ways of overcoming these obstacles. As well, social workers can organize or take part in community-based responses that work to increase newcomers' access to the labour market. For example, the Pinecrest-Queensway Health and Community Services organization in Ottawa, Ontario, offers free employment workshops for immigrants and foreign-trained professionals. These sessions provide useful information about what employers want, how to market one's skills and experiences, and concerning career planning and development more generally.

At the level of society's systems, social workers can participate in efforts to shape or enhance equity policies and programs designed to remove barriers to hiring that are based on racism and discrimination. In addition, social workers can lobby for legislative changes that address the devaluation of foreign-obtained skills and credentials. By streamlining the recredentialization process, a considerable amount of time and resources might be saved, and newcomers would be able to move into suitable employment arrangements more efficiently and effectively, thus contributing to the Canadian economy.

Conclusion

This chapter has provided an overview of issues related to the growing rates of low-income among new immigrants to Canada. In addition to the broad challenges that typically surface during the period of immigration and settlement, newcomers also confront particular challenges when trying to find and keep suitable employment. This chapter focused on describing the various barriers that contribute to unemployment and underemployment among newcomers (especially those from visible minority groups). Social workers providing support in an increasingly diverse Canada need to understand this issue and be able to identify helpful ways of responding to these obstacles.

Chapter Summary

Key Concepts

- ☐ **Anti-racist approach**
- ☐ **Canadian Multicultural Policy**
- ☐ **Chinese Head Tax**
- ☐ **Continuous Journey Requirement**
- ☐ **Culturally biased hiring practices**
- ☐ **Culture**
- ☐ **Devaluation of credentials**
- ☐ **Economic class**
- ☐ **Ethnicity**
- ☐ **Family class**
- ☐ **Human capital perspective**
- ☐ **Labour market approach**
- ☐ **Permanent residents**
- ☐ **Personal resources**
- ☐ **Points system**
- ☐ **Race**
- ☐ **Racism**
- ☐ **Refugee class**
- ☐ **Visible minority**

Review Questions

1. According to the Canadian *Immigration Act*, what are the three main goals of immigration today?

2. Presently, what are the three categories under which newcomers can apply to immigrate to Canada? What are the criteria used in each of these categories?

3. According to researchers looking at unemployment and underemployment in newcomers to Canada, what are the main barriers that prevent these individuals from finding and keeping suitable jobs?

4. This chapter provided a summary of how a labour market approach, a human capital perspective, and an anti-racist approach might be used to understand unemployment and underemployment among immigrants to Canada. How might a political

ideology perspective (described in Chapter 3) be used to look more deeply at the economic, social, and political forces underlying this issue?

5. A range of responses to unemployment and underemployment among newcomers was described in this chapter. Suppose you are hired by a non-profit organization to work with local business-owners to support them in hiring newcomers. How would you go about doing this?

Exploring Social Welfare

1. Some of the main critiques of Canada's Multicultural Policy are described in this chapter. In your view, what are some other challenges that multiculturalism introduces into Canadian society? What are some of the benefits of multiculturalism? On the whole, do you think this policy is a good one? Why or why not?

2. Use the Internet to find three community-based supports that are being developed to assist foreign-trained professionals to find and keep appropriate employment. In your opinion, do you think these initiatives are helpful for newcomers? If so, what do you think makes them effective? If not, how might they be made more effective?

Websites

Department of Justice Canada
http://laws.justice.gc.ca

This website provides an overview of Canada's *Employment Equity Act*, and includes information about its purpose, how it can be used, and the details of its provisions.

Toronto Region Immigrant Employment Council (TRIEC)
www.triec.ca

TRIEC works to address barriers that prevent immigrants from participating in the labour market. Membership includes workers, employers, occupational regulatory bodies, post-secondary institutions, assessment service providers, community organizations, and all three levels of government.

Canada Immigrants Job Issues
http://www.canadaimmigrants.com/

This website is a support resource for immigrants in Canada; founded by an immigrant in 2002, the site runs a job matching program, provides information to potential immigrants and support to new Canadians. The site also publishes an on-line magazine that explores issues of systemic racism in the Canadian labour market.

References

Canadian Research Institute for the Advancement of Women. 2003. *CRIAW Fact Sheet: Immigrant and Refugee Women.* www.criaw-icref. ca/factSheets/Immigrant%20&%20refugee%20women/Immigrant_fact_ sheet_e.htm.

Department of Justice Canada. 1995. *Employment Equity Act, 1995 c.44 E-5.401.* Ottawa: Department of Justice Canada. http://laws.justice.gc.ca/en/ E-5.401/index.html.

Isajiw, W. 1999. *Understanding Diversity: Ethnicity and Race in the Canadian Context.* Toronto: Thompson Educational Publishing.

James, C. 2003. *Seeing Ourselves: Exploring Race, Ethnicity, and Culture,* 3rd ed. Toronto: Thompson Educational Publishing.

Kelley, N., and M. Trebilcock. 1998. *The Making of the Mosaic: A History of Canadian Immigration Policy.* Toronto: University of Toronto Press.

Mahtani, M. 2004. Interrogating the hyphen-nation: Canadian multicultural policy and "mixed race" identities. *Policy Matters (CERIS)* 5: 1–6.

Pendakur, K. and R. Pendakur. 1998. The colour of money: Earning differentials among ethnic groups in Canada. *Canadian Journal of Economics* 31 (3): 518–48.

Picot, G. and F. Hou. 2003. *The Rise in Low-Income Rates among Immigrants in Canada.* Analytical Studies Branch Research Paper Series. Ottawa: Statistics Canada.

Reitz, J. 2001. Immigrant skill utilization in the Canadian labour market: Implications of human capital research. *Journal of International Migration and Integration* 2 (3): 347–78.

Saunders, R. 2006. *Making Work Pay.* Ottawa: Canadian Policy Research Networks. www.cprn.com/documents/46773_en.pdf.

Poverty and Inequality

9

How Much Is Too Much?

One in six Canadians lives in "straitened circumstances," the Canadian government's euphemism for poverty. And statistics do not tell the whole story — most Canadians would be shocked if they knew how a large number of fellow Canadians survive. This chapter explores the extent of poverty and why poverty persists.

Canada is one of only a few countries without an official poverty line. However, Statistics Canada produces something called the Low Income Cut-off (LICO). These statistics on low income reveal that in 2004 around 3.5 million Canadians, or 11.2 percent, lived below the after-tax LICO level, including 1 million children (Statistics Canada 2006). Of course, certain populations, such as single mothers, unattached individuals, Aboriginal peoples, and recent immigrants, have a much greater risk of poverty. According to the 2001 census, for

> "Today, 826 million people are chronically and seriously undernourished although the world can nourish 12 billion human beings — twice its present population — without any problem."
>
> — *Shukor Rahman, World Food Programme*

Table 9.1: Poverty Rates in Eight Rich Countries, by Age Group

Nation (Year)	Overall	Families with Children		Childless	Elders
		1 Parent	2 Parent		
United States (2000)	17.0	41.4	13.1	11.1	28.4
United Kingdom (1999)	12.3	31.3	8.9	7.7	24.6
Canada (1997)	11.9	38.9	9.5	12.1	5.2
Netherlands (1999	8.9	26.8	7.9	9.5	3.2
Germany (2000)	8.2	31.6	2.8	9.0	12.2
Belgium (1997)	7.9	12.5	6.6	7.3	13.1
Sweden (2000)	6.4	11.3	2.1	9.7	8.2
Finland (2000)	5.4	7.3	2.2	7.6	10.1

Source: Smeeding, Timothy M. Table 4.2, "Poverty Rates in Eight Rich Countries, by Age Group, at the End of the Twentieth Century." In *Public Policy and the Income Distribution*, edited by Alan J. Auerbach, David Card, and John M. Quigley. © 2006 Russell Sage Foundation, 112 East 64th Street, New York, NY 10021. Reprinted with permission.

International Council on Social Welfare (ICSW)

www.icsw.org

Founded in Paris in 1928, the ICSW is a non-governmental organization that represents organizations in more than fifty countries around the world. The ICSW undertakes research and organizes consultations to help analyze social problems and develop policies.

example, the poverty rate of lone-parent families with children has dropped below the 50 percent mark for the first time in at least twenty years. For seniors, on the other hand, things have recently improved dramatically. The current poverty rate for seniors is 17 percent, which is nearly half that of the 1980s rate of 30 percent.

The factors that result in poverty are varied and complex. Poverty is usually brought on by an unexpected turn of events, such as loss of employment, death or disability of a family breadwinner, family breakup, or increased costs from a major illness or mishap. Changes in the economy and problems in the labour market can also result in limited employment opportunities, not enough hours of work, declining real value of minimum wages, or wages so low that people cannot earn enough to live on. Furthermore, members of some groups in our society face a greater risk of poverty than others due to such things as discrimination, unequal opportunities, lack of recognition for their work (paid or unpaid), and inadequate income support for people who are unable to work or to find paid employment. In this chapter, we examine ways of measuring poverty and inequality, which sectors of the Canadian population live in poverty, and possible explanations for this. We will also look at homelessness, hunger and global poverty.

For the past century, governments and international bodies have attempted to reduce or eradicate poverty. Despite this, poverty at the national and international levels has persisted, and indeed is rising overall. Increasingly, many are arguing that poverty is perhaps an impossible problem to solve, while others put forth the view that only a fundamental restructuring of the global economy will allow us to begin to address such deep-seated social problems.

Poverty

It seems that poverty is continually discussed, defined, and measured in an infinite number of ways. The United Nations Development Programme (UNDP) describes "human poverty" as "a denial of choices and opportunities for living a tolerable life," and the World Bank speaks of "income poverty" as living on less than $1 per day. There is also "absolute poverty," or those without the bare necessities, and "relative poverty," or those who are poor in relation to others. For governments, the latest term is "social exclusion," which is supposed to define what poor people experience. It seems that more time and money may be spent discussing poverty than actually trying to eradicate it. It is hoped that this chapter will not add to the malaise.

Certainly, one of the great failures of societies around the world, including Canada, is the perpetuation of poverty. Poor nutrition, poor health, a lack of shelter, and in some cases death are directly related to poverty and contribute to the degradation of our social structures. The different approaches to addressing poverty have a long history in Canada and in the international community. We will explore the different aspects of poverty, including how it is defined and the diverging explanations for its continued existence.

Measuring Poverty

Poverty traditionally has been defined using two different measurements: an absolute measure and a relative measure. The absolute measure of poverty is based on an essential basket of goods and services deemed necessary for survival or well-being. Using the term *absolute* is misleading, however, as there is not one "absolute" standard of needs. The bundle of goods and services considered essential to well-being is subject to numerous value judgements and is relative to local culture and context.

A measure of poverty based on the absolute approach generally leaves the door open as to what should be included in the essential basket for survival. Critics claim that the basket of goods and services should include items that bring a household beyond mere physical survival and up to a state that meets some kind of social or community norm. The essential basket may include adequate space, cooking facilities, storage for fresh food, furniture, transportation, and even recreation and leisure. Other critics place strict boundaries on what should be included, based on the absolute approach. Christopher Sarlo, an analyst with the Fraser Institute, believes that poverty figures are exaggerated because of the level of poverty lines. He developed a new lower measure of absolute poverty by limiting the basket of goods and services to those deemed necessary. With this new lower poverty line, he found that only 4 percent of Canadians were actually living in poverty (Sarlo 2001).

Absolute measure of poverty

■ based on an essential basket of goods and services deemed necessary for survival or well-being, relative to cultural context and value judgements.

■ Open for debate because people do not agree on what should be included in the "basket"

Relative measure of poverty

■ based on how low one's income is relative to other people, and it relies on the income distribution within a particular society.

■ those who fall below a fixed percentage of the average or median income in a particular community are considered to be living in poverty

U.S. Department of Health and Human Services

http://aspe.hhs.gov/poverty/06poverty.shtml

Explore how the United States government classifies and measures poverty and the country's current poverty rates.

On the other hand, the relative measure of poverty is based on how low one's income is relative to other people. It measures the number and proportion of persons and households whose incomes fall below some fixed percentage of the average or median for the same household size and configuration. This measure reflects the differences in income between the poor and the majority of society, rather than being an abstract standard. Relative poverty is based on the income distribution within a particular society, and it is established by setting a poverty line that is some fraction of either the mean or median income for a country or other reference group. When the mean income is used for the calculation, the poverty line changes when the incomes of the richest change. For this reason, many prefer to use the median income.

Some measures of poverty, such as Statistics Canada's Low Income Cut-off (LICO), are based on both absolute and relative measures. This combined measure is often referred to as a "relative necessities" approach. It is based on the percentage of income that individuals and families spend on basic needs or necessities in comparison with the rest of Canadians. LICO is not explicitly put forth as a poverty line by the Canadian government, but rather as a level of low income.

Other jurisdictions use other measures. For example, the European Commission sets an explicit poverty measure at a poverty line of 60 percent of the national mean income. The United States, on the other hand, still uses an absolute measure of poverty, and the World Bank defines absolute poverty as living on less than $1 per day. In 2006, for example, the U.S. official poverty line for a family of four was US$20,000 (Federal Register, 2006). According to this measure, 10.8 percent of U.S. families live in poverty.

One of the key debates concerns the use of pre-tax or after-tax income when comparing to LICOs. The government argues that we should use after-tax income, as the tax system has a redistributive effect from higher income earners to lower income earners. This is true, in that the poverty rates using after-tax figures are lower than when one uses before-tax incomes (see Table 9.2). The use of pre-tax income presents a measure of market poverty or how well families are doing earning income in the marketplace, but it ignores government transfers through income security programs. For groups such as seniors, the two measures are quite different (see Table 9.2) due to the high amount of income transferred to seniors through programs such as CPP and OAS.

Despite the continuous debate over poverty measures, it is safe to say that those scholars who research the causes of poverty are increasingly seeing a relative measure as appropriate for advanced capitalist countries. Although Canada does not have an official poverty line, most, including the United Nations, consider the LICOs to be an adequate measure.

Defining the Poverty Line

For the past thirty years, Statistics Canada has produced LICOs for different household sizes in different regions. According to Statistics Canada, LICOs are used to distinguish "low income" families from "other" families. A family is considered to have a low income when it falls below the LICO for its family size and community population.

LICOs are set by taking what the average household spends on food, clothing, and shelter and adding 20 percent. According to the most recent base data, the 1992 Family Expenditure Survey, the average Canadian household spends 43 percent of its income on food, clothing, and shelter. Twenty percentage points are added to this to obtain a 63 percent threshold. This 63 percent threshold is then converted into a set of LICOs that vary with family and community size. The process is carried out for seven family sizes and five community sizes, providing a matrix of thirty-five cut-offs. In addition, Statistics Canada produces cut-offs for before-tax and after-tax incomes.

For example, the 2005 LICO for a family of four in a medium-sized city of 100,000–500,000 is $33,251. A family of four living in a very large Canadian city with a before-tax income of less than $38,610 in 2005 would have been living below the LICO.

Statistics Canada has another measure called the Low Income Measure (LIM), which is widely used for international comparisons of child poverty. It measures the relative low-income rates as one-half of the median adjusted income of the country. The calculation is adjusted for family size, as larger families have increased needs. Because it is a straightforward calculation and can be collected in all nations, it allows for simple comparisons between countries.

Table 9.2: Prevalence of People Living on Low Income

Prevalence (%) of Low Income in	Before Tax 2000	After Tax 2000	Before Tax 2002	After Tax 2002	Before Tax 2004	After Tax 2004
All persons	16.4	12.5	16.2	11.6	15.5	11.2
Persons under 18 years of age	18.1	13.8	18.0	12.2	17.7	12.8
Persons 65 and over	16.6	4.6	15.8	4.9	14.0	3.5
Unattached individuals	41.3	32.9	37.7	29.5	37.6	29.6

Note: Prevalence of low income shows the proportion of people living below the LICO within a given group. It is expressed as a percentage. The before-tax incidence does not include tax-based income security transfers, such as the CCTB, CPP, and OAS.

Source: Adapted from Statistics Canada. 2006. *Table 202-0802 Persons in low income (before and after tax), by prevalence in percent.* CANSIM (database) Last modified: 2006-03-28. http://www40.statcan.ca/l01/cst01/famil19a.htm and http://www40.statcan.ca/l01/cst01/famil41a.htm

In 2005, a family of four in a large Canadian city would have been living below the Low Income Cut-off if they earned less than $38,610; that's less than $750 per week before taxes.

Human Resources Development Canada (HRDC), in conjunction with a federal, provincial, and territorial working group, has proposed yet another measure of poverty called the *Market Basket Measure* (MBM). First published in 2003, the MBM is an absolute measure of poverty based on the cost of purchasing a basket of goods and services in forty-eight different geographical areas. HRDC intended the MBM to represent a level of consumption that was closer to median standards, and it goes beyond the bare minimum of other measures (HRDC 2003). The MBM calculates the amount of income needed by a given household to meet its needs based on "credible" community norms, so the measure will therefore reflect changes in the cost of consumption rather than changes in income. The basic issue raised by the MBM is what to include and what not to include in the market basket. A limited market basket will result in a low poverty line, thus creating the assumption that fewer people are living in poverty. The overall incidence of low income in 2000 for the ten provinces combined using the MBM was 13.1 percent. This is slightly lower than it was for the before-tax version of the LICOs (14.7 percent).

In Canada, there is an ongoing debate about what the correct poverty line should be. Clearly, to some extent, what one person may consider to be adequate for survival will be different from what another person believes is necessary. In 1988, for example, Gallup conducted a survey asking what people thought was the minimum weekly amount of income required for a family of four. The amount was about $3,000 less than LICO, but well above welfare rates. If one takes the approach that poverty is entirely based on the subjective belief of the citizens of a country, then LICO is fairly close to what Canadians believe is poverty.

In 1992, the Fraser Institute published *Poverty in Canada* by Chris Sarlo, a Nipissing University professor. He proposed an alternative measure of poverty based on the costs of a list of necessities. The Basic Needs Lines (BNLs) were widely criticized for being below most Canadians' ideas of an adequate amount for survival. According to Richard Shillington, a social policy consultant, Sarlo's calculations of the costs of a body's minimum caloric requirements are chilling. In 1998, the amount for food for a single elderly women was $17.48 per week. This includes $2.11 for fruit and $1.33 for vegetables. For a single mother with two children, he allocates $50.47, including $7.82 for milk (including powdered milk) and $4.00 for vegetables (Sarlo 1992, 66).

He provides no funds for school supplies, which are "assumed to be offset by part-time or summer earnings."

Sarlo recently updated the BNLs. To address some of the critics, he scrutinized every item on the original list and reconfigured it from scratch. His new BNLs are higher and therefore find that income poverty in Canada is now in the range of 8 percent, compared to 4 percent with the old BNLs. He has set an annual food budget of $5,306, or $442 per month, for a family of four (Sarlo 2001, 20). He does not provide a breakdown of the amount spent on each food item, as he did in the 1992 calculations. The BNLs are not generally taken seriously by the academic or international communities, and few Canadians would agree that people could actually survive on the amounts that are proposed for basic survival.

Precise poverty lines are by and large arbitrary. As we have seen, there is not even a basic conceptual agreement among the experts on what poverty means. Some, such as the Fraser Institute, argue for an absolute approach, while others, such as the Canadian Council for Social Development, argue for a relative approach. The Organisation for Economic Co-operation and Development (OECD) believes that absolute poverty measures have little meaning in advanced industrialized societies. They maintain that poverty should not be seen as a deprivation of very basic needs, but as an exclusion from the standards of living broadly available to others in the same society (OECD 2001, 41).

Two things are clear, however. First, underlying these various academic debates about poverty and poverty lines are many unstated beliefs and assumptions about exactly how much inequality we should permit in our society. And, second, it is clear that there can be no debate that serious poverty exists in Canadian society today.

Table 9.3: Before-Tax LICOs, 2005

Family Size	Population of Community of Residence				
	500,000 or More	100,000–499,999	30,000–99,999	Less than 30,000*	Rural
1	$20,778	$17,895	$17,784	$16,273	$14,303
2	$25,867	$22,276	$22,139	$20,257	$17,807
3	$31,801	$27,386	$27,217	$24,904	$21,891
4	$38,610	$33,251	$33,046	$30,238	$26,579
5	$43,791	$37,711	$37,480	$34,295	$30,145
6	$49,389	$42,533	$42,271	$38,679	$33,999
7 or more	$54,987	$47,354	$47,063	$43,063	$37,853

Note: This table uses the 1992 base. Income refers to total before-tax household income.

*Includes cities with a population between 15,000 and 30,000, and small urban areas (under 15,000).

Source: Prepared by the Canadian Council on Social Development (www.ccsd.ca) using Statistics Canada's Low Income Cut-Offs, from *Low-income cut-offs for 2005 and low income measures for 2004*, Catalogue #75F0002MIE. Reprinted with permission.

Social exclusion

■ A person living in poverty is not only lacking in basic resources—food, shelter, clothing—but also has limited opportunities to participate in the social, economic, and cultural activities of his or her society, thereby experiencing social exclusion.

Beyond Income

Many scholars, particularly in Europe, are increasingly conceptualizing poverty in terms of social exclusion. The concept refers to marginalization – having limited opportunities or abilities to participate in the social, economic, and cultural activities of society. The use of social exclusion is an attempt to broaden the definition of poverty beyond simple income level calculations. It includes measuring the extent to which people have freedom of choice to achieve security. In short, social exclusion views poverty not as a matter of a low degree of well-being, but as the inability to pursue well-being because of the lack of opportunities.

How people themselves, particularly the poor, define poverty varies by gender, age, culture, and other social aspects. For example, a young person may define poverty as a lack of job opportunities, while an elderly person may see it in terms of food security and health care. It becomes apparent, however, that poor people are acutely aware of their lack of power, voice, and independence. Many poor people speak of poverty in terms of humiliation, isolation, safety, and inhumane treatment, and, in some cases poor people speak about these negative social aspects of poverty as being worse than the lack of income. Poor people also speak more about assets and less about income – having assets is perceived as providing opportunities to gain well-being. Clearly, poverty is more than a mere lack of income, and this suggests the need for more coordinated, comprehensive solutions. Increasingly, the solutions are being viewed in the context of human rights.

How Much Poverty?

In discussing how much poverty exists, three dimensions need to be considered: how many people are poor (the headcount measure), by how much they fall below the poverty line (the poverty gap measure), and for how long they are poor (the poverty duration measure). Social workers and social policy analysts need to examine all three aspects of the problem to develop coherent and comprehensive income programs.

The poverty headcount measures the number and proportion of persons in poverty. Poverty is much more widespread than most people realize. Based on the 2004 LICOs, there are 3.5 million people living in poverty, or 11.2 percent of the total population. These numbers likely underestimate the number of poor Canadians, as they do not include Aboriginal peoples on reserves, residents of the Yukon, Nunavut, and Northwest Territories, and people who live in homes for the aged or other institutions.

Provincial poverty rates for 2003 also vary. Quebec has the highest rate (21.3 percent) and Prince Edward Island has the lowest (12.8 percent). Because so many Canadians reside in Ontario and Quebec, more than half of Canada's poor can be found in these two

THE HUMAN DEVELOPMENT INDEX (HDI)

In 2006, Canada ranked sixth in the Human Development Index (HDI) annual survey by the United Nations Development Programme (UNDP). A component of the overall HDI is a poverty ranking.

On this aspect, Canada scored eighth. An eighth place ranking is in the middle of the pack of developed nations — scoring behind countries like Norway and Sweden, but well above the United States and the United Kingdom. Canada has fared better in the past: it ranked first on the overall index in 1992, but has steadily declined since then.

For more on the Human Development Index, see Chapter 5, p. 109.

Note: The human poverty index is calculated for selected high-income OECD countries only.

Source: Watkins, Kevin. **Human Development Report 2006.** *Reproduced with permission of Palgrave Macmillan.*

Overall ranking		Poverty ranking
1	Norway	2
2	Iceland	..
3	Australia	14
4	Ireland	17
5	Sweden	1
6	**Canada**	**8**
7	Japan	11
8	USA	16
9	Switzerland	7
10	Netherlands	3
11	Finland	4
12	Luxembourg	9
13	Belgium	12
14	Austria	..
15	Denmark	5
16	France	10
17	Italy	18
18	UK	15
19	Spain	13

provinces. To determine whether these rates are high or low, it is useful to compare them with those of different countries using a comparable measure. With poverty defined as 50 percent of the median income (adjusted), we find that Canada (11.9 percent) ranks sixteenth out of twenty-two countries (Jesuit and Smeeding 2002, 13). All European countries rank ahead of Canada, with the exception of Italy. Canada ranks ahead of the United States, Australia, and the United Kingdom.

Another dimension of poverty can be calculated as the total shortfall from the poverty line – that is, the depth of poverty. Poverty rates do not show whether poor people are living in abject poverty or merely a few dollars below the poverty line. To determine this, we need to measure the poverty gap. The poverty gap is a measurement of how much additional income would be required to raise an individual or household above the LICO. Statistics Canada refers to this as the "average income deficiency." The number of people in Canada living at less than 50 percent of the LICO changed from 143,000 families and 287,000 individuals in 1989, to 140,000 families and 552,000 individuals in 2003 (National Council of Welfare 2006, 4).

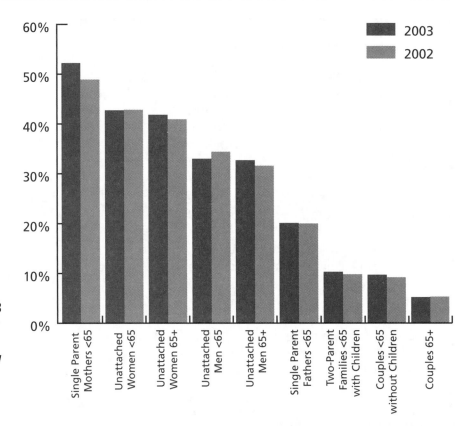

Figure 9.1: Poverty Rates by Family Type, 2002 and 2003

Source: National Council of Welfare. Poverty Profile 2002 and 2003. Reproduced with the permission of the Minister of Public Works and Government Services Canada, 2007.

In 2003, the average income for female-led lone-parent families was $9,600 below the poverty line (National Council of Welfare 2006, 58) and two-parent families with children had the largest depth of poverty, living $9,900 below LICO.

Finally, it is important to consider poverty duration, or how long people experience low income. The Statistics Canada Survey of Labour and Income Dynamics (SLID) enables analysis of the duration of poverty. SLID follows the same set of people for six consecutive years and is designed to capture changes in the economic well-being of individuals and families over time. This data shows that, over the long term, poverty affects a greater number of Canadians than yearly poverty rates suggest. More than 7.6 million, or 30.7 percent, of all Canadians had experienced poverty in at least one of the six years between 1996 and 2003 (National Council of Welfare 2006). Lone parents, persons with disabilities, members of visible minority groups, recent immigrants, individuals with low levels of education, and unattached individuals are more likely to experience lengthy spells of poverty.

Statistics Canada's survey of poverty duration, reported in *The Canadian Fact Book on Poverty 2000* (Ross, Scott, and Smith 2002, Chapter 7), finds that, for roughly 60 percent of those in poverty in any given year, poverty proves to be a temporary situation, while it is a recurrent problem for the remaining 40 percent. On average, after counting both single and multiple spells, a poor individual will spend approximately five years in poverty, while 5 percent will stay in poverty for ten or more years.

Inequality and Income Distribution

Poverty and inequality are different concepts that should not be confused. As has been described, poverty refers to some benchmark standard and how many people live below that standard. Inequality is concerned with the differences between income groups. The way in which total income in a country is divided between households is a measure of inequality (also known as income distribution).

Analysis of income distribution data illustrates that income is shared very unequally in Canada. First, we can examine the quintile income distribution. A quintile represents one-fifth (20 percent) of the total number of people being studied. If you took all Canadians and ranked them according to income, you could then divide them into five equal quintiles. The top quintile is the one-fifth (or 20 percent) of people with the highest incomes. The fourth quintile is the one-fifth with the second-highest incomes, and so on down to the bottom quintile, which is the one-fifth (20 percent) of Canadians with the lowest incomes. The quintile income distribution calculates the share of total income that goes to each quintile. If the Canadian population is divided into five sections (quintiles), the richest 20 percent (the richest fifth) of Canadians receives around 40 percent of the total income; the poorest fifth receives only 6 percent of the income.

Another measure of income inequality is the Gini coefficient, which measures the degree of inequality in income distribution. Values of the Gini coefficient can range from 0 to 1. A value of 0 indicates that income is equally divided among the population, with all units receiving exactly the same amount of income. At the opposite extreme, a Gini coefficient of 1 denotes a perfectly unequal distribution, where one unit possesses all of the income in the economy. A decrease in the value of the Gini coefficient can be interpreted as reflecting a decrease in inequality, and vice versa.

Another method for determining inequality is to measure the amount of wealth or net worth of each quintile. *Net worth* is the amount that a household would have after selling all assets, such as residences, stocks, and registered retirement savings plans; and paying off all debts, such as mortgages, car loans, and student loans. According to a Statistics Canada study, those in the top 20 percent of the wealth distribution had a median net worth of $551,000 in 2005 (see Table 9.5). In other words, half of the families in the top 20 percent of the wealth distribution had a net worth more than this figure and half had less. In comparison, the median net worth of the families in the bottom fifth decreased, resulting in a negative worth of $1,000 in 2005. This means that they have more debt than assets.

Who Is Hungry?

You might be surprised to know who uses your local food bank. The Daily Bread Food Bank in Toronto tracks food bank usage and found that, in 2002, 19 percent of those using food banks were working, 33 percent had at least some college or university education, 41 percent had a disability or long-term illness, and 37 percent were children. But the food banks cannot possibly meet existing needs — 42 percent say they go hungry at least once a week.

Source: Daily Bread Food Bank. 2002. **Who Is Hungry Now? The Demographics of Hunger in Greater Toronto.**

What is really striking is that the gap in average market income between the lowest 20 percent of families and the highest 20 percent increased by over $4,600 between 1998 to 2000, because the highest quintile increased by $6,900, but the lowest quintile increased by only $2,300 – a significantly larger gain for the top earners, and a significant widening of the income gap (Statistics Canada 2004).

Some analysts have attributed this increase in income and wealth inequality to the effects of globalization (the increased integration of global markets and trade liberalization). In 2001, Bourguignon and Morrisson (2001) produced a benchmark study of world income inequality trends over the past two centuries. The study makes comparisons for thirty-three groups of countries between 1820 and 1992. They found that world inequality increased by 50 percent between 1820 and 1910, a period of rapid growth and globalization. Between 1919 and 1960, inequality remained stable, dipping in the 1950s before resuming the rise after 1960. The period between 1960 and 1992 saw another era of rapid growth and globalization as well as substantial increases in inequality.

Table 9.4: Percentage Distribution of Total Income of Families by Quintiles, Canada, 1974, 1984, 1994, 2003 (Includes Market Income, Government Transfers, and Income Tax)

Quintile	1974 (%)	1984 (%)	1994 (%)	2003 (%)
Bottom	6.3	6.1	6.4	5.0
Second	13.1	12.3	12.2	10.8
Middle	18.2	18.0	17.7	16.5
Fourth	23.6	24.1	24.1	24.1
Top	38.8	39.5	39.6	43.7

Source: Data for 1974, 1984, and 1994 prepared by Centre for International Statistics at the Canadian Council on Social Development, using Statistics Canada, *Income Distributions by Size*, Cat. no. 13-207 (various years); data for 2003 from National Council of Welfare. 2006. *Poverty Profile 2002 and 2003*. Ottawa: National Council of Welfare, p. 130.

Table 9.5: Median Wealth of Families (Including Unattached Individuals), by Quintile, 1984 to 2005

Quintile	1984	1999	2005	1999 to 2005	1984 to 2005
	(2005 Dollars)			% Change	
Bottom	0	–700	–1,000	–43	Not applicable
Second	14,100	14,400	12,500	–13	–11
Middle	67,300	74,400	84,800	14	26
Fourth	143,400	181,400	212,600	17	48
Top	335,500	464,900	551,000	19	64

Note: This table excludes the value of registered pension plans.

Source: Morisette, René and Xuelin Zhang. 2006. "Study: Inequality in Wealth." Statistics Canada, *The Daily*. Release date: December 13, 2006. Catalogue 11-001. http://www.statcan.ca/Daily/English/061213/d061213c.htm

Others have criticized the premise of the study, maintaining that the growth in inequality during periods of economic growth and globalization may be merely a coincidence. But whatever the verdict, the promise of help for the poor trickling down from the rich when economic growth is strong seems unlikely.

Who Is Poor?

The Working Poor

There is a widespread assumption that people who are poor are unemployed, and that many of those who are unemployed are single parents staying at home with children. The reality is that many of the poor, including single mothers, are employed. It is important to define some terms here, as there is a difference between low-paid workers and the working poor.

A low-paid worker is an individual whose annual earnings are low, while a working poor person is an individual whose economic family income is below the poverty threshold. In the second case, the incomes of all family members determine whether they are poor. (Some consider only those who are employed full-time to be the working poor, while others include those people with strong ties to the labour force, regardless of their hours of work.) A Human Resources and Social Development Canada (HRSDC) report provides operational definitions of both terms. *Working poor individuals*, they say, are those individuals aged 18 to 64 who have worked for pay a minimum of 910 hours in the reference year, who are not full-time students, and whose family income falls below LICO. *Working poor families* include at least one working poor individual (Fleury and Fortin 2006, 16). According to this definition, there were 653,300 working poor persons in Canada in 2001, accounting for 5.6 percent of all workers (Fleury and Fortin 2006, 17). And, a total of 1.5 million Canadians were living in a working poor family (Fleury and Fortin 2006, 93). These individuals account for almost 40 percent of all low income Canadians. In other words, 40 percent of low income Canadians are in working poor families.

Employment offers some protection from poverty, but having one income is not enough. Two-parent families with one earner have a 25.2 percent poverty rate, well above the 6.2 percent rate for two-earner families. These statistics indicate that a large portion of those living with low incomes are employed, but working at jobs that provide such a low wage that they remain in poverty. As governments cut back on income security programs and tighten eligibility requirements, many find that the job opportunities do not provide an income sufficient for their family's well-being or even survival. The lack of good paying jobs has propelled increasing numbers of working Canadians into the category of the working poor.

Canada's Income Gap

According to a recent study (CCPA 2007), Canada's income gap is growing. In 2004, the wealthiest 10 percent of families in Canada earned 82 times more than the poorest 10 percent in 2004. This is almost three times the ratio between rich and poor found in 1976. After tax, the gap between rich and poor has reached a 30-year high. And, with the exception of the richest 10 percent, all Canadians are working more with no significant increase in wages.

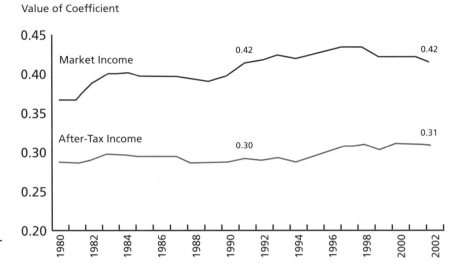

Figure 9.2: Gini Coefficients for Families, 1980 to 2002

Source: Statistics Canada. 2004. **Analysis of Income in Canada 2002.** *Catalogue 75-203. Ottawa, p. 41. http://www.statcan.ca/english/freepub/75-203-XIE/0000275-203-XIE.pdf*

The State of the World's Children

www.unicef.org/sowc06

UNICEF produces an annual report called *The State of the World's Children* that compares, among other items, child poverty rates throughout the world.

Child Poverty

In 1989 the Canadian federal government declared its commitment to "seek to achieve the goal of eliminating poverty among Canadian children by the year 2000." Campaign 2000, a national anti-poverty coalition, annually releases *The Report Card on Child Poverty in Canada*, which indicates that one in five of Canada's children lives below the Statistics Canada LICO. Campaign 2000's 2005 report summarizes the deteriorating economic situation of Canada's children since 1989. It further demonstrates that 1,202,000 children, or nearly one in six, remain below the LICO. Child poverty remains stuck at 17.6 percent.

According to Statistics Canada's 2004 LICO, 8.1 percent of children in two-parent families and 40 percent of children in single-parent families were living in poverty. Infants were over 20 percent more likely than 11-year-old children to be living in poverty, primarily because statistics indicate that younger families have higher poverty rates. In Canada, 513,754 children rely on Social Assistance, which does not reach the LICO in any province (Campaign 2000, 2005, 2). The odds of poverty are again increased by 56 percent if one family member is an immigrant, even when one equalizes other factors such as education, language skills, and age (Kazemipur and Halli 2001, 231).

All of this indicates that different sectors in Canadian society are more likely to find themselves living in poverty. Simply put, the risk of being poor is higher when the head of the family is single or unattached, is a woman, lives with a disability, is a member of a visible minority, is an Aboriginal person, or immigrated to Canada after 1979.

The Colour of Poverty

As noted in Chapter 8, aside from Canada's Aboriginal peoples, we are a nation of immigrants. Moreover, "visible minority" groups now

Case Study:

Mary-Anne and Clarisse

The real issues facing people living in poverty frequently get lost in the barrage of statistics. The numbers are important, but stories such as Mary-Anne's do more to illustrate the situation of the working poor.

Mary-Anne became ill when she was pregnant with her daughter, Clarisse. She lost her job, where she earned $1,600 a month. She did not have enough hours to qualify for EI, so she applied for assistance, and received $1,200 per month. It was difficult having her income decreased $400 per month, along with the expenses of a new baby. After the Ontario Social Assistance cutbacks in 1995, her benefits were cut to $957 per month. She lost her apartment and moved in with her mother, but living in poverty drove Mary-Anne and her mother apart. They found themselves accusing each other of spending too much on food.

What Mary-Anne wanted most was to find a well-paying job to support herself and her daughter. She voluntarily entered the workfare program of Ontario Works, even though she was exempt because of Clarisse's age. Eventually, she located a job without the help of workfare, earning $1,235 per month. She receives $200 per month in child support, and her Canada Child Tax Benefit amounts to $150 per month. Her total income is $20,120 per year, about 10 percent below LICO.

Mary-Anne's apartment consumes almost half of her income, leaving little for other necessities. It is cramped, and she sleeps on a pull-out couch in the living room so that Clarisse can have her own room. After paying for phone, food, transportation, clothes, and her student loan, nothing is left. She feels lucky to have a substantial child care subsidy, leaving her to pay only $30 per month. After paying $200 per month in payroll taxes, she cannot make ends meet.

She would like to save for Clarisse's education and open a Registered Education Savings Plan (RESP), but that is not possible with her income. She cannot even afford a drug prescription that her doctor recommended. She knows that, above all else, they have to pay the rent on time or risk losing their apartment. The only item that she can cut back on is food. ■

The 2007 WITB

The federal budget in 2007 included some new measures to assist Canada's lowest income earners. The proposed Working Income Tax Benefit (WITB) would provide families earning less than $21,167 a year a maximum tax credit of $1,000. However, many critics allege that such an initiative will do little to truly help those who live below LICO.

make up about 11 percent of the total Canadian population, compared to 6 percent in 1986. Poverty among racialized groups in Canada, particularly recent immigrants, is higher than for other Canadians. Census data from 1996 shows that the poverty rate for Canadians was 21 percent, whereas the rate for "visible minority persons" was 38 percent.

York University professor Michael Ornstein has researched poverty levels among racialized groups using the 1996 census. The

Persistent Poverty

Persistent poverty is highly concentrated in high at-risk groups, which include people with work-related disabilities, recent immigrants, single mothers, unattached older people (until they reach pension age), and Aboriginal peoples.

report, *Ethno-Racial Inequality in the City of Toronto: An Analysis of the 1996 Census*, found that, while 14 percent of European families live below the LICO, the percentage is much higher for non-Europeans: 32.1 percent for Aboriginal peoples; 35 percent for South Asians; 45 percent for Africans, Blacks, and Caribbeans; and 45 percent for Arabs and West Asians (Ornstein 2000). Similarly, a study by two university professors (Kazemipur and Halli 2001, 231) found that with everything else (such as education and language) being equal, the odds of poverty increase by 56 percent if one is an immigrant.

Statistics Canada recently released the research paper by Garnett Picot and Feng Hou: *The Rise in Low-Income Rates among Immigrants in Canada*. Picot and Hou (2003) found that the low-income rate among the most recent immigrants to Canada almost doubled from 1980 to 1995, before easing back during the last half of the 1990s. Among all immigrants as a group, the low-income rate rose from 17.0 percent in 1980 to 20.2 percent in 2000. Among recent immigrants, it rose from 24.6 percent to 35.8 percent. The gap in low-income rates between the Canadian-born and recent immigrants was highest among those who had a university degree, particularly those with applied science degrees. A "credentialism" issue may exist as degrees and certification from the non-traditional source countries may not be as readily recognized.

Many studies have analyzed the possibility that the lower economic achievement of recent immigrants and racialized groups may be attributed, not to their lower level of education, language, or skill (also known as human capital), but to diminishing returns for these factors. Immigrants have higher levels of education than Canadians overall, but do not earn income usually associated with their level of education. Some have attributed this to discrimination and to non-recognition of or the undervaluing of foreign education, skills, and credentials.

A major implication of this body of research is that labour market forces alone will not address such deep-seated problems, and a variety of initiatives are needed. Such policies include employment and pay equity, the recognition and promotion of the "hidden skills" of new immigrants to prospective employers, the provision of language and skills training to new immigrants, and the expedited recognition of foreign credentials. These policies are especially needed to address the social exclusion of recent immigrants and racialized communities. Without such policies, the major social inequalities that currently exist will persist and even grow deeper as time goes on.

Three Explanations for Poverty

There are three explanations for the existence of poverty in Canada. Each takes a different viewpoint on how the economy and society interact, and therefore on how people end up in poverty. The first approach places more emphasis on the individual attributes of the

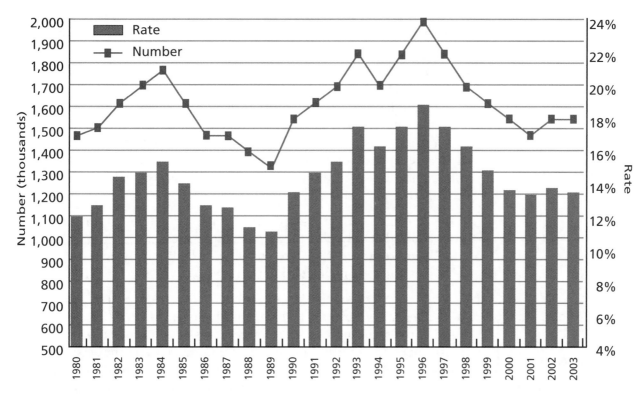

Figure 9.3: Child Poverty in Canada, 1980–2003

With permission from Campaign 2000, quoting its annual report card on child poverty (2005, p. 2). www. campaign2000.ca.

person in poverty – what it calls *human capital*. The second explanation highlights the conditions of the labour market, such as the availability of jobs. The third, critical perspective takes aim at the unequal distribution of power and ownership within the economy and political institutions.

Human Capital Perspective

The human capital perspective focuses on how the endowments of individuals determine their economic performance. Thus, low earnings that lead to poverty can result from factors such as less education, fewer job skills, old age, poor health, and low geographic mobility. Beyond this, differences in earnings are ascribed to differences in individual preferences between income and leisure. This is known as the *income-leisure choice theory*: the view is that people will choose between paid employment and unpaid leisure. Those with lower incomes are said to have chosen the latter.

In this approach, it is thought that income distributions depend largely on the interaction of supply and demand in the market for labour. As such, workers receive what they contribute. The approach perceives income inequality as a result of the quality of labour supplied. Poverty largely results from a lack of skills or education; inability to plan for old age or unemployment; unwillingness to work, move, or retrain; or an unwillingness to compete. This approach places emphasis on education and job training in order to break the poverty cycle.

Labour Market Perspective

In the labour market perspective, the emphasis is on the characteristics of society (demand-side) rather than the individual. Its historical basis is in Keynesian economics, as outlined in Chapter 3. It takes into consideration the barriers people face as a result of location, discrimination, and lack of demand for their labour. This explanation emphasizes that the characteristics of the labour market determine income. Adherents to this perspective believe that both supply and demand in the market for labour are important. Markets are viewed as limited or constrained by institutional factors, social norms, and other non-economic factors, such as:

- **SOCIALIZATION.** People are conditioned to believe certain things about themselves and their position in society.
- **DISCRIMINATION.** Negative stereotypes and employment barriers may limit employment opportunities.

Within the labour market perspective, there is a variant referred to as *dual labour market theory*. This theory postulates that administrative rules and processes structure and shape labour markets into non-competing groups: the primary labour market and the secondary labour market. The primary labour market is composed of unionized or professional employment, with high wages, benefits, good working conditions, and opportunities for advancement. It is generally closed to external competition or highly limited by qualifications. It is predominantly men who hold these jobs. The secondary labour market is composed of low-wage jobs with few benefits, and it is open to external competition. Most often, women with part-time and unstable jobs occupy this market. According to this perspective, the large pool of unemployed workers keeps the wages down in the secondary labour market, and poverty is generally associated with the secondary labour market.

In today's society, there are fewer primary jobs and significantly more secondary jobs. The primary jobs are becoming increasingly knowledge based; however, these jobs have become less stable, and more people are working on contracts. One explanation for low incomes, therefore, is the growth of the secondary labour force. As well, many families living on one income are now considered low income. At the same time, the Canadian labour force is being pitted against the labour forces in other low-wage countries, driving Canadian wages and benefits down.

Political Economy Perspective

The political economy perspective presupposes a relationship between politics and economics (for more information on this perspective, see Chapter 3). The large concentration of ownership of major corporations affects the way governments operate in the regulation of

Dual Labour Market Theory

■ **Primary labour market**: unionized or professional employment with high wages, benefits, good working conditions and opportunities for advancement, and a relatively small number of qualified workers

■ **Secondary labour market**: low-wage jobs with few benefits, part-time hours, lack of job-security, and competition between the large pool of available workers, all of which help keep wages down

industry and the labour market. Those who control the labour market control the wages of workers. Thus, there is a large spread and great inequality between owners at the top and workers at the bottom, leading to the poverty of some and the affluence of others.

Within this perspective, labour markets are segmented into competing camps. This enables employers to keep wages down. Stratification in the labour market is useful, it is argued, because employers pay some workers less than others pay, and create a group of flexible low-paid workers who can be moved in and out of employment as needed. Some feminist theories, for example, suggest that women are trapped in low-paying "women's work" in the labour market, which is viewed as an extension of their domestic work in the home.

Another factor that falls within the political economy explanation is discrimination. Discrimination based on race and ethnicity, both at interpersonal and at institutional levels, negatively affects the economic achievement of immigrants and people of colour. Some researchers have found that, even when immigrants are highly educated, their achievements are not recognized in the labour market.

Increasingly, social policy analysts are advocating an approach that considers all three perspectives. This three-track method emphasizes accessible and quality education and training opportunities, job creation, employment equity, and public participation in labour policy discussion and development.

Some Dimensions of Poverty

Homelessness

Symptomatic of the growing problem of poverty in Canada, homelessness is also on the rise. Simply defined, it is the absence of a place to live. A person who is considered to be homeless has no regular place to live, and stays in an emergency shelter, in an abandoned building, in an all-night shopping area, in a laundromat, outdoors, or any place where they can be protected from the elements.

Two types of homelessness can be distinguished: absolute homelessness and relative homelessness. Absolute homelessness is a situation in which an individual or family has no housing at all, or is staying in a temporary form of shelter. Relative homelessness is a situation in which people's homes do not meet the United Nation's basic housing standards, which are that a dwelling must:

- have adequate protection from the elements
- provide access to safe water and sanitation
- provide secure tenure and personal safety
- not cost more than 50 percent of total income
- lie within easy reach of employment, education, and health care

The homeless you see on the streets are long-term or "chronically" homeless people who represent less than 20 percent of the homeless.

Types of Homelessness

- **Absolute homelessness:** when an individual or family has no housing
- **Relative homelessness:** when housing does not meet the UN's basic standards for safe and adequate housing

Make Poverty
History

www.makepovertyhistory.ca

This new global campaign
summarizes its aims in
fourteen words: "More and
better aid. Trade justice.
Cancel the debt. End child
poverty in Canada."

Learn more, take
action, sign on or wear
a white band . . .

The rest are families and individuals who find themselves without a place to live for a period of time.

People become homeless for a variety of reasons. The major reasons appear to be economic crises due to unemployment or low income, mental health problems, other severe health problems, violence or abuse in the home, eviction, a lack of support from family and friends, and substance abuse problems. In some cases these factors can overlap and are precipitated by unemployment, health problems, or a family crisis. Changes to government policy, such as the *Tenant Protection Act* in Ontario, have removed rent controls and made it easier to evict tenants. When combined with a decrease in affordable housing, homelessness becomes a growing problem.

According to Statistics Canada, about two-thirds of Canadians own their own homes — half without a mortgage. This is a testament to the wealth in Canada, for some. The problem, however, is for those with low incomes. Only 40 percent of households in the lowest quintile (the bottom 20 percent of income recipients) own their own homes. A report by the City of Toronto found that the number of families living in shelters is dramatically increasing. While the majority of people staying in Toronto's emergency shelters are still single men, the number of families is growing. The number of people using Toronto's shelters rose from 22,000 in 1988 to 32,700 in 2003 (City of Toronto 2006, 1).

However, such numbers do not capture the extent of the problem of homelessness. They do not include women staying in emergency battered women's shelters, people who are living in substandard situations (a relative's basement), or women who use sexual contracts to find shelter with a man (the latter is an increasingly common phenomenon, showing the extent to which women are desperate to avoid life in emergency shelters).

The first Canadian food bank opened in 1981 in Edmonton as a temporary measure. Toronto's Daily Bread Food Bank, pictured here, is an organization that advocates for welfare reform and eliminating the need for food banks.

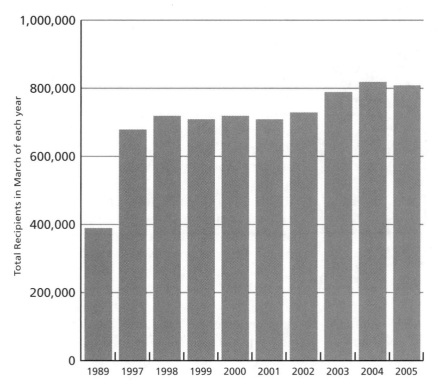

Figure 9.4: Monthly Canadian Food Bank Use: 1989–2005

Source: Canadian Association of Food Banks. HungerCount 2005. p. 9. Toronto. Reprinted with permission.

Homelessness has increased over the past decades as governments have cut back on social housing. In many cases, people simply cannot afford the housing that is available in their community. What is called for is a program of investment in low-cost affordable housing.

Food Insecurity

With cutbacks in many income security programs, Canadians are having to rely on food banks and feeding programs in order to survive. In 2005 there were over 650 food banks in Canada, and 823,856 people received emergency food in these food banks in a one month period (Canadian Association of Food Banks 2005). The number of people who utilized food banks increased by 118 percent since March 1989. Over 40 percent of those being helped are under the age of 18.

Of those Canadians using food banks, 68.7 percent relied on income security programs as their income source (51.6 percent Social Assistance, 4.5 percent Employment Insurance, and 12.6 percent Disability Benefits). Only 13.1 percent were employed, and 6.7 percent reported no income. As Social Assistance rates decrease and eligibility requirements for EI tighten, it is estimated that food bank usage by Canadians will continue to increase.

Feeding programs provide cooked meals at specified times during the day. They often operate out of shelters or church basements and provide two meals per day. Such programs are operated by volunteers and by those who use the service. For example, The Well in Ottawa

One-quarter of the world's population lives on less than $1 per day. The effects of global poverty include high rates of infant mortality and major health crises.

does not start providing meals until enough people volunteer to help. Many feeding programs are run in conjunction with emergency shelters. Feeding programs often also provide additional services, such as free laundry facilities, telephone access, newspapers, and clothing. In certain instances, access to computers and the Internet is also available. At most times, social workers are available and may even work directly from within the feeding program.

There is difficulty in keeping pace with demand. Almost half, or 49 percent, of food banks report that they often run out of food and must turn people away. Many believe that the steady unravelling of the social safety net means that access to basic food is in jeopardy. Food security is a basic right, and all people in their community should have access to good, nutritious food at all times. Fundamental changes in benefit levels and eligibility requirements are still needed to address the hunger problem.

Global Poverty

The circumstance of so many Canadians living in poverty is certainly appalling; however, the extent of global poverty and world inequality is infinitely worse. According to the World Bank, about one-quarter of the world's population lives on less than $1 per day, and over half live on $2 per day. Such figures do not capture the suffering that can accompany poverty of this magnitude. While some people can adequately survive on such meagre incomes given the cost of living in their home countries, many suffer with health problems, low life expectancies, high infant mortality rates, low levels of education, and malnutrition.

What is most startling about the situation of global inequality is that it is getting worse. Free trade and increased global investments have not decreased the gap between the rich countries and the poor countries. The World Development Reports of the World Bank state that the gap has widened considerably between 1960 and 1990. In 1960, the rich world average income was 20 times that of the poor world average income, whereas in 1990 the ratio had increased to 55 times.

The impacts of global poverty are enormous. According to the World Health Organization (WHO), more than 11 million children die each year before reaching the age of five; of them, 70 percent, or around 8 million children, die from one or more of five preventable causes of death that are all related to poverty: pneumonia, diarrhea, measles, malaria, and malnutrition.

Beyond individual suffering, the existence of poverty affects world politics, warfare, and terrorism. One year after the September 11 attacks on the World Trade Centre, Jean Chrétien, then prime minister, made several comments to the media regarding the link between poverty and world security. In a CBC interview, he said the attacks made him aware that the Western world faces a lot of resentment because of the growing divide between rich and poor nations.

Human development challenges remain large in the new millennium. Around the world we see unacceptable levels of deprivation in people's lives. Of the 4.6 billion people in developing countries, more than 850 million are illiterate, nearly a billion lack access to improved water sources, and 2.4 billion lack access to basic sanitation. Nearly 325 million boys and girls are out of school. And 11 million children under the age of five die each year from preventable causes – equivalent to more than 30,000 a day. Approximately 1.2 billion people live on less than $1 a day, and 2.8 billion on less than $2 a day.

Such deprivations are not limited to developing countries. In OECD countries, more than 130 million people are income poor, 34 million are unemployed, and adult functional illiteracy rates average 15 percent. Indeed, the late twentieth century may go down in world history as a period of increasing global impoverishment. Some believe that the new economic order feeds on cheap labour and, with the freer movement of capital, corporations pick up and move when citizens begin to increase their earnings, leaving many people without a stable source of income.

Conclusion

Regardless of how it is defined, serious poverty exists in Canada. People can find themselves in poverty due to the lack of employment, employment that pays inadequately, or obligations to care for children or other family members. Economists and social scientists have put forth different explanations for the existence of poverty, so a variety of proposed solutions have emerged. Over the past few decades, Canadian policy has adhered to a human capital perspective.

While social scientists argue about the merits of their various measures of poverty, people must live in misery and with the problems created by poverty. Without a doubt, a market economy excels at maximizing the production of goods and services (as compared to other historical relations of production). However, the system, as it currently exists in Canada and most other industrialized countries, has not figured out how to address poverty. Some argue that with the new-found ability of corporations to move production from Canada to low-wage countries, the situation could get worse. What is alarming is that even with this shift in production, poorer countries on the whole are growing poorer, and the gap between rich and poor countries is widening.

Global Poverty Quiz

http://unpac.ca/economy/wei_main.html

UNPAC is a Manitoba group dedicated to the UN's Platform for Action for the equality of women. On their advocacy website called Women and the Economy, there is a Global Poverty Quiz. You may be shocked to learn that one in four people around the globe live on less than $1 per day.

Chapter Summary

Key Concepts

- ☐ Absolute homelessness
- ☐ Absolute measure of poverty
- ☐ Basic Needs Lines (BNLs)
- ☐ Food banks and feeding programs
- ☐ Gini coefficient
- ☐ Global poverty
- ☐ Inequality
- ☐ Low Income Cut-off (LICO)
- ☐ Low Income Measure (LIM)
- ☐ Low-paid worker
- ☐ Market Basket Measure (MBM)
- ☐ Poverty duration
- ☐ Poverty gap
- ☐ Poverty headcount
- ☐ Quintile income distribution
- ☐ Relative homelessness
- ☐ Relative measure of poverty
- ☐ Social exclusion
- ☐ Working poor

Review Questions

1. How do the absolute and relative measures of poverty differ? Which one do you think produces a more accurate measure of poverty?

2. What is LICO, how is it calculated, and what does it intend to measure? How is it different from the Low Income Measure and the Market Basket Measure? Which of these measures is an absolute measure?

3. Other than the rate of poverty, what other aspects of poverty are important to measure, and why?

4. What is inequality, and how is it measured? What share of total income goes to the top quintile of income earners in Canada? How does this compare to the bottom quintile?

5. What are the three explanations for poverty, and how would each differing explanation affect the method the government chooses to tackle poverty?

6. What are the two types of homelessness? What are the causes of homelessness? What do you think can be done to solve the homelessness situation?

Exploring Social Welfare

1. Visit the Make Poverty History website (www.makepovertyhistory. ca) to explore its four-part mission: more and better aid, trade justice, cancel the debt, and end child poverty in Canada.

   a. Research and describe each of the four aims of Make Poverty History.
   b. Write a short essay describing how an individual such as your self might take action to help promote those aims.
   c. Share your findings with a group of people.

2. As you have discovered in this chapter, there are a variety of measures of poverty in Canada. Go to the Canadian Social Research website (www.canadiansocialresearch.net/poverty.htm) and read a few articles in the "Overviews of poverty measurement in Canada" section. Based on your reading, what poverty measure do you think best captures the phenomenon of poverty? Give a rationale for your viewpoint.

3. Research the issue of the working poor in Canada. Why has the number of working poor increased in the past five years? What income security program(s) are responsible for this?

Websites

Centre for Equality Rights in Accommodation
www.equalityrights.org/cera/

The centre's website has reports on housing issues from a human rights perspective.

Toronto Disaster Relief Committee
www.tdrc.net/

The Toronoto Disaster Relief Committee has a good collection of resources on homelessness.

PovNet
www.povnet.org

For people involved in anti-poverty work, this site has up-to-date information on a variety of pertinent issues related to the persistence of poverty in Canada.

References

Bourguignon, François, and Christian Morrisson. 2001. Inequality among world citizens: 1820–1992. Working Paper 2001-25. Department and Laboratory of Applied and Theoretical Economics, École Normale Superieure, Paris.

Campaign 2000. 2005. *Decision Time for Canada: Let's Make Poverty History, 2005 Report Card on Child Poverty in Canada.* Toronto: Campaign 2000. www.campaign2000.ca/rc/index.html.

Canadian Association of Food Banks. 2005. *HungerCount 2005.* Toronto: Canadian Association of Food Banks. www.cafb.ca.

Canadian Centre for Policy Alternatives (CCPA). 2007. *The Rich and the Rest of Us: The Changing Face of Canada's Growing Gap.* Toronto: Canadian Centre for Policy Alternatives. www.growinggap.ca

City of Toronto. 2006. *Quick Facts.* Toronto: City of Toronto. www.toronto. ca/housing.

Federal Register. 2006. *Federal Register* 71 (15): 3848–49.

Fleury, Dominique, and Myriam Fortin. 2006. *When Working Is Not Enough to Escape Poverty: An Analysis of Canada's Working Poor.* Ottawa: Human Resources and Social Development Canada.

Human Resources Development Canada (HRDC). 2003. *Understanding the 2000 Low Income Statistics Based on the Market Basket Measure.* Ottawa: HRDC.

Jackson, Andrew. 2004. Precarious jobs and social exclusion: key issues and new policy directions. *Policy Research Initiative* 7 (2). http:// policyresearch.gc.ca/page.asp?pagenm=v7n2_art_07.

Jesuit, David, and Timothy Smeeding. 2002. Poverty levels in the developed world. Luxembourg Income Study Work Paper No. 321. Luxembourg: Luxembourg Income Study. www.lisproject.org.

Kazemipur, A., and S. Halli. 2001. The changing colour of poverty in Canada. *Canadian Review of Sociology and Anthropology* 38 (2): 217–38.

National Council of Welfare. 2006. *Poverty Profile 2002 and 2003.* Ottawa: National Council of Welfare. www.ncwcnbes.net.

Organisation for Economic Co-operation and Development (OECD). 2001. *Economic Outlook 2001.* Paris, France: Organisation for Economic Co-operation and Development.

Ornstein, Michael. 2000. *Ethno-Racial Inequality in the City of Toronto: An Analysis of the 1996 Census.* Toronto: Chief Administrator's Office, City of Toronto.

Picot, Garnett, and Feng Hou. 2003. *The Rise in Low-Income Rates among Immigrants in Canada.* Ottawa: Statistics Canada.

Ross, David P., Katherine Scott, and Peter Smith. 2002. *The Canadian Fact Book on Poverty 2000.* Ottawa: Canadian Council on Social Development.

Sarlo, Christopher. 1992. *Poverty in Canada.* Vancouver: The Fraser Institute.

Sarlo, Christopher. 2001. *Measuring Poverty in Canada.* Vancouver: The Fraser Institute.

Statistics Canada. 2004. *Analysis of Income in Canada 2002.* Ottawa: Statistics Canada. Cat. no. 75-203.

Statistics Canada. 2006. *Persons in Low Income After Tax, by Prevalence in Percent (2000 to 2004).* Ottawa: Statistics Canada. CANSIM 202-0802 and Cat. no. 75-202-X.

10

People in the Labour Force

Understanding Income Security

Two pillars of our income security system, Employment Insurance and Workers' Compensation, provide income loss protection for those in the labour force. Without these benefits, both employees and employers would face uncertainties, and the operation of our economy would be hindered. They not only insure workers, but protect employers from lawsuits and enhance their competitiveness through labour market flexibility.

Since the postwar years, the recommendations of the 1943 *Report on Social Security for Canada* (known as the *Marsh Report*), and the rise of Keynesian economic ideas, there has been considerable debate about how the government should address the problem of unemployment. Debates centre on how much the government should interfere with a free market economy and whether emphasis should be on job creation, employment training, or income support. In a market

> "Workers' rights are human rights as well. The lives of 115 trade unionists who were murdered worldwide . . . in 2005, and the 1,600 who were violently assaulted, the 9,000 arrested, the 1,700 detained and the 10,000 who were sacked for trade union involvement each stood up for Article 23 — The Right to Desirable Work and to Join Trade Unions."
>
> —*Canadian Labour Congress, Statement on United Nations Human Rights Day, December 10, 2006.*

How Much Would I Get on EI?

Province/ Territory	Average Weekly Benefit
NL	$313
PEI	$301
NS	$297
NB	$299
QC	$310
ON	$326
MB	$300
SK	$307
AB	$329
BC	$318
NU	$346
NT	$372
YT	$356

Source: Adapted from The Canada Employment Insurance Commission. 2006. Employment Insurance: 2005 Monitoring and Assessment Report. Ottawa: Human Resources and Social Development Canada, 10.

economy such as ours, unemployment is one of the most important risks faced by Canadians. Without a job, a person confronts poverty: loss of social status, less access to health care, possible loss of housing, and a multitude of other problems. In fact, many difficult social problems in our society can be attributed, to a large extent, to the repercussions of unemployment (or low wages).

Two income security programs provide social insurance against interruption in earnings: Employment Insurance (EI), delivered by the federal government, and Workers' Compensation (WC), offered by the provinces. Employment Insurance insures against a short-term loss of employment income; Canadians unemployed for longer periods will exhaust their EI benefits and will turn to Social Assistance (SA), which is discussed in detail in Chapter 11. Workers' Compensation, on the other hand, protects the employed from the consequences of work injuries and health-related risks. It was the first social insurance program in Canada — and in many other industrialized countries.

The fundamental element of a modern welfare state is its **social insurance schemes**. You pay your premiums and you have a right to benefits. This chapter outlines the historical and current EI programs and provides an overview of Workers' Compensation.

Employment Insurance and Workers' Compensation: An Overview

In Canada over the past fifty years, overall unemployment has risen fairly steadily. The unemployment rate has increased from under 2 percent in 1942 to over 9 percent through the 1980s, and over 7 percent through the 1990s and into the 2000s. Employment Insurance (EI) is a social program that contributes to the security of all Canadians by providing assistance to workers who lose their jobs and by helping unemployed people get back to work. However, Employment Insurance is much more than protection from unemployment. It provides temporary financial help to eligible unemployed Canadians while they look for work or upgrade their skills, while they are pregnant or caring for a newborn or adopted child, while they are sick, or while they care for a gravely ill family member. It also provides employment assistance to help people return to the workforce. Individuals who have paid into the EI account can qualify for regular benefits of 55 percent of their average weekly insured earnings, to a maximum of $413 per week — provided they have worked the minimum required number of insurable hours within the last fifty-two weeks or since the start of their last claim, whichever is shorter.

But EI does not cover all unemployed Canadians. In fact, fewer and fewer people are finding that they can draw benefits when they need them. This can be a shock for someone who has paid into the insurance fund for years. Changes to EI eligibility requirements during the 1990s have severely limited the number of people who are eligible for benefits. From 1989 to 1997, the percentage of unemployed people that actually received benefits dropped from 83 to 42 percent (Human Resources Development Canada 1998), remaining at 43.6 percent in 2004 (Human Resources and Social Development Canada 2005, ii). This increasingly affects women who, due in part to additional family responsibilities, work less than the required 35 hours per week. In 1999, 68 percent of employed women were ineligible for EI benefits (Canadian Labour Congress 2000a, 3). Details on the program and how it has changed are discussed later in the chapter.

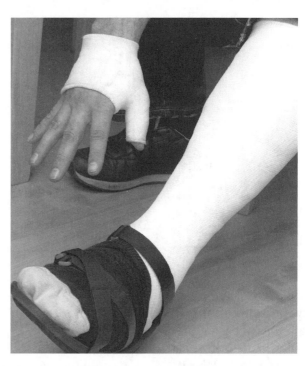

Workers' Compensation (WC) is an insurance system for employers and workers, established to replace the tort system (the courts) in determining compensation for workplace injuries and health-related risks. It provides no-fault compensation. This means that benefits are paid to injured workers whether or not negligence on the part of the worker or employer is considered to have contributed to the accident. With this coverage, workers give up their right of legal action in return for certainty of compensation. A worker injured in the course of employment cannot sue his or her employer for damages. Early programs were instituted due to employers' concerns about lawsuits resulting from injuries in the workplace where the employers were negligent. Factories in the late 1800s and early 1900s were dangerous places, and injuries and work-related illnesses were commonplace. Earlier programs were called "Workmen's Compensation," but they have since been renamed with gender-neutral terms.

Workers' Compensation guarantees benefits to employees injured at work and protects employers from being sued.

Roughly 85 percent of the Canadian labour force is covered by provincial Workers' Compensation programs (Human Resources Development Canada 1999, 5). First, WC covers the risk of incurring costs for the rehabilitation from an injury or illness contracted at or caused by the workplace or because of working. Secondly, WC provides insurance against the interruption of income or the impairment of earnings capacity, whether temporary or permanent, that arises from an illness or accident at work. This includes support for dependants in the case of the death of a worker at the workplace or arising out of work.

On average, one Canadian worker out of sixteen was injured at work in 1997, and one worker out of thirty-one was injured severely enough to miss at least one day of work. In 2003, Workers' Compensation Boards (WCBs) paid over $5.2 billion in benefits. If the indirect costs (the time lost by uninjured workers trying to help an injured worker, lowered staff morale, and damage to materials and equipment) are included, the total cost of occupational injuries to

Unemployment Insurance was first introduced in the post-World War II era.

Workplace Safety and Insurance Board

www.wsib.on.ca

The WSIB administers the Workers' Compensation system in Ontario and advocates for workplace safety, health, and injury prevention.

the Canadian economy could be estimated at over $9.1 billion (Statistics Canada 2003). These rates do not include those not covered by Workers' Compensation and may be underestimating injuries and costs by 15 to 20 percent.

Every province has its own Workers' Compensation program. Eligibility criteria, benefit levels, and coverage all vary considerably between provinces. Coverage, for example, varies from 60 to 90 percent of the workforce between provinces. Quebec and Manitoba have even used WC to indemnify victims of criminal acts. This covers the costs of injury of victims of criminal acts or innocent bystanders. Programs are generally financed by employer contributions. The Workplace Safety and Insurance Board (WSIB) in Ontario is entirely financed by employer premiums. It receives no money from the Ontario government.

Through the changes introduced by the *Workplace Safety and Insurance Act* (1998), the WSIB in Ontario oversees workplace safety education and training. Some provinces and territories, such as the Yukon, the Northwest Territories, Nunavut, and Newfoundland and Labrador have added both workplace health and safety to the titles of their organizations reflecting the expansion of their missions. Other provinces, such as Manitoba, Alberta, Nova Scotia, and British Columbia, work exclusively in injury compensation, and they have retained the traditional organization title of Workers' Compensation Board.

Workers' Compensation programs nationwide are facing new challenges. Knowledge of work-related injury and disease causation has changed the nature of claims. When Workers' Compensation systems first began, far less was known about the intricate relationship between work and health. In the early days, work injuries were usually readily identifiable by specific traumatic incidents. Today, many claims relate to occupational diseases. Claims for items such as occupational cancer due to prolonged exposure to tobacco smoke at the workplace are more common than they used to be.

This new knowledge has implications for prevention. We are discovering the relevance of work factors that have not been adequately addressed by our prevention and compensation systems. There is a widening gap between our knowledge of how work causes disease and our strategies in preventing and compensating for it. Ontario is one of the few provinces that has begun to address prevention issues as part of its WSIB program, but so far programs have related more to educating workers on how to avoid workplace disease rather than directly addressing its occurrence.

The History of Unemployment Insurance

Unemployment Insurance (UI) — now called Employment Insurance (EI) — came into being during the high-employment era of World War II. It began with a narrow focus on the income support needs of regular, full-time, year-round workers who might find themselves temporarily without work. Over the next thirty years, it expanded to cover almost all employed workers and became the federal government's primary vehicle for addressing a wide range of income support and social policy issues.

The history of Employment Insurance begins in 1940 with the *Unemployment Insurance Act*. The federal government obtained the unanimous consent of the provinces to amend the *British North America Act*, making a national UI program possible. Before this amendment, such an insurance system was the exclusive domain of the provinces. On August 7, 1940, the *Unemployment Insurance Act* was given royal assent and, with it, Canada became the last Western industrialized nation to institute Unemployment Insurance. As mentioned, the 1940 program was narrow in scale, and eligibility requirements were limiting. For example, weekly benefit rates for a single person were between $4.08 and $12.24. Throughout the period between 1940 and 1960, numerous amendments to the UI legislation expanded eligibility and increased benefits and coverage. In general, the 1950s and particularly the 1960s, saw greater involvement of government in most areas of Canadian life. Growth in government revenues and increased expectations from Canadians led to an expansion of the social safety net, and this included UI.

The 1970 White Paper on Unemployment Insurance recommended an extended and enhanced UI program, including universal coverage for all workers who could be considered employees, increased benefits that should be related to income, and lower contribution rates. Sickness and pregnancy benefits were also recommended. Bill C-229, introduced early in 1971, legislated a revamped UI that followed many of the White Paper recommendations. This was part of Prime Minister Pierre Elliott Trudeau's Just Society initiative. Due to these changes, 80 percent of unemployed workers were covered by UI.

New maternity and sickness programs were also introduced, providing financial support to new mothers who worked before they had their children, and to workers with short-term illnesses. The government assumed full responsibility for the cost of extended UI benefits due to high unemployment (above 4 percent). In 1977 the government introduced a number of training measures for unemployed workers drawing benefits, such as work sharing and job creation programs.

The introduction of Bill C-21 in 1990 reversed several of these enhancements. The bill increased the number of weeks of work required to receive benefits, reduced the maximum duration of benefits for most regions, and reduced the replacement rate from 60 to 50 percent

HRSDC

www.hrsdc.gc.ca

The Human Resources and Social Development Canada (HRSDC) website provides a complete overview of Employment Insurance. It also has a superb history section at www.hrsdc.gc.ca/en/ei/history/unemployment_insurance.shtml.

Canadian Labour Standards

The *Canada Labour Code* applies only to employment under federal jurisdiction — just 10 percent of the Canadian workforce. Provincial laws apply to the other 90 percent of workers. The *Canada Labour Code* differs in many areas from the provincial legislation. The codes deal with issues such as hours of work, minimum wage, general holidays, termination or severance pay, unjust dismissal, and various types of leave such as vacation, maternity, bereavement, or illness.

of insurable earnings for those who declined "suitable employment," quit "without just cause," or were fired. In 1993 benefits were tightened further. Bill C-113 cut the regular benefit rate from 60 percent of insurable earnings to 57 percent, and benefits for workers who quit or were fired from their jobs were eliminated.

A much-touted 1994 review of social security in Canada resulted in numerous changes to UI. The review resulted in the Green Paper called *Agenda: Jobs and Growth — Improving Social Security in Canada*. The Green Paper recommended the name change from Unemployment Insurance to Employment Insurance to represent the goal of encouraging employment (Human Resources Development Canada 1994, 42). The paper recommended a smaller, better-targeted program with tighter rules and lower premiums. With this in hand, the Liberal government announced a round of cuts to UI to save a projected $5.5 billion over three years. The changes included a reduction in benefits for most claimants from 57 to 55 percent of insured earnings, a further increase in the number of weeks needed to qualify, and a decrease in the benefit period — in sum, extensive alterations to the benefit structure. Perhaps most controversial was the two-tier system of benefits that had lower benefits for frequent claimants — known as the *intensity rule*. (This was discontinued in 2001 due to findings that it was ineffective in discouraging repeat use, and was also seen as being punitive.)

On January 5, 1995, changes to the Employment Insurance system took effect with Bill C-12, the new *Employment Insurance Act*. The new system replaced the previous Unemployment Insurance system on July 1, 1996. Beyond the name change, there were five key differences:

- **HOURS.** Income benefits are based on hours worked rather than weeks worked.
- **EARNINGS.** Benefits are more closely tied to earnings.
- **INTENSITY RULE.** The basic benefit rate of 55 percent declines according to the number of weeks of benefits drawn in a five-year period (lowering benefits for frequent recipients).
- **EMPLOYMENT BENEFITS.** There is an increased concentration on benefits intended to equip an unemployed person to return to work.
- **FAMILY INCOME SUPPLEMENT.** There is enhanced protection for low-income families.

The new bill also reduced the dollar benefits payable, reduced the premiums to be paid into the EI fund by employees and employers, increased the length of work time required to be eligible, and shortened the maximum periods for which benefits can be paid. These changes have been criticized by the labour community and by social welfare advocates for hurting those who need the program most — single-parent families (mostly led by women) and children.

In its report entitled *Analysis of UI Coverage for Women*, the Canadian Labour Congress (CLC) found that the gap in UI coverage between men and women has widened due to the 1997 changes. The CLC claims that the portion of women now getting UI is 10 percent lower than for men, and that women under the age of 45 have lost most heavily, since only 28 percent of them are covered (Canadian Labour Congress 2000a).

The History of Workers' Compensation

The concept of Workers' Compensation originated in England and the United Sates in the late 1800s and early 1900s. Early laws in England made it extremely difficult for workers to successfully sue an employer for negligence. The employers' defences, which developed earlier in the nineteenth century, were based on the assumptions that contracts between workers and their employers were the same as commercial contracts between people of equal bargaining power. If workers did not like the employers' terms and conditions, they could simply find work elsewhere. The defences later became known as the "unholy trinity":

- **VOLUNTARY ASSUMPTION OF RISK.** The worker assumed the usual risks of the job. The rate of pay for each job was assumed to reflect its level of risk.
- **FELLOW SERVANT RULE.** A worker's injury was related to a co-worker's negligence, and the employer was not responsible. This second defence was a variation on voluntary assumption of risk – one of the risks a worker assumed was the possible negligence of a co-worker. The injured worker could sue the co-worker, but considering the income levels of workers at the time, that was an ineffective option. It also pitted worker against worker.
- **CONTRIBUTORY NEGLIGENCE.** If the injured worker's own conduct contributed to the injury in even the slightest way, the employer completely escaped legal responsibility.

By the end of the nineteenth century, the situation began to change. Unions were becoming more powerful, and political parties of the day competed for the labour vote. The government passed legislation that slightly loosened the hold of employers' defences, and it became somewhat easier for workers to succeed in the courts. A spate of successful lawsuits concerning the dangerous factories of the era put many employers in a panic. Employers began to push for legislation that protected them from these lawsuits.

To some extent, this was a worldwide problem, and it resulted in England's 1897 *Workmen's Compensation Act* and numerous state acts in the United States between 1908 and 1915. Germany enacted the first Workers' Compensation law in 1884, followed by Poland the same year, and England, Czechoslovakia, and Austria in 1887. The new laws were the first instance in history of a compulsory social insurance program. The German program was based on a non-profit system that required employers, through trade associations, to operate a collective liability system of insurance guaranteed by the government.

Meredith principle

■ a 1913 compromise in which workers give up their right to sue employers for work-related injuries in exchange for guaranteed compensation

In Ontario, increasing accident rates and pressure from labour unions led the government to appoint a Royal Commission, headed by William Meredith, to study the matter. The Royal Commission report was submitted in 1913. Meredith rejected the assumptions underlying employers' legal defences. He maintained that workers had few choices concerning their place of work. He condemned the fellow servant rule as a "relic of barbarism." Meredith recommended abolishing what he called "this nuisance of litigation" and proposed the "historic compromise" that became known as the *Meredith principle*. The **Meredith principle** is a compromise in which workers give up the right to sue for work-related injuries, irrespective of fault, in return for guaranteed compensation for accepted claims. He concluded the Meredith Report as follows:

> In these days of social and industrial unrest it is, in my judgement, of the gravest importance to the community that every proved injustice to any section or class resulting from bad or unfair laws should be promptly removed by the enactment of remedial legislation and I do not doubt that the country whose Legislature is quick to discern and prompt to remove injustice will enjoy, and that deservedly, the blessing of industrial peace and freedom from social unrest. (Meredith 1913)

As a result of Meredith's report, Ontario's *Workmen's Compensation Act* received royal assent in 1914 and was implemented in 1915. The *Workers' Compensation Act of Manitoba* quickly followed suit and was enacted in 1916. British Columbia's *Workmen's Compensation Act* was passed in 1902, but it did not come into force until 1917, when the Workmen's Compensation Board was created. Legislation followed in all other provinces and territories over the next forty years. The Yukon did not institute legislation until the 1958 *Workmen's Compensation Ordinance*; Saskatchewan's legislation came in 1930, Prince Edward Island's in 1949, and Newfoundland's in 1950.

The passage of these early acts in Ontario, British Columbia, and Manitoba was revolutionary. At the time, no social welfare programs existed in Canada – nor did the income taxes to fund them. The social welfare programs were also revolutionary in that they broke away from the principle of individual fault and prescribed a collective responsibility. The Meredith principle still forms the basis of Workers' Compensation systems across Canada. It was the first legislative challenge to the idea that free enterprise without government interference would be just and fair.

Until the 1960s, changes to programs consisted mostly of revising benefit levels and clinical rating schedules to enable the boards to more easily determine benefit rates and prevent litigation. The use of schedules provided a kind of rough-average justice, but also provided benefits based on a presumed wage loss related to the nature and extent of the injury – rather than the impact of the injury on one's earnings.

In the 1960s, compensation was expanded to include injuries that developed over time, as long as they were work related. This means that conditions such as occupational cancer and chronic stress could now be claimed. Conditions such as these are currently giving the boards difficulty, because it is hard to be sure whether or not such conditions are work related. Some governments are removing such items from their lists and refusing to accept related claims. The problem with this approach is that it merely places the problem back into the courts, and employers find themselves in litigation — situations Workers' Compensation Boards were created to avoid.

Employment Insurance: The Details

There are different types of Employment Insurance benefits:

■ **REGULAR BENEFITS.** These are paid to people who have lost their job and want to return to work. To receive them, one must be actively looking for another job and be willing and able to work at all times. In October 2003, 579,900 Canadians were receiving benefits.

■ **MATERNITY/PARENTAL AND SICKNESS BENEFITS.** In addition to regular benefits, Employment Insurance provides maternity/parental and sickness benefits to individuals who are pregnant, have recently given birth, are adopting a child, are caring for a newborn baby, or are sick. Maternity benefits are payable to the birth mother (or surrogate mother) for a maximum of fifteen weeks. To receive maternity benefits, you are required to have worked for 600 hours in the last fifty-two weeks or since your last claim. You need to prove your pregnancy by signing a statement declaring the expected due date or actual date of birth. Sickness benefits may be paid for up to fifteen weeks to a person who is unable to work because of sickness, injury, or quarantine. To receive these benefits, you are required to have worked for 600 hours in the last fifty-two weeks or since your last claim.

■ **COMPASSIONATE CARE BENEFITS.** In 2004, a new type of EI benefit was introduced, called the *compassionate care benefits*. These benefits are paid for a maximum of six weeks to workers who have to be away from work temporarily to provide care or support to a member of their family who is gravely ill with a significant risk of death within six months. To qualify, you must have 600 hours of insurable employment during your qualifying period.

■ **FAMILY SUPPLEMENT.** The Family Supplement (FS) provides additional benefits to low-income families with children. Families with children with a net income up to a maximum of $25,921 per year have the FS benefit automatically added to their Employment Insurance payment. As income increases, the FS gradually decreases.

■ **FISHING BENEFITS.** These are paid to self-employed persons engaged in fishing, and who earn insufficient earnings from that activity.

Compassionate Care Benefits

Bill C-28 amends the *Employment Insurance Act* to provide up to six weeks of compassionate care benefits for workers with 600 hours of insurable earnings. Workers can leave work to care for

■ a spouse or common-law partner
■ a child or the child of their spouse/partner
■ a parent or the spouse/partner of their parent
■ any other person who may be defined as a "family member" in subsequent regulations.

The person requiring care must have a serious medical condition with significant risk of death within twenty-six weeks and must require care.

The Employment Insurance program has a few other special features, such as skills development assistance, self-employment assistance, and EI for Canadian workers or residents outside Canada. The skills development assistance aims to help individuals obtain skills for employment, ranging from basic to advanced, by providing them with financial assistance to select, arrange, and pay for their own training. Self-employment assistance helps provide unemployed individuals who are eligible for EI with financial support, planning assistance, and mentoring to help them start a business. Finally, Employment Insurance for workers and residents outside Canada provides EI benefits to people working outside Canada for a Canadian company or with the Canadian government.

Benefit Levels

The amount of EI benefits paid has dropped dramatically since the 1996 changes to the act, with a 50 percent drop between 1993 and 1999. During the height of the recession in 1993, EI (then called UI) provided $19.6 billion in benefits. In 2004/05, total benefits amounted to $12.7 billion (Human Resources Development Canada 2003). This figure breaks down as follows:

■ Regular benefits: $8.2 billion
■ Employment benefits: $385 million
■ Work-sharing benefits: $25 million
■ Fishing benefits: $289 million
■ Special benefits: $3.8 billion (includes sickness, maternity, and parental)

Regular benefits can be paid if you lose your job through no fault of your own (for example, due to shortage of work or seasonal or mass layoffs), and you are available and able to work but cannot find a job.

In 2003, $18.5 billion was paid in EI premiums, but less than $12 billion was paid out as benefits. This overcontribution is a hot issue with both labour and business groups.

Insurable Hours

If you have paid into the Employment Insurance account and you have worked a minimum number of hours of work (420–700 hours in the past fifty-two weeks) you are eligible for EI; however, you are required to have 910 hours if you are in the workforce for the first time, or have left for the past two years. The number of insurable hours needed to qualify for EI depends on the rate of unemployment in your region. A 2001 change to the EI legislation allows EI claimants to exclude low-earning weeks (less than $150) for benefit calculation purposes, which encourages people to accept all available work.

Regular benefits are 55 percent of average weekly insured earnings to a maximum of $413 per week. You may receive a higher or a lower benefit rate depending on your personal circumstances. If you are in a low-income family (an income of less than $25,921) with children and you receive the Child Tax Benefit (CTB), you could receive a higher benefit rate. The average was $315 in 2005.

The allowed amount of time you can be on EI, known as the claim period, varies depending on the number of weeks you have worked and the local unemployment rate. The maximum claim period is forty-five weeks.

The government is running an EI pilot project for three years ending in 2008. The pilot aims to help Canadians who face sporadic or seasonal work patterns. Benefits are calculated based on the best fourteen weeks of earnings. All insurable hours are still used to determine the duration of the claim. Additional information regarding the pilot project is available at www.hrsdc.gc.ca/en/ei/information/best14weeks.shtml.

Clawback Rule

The new Employment Insurance system has a clawback rule, which specifies that benefits must be repaid if net income is over $48,750. The maximum repayment is limited to 30 percent for a person with a net income in excess of $48,750. Claimants are exempt from benefit repayment (clawbacks) if they have received maternity/parental and sickness benefits. This is meant to ensure that parents who stay home with their newborn or newly adopted children, or workers who are too sick to work, are not penalized. The intent of the clawback is to discourage individuals with higher annual incomes from repeatedly collecting benefits.

Premiums paid are reported as being part of a special EI account, but in reality they are lumped in with all other government revenues. The Auditor General of Canada (2002) reports that EI premium revenue has exceeded program costs since 1994, resulting in a surplus of $46 billion. This surplus was over $50 billion in 2004. According to the Auditor General, these funds have contributed to a large part of other government expenditures, including tax cuts and paying down

Table 10.1: Average Weekly Employment Insurance Benefits

	2002	2003	2004	2005	2006
All benefits	**$288.78**	**$293.63**	**$296.87**	**$300.01**	**$308.73**
Regular	$257.61	$291.00	$293.24	$295.58	$305.78
Sickness	$297.00	$264.69	$269.50	$275.51	$286.75
Maternity	$297.00	$303.55	$309.24	$314.01	$321.86
Fishing	$398.21	$447.72	$381.27	$374.94	$371.49
Work sharing	$86.47	$93.37	$90.79	$95.15	$95.48
Adoption	$353.90	$358.23	$365.57	$367.05	$372.83

Source: Statistics Canada. 2007. *Table 276-0016 Average weekly employment insurance benefits.* CANSIM (database) Last modified: 2006-02-27. http://www40.statcan.ca/l01/cst01/labor17.htm

government debt. Some question the practice of collecting premiums for designated insurance benefits, but actually using the monies for other purposes. Others believe that collecting premiums from working people and then using the funds for tax cuts that predominately benefit wealthier Canadians is a form of income redistribution from the poor to the rich.

Workers and employers both criticize the use of the EI surplus for other purposes. Employers complain that artificially high EI rates place a burden on labour-intensive industries and penalize employers for creating jobs. They want the premium rates lowered. Workers and their unions, on the other hand, criticize what they call the theft of EI premiums, and they want decreased eligibility requirements and higher benefits.

Maternity and Parental Benefits

In Canada women can claim up to fifteen weeks of maternity leave when giving birth, and both men and women can claim an additional thirty-five weeks of parental leave for newborns or adopted children.

In 1984, the Unemployment Insurance legislation began to provide for the payment of benefits to a claimant, man or woman, who remained at home to care for a child who was being adopted. Three years later, paternity benefits were introduced so as to provide support (under very specific conditions) for the father of a newborn who stayed at home to care for his child. In 1990, adoption and paternity benefits were replaced by parental benefits, which allowed payment of benefits for ten weeks, with the possibility of extension to fifteen weeks.

Important changes to the *Employment Insurance Act* were introduced in 2000 that increased **parental leave benefits** from ten weeks to thirty-five weeks. In addition, the threshold for eligibility was lowered from 700 to 600 hours of insurable employment. The thirty-five weeks of benefits can be taken by one qualifying parent, or split between both qualifying parents, with only one waiting period required between them. The benefit entitlement remains at 55 percent of average insured earnings, up to a maximum of $413 per week. In 2003, maternity benefits paid amounted to $873 million, with parental benefits totalling $1.9 billion.

Only women can claim maternity leave benefits, administered in the same way as parental leave, for fifteen weeks. The combination of maternity and parental benefits now enables parents to receive up to one year of paid leave to care for their infants. Parental benefits are payable either to the biological or adoptive parents while they are caring for a newborn or an adopted child. To receive either benefit, one is required to have worked 600 hours in the last fifty-two weeks or since the last claim.

Social policy author Richard Shillington, in his survey of maternity and parental benefits, found that recent significant increases in duration of benefits (now up to fifty weeks) has benefited families with newborn children. In researching maternity benefits, he found that only 58 percent of new mothers reported receiving EI benefits in 2001 (2001, 6). Of those who did not receive maternity benefits, about half reported that they did not work in the year before, and half did not have enough hours or had jobs that were not insured (12).

Some have said that recent enhancement to parental benefits has brought Canada close to the Swedish model of family policy. In Sweden the benefits are universal and administered through health insurance, unlike Canada, where only about 58 percent of parents are eligible. Sweden also includes coverage for 450 days for 80 percent of previous salary up to a maximum ceiling. Parents who continue to stay off work after the 450 days can receive a so-called guarantee amount of $60 per day. Parents with no previous income receive the guaranteed amount for all the 450 days (Swedish Institute 2001). Clearly, Canada's parental leave EI policy has a long way to go before it mirrors the Swedish model.

In 2004, six weeks of EI compassionate care benefits (CCB) were introduced. Job protection in the federal and most provincial labour codes was simultaneously introduced. In 2004/05, only 4,782 claimants received compassionate care benefits with an average weekly benefit of $314. Overall, $6.9 million was paid in benefits, and the majority of new compassionate care claims was established by women (73.7 percent) (Office of the Auditor General, 2005, Annex 2).

Canada is one of the few countries that has compassionate care benefits for all workers with insurable employment. Most other countries that offer such benefits restrict them to parents who are caring for sick children. Canada's program does not have these restrictions. A person can access the benefit to care for any gravely ill family member at risk of dying within twenty-six weeks. The definition of *family member* includes a wide range of people, such as grandchildren, uncles or aunts, nephews and nieces, foster parents, or even neighbours who might consider you like a family member. One needs 600 insured hours in the last fifty-two weeks or since the start of your last claim to qualify.

Maternity Leave for Canadian Women

Since the extension of parental benefits in 2001, qualifying mothers are staying home longer with their newborn infants, and more fathers are claiming benefits. Canada is tied with Denmark as the fifth-best country for parents wanting time off, following Sweden, Norway, New Zealand, and Australia. Canada offers one year of maternity leave for mothers to raise their newborns, but Canada ranks fifteenth when it comes to the amount of benefits offered. During the year allowed for maternity leave, the government pays Employment Insurance to a maximum of $423 per week (Human Resources and Social Development Canada 2006a).

EI Benefit Coverage

One way to measure the extent to which people who become unemployed in Canada are covered by Employment Insurance is to calculate the proportion of unemployed who actually receive EI benefits. This is known as the B/U ratio — the ratio of unemployed EI beneficiaries to the unemployed without benefits.

In 1998, a study released by Human Resources Development Canada found that the B/U ratio declined by almost 50 percent in the 1990s. Figure 10.1 shows the extent of the decrease in UI/EI coverage. It has plummeted from 82.9 percent of the unemployed in 1989 to 43.4 percent in 1997 and has remained fairly constant to 2004 (Human Resources and Social Development Canada 2005, ii). This means that only 43 percent of the unemployed in 2004 actually received regular benefits.

The 2005 *Employment Insurance Monitoring and Assessment Report*, prepared by the Canada Employment Insurance Commission (Human Resources and Social Development Canada 2005, ii), reports that the B/U ratio was 43.6 percent for 2004. However, the commission has problems with the measure because it includes people who are not eligible to pay into EI. Their alternative ratio comparing the number of EI beneficiaries to unemployed EI contributors (the B/UC ratio) was 63.5 percent in 2004 (Battle, Mendelson, and Torjman 2006, 18).

There are wide provincial differences in EI coverage, with a B/U ratio of 29.7 percent in Ontario and 93.3 percent in Newfoundland. These provincial differences reflect in part the wide variation in work requirements and maximum duration of benefits according to the program's fifty-eight regional unemployment rates. There is a gender gap, with the 2004 B/U ratios for men being 47.3 percent and 39.7 percent for women (Battle, Mendelson, and Torjman 2006, 18).

Moreover, it is largely the growing number of Canadians who are unemployed but do not have recent work experience (and are therefore not eligible for EI) that is lowering the B/U ratio so dramatically. The category of unemployed without recent work, which includes young people looking for their first job and those looking for a job after an extended period of absence from the labour market, is the largest category of unemployed workers ineligible for Employment Insurance; it is also the group that grew the fastest during the 1990s. Their percentage doubled between 1989 and 1997 from 19 percent to 38 percent, before dropping to 34 percent in 1999 (Bédard, Bertrand, and Grignon 2000).

According to the Canadian Labour Congress, the drop in EI protection has the most impact on the lowest-paid workers and women. Their data indicates that 41 percent of the $7.4 billion in reduced benefits (from 1993 to 1999) came from workers earning less than $15,000 per year, and two-thirds came from workers earning less than $20,000 (Canadian Labour Congress 2002, 2).

The Current State of the Labour Market

Jobs can be defined as standard and non-standard. Standard jobs are those that are full-time, full-year with a single employer. They usually offer benefits and career opportunities. Under one-half of Canadian workers hold standard jobs. The rest are part-time workers, self-em-

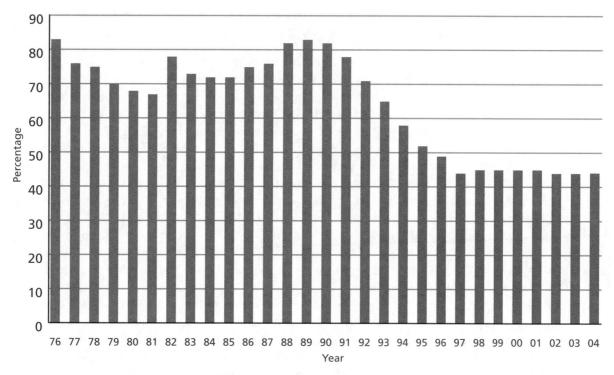

**Figure 10.1:
Percentage of
Unemployed
Receiving Regular
UI/EI Benefits,
Canada, 1976–2004**

*Source: Battle, Ken, Michael
Mendelson, and Sherri
Torjman. 2006.* **Towards
a New Architecture for
Canada's Adult Benefits.**
*Ottawa: Caledon Institute of
Social Policy, 16. Reprinted
with permission.*

ployed contract workers, and temporary help. The just-in-time work-force is a new reality. Employers are hesitant to commit to full-time, full-year "permanent" jobs and increasingly prefer to hire on a project-by-project basis.

In his book *Job Shift*, William Bridges (1994) coined the phrase "dejobbing" to describe this trend to non-standard employment. He says that workers are going to become more like independent business people (or one-person businesses) than conventional employees. Not only are there fewer standard jobs, but those that remain are chang-ing. No longer do people have stable 9-to-5 jobs with good pay. Peo-ple are left with what are called "McJobs," a term meant to reflect the substandard nature of jobs at McDonalds.

EI: The Economy Stabilizer

A major portion of contemporary social welfare has to do with people who are out of work or are not making a wage that permits them, or those who depend on them, to live at the standards established in our society. People may be unable to work for a wide range of reasons. It may not have anything to do with their individual capacity to be em-ployed, and instead may be based on the labour market's capacity to employ them. The Canadian UI/EI system has generally played a posi-tive role as an automatic stabilizer for the economy. In employment terms, this translates into 11 to 14 percent of job losses being averted because of UI/EI.

THE ATTORNEY GENERAL OF CANADA V. KELLY LESIUK

The introduction of more restrictive eligibility rules in the 1996 *Employment Insurance (EI) Act* has been a major step backward for unemployed people across Canada. Between 1989 and 1999, the percentage of unemployed people who were receiving benefits dropped dramatically from 74% to 37%. Over the same period, a huge surplus has accumulated from the premiums paid by workers who are increasingly unable to access any benefits. Part-time and low-income workers have been particularly hard hit by the change from using insurable weeks to insurable hours as the basis for meeting minimum eligibility requirements. Women constitute 70% of the growing part-time labour force in part because they still perform two-thirds of unpaid work in the home and are overwhelmingly responsible for childcare. As a result, in 1999, only 32% of unemployed women in Canada qualified for benefits — 10% lower than the comparable figure for men.

In 1998, Kelly Lesiuk moved from Brandon to Winnipeg, Manitoba where her husband had recently found employment. For almost five years prior to the move, Ms Lesiuk had been a part-time registered nurse at the Brandon General Hospital. She was also the primary caregiver for the couple's daughter. When Ms Lesiuk applied for EI benefits shortly after arriving in Winnipeg, the Employment Insurance Commission determined that she had worked fewer than 700 insurable hours in the previous 52 weeks and therefore could not qualify for regular, pregnancy or sickness benefits. Under the new EI rules, she was 33 hours short. Significantly, under the old Unemployment Insurance Act she would have had enough insurable weeks to qualify.

Assisted by the Community Unemployed Help Centre in Winnipeg and the Public Interest Law Centre, Ms Lesiuk appealed the Commission's decision to the Employment Insurance "Umpire," arguing that the new EI eligibility rules discriminated against women and parents. In March 2001, she won a dramatic victory when the rules were found to violate the equality guarantee in section 15 of the Charter of Rights and Freedoms. Kelly Lesiuk's case represents an important achievement for the equality rights of unemployed women in Canada. Finally, the federal government is being taken to task for its punitive, regressive and discriminatory unemployment insurance legislation — legislation that denies hundreds of thousands of unemployed women adequate income security.

Disappointingly, the federal government continues to defend their discriminatory rules. It appealed the Umpire's decision to the Federal Court and the case was heard on November 19 and 20, 2002. ISAC [Income Security Advocacy Centre] appeared as an intervener to support Ms. Lesiuk's efforts at the hearing. On January 8, 2003, the Court released its decision, overturning the Umpire's verdict that EI rules violate the Charter . . . Ms. Lesiuk appealed this decision to the Supreme Court of Canada, but on July 16 the Court denied her leave to appeal, closing off the legal system as an avenue to address this injustice. Shockingly, the Supreme Court also ordered Ms. Lesiuk to pay the costs associated with her appeal application. This will certainly cast a chill over low income people hoping to use the Supreme Court to enforce their rights.

Source: Excerpt from Income Security Advocacy Centre, www.incomesecurity.org. Reprinted with permission.

There is indeed a strong correlation between the net UI/EI spending and the performance of the economy. This is especially true with respect to UI/EI benefit payments but much less so with respect to UI/EI premiums. The analysis suggests that the UI/EI premium rate (which is, arguably, not automatic but changed by policy choice) appears to have moved pro-cyclically — that is, its rate has been raised in downturns and reduced in upturns. The stabilizing impact of the UI/EI system has varied over the last fifteen years, reflecting the changes in the size of the program relative to that of the economy. An average estimate of the stabilizing effect of the program is about 10 to 13 percent. This means that the existence of EI reduced the decline in employment of the last economic turndown in 2001/02 by 10 to 13 percent (Dungan and Murphy 2003 as referenced in Human Resources and Social Development Canada 2006b, 47).

Conclusion

Social insurance programs for those in the labour force are meant to protect workers from the consequences of particular risks, such as injury on the job or unemployment. Workers' Compensation programs represent the first legislated recognition of collective responsibility for social welfare in the world. A healthy, well-trained, and secure labour force is essential for our economy to grow. Cuts to Canada's EI program threaten to weaken these positive aspects of our labour force. As the Canadian government strives to cut back expenditures, it has tightened and targeted the EI program. It is clear, however, that Canada requires a strong EI program in order to maintain a vibrant workforce.

In the past two decades, Canada has faced new challenges as the world economy shifted to an information- and knowledge-based economy with rapid globalization. Throughout the 1980s and 1990s, governments cut social spending, pushed people off income security programs into paid employment, and moved towards free trade in the hope that this would solve the problem. It is clear at the beginning of the twenty-first century that this is not sufficient.

New ideas are emerging that respond to these changing circumstances. Labour market participation does not guarantee an exit out of poverty. Governments are recognizing that families have particular needs, and there is new activity in the area of income supplements for low wages. There is a clear need to have better integration of EI, Social Assistance, and child benefits.

Chapter Summary

Key Concepts

- B/U ratio
- Claim period
- Clawback rule
- Contributory negligence
- Employment Insurance (EI)
- Fellow servant rule
- Meredith principle
- Parental leave benefits
- Social insurance schemes
- Types of Employment Insurance benefits
- Voluntary assumption of risk
- Workers' Compensation (WC)

Review Questions

1. Who in Canadian society benefits from EI and WC, and in what ways do they benefit?
2. What was the primary impetus for the introduction of Workers' Compensation in the rising industrialized countries of the world, including Canada? Explain.
3. What are the "unholy trinity" defences that made it extremely difficult for employees to successfully sue an employer? Define and explain each defence.
4. What is the Meredith principle, and what is its significance?
5. In what ways did Bill C-12, the new *Employment Insurance Act*, change Unemployment Insurance in Canada in 1995? What have been two significant negative impacts on employees?
6. What maternity and parental benefits are available to Canadians?
7. What is the B/U ratio, and how has it changed over the past decade?

Exploring Social Welfare

1. Go the HRSDC website for a review of the history of Unemployment Insurance (www.hrsdc.gc.ca/en/ei/history/unemployment_insurance.shtml). Pick one of the major bills that enacted EI/UI, such as Bill C-229, C-69, C-21, and so forth, and outline the important attributes of the EI/UI program at the time of this bill. How does the program differ now? Is the current EI program better or worse, and how so?

2. Visit the Government of Canada's Youth Employment Strategy website (available from www.youth.gc.ca). What are the major components of the strategy? Do you think that it will address the major issues facing youth? Write a brief review of the strategy outlining your opinion.

Websites

Social Policy in Ontario
    http://spo.laurentian.ca/
The online guide to social policy in Ontario has information on a variety of topics including service sectors, policy issue round-tables, the history of program development, Ontario's social context, and social planning.

The History of Unemployment Insurance
    www.hrsdc.gc.ca/en/ei/history/unemployment_insurance.shtml
This site offers a complete history of EI online.

Canadian Policy Research Networks (CPRN)
    www.cprn.org
Founded in 1994, CPRN's mission is to create knowledge and lead public debate on social and economic issues important to the well-being of Canadians. It currently has four themes or networks in the areas of family, health, public involvement, and work.

References

Battle, Ken, Michael Mendelson, and Sherri Torjman. 2006. *Towards a New Architecture for Canada's Adult Benefits.* Ottawa: Caledon Institute of Social Policy.

Bédard, Marcel, Jean-François Bertrand, and Louis Grignon. 2000. *The Unemployed Without Recent Employment.* Ottawa: HRDC.

Bridges, W. 1994. *Job Shift — How to Prosper in a Workplace Without Jobs.* Reading, Massachusetts: Addison-Wesley Publishing Company.

Canadian Labour Congress. 2000a. *Analysis of UI Coverage for Women.* Ottawa: CLC. http://action.web.ca/home/clcpolcy/attach/wom-ui-00e.pdf.

Canadian Labour Congress. 2000b. *Left Out in the Cold: The End of UI for Canadian Workers.* Ottawa: Canadian Labour Congress (CLC). http://canadianlabour.ca/index.php/Unemployment_Insuran/556.

Canadian Labour Congress. 2002. *Unemployment Insurance Bulletin.* Ottawa: Canadian Labour Congress (CLC).

Human Resources and Social Development Canada. 2005. *Employment Insurance Monitoring and Assessment Report.* Ottawa: HRDC.

Human Resources and Social Development Canada. 2006a. *Employment Insurance (EI) and Maternity, Parental, and Sickness Benefits.* www.hrsdc. gc.ca/en/ei/types/special.shtml.

Human Resources and Social Development Canada. 2006b. *Summative Evaluation of EI Part I: A Summary of Evaluation Knowledge to Date.* Ottawa: Human Resources and Social Development Canada. www.hrsdc. gc.ca/en/cs/sp/hrsd/evaluation/reports/sp-ah-685-06-06/page00.shtml.

Human Resources Development Canada. 1994. *Agenda: Jobs and Growth — Improving Social Security in Canada.* Ottawa: HRDC.

Human Resources Development Canada. 1998. *An Analysis of Employment Insurance Benefit Coverage.* Ottawa: HRDC.

Human Resources Development Canada. 1999. *Occupational Injuries and Their Cost in Canada, 1993–1999.* Ottawa: HRDC.

Human Resources Development Canada. 2003. *Employment Insurance Monitoring and Assessment Report.* Ottawa: HRDC.

Meredith, W.R. 1913. *Meredith Report.* Toronto: Legislative Assembly of Ontario.

Office of the Auditor General. 2002. *Report of the Auditor General of Canada.* Ottawa: Office of the Auditor General.

Office of the Auditor General. 2005. *Report of the Auditor General of Canada.* Ottawa: Office of the Auditor General.

Shillington, R. 2001. *Access to Maternity Benefits.* Ottawa: Trisat Resources.

Statistics Canada. 2003. *Government Transfer Payments to Persons, Provincial Economic Accounts, Annual (Dollars).* CANSIM Table 384-0009.

Swedish Institute. 2001. *Fact Sheets on Sweden: Taxes in Sweden.* The Swedish Institute. www.sweden.se/upload/Sweden_se/english/factsheets/SI/SI_FS35y_Taxes_in_Sweden/fs35y.pdf.

11 People Living in Poverty

The Policy Context

Why do some people in Canada continue to live in poverty when public income security programs exist? Many believe that a new approach to poverty is needed. Building the labour market is obviously important, but financial support for families that are undergoing difficult transitions in their lives is also vital. This is largely the role of minimum income programs such as Social Assistance. But are they doing what is needed?

Many families and individuals experience difficult life events, challenges, or changes that may affect their capacity to function effectively in their private and public lives. Incidental and unexpected events in any aspect of an individual's life can lead to stress, coping difficulties, and loss of employment. The reaction of individuals and families to stress will vary. People may lack coping mechanisms, they may come up against a particular type of challenge that is too serious

> **"** In 2005 almost half a million of the 1.7 million people on welfare were children."
>
> *— National Council of Welfare,* Welfare Incomes 2005, Fact Sheet #9: Number of People on Welfare, *revised October 2006 (Ottawa: National Council of Welfare, 2006)*

or difficult to deal with, or they may lack internal and external support systems. In some cases, these difficulties result in job loss, alienation, and isolation.

When a person has no source of income, he or she is entitled to what is commonly known as Social Assistance (SA), otherwise known as *welfare*. SA is a province-based minimum income program for people who are defined as "in need." Strict eligibility criteria, known as *needs tests*, are applied to determine whether people are in need. If the person has a disability, he or she is entitled to disability support, normally with higher benefits. In Ontario this is called the *Ontario Disability Support Program (ODSP)* (see Chapter 13). Social Assistance is a program of last resort with roots in early charity relief and the English Poor Laws.

Generally, Canadians access Social Assistance only when all other public and private means of support are exhausted. In 2005, 1.8 million Canadians, or 6.6 percent of the Canadian population, received Social Assistance. This compares to 2.9 million in 1996, or almost 10 percent of the Canadian population (HRSDC 2006, Table 435). The cost of these benefits was $20.5 billion in 2003, compared with $21.2 billion in 1997 (HRDC 2000, Table 524).

Each of Canada's ten provinces and three territories designs, administers, and delivers its own Social Assistance program. Entitlement is based on a test, which takes into account the assets and income of the applicant's household and its basic needs (food, clothing, shelter and utilities, household necessities, and personal needs) as defined in provincial legislation. Each province also establishes its own administrative and categorical eligibility requirements for those applying for benefits.

The federal Department of Indian and Northern Affairs is responsible for the Social Assistance for Registered Indians living on reserves. Programs are delivered either by the provincial government or by an Aboriginal agency (depending on the province) in accordance with the prevailing Social Assistance rules and regulations of that province. The Department of Indian and Northern Affairs covers the entire cost of such assistance.

The Rise of Poor Relief and Social Assistance

Before the twentieth century, the dominant explanation for poverty was that people who were poor had a defect in their character. The general public consensus was that persons living in poverty were unwilling to seek employment and had to be forced to work.

As we saw in Chapter 2, after the Elizabethan Poor Law legislation of 1601, unemployed people were harshly punished to discourage vagrancy and begging. If people could not be coerced to work through punitive efforts, they were forced into corrective and common jails (Guest 1999). Another widespread belief was that offering relief to the poor encouraged them not to work and, as a result, it was illegal to assist the able-bodied poor. In the nineteenth century, after the reform of the Poor Laws, relief was available only through the almshouse (commonly referred to as the *poorhouse* or the *workhouse*). In the 1800s and earlier, caring for the poor in Canada was the responsibility of the family, churches, or the local community. In Quebec, the Catholic Church was responsible for income security for the poor, whereas in the Maritimes, the application of Elizabethan Poor Laws gave the responsibility to the local authorities. Collective self-help was essential to survival in sparsely settled pioneer communities in the West. The western provinces relied on public programs run by municipalities for health care and aid to the poor. Towards the end of World War I, Manitoba and British Columbia offered Mothers' Allowance programs. These programs were the first provincial measures to aid the poor in the West.

Canada's first public income security provisions for the poor were based on the Elizabethan Poor Laws. This style of relief was implemented in Nova Scotia in 1758, in New Brunswick in 1783, and in Ontario in 1791. There were two styles of relief offered by private charities and municipalities — indoor and outdoor relief. Outdoor relief was available to the recipient in his or her own home, and indoor relief was given in an institution, such as a House of Industry. Rather than cash, most relief during the 1700s was in the form of food or food vouchers, clothes, and fuel.

The concept of "less eligibility" was established in the English system of poor relief. According to the concept of less eligibility, relief benefits had to be lower than what could be earned by the lowest paid labourer. Relief administrators were concerned that higher levels of relief would encourage workers to become dependent on the benefits. During this era, not only did less eligibility ensure that no one would receive in relief more than what might be available from the poorest paying job, but it also kept people poor and provided few employment options other than low-paying and often dangerous jobs. Workers during the time of less eligibility described their workplaces in terms of detention rather than employment. Records from the labour commission reveal a pattern of exploitation, unhealthy workplaces, and immutable laws of supply and demand (Guest 1999).

Welfare systems were dominated by political practices in which social policies were used as instruments to regulate the poor (Rice and Prince 2000). The earliest studies of poverty were not concerned with how the poor lived in relation to those better off; they were concerned with establishing the minimum income necessary for survival. The early laws of poor relief were not intended to raise the standard of the poor; they were intended to keep that standard low to ensure a plentiful supply of cheap labour. This attitude is evident throughout history. It is especially evident during periods of economic growth and increased immigration; foreign workers were expected to roam

The National Council of Welfare

www.ncwcnbes.net

The National Council of Welfare (NCW) is a citizen's advisory body to the Minister of Human Resources and Social Development Canada on matters of concern to low-income Canadians. Their annual *Welfare Incomes* report details welfare rates by province and compares this to LICOs.

the country, take work wherever it was available, and be thankful for the wages offered. A typical example of this occurred during the advancement of the railway system. The Canadian Pacific Railway felt that immigrants could serve as a cheap and plentiful source of labour in the expansions of new branch lines.

In Canada during the nineteenth century, this view was accompanied by the idea that there were unlimited work opportunities, and therefore there was no need for poor relief. The first constitution of Ontario, for example, did not carry any provision for poor relief. But conditions of misery became increasingly obvious in cities and towns during the industrial revolution of the late-nineteenth and early-twentieth centuries. Canadian people reacted accordingly. Social unrest led to the Canadian trade union movement and the widespread appeal of radical political ideas and parties. Poverty and inequality became an important issue in churches in Canada, and this spawned the Social Gospel movement. As a result, committees were formed, conferences were held, and coalitions such as the Moral and Social Reform Council of Canada were organized to denounce capitalism and its effects on wages, sweatshops, and child labour (Guest 1999).

To an extent, the wealthy began to fear the consequences of poverty, which led to efforts to deal with the problem in Canada. One of the first efforts to look at the conditions of the poor was initiated by the Royal Commission on the Relations of Labour and Capital in 1889. This report contained numerous pages of testimony about the deplorable living and working conditions prevalent at the time. These testimonies and other observations led reformers to demand the involvement of the state and the public in a wide range of activities to curtail poverty.

Industrial development and the growth of poverty eventually led to demands for the development of public social welfare. In the early part of the century, a transition took place from private to public social welfare – social welfare was no longer seen as the private domain of families. Before the Great Depression of the 1930s, the country had very limited public Social Assistance measures. The government avoided intervening in the economy, believing that the free market would look after everyone. However, lessons learned from the Depression changed this outlook. During the Depression, people began to see that poverty was due less to individual inadequacy or laziness, and was more the result of common and insurable threats to the livelihood of all people. Following the two world wars, there was a desire for economic security and more acceptance of government intervention in society. After World War II, Keynesian economic ideas (discussed in detail in Chapter 3) provided an economic rationale for substantial government intervention in the economy. At this time, there was a communal desire by citizens and governments to devise government-funded income security assistance for the poor. Eventually, welfare or Social Assistance was instituted in all provinces as a program of last resort.

By the 1960s, a wide range of programs had been instituted to assist the poor. Each province had a different program, and there was little coordination and consistency between provinces. In an effort to consolidate Social Assistance and other income security and social service programs, the federal government introduced a new cost-sharing arrangement with the provinces in 1966 – the Canada Assistance Plan (CAP). CAP brought together a range of cost-shared income security and social services into one system. It also included several national standards. In April 1996, the Canada Health and Social Transfer (CHST) replaced CAP as a vehicle for federal funding. It was a block grant and includes health and post-secondary education. As described in Chapter 2, the CHST is now two separate grants, the Canada Health Transfer (CHT) and the Canada Social Transfer (CST).

Current welfare programs, now called Social Assistance, income support, or employment and financial assistance, provide additional support in the form of cash to help recipients meet expenses over and above basic needs, depending on the province.

Myths about the Poor

Programs of income security for the poor often have been based on myths about the poor. The 1988 *Transitions* report by the Social Assistance Review Committee in Ontario discovered a series of common misperceptions about people who use Social Assistance. As well, the National Anti-Poverty Organization (NAPO) and the Canadian Council on Social Development (CCSD) have documented a variety of myths. The following myths are prevalent today:

■ **POVERTY IS THE FAILURE OF THE INDIVIDUAL.** This is a stereotype or blame-oriented belief that has a long history. It began with early religious attitudes of the sixteenth century and was reinforced by Calvinist ideas. The reasoning was that paupers were being punished for hidden sins. This perception gradually shifted to beliefs underpinned by the Social Darwinism of the nineteenth century, which applied Darwin's biological theories to social life. This blame-oriented idea proposed that people of any energy and ability could make their way in life, and that incompetence and poverty were clear signs of biological and social inferiority. Although it is clear that increases in unemployment in Canada during the Depression and over the last few decades did not result from personal inadequacy, but rather from economic factors, there is still a sense that poverty results from personal failure. Many workers have lost their jobs for reasons beyond their control and cannot find work because it is not available. Many people are on welfare because they are temporarily unable to provide for themselves, often due to some personal or economic crisis beyond their control.

Canadian Council on Social Development

www.ccsd.ca

The CCSD is a non-governmental, non-profit organization founded in 1920; it seeks to develop and promote progressive social policies through research, consultation, public education, and advocacy. The publications catalogue provides an extensive list of publications that analyze poverty in Canada.

We often think that Canada provides all children with a decent start in life, but children who grow up in poor families are most likely to suffer chronic health problems and drop out of school.

- **THE MAJORITY OF WELFARE RECIPIENTS ARE ABLE-BODIED MEN WHO ARE SIMPLY LAZY.** There is a straightforward rebuttal to this myth. One needs only to examine the demographic characteristics of individuals on Social Assistance. Studies have found that less than 15 percent of Social Assistance recipients are "employable" men. Many more are children (in the range of 30 to 40 percent) or people with a disability (25 to 30 percent) (CCSD 1998).

- **THE POOR DO NOT WANT TO WORK.** Most poor people do work full- or part-time, including over 60 percent of heads of poor households, and over 70 percent of poor unattached individuals. Of this population, 26 percent worked full-time, 34 percent worked part-time, 31 percent did not work at all, and 10 percent were unable to work. If we look at the people who are dependent on welfare, we see that about 38 percent are children. Another 16 percent are single mothers, many still caring for young children. If we look at the number of welfare cases, we find that about 27 percent are disabled people (National Council of Welfare 2002).

- **LONG-TERM DEPENDENCE ON WELFARE IS RARE IN CANADA.** In March 1997, 54 percent of the people on welfare had been on welfare continuously for 25 months or more (National Council of Welfare 1998, 24). According to the National Council of Welfare, there had been a rise in long-term cases in the years after 1990. The shorter-term cases tend to rise in bad economic times and fall in good times. A study by the HRDC called *Low Income (Poverty) Dynamics in Canada* (Finnie 2000) found that half of those earning low incomes from 1992 to 1996 were doing so temporarily. By contrast, 40 percent were in poverty throughout the entire period.

■ **Most female-led, single-parent families depend on Social Assistance.** In 1997, about one-third of single-parent families led by women relied on Social Assistance (National Council of Welfare 1998, 24). The other two-thirds were in the labour force. The labour force participation rate of lone parents has increased from 56 percent in 1973 to 66 percent in 1997 (Phipps and Lethbridge 2002, 6) to 68 percent in 2004 (Statistics Canada 2006b, 109).

■ **People on Social Assistance do not pay very much rent because they all live in subsidized housing.** There is not nearly enough public or assisted housing, therefore a very small portion of people on welfare live in subsidized housing.

■ **Poor people do not pay taxes.** In a 2004 report for the National Anti-Poverty Organization (NAPO), Andrew Mitchell and Richard Shillington found that low-income people would pay over $4 billion dollars in federal taxes in 2004. Of this, approximately 70 percent would come from federal commodity taxes. The remainder was from income taxes (12 percent), CPP/QPP contributions (12 percent), and EI contributions (5 percent) (Mitchell and Shillington 2004).

■ **Welfare rates are too generous.** All welfare rates are well below LICO and always have been. Some provinces are worse than others. Welfare benefits for single employable people are the least adequate, with 2005 rates ranging from 19 percent of LICO in New Brunswick to 46 percent of LICO in Newfoundland and Labrador. Welfare benefits for single-parent families ranged from 48 percent of LICO in Alberta to 73 percent of LICO in Newfoundland and Labrador (National Council of Welfare 2006, 10–14). Even using the Basic Needs Lines (BNLs), developed by Chris Sarlo at the Fraser Institute, welfare income is either below the BNL for single employable people or just above it. The BNLs are the lowest poverty lines ever calculated in Canada and are not taken seriously by Canadian policy experts or the international community.

■ **Poor people need to be taught basic life skills, such as budgeting.** Many who live far below the poverty line must spend all or most of their income on basic needs. Anyone who manages to feed and clothe a family on a very limited income already has budgeting skills.

■ **The welfare system is rife with cheating and fraud.** A study conducted by a national auditing firm estimated fraud to be within the range of 3 percent of the welfare budget (on the other hand, there are estimates that income tax fraud is in the order of 20 percent). The Ontario government reports that $46 million was saved due to catching people committing welfare fraud. Analysis of the government's claim (see the discussion later in this chapter) reveals that, of the 15,680 reductions or terminations due to "fraud," very few were actually convicted of fraud. Most of what the government reports as fraud is actually administrative error.

■ **WE CANNOT AFFORD THE SOCIAL PROGRAMS NEEDED TO ELIMINATE POVERTY.** This statement stems from the efficiency/equity trade-off concept discussed in Chapter 4. Canada is a very prosperous country with high rates of economic growth and GDP per capita. But Canada spends less on social security and other income support measures (including EI and welfare) as a share of the GDP than most European countries. In Canada, all "social protection" government transfers add up to only 18 percent of the GDP whereas France transfers 29 percent, Germany transfers 27 percent, the Netherlands transfers 33 percent, Finland transfers 36 percent, and Sweden transfers 40 percent (Bohácek 2002, 26). Countries with economies similar to ours have refused to tolerate high levels of family poverty. These countries provide more income and employment support to help families with children, and their economies still grow and thrive.

■ **ALL CHILDREN IN CANADA ARE ASSURED A DECENT START IN LIFE.** Recent studies show strong links between poverty and poor health and poor achievement at school. While infant mortality rates for all income groups are about half of what they were twenty years ago, according to the census, the rate for the lowest income group was still about double that of the highest. Children in poor families are more likely to suffer chronic health problems than other children. They are almost twice as likely to drop out of school. According to the Canadian Council on Social Development, there is finally hard statistical data showing that family income has a major effect on a child's well-being. To date, they have examined thirty-one outcomes and living conditions, and in each case they found a statistical association with family income levels. Recent studies by Statistics Canada have found that "higher income is almost always associated with better outcomes for children" (2006a, 4).

The list is long, but these are not the only myths about individuals and families that receive Social Assistance or live in poverty. It is important to be aware of such stereotypes and blame-oriented beliefs and to explore the possible reasons for their existence. The preceding points, and other information and data throughout the text, should provide facts that help to refute myths about the poor.

Social Assistance: A Minimum Income Program

As noted in Chapter 1, there are four broad categories of public income security programs: social insurance, minimum income, demogrants, and income supplementation. Social Assistance belongs in the minimum income category. It transfers income to people who have little or

Number of People

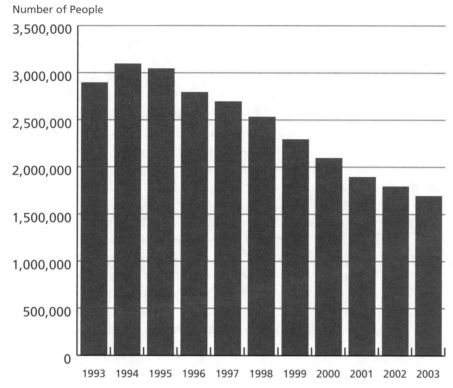

Figure 11.1: Estimated Number of People Receiving Welfare in Canada, 1993–2003

Source: Kerr, D., and Michalski, J. (2005). Income Poverty in Canada: Recent Trends among Canadian Families 1981–2002. *(London: Population Studies Centre at the University of Western Ontario), 9. Reprinted with permission.*

no employment or other income, and it supplies a bare minimum of funds for survival. The transfer is conditional, based on a needs test. A needs test looks at what the person needs in terms of both expenditure and income — or the difference between what they have and what they are required to spend to survive. It also considers the assets that could be sold to provide an income.

Figure 11.1 illustrates the dramatically declining use of Social Assistance in Canada. For example, between 1996 and 2003, the number of one-parent families relying on Social Assistance decreased by 51.8 percent (from 454,500 to 219,700 households). Similarly, the number of two-parent families with children relying on Social Assistance decreased by 57.8 percent (from 177,400 to 74,900 households). The overall number of children living in families relying on Social Assistance decreased by 50.4 percent (from 1,096,900 to 544,200 children).

Two factors are likely central in this decrease of Social Assistance use. First, economic growth in the late 1990s enabled many who were previously on Social Assistance to obtain employment. Historically, Social Assistance use has mirrored employment trends in this way. As discussed in Chapter 9, many people who stopped using Social Assistance found extremely low-paying jobs that did not elevate them out of poverty. The second key reason for the overall reduction in welfare recipients is welfare reform, which restricted eligibility. By making it harder to get Social Assistance, many provinces dramatically decreased caseloads.

Ontario Works Act

www.e-laws.gov.
on.ca/DBLaws/Statutes/
English/97o25a_e.htm

The *Ontario Works Act* is available through Ontario's e-Laws website (www.e-laws.gov.on.ca).

Constitutionally, Social Assistance is the jurisdiction and responsibility of the provinces. Although people talk about welfare as a single entity, there are really thirteen welfare systems in Canada: one in each province and territory, including the new territory of Nunavut. Despite the fact that each of the thirteen systems is different, they have many common features. They all have complex regulations, including regulations about the eligibility for assistance, the rates of assistance, the amounts of other income recipients are allowed to keep, and the appeals process for applicants and recipients to question decisions regarding their cases. In Ontario, Social Assistance is currently legislated through the *Ontario Works Act*, 1997. Ontario is the only province where municipalities are responsible for delivering the program.

Welfare is a provincial responsibility, but all three levels of government fund it: the city or municipality, the province, and the federal government. For example, in Ontario, a typical city paid approximately 15 percent of the costs, the province paid approximately 57 percent, and the federal government paid approximately 28 percent.

Eligibility for Social Assistance is based on general administrative rules that vary widely throughout the country, such as the following:

- Applicants must be of a certain age (usually between 18 and 65).
- Full-time students of post-secondary educational institutions may qualify for assistance in some provinces and territories, if they meet stringent conditions. In other provinces and territories, students cannot apply for assistance without leaving their studies.
- Parents must try to secure any court-ordered maintenance support to which they are entitled.
- People who are disabled require medical certification of their conditions.
- Strikers are not eligible in most jurisdictions.
- Immigrants must try to obtain financial assistance from their sponsors.

The Poverty Gap

One way the adequacy of Social Assistance benefits can be calculated is to compare the welfare rates to LICO. The difference between the two is the poverty gap (see Chapter 9). Table 11.1 shows the total Social Assistance income per type of household as a percentage of LICO.

Researchers calculating the adequacy of Social Assistance compare benefits with the costs of basic necessities, such as food and shelter. According to professors at the Department of Nutritional Sciences at the University of Toronto, a nutritional diet — as defined by the Ontario Ministry of Health standards — is out of reach for Toronto's Social Assistance recipients (Vozoris, Davis, and Tarasuk 2002, 38). The professors calculated the affordability of a nutritious diet by comparing the monthly costs considered essential for a basic standard of living with the average monthly income of three household types: one-person, single-parent, and two-parent households. They found that if households live in market rental accommodations, income was insufficient to purchase a nutritious diet along with all the other essential items (36). "This speaks to the need for a review of welfare benefit levels and housing policies to ensure that people on these programs are not put at risk," says Tarasuk (email correspondence, October 2003).

The large discrepancies between welfare incomes and the cost of basic needs puts the health and well-being of Canadian children at risk. This not only affects their daily lives, but also their ability to keep pace with classmates in school and their future opportunities.

A Sample Calculation of Social Assistance Benefits

To provide an example, let us examine the benefit amounts in Ottawa, Ontario. In Ottawa, the Ontario Works calculations for establishing financial eligibility are based on basic needs, the presence of a spouse or same-sex partner, the number of members in the benefit unit, and the age of any dependent children. Shelter allowance is then added to this amount. It includes actual costs for rent, mortgage, taxes, board and lodging, and utility and fuel costs, up to the maximum levels. Emergency assistance is also considered. Table 11.3 is used by welfare workers (who are generally called case workers or case coordinators) in Ontario to calculate the amount that an individual or family would receive for basic needs. By adding this basic need amount with the basic shelter allowance amount in Table 11.2, the total monthly benefit is determined. Shelter is calculated based on the maximum amount payable in accordance with the benefit unit size. This is a maximum amount – one would get a lower amount if their actual shelter costs were lower.

Using the two charts, you can calculate the maximum total Social Assistance benefits as follows: single person at $520 per month ($195 basic allowance plus $325 maximum shelter allowance); family of four with two children under 12 at $1,178 ($576 basic allowance plus $602 maximum shelter allowance).

Child Tax Benefit

In addition to Social Assistance or welfare, families with children living on low income are eligible for the **Canada Child Tax Benefit (CCTB)** basic benefit. In addition, some low-income families received the National Child Benefit Supplement (NCBS), where the clawback was not applied. Chapter 12 provides additional details on child benefits.

As detailed in Chapter 12, the federal government began paying child-related benefits to low-income families in 1998. In 2007, families with a net income under the threshold of $36,378 received the CCTB tax credit benefit of $1,255 per child, with additional amounts for children under age seven and for families with more than two children. Fami-

Table 11.1: Welfare Incomes as Percentage of LICO, 2005

Type of Household	Percentage of LICO
Single, employable	34%
Single, disabled	58%
Single parent, one child	56%
Two parents, two children	50%

Source: Adapted from the National Council of Welfare. 2006. *Welfare Incomes 2005*. Ottawa: National Council of Welfare, 75. www.ncwcnbes.net.

Table 11.2: Basic Shelter Allowance

Benefit Unit Size	Maximum Monthly Shelter Allowance
1	$342
2	$538
3	$583
4	$634
5	$683
6 or more	$708

Source: O. Reg. 134/98, as amended to O. Reg. 464/06, s. 42 (2) 2. © Queen's Printer for Ontario, 2006.

Table 11.3: Basic Need Allowances

No. of Dependants Other than a Spouse	No. of Dependants 13 Years and Over	No. of Dependants 0–12 years	Recipient	Recipient and Spouse or Same-Sex Partner
0	0	0	$206	$411
1	0	1	$470	$501
1	1	0	$512	$539
2	0	2	$559	$606
2	1	1	$602	$644
2	2	0	$640	$682

Note: For each additional dependant, add $144 if the dependant is 13 years of age or over, or $106 if the dependant is less than 13 years of age.

Source: O. Reg. 134/98, as amended to O. Reg. 464/06, s. 41 (1) 1. © Queen's Printer for Ontario, 2006.

Table 11.4: Annual Social Assistance Amounts by Type of Household, Ontario, 2005

Type of Household	Social Assistance	Other Benefits*	Total
Single, employable	$6,400	$607	$7,007
Single, disabled	$11,450	$607	$12,057
Single parent, one child	$10,120	$4,130	$14,451
Two parents, two children	$12,321	$7,071	$19,302

*Other benefits include additional Social Assistance benefits, the Federal Child Tax Benefit, the Provincial/Territorial Child Benefits, the Federal GST Credit and Provincial tax credits.

Source: Adapted from the National Council of Welfare. 2006. *Welfare Incomes 2005*. Ottawa: National Council of Welfare, 11. www.ncwcnbes.net.

lies with incomes under $20,435 are also eligible for the full NCBS of $1,945 for the first child. The amount drops slightly for additional children. The NCBS amount decreases as income increases over $20,435. Families are no longer eligible for the NCBS when their income reaches $36,378.

A controversial aspect of these benefits is the clawback of the NCBS portion for Social Assistance recipients. The CCTB portion is received by all families with children whose net income is below a certain level, including families on Social Assistance, but the NCBS is taken away from families on Social Assistance (in most provinces). The term "clawback" refers to this taking back of the monies.

Only those families on welfare who live in Newfoundland, New Brunswick, Nova Scotia, Manitoba, and Quebec see an increase in their incomes because of the NCBS. The other provinces and territories claw back the money in different ways. In Prince Edward Island, Ontario, British Columbia, the Yukon, and the Northwest Territories, the welfare departments consider the supplement to be non-exempt income that triggers a cut in the family welfare cheque. In Saskatchewan and Alberta, the provincial governments have actually cut welfare benefits by the amount of the supplement (see Chapter 12 for more information). In 2006, Prime Minister Stephen Harper's government introduced "Choices in Child Care," now called the *Universal Child Care Benefit (UCCB)*, which provides $100 per child per month. However, several groups criticize this program, including the Caledon Institute for Social Policy, because the benefit will be considered taxable income in the hands of the lowest income earners, and because the Canada Child Tax Benefit, which supports low-income families, will be cancelled.

Ontario Child Benefits

The 2007 provincial budget announced a new Ontario Child Benefit (OCB) of $250 per child for all low-income families, whether the parents work or receive social assistance. The benefit will increase to a maximum of $1,100 per child by 2011. In 2007 the benefit will be adjusted by 3.4 cents for every dollar of adjusted family net income above $20,000. In 2008 this will increase to 8 cents. With this new program, the Ontario government claims that it has effectively eliminated the NCBS clawback by "flowing through" more money than it takes in.

Case Study:

Mary, Amira, and Marie: Different Women Surviving

Mary, a single woman, spends $350 per month on rent for her bachelor apartment. She spends a further $30 per month on utilities. Since Mary lives in Ontario, she will receive a maximum of $195 per month for basic living expenses and a maximum of $325 per month for rent, even though her rent exceeds this. She will receive a total of $520 per month — this is the provincial maximum (or the maximum barring exceptions — more money could be possible if a physician recommended a special diet, or if Mary lived in the far north of Ontario, for example). After rent and utilities, this leaves Mary with $140 each month with which to pay for food, clothing, transportation, and other expenses.

Amira, a single mother, has one five-year-old daughter. Their one-bedroom apartment costs $450 per month, **continued›**

Case Study:

Mary, Amira, and Marie: Different Women Surviving (continued)

and their utilities cost a further $50 per month. Amira receives $446 per month as a basic needs allowance and another $500 to pay for shelter. The maximum she can receive is $957 per month. Amira also receives a back-to-school allowance for her daughter each July. She receives $69 for this allowance because her daughter is under age 13 — when she is over age 13, Amira will receive $128 to pay for her school-related costs. Each November, Amira receives $105 as a winter clothing allowance for her child. For all other expenses, including child care, Amira must rely on the $446 dollars per month she has left after paying her rent.

Marie is homeless. Although she is eligible for the $196 per month in basic needs allowance, in order to receive her $325 per month shelter allowance, Marie must provide receipts to prove she is using the money to pay for shelter. If Marie does find housing, she will become eligible for the Community Start-Up Fund, which will help her with paying the last month's rent and other start-up costs, such as new dishes and furniture. She will only be eligible for this fund once within a twelve-month period and is allowed to draw a maximum of $799 from the fund within that year. A family moving into new housing would be able to request up to $1,500 within a twelve-month period. ■

Dorothy: Working on Welfare

Dorothy and her husband Harry managed to survive on their combined earned income along with some Social Assistance. Dorothy wanted to leave her husband because of his alcoholism and his "temper fits." She could not afford to rent her own apartment, so she applied for subsidized housing and was placed on the waiting list. Five years later, her name came up on the list and she separated from her husband.

Dorothy and her four children now live on $950 per month from Social Assistance and $550 per month from the Canada Child Tax Benefit — $1,500 in total (as of 2005). Recently, Dorothy obtained part-time employment at a hamburger chain and makes about $350 per month. Welfare recipients are allowed a certain earnings exemption, so she is allowed to keep her entire earnings. In her case, with the four children, she is allowed to keep up to $423 per month. If she were single, her flat-rate exemption would only be $143. If Dorothy earns more than her exemption, she will lose some of her income. For the first twelve months that she has earnings, a full 25 percent variable   **continued⟩**

Case Study:

Dorothy: Working on Welfare (continued)

exemption applies. This means that she retains 25 percent of her earnings above $423. Between the thirteenth and the twenty-fourth month, the variable exemption falls to 15 percent, and for the months over twenty-four it falls to zero.

The extra earnings allow Dorothy to survive, especially given the health problems of her youngest child. He has asthma, and the extra medical supplies and transportation cause her expenses to exceed her income. Dorothy's ex-husband is supposed to pay $900 per month in child support, but Dorothy has yet to see a cheque. He says that he does not have any income, but Dorothy suspects that he is working in construction and is being paid in cash. Even if she did get support from her husband, her welfare benefits would be reduced dollar-for-dollar. Dorothy wants to find a job that pays more or offers more hours. She has been on Social Assistance for over two years now, so she knows that even if she finds a job that pays well, she will only be able to keep $423. She feels trapped and wonders if her situation will ever change. ■

Carlos: Educated Poor

Carlos is 26 and came to Canada as a refugee five years ago, settling in Toronto. His homeland had been completely destroyed and he fled for his life. His younger sister is developmentally challenged and she lives with him. Any job that he gets just barely covers the cost of paying for someone to take care of his sister. She needs special care and does not speak English, so it is very difficult to find care.

He is a well-educated man and worked as a physician in his home country. When he arrived in Canada, he found that the Canadian Medical Association did not recognize his medical degree, and he was forbidden to work in his profession. He was immediately placed on Social Assistance, and encouraged to "upgrade his skills." He was unable to find a way to gain Canadian medical credentials, so he enrolled in a college nursing program.

He was enrolled as a full-time student, but found it impossible to dedicate himself to full-time work and full-time study. He did get a $2,500 Special Bursary, but that made him ineligible for the Ontario Student Assistance Program (OSAP) loans. Eventually, Carlos changed to part-time studies. His job pays $7.50 per hour — that is only $14,625 per year without holidays. He found that it was impossible to live in Toronto on that money, and pay tuition on top of it. He was left with no choice but to postpone his studies. ■

Living on Welfare

Bare numbers do little to illuminate the challenges facing people on Social Assistance. The following cases may reveal what life on welfare or disability benefits is actually like.

Determining Eligibility

In order to qualify for Social Assistance, Canadians must meet the criteria for three eligibility tests: financial eligibility, administrative eligibility, and categorical eligibility.

- To meet the financial eligibility requirement, an applicant must show the need for Social Assistance. A needs test compares the household's assets with its needs. Initially, the household's non-exempted assets are examined to confirm that they do not exceed the maximum level set by provincial regulation. These levels vary both among provinces and across application categories. For example, a single person must have fewer assets than a single parent in order to qualify for Social Assistance. Once it has been established that an applicant's assets do not exceed the maximum, the household's income is compared with its needs. When the cost of a household's needs is greater than its available income, Social Assistance may be granted. In some provinces, Social Assistance may be granted even if the household has surplus income. An applicant must prove that the surplus is necessary in order to pay for recurring special needs.

- Administrative eligibility calls for Social Assistance applicants to fulfill certain administrative requirements. In most provinces, this entails the completion of an application (although, in Ontario, the process is now undertaken through an automated phone system). In addition, applicants are required to provide evidence that they meet other eligibility criteria. Evidence may be in the form of bank books, pay stubs, or doctors' notes to support claims of disability. An applicant must meet with a worker in order to discuss his or her situation and must sign a waiver giving permission for the worker and the Social Assistance authority to contact other agencies to verify information. Finally, an applicant must agree to contact the office immediately should any change in circumstances result in an increase of household income.

- Categorical eligibility refers to the different types of reasons why applicants might request assistance. While all applicants are presumed to be in need, different criteria for needs are considered. Criteria can depend on whether the applicant is elderly, disabled, a single parent, or otherwise employable. There are consistent policies across all provinces with regard to individuals in certain categories. For example, in the case of a single parent who is in need due to lack of child support payments, the parent must take on the responsibility of pursuing the absent parent. "Employable" applicants must agree to undergo training (or community work projects in Ontario) in order to receive assistance. Some categories of people are ineligible for Social Assistance. For example, sponsored immigrants and nominated relatives are considered the responsibility of the sponsor and would only be granted Social Assistance under very special circumstances. Students and the elderly are generally considered categorically ineligible.

The Legislative and Policy Context

The nature of Canadian federalism and disputes over funding and delivery of income security programs have led to legislation that attempts to define federal-provincial responsibilities.

The **Canada Assistance Plan (CAP)**, mentioned earlier, was instrumental in standardizing and funding Social Assistance nationwide and was in effect between 1966 and 1996. From the plan's inception until 1991, the federal government paid 50 percent of the cost of welfare in all the provinces and territories. Further details on the history and development of CAP can be found in Chapter 2.

Under CAP, provincial Social Assistance legislation contained conditions that clients had to respect to stay eligible for welfare. With regard to Social Assistance, the federal government established certain rules or standards that the provinces had to adhere to in order to receive CAP funding:

- Welfare must be given on a test of need (not means).
- No work for welfare. When somebody applies for welfare, they cannot be told that they must take a specific job offered by the welfare agency in order to get a cheque. This does not mean that there is no obligation on the part of the recipient to work. If an "appropriate" job comes along, the recipient must take it. In addition, work activity or training is permitted.
- No residence requirement is involved. This means that a person needing welfare can claim it in any city or province.
- There must be an appeals system, formalized in provincial law.

Beginning in 1991, the Canada Assistance Plan began to change. The first change was the so-called "cap on CAP" under which the three wealthiest provinces received a limited amount of federal support rather than the full 50 percent initially guaranteed by CAP. The amount contributed by the federal government was clawed back until 1996, at which point the Canada Assistance Plan was replaced with the **Canada Health and Social Transfer (CHST)**.

The replacement of one federal subsidy program with another may not seem like a dramatic change, but the major drop in federal

WELFARE IN BRITISH COLUMBIA

The British Columbia government introduced two bills in 2002 that dramatically changed welfare legislation in British Columbia: Bills 26 and 27. BC is the latest province to restrict and cut welfare.

Bill 26, the Employment and Assistance Act, includes the following changes:

- Eligible employable persons will receive assistance for a maximum of two years out of every five years.
- People convicted of welfare fraud will be permently ineligible for assistance.
- The independent Income Assistance Appeal Board will be eliminated and replaced with a tribunal directly appointed by the Minister of Human Resources.

These legislative changes are being made in the context of other dramatic cuts to welfare:

- Individuals must job seek for three weeks before being eligible to apply for welfare.
- University and college students are no longer eligible for income assistance.
- Seniors aged 55–59 will have their rates reduced by $50 a month, while seniors aged 60–64 will have their rates reduced by nearly $100 a month.
- Benefits for employable individuals aged 60–64 are reduced by $98 per month, and for employable couples age 55–59 are reduced $94 per month.
- The benefits of employable couples aged 60–64 have dropped by $145 per month.
- Single parents have seen their benefits reduced by $43 per month, while payments to employable individuals aged 55–59 have fallen $47 per month.
- Single parents will now be expected to seek work when their children are three years old, not seven.
- Shelter allowances were also reduced by between $55 and $75 per month.
- Homemaker services have been entirely eliminated.

Bill 27, the Employment and Assistance for Persons with Disabilities Act, includes the following changes:

- There is now a reassessment of all people on disability benefits.
- There are new, stricter definitions of "disability."
- The disability designation is no longer be permanent.

One of the most punitive changes to the BC legislation is the assistance limit of two years out of every five years. This two-year maximum rule is unprecedented in Canada, and denies assistance when in need as a human right. The rule would force people without income into emergency shelters and food banks. The only possible benefit from such a policy is a decrease in welfare caseloads and government expenditures. Many analysts question whether this is the correct way to cut government spending.

As severe opposition to the time-limit rule increased, the BC government issued twenty-five exemptions that virtually exempted everyone from the rule. However, the reforms still had the expected result of dropping thousands off assistance. According to *BC Employment and Assistance Month Statistics* (2007), total welfare recipients for 2001 were 191,937, and by 2006 there were only 60,823, (Government of British Columbia 2007, 1).

Another rule states that applicants aged 19 and over must demonstrate that they have been financially independent for two consecutive years (including any time spent receiving Unemployment Insurance benefits) before they are eligible to apply for welfare. There is no defensible rationale for this rule, except perhaps to send a message to youth that they should either be in school or working at any available job. Some believe that it is causing an increase in the numbers of youth living on the streets. David Carrigg reported in the January 22, 2003, edition of the *Vancouver Courier* that, in the winter of 2003, the Dusk to Dawn youth drop-in centre in downtown Vancouver stated that the number of youths using its facilities had reached seventy-five per night, up from an average of from forty to fifty per night six months earlier (itself an increase over the previous year). Deena Franks of Family Services of Greater Vancouver attributes this jump in part to BC's new welfare rules.

monies to the provinces resulted in the federal government's inability to maintain the national standards. A key change is the shift from cost-sharing with CAP, where the federal government paid a 50 percent share of the province's social spending, to a per-person transfer that is fixed regardless of actual costs. In addition, Social Assistance funds were now being drawn from the same pool as money for education and health. As a result, four of five standards previously outlined under the Canada Assistance Plan were dropped under the CHST.

The most notable and immediate change was the introduction of "workfare" in Ontario. Work for welfare was not allowed under CAP, but this standard was dropped under the CHST funding plan. Ontario immediately adopted a workfare scheme in the wake of this change.

The CHST had profound impacts on welfare. There is a fundamental difference in the "extent of compulsion" between the reciprocity condition that was inherent in programs under CAP, and the workfare that emerged after the CHST was implemented. CAP supported provincial rules that required employable people on welfare to do something to help themselves. This could involve participating in an activity to improve their employability, such as going back to school, participating in a training program, or even working in a job placement or apprenticeship. It might also involve actively looking for a job. In the latter case, CAP even tolerated provincial rules requiring proof of job search efforts by clients. What CAP did not support was workfare in its formal sense — the requirement to work for a specific number of hours in a designated job for basic welfare benefits. The CHST allows provinces to implement formal workfare (to be discussed shortly).

In 1999 the **Social Union Framework Agreement (SUFA)** was introduced. This is an agreement based upon mutual respect between the federal and provincial orders of government and a willingness to work more closely together. After the unilateral discontinuation of CAP by the federal government, SUFA aimed at reducing the fallout and smoothing out relations. SUFA covers a range of programs such as medicare, social services, education, and the manner in which these programs are funded, administered, and delivered (policy). Three major social policy initiatives have been launched using the SUFA: the National Child Benefit, early childhood education, and services for persons with disabilities. Further information is available at www.socialunion.ca.

In 2004, the CHST was divided into two separate transfers: the Canada Health Transfer (CHT) in support of health, and the Canada Social Transfer (CST) in support of post-secondary education, Social Assistance, and social services (including early childhood development).

Welfare Reform Debates

Several reforms of Social Assistance have been tried or considered over the past few decades. In some cases these reforms have sparked controversy. Three of these reforms will be discussed here: workfare, the "spouse-in-the-house" rule, and the zero-tolerance rule concerning welfare fraud. Many of the recent reforms have been directed at increasing work incentives or decreasing eligibility.

Workfare

Some provincial welfare programs require applicants to work as a term of eligibility. This is commonly known as workfare, and it has drawn criticism. Refusal to participate in the program results in some sort of penalty. For example, workfare could require people to work at specific jobs in order to get a government cheque, or it could mean that people receive a smaller cheque if they refuse to accept work through a government program. It might also require applicants to select retraining or pursue self-employment programs. Workfare placements could involve working in a community or social service agency. Applicants may also choose community work placements as a workfare option for the purposes of increasing skills, knowledge, and networks in the labour market.

Critics equate workfare as a return to the "work test" of the Elizabethan Poor Laws. Others cite research to show its failure in other countries — particularly the United States. It has also been criticized for being expensive to administer, and for taking away jobs from the paid labour force. Others see workfare as a blame-oriented approach that ignores job creation, arguing that people want to work, but that there are not enough good jobs.

It is difficult to discuss the issue of welfare without confronting the concept of workfare. Most of what is discussed under the rubric of workfare is actually a combination of tighter eligibility criteria, benefit cuts, a broadening of the definition of "employable," and more stringent enforcement of job search rules. These requirements are generally

Table 11.5: Estimated Annual Basic Social Assistance Income by Type of Household and Province/Territory, 2005

Newfoundland and Labrador		Saskatchewan	
Single, employable	$7,189	Single, employable	$6,328
Person with disability	$7,189	Person with disability	$7,680
Single parent, one child	$11,461	Single parent, one child	$9,052
Couple, two children	$11,941	Couple, two children	$12,488
Prince Edward Island		**Alberta**	
Single, employable	$5,988	Single, employable	$4,824
Person with disability	$7,848	Person with disability	$6,684
Single parent, one child	$10,061	Single parent, one child	$8,784
Couple, two children	$14,723	Couple, two children	$12,996
Nova Scotia		**British Columbia**	
Single, employable	$5,196	Single, employable	$6,120
Person with disability	$8,646	Person with disability	$10,277
Single parent, one child	$8,826	Single parent, one child	$10,147
Couple, two children	$11,652	Couple, two children	$11,893
New Brunswick		**Yukon**	
Single, employable	$3,201	Single, employable	$11,990
Person with disability	$6,762	Person with disability	$11,990
Single parent, one child	$8,860	Single parent, one child	$15,474
Couple, two children	$9,927	Couple, two children	$21,307
Quebec		**Northwest Territories**	
Single, employable	$6,721	Single, employable	$13,280
Person with disability	$9,793	Person with disability	$13,330
Single parent, one child	$8,089	Single parent, one child	$18,672
Couple, two children	$10,405	Couple, two children	$25,103
Ontario		**Nunavut**	
Single, employable	$6,400	Single, employable	$10,686
Person with disability	$11,540	Person with disability	$10,826
Single parent, one child	$10,321	Single parent, one child	$18,178
Couple, two children	$12,231	Couple, two children	$31,515
Manitoba			
Single, employable	$5,592		
Person with disability	$7,397		
Single parent, one child	$9,636		
Couple, two children	$14,057		

Source: Adapted from National Council of Welfare. 2006. *Welfare Incomes 2005*. Ottawa: National Council of Welfare, 10–14. www.ncwcnbes.net.

WORKFARE IN THE COURTS: THE GOSSELIN CASE

Between 1985 and 1989, the Quebec government slashed welfare benefits to all those under 30 deemed able to work. Louise Gosselin, a Montreal woman on Social Assistance, had her welfare benefits reduced. Gosselin saw her benefits plunge from $434 to $170 per month, which she says forced her into soup kitchens and into prostitution. She took the Quebec and Canadian governments to the Supreme Court. Her lawyer asked the court to grant compensation, arguing that Quebec violated Gosselin's fundamental right to a decent standard of living, and that under section 7 of the *Canadian Charter of Rights and Freedoms*, everyone has the right to "security of the person and the right not to be deprived thereof."

This was the first claim to the right to an adequate level of Social Assistance for those in need under the *Canadian Charter of Rights and Freedoms* and the first claim under any Canadian human rights legislation.

The Gosselin case provided the first opportunity for the Supreme Court to consider whether denying members of a disadvantaged group adequate financial assistance, which results in homelessness and deprivation of other basic necessities, is a violation of the *Canadian Charter of Rights and Freedoms*. The case raised the critical issue of whether the right to "security of the person" in section 7 of the Charter and the right to equality under section 15 oblige positive legal responsibilities upon governments to ensure an adequate level of income for Canadians when they are unable to provide for themselves.

In 2002 the Supreme Court ruled against Louise Gosselin, but many social rights advocates saw positive elements in the ruling. For example, the decision overruled the lower courts, which were reluctant to review compliance of government policies with economic and social obligations under the *Quebec Charter of Rights*.

In future cases, economic and social rights will be interpreted to include positive obligations on the part of the government.

not new. Before we can debate whether workfare helps or hinders the poor, we need to delineate what workfare really is.

It is important to distinguish between two types of workfare: formal workfare and de facto workfare. Formal workfare is officially prescribed in policy and procedures. It states that employable benefit recipients must work for a specific minimum number of work units (usually measured in hours per week) in a job that is approved by the welfare authority.

As of 2003, the province of Ontario is the closest to requiring formal workfare. All employable people in the Ontario Works program (single people, couples with and without children, single parents, and people aged 60 to 64 years) must agree to participate in one of the program's three active parts: employment supports (job-search services, referral to basic education, and job-specific skills training), employment placement (referral to job placement or self-employment development agencies), or community participation (unpaid community service activity). Community participation is the stream most readily identified with the concept of workfare. In this stream, welfare recipients can be required to work from 17 to 70 hours per month in a non-profit or public sector workplace approved under the program, in order to receive their basic welfare benefit.

Examples of community placement can include working with non-profit organizations: this may require helping with administration, fundraising, or marketing and promotional strategies, or working as support staff in child care. Other duties may include assisting the program staff with the delivery of specific programs, such as supervising youth or providing transportation to seniors.

De facto workfare is more common and occurs when provinces stringently enforce job-search and training requirements for employable people. The government pays monthly supplements to people who actively train for and find employment. Some provinces pay extra benefits to recipients who are participating in an approved training program or job-search activity. Other provinces deduct benefits from those who do not participate in mandated employment-related programs.

Workfare is hotly debated, and a variety of terms are used to describe it, such as formal or de facto workfare, welfare-to-work, and even trainfare. All provinces except Ontario like to call their programs "welfare-to-work" programs.

Terminology aside, it is clear that across the country, a significantly more coercive and disciplinary approach is being used in employment and training programs for welfare recipients. The programs are defining increasing numbers of people as employable. For example, in most provinces, single parents with children are now considered employable depending on the ages of their children. In addition, the programs have mandatory participation requirements and sanctions for non-compliance, and they generally operate with the mindset of "any job is a good job."

Sadly, most workfare schemes, whether de facto or formalized, rely on the same myths that have always plagued Social Assistance policy-making: that the average user is lazy and unmotivated and will stay on Social Assistance indefinitely if not forced to do useful work. On the contrary, Christopher Clark (a policy analyst for the Canadian Council on Social Development) points out that most households are simply finding it impossible to support basic needs while working in low-income jobs. As Clark writes, "if the alternative for most people on Social Assistance is a minimum-wage job, the labour market offers little hope for avoiding the poverty trap" (Clark 1995).

National Welfare to Work Study

http://publish.uwo.ca/~pomfret/wtw/#

The National Welfare to Work Study produced a comprehensive inventory of the different types of welfare-to-work programs across Canada.

Consider the scenario of a single mother with an eight-month-old child who is offered a minimum paying job. In order to take the job, she must find child care and pay for her own transportation. The parent must deal with the increased stress of not being with the child, the increased expenses related to child care and employment needs, and the discouragement of making the same or less income than she was receiving from assistance. The parent then begins to question the sense of working and succumbs to feelings of being trapped.

The "Spouse-in-the-House" Rule

Social workers and welfare advocacy groups have long been critical of the so-called spouse-in-the-house rule. In some cities, welfare workers were trained to determine whether a person of the opposite sex had stayed overnight at a welfare recipient's home (they looked for things such as an extra toothbrush or shoes). If it was determined that there was someone staying in the home, that person could have been deemed financially responsible for the person receiving welfare. The rule is still applied (as described below) in a modified way.

Until 1986, the definition of "spouse," under Social Assistance legislation, required a determination of whether opposite-sex co-residents were living together as "husband and wife." A *Canadian Charter of Rights and Freedoms* challenge to this definition prompted the Ontario government to bring in a new definition in 1987, which allowed welfare recipients to have up to three years of cohabitation before an economic interdependence was deemed to exist. This three-year rule matches the rule in the *Family Law Act*, which views unmarried couples as spouses if they have cohabited for at least three years.

Thus, under the 1987 definition, an individual welfare recipient co-habitating with a person of the opposite sex had a grace period of up to three years before being considered a spouse. After three years, to maintain an individual entitlement to Social Assistance, the recipient had to produce evidence to show that the social, familial, and economic aspects of the relationship did not amount to cohabitation. No legal challenge was made to the 1987 definition.

In 1995 the Ontario government replaced the 1987 definition of spouse with a new definition. A person could be a spouse in one of four ways. Three of those ways were similar to the previous definition: a person could be a spouse by self-declaration, by being required to pay support under a court order or domestic contract, or by having a support obligation under the *Family Law Act*. The Ontario government defined the fourth way to be a spouse more expansively than it had in the past. Under this provision, economic interdependence is deemed to exist as soon as there is evidence of cohabitation. This is the provision that is at issue.

This policy was deemed unconstitutional in 2000 by the Divisional Court and in 2002 by the Ontario Supreme Court. The definition of "spouse" is overly broad, and captures relationships that are not spousal or marriage-like. The 2002 court decision has ruled that citizens on welfare cannot be discriminated against just because they collect Social Assistance. The Ontario government began to appeal the case to the Supreme Court but dropped the appeal in 2004.

When the Ontario government announced that it would not pursue its appeal of the case, Ontario Attorney General Michael Bryant said, "It's not the business of government to decide when a family is a family." While the government has abandoned the appeal, welfare departments are still enforcing a variant of the spouse-in-the-house rule. A welfare recipient's benefits are reassessed after he or she has lived with an income-earner for three months. This is a shift from previous policy that terminated benefits. It appears that the revised policy might be unconstitutional as well.

The Women's Legal Education and Action Fund (LEAF), a national, non-profit organization working to promote equality for women and girls in Canada, agrees and further maintains that it directly affects single mothers who may want to form relationships. They believe that the law forces women and their children to be economically tied to a man, or that women must give up having live-in relationships or even sharing accommodations with men. The Charter Committee on Poverty Issues, an anti-poverty organization, says that Canada falls short in a number of areas stipulated in international human rights law, and this regulation is just one example.

This is an issue that has been debated by social policy analysts for decades, and it seems that whenever governments aim to cut spending on Social Assistance, they turn to this rule.

In August 2001, Kimberly Rogers died while under house arrest for committing welfare fraud. At a rally to remember Kimberly Rogers outside the provincial building in Sudbury, Ontario, protesters call for changes to welfare policies.

Kimberly Rogers

Sudbury resident Kimberly Rogers died on August 11, 2001, while confined to her overheated apartment; she was eight months pregnant. She had been convicted of welfare fraud for not declaring the student loans she received while collecting Social Assistance. She was sentenced to:

- ■ six months under house arrest
- ■ only three hours per week could be spent outside of her apartment
- ■ repayment to welfare of $13,648.31
- ■ 18 months' probation
- ■ loss of the right to have part of her student loan forgiven
- ■ no income at all for three months

At the time of her conviction, she was five months pregnant. A coroner's inquest into her death concluded that the zero-tolerance lifetime ineligibility for Social Assistance, as a result of the commission of welfare fraud, pursuant to *Ontario Works Act,* 1997, O. Reg. 134/98 Section 36, should be eliminated.

Welfare Fraud

Welfare fraud is not defined in provincial Social Assistance policies, but the courts have defined it generally as the deliberate attempt to deceive the government to obtain or increase welfare benefits. The courts have not prosecuted cases of overpayment that are caused by welfare recipients or caseworkers misinterpreting complex and changing rules. The *Ontario Welfare Fraud Control Report 2001–2002* shows 38,452 fraud investigations. This resulted in 12,816 terminations of assistance and 393 criminal convictions. The government report says that $46 million was saved as a result of reducing or terminating assistance. They do not state the cost of tracing these funds. The most prevalent reason for the reduction or termination of assistance is listed as "incarceration" (45.5 percent of cases in 1999–2001 and 43.6 percent in 2001–02). This means that most of the savings comes from terminating people who were receiving assistance while in prison. Other reasons include "spouse not declared" (10.9 percent), "undeclared income" (14.8 percent), "undeclared earnings" (9 percent), and "not at a stated address" (8.5 percent).

Several problems become evident when one analyzes the Ontario welfare fraud statistics. First, almost half of the fraud cases were instances of people collecting welfare while in prison. Many of the other reported frauds were overpayments and administrative errors, or cases where documents were missing.

It is safe to say that no one knows all the rules surrounding welfare. The rules are so complex, unrealistic, and impossible to follow that recipients are in a situation where they are always breaking some rule at some time. And it is not only recipients breaking the rules – welfare workers cannot possibly know, and therefore follow, all of the rules and are left breaching key ones daily. In the eyes of some provincial governments, this amounts to fraud. The use of the term "fraud" to cover a wide range of non-criminal conduct builds upon and perpetuates myths about welfare recipients as criminal, who prefer to rip off the system rather than work.

Conclusion

Provincially delivered Social Assistance programs intend to provide a minimum income, as a last-resort measure. The costs of these programs are the responsibility of all levels of government. With the 1996 discontinuation of CAP and its replacement with the CHST, and the 2004 CHT/CST split, the federal government ceased to play a role in setting national standards for Social Assistance, and cut transfers to the provinces that would cover Social Assistance. This opened the door to the workfare that several provinces have instituted.

Social Assistance rates in all provinces are below LICO. Rates in some of the provinces and territories, especially rates for single "employables," reach only one-fifth or one-third of LICO. The situation

Table 11.6: Welfare Fraud in Ontario		
Year	**Convictions**	**Investigations**
2001–2002	393	38,452
2000–2001	430	52,582
1999–2000	557	43,900
1998–1999	747	49,987

Source: Government of Ontario Ministry of Community and Social Services, Welfare Fraud Control Reports from 2001–02, 2000–01, 1999–2000, 1998–99.

of single-parent families on Social Assistance is particularly dismal. Incomes for 2001 were at least $10,000 below the estimated average total income for all single-parent families.

The cost of poverty to all Canadians is high. There is evidence that poverty causes individual problems and lost opportunities and that it harms a nation's economic performance. In The *Cost of Poverty* (National Council of Welfare 2001), a number of studies in the areas of health, justice, human rights and human development, work and productive capacity, and child development are reviewed. The report found that reducing inequality between rich and poor, and especially helping the extremely poor, has positive individual and societal effects. According to the National Council of Welfare, this would help Canada better manage the cost of health care, reduce crime, develop a productive labour force, advance human well-being, and foster social cohesion and public confidence in governments and in the economy.

Chapter Summary

Key Concepts

■ **Administrative eligibility**

■ **Canada Assistance Plan (CAP)**

■ **Canada Child Tax Benefit (CCTB)**

■ **Canada Health and Social Transfer (CHST)**

■ **Canada Health Transfer (CHT)**

■ **Canada Social Transfer (CST)**

■ **Categorical eligibility**

■ **Financial eligibility**

■ **Poverty gap**

■ **Social Assistance (SA)**

■ **Social Union Framework Agreement (SUFA)**

■ **Spouse-in-the-house rule**

■ **Workfare**

■ **Welfare fraud**

Review Questions

1. What factors or events in Canadian society led to the implementation of public social welfare for the poor?

2. List and explain five myths or blame-oriented beliefs about the poor. Why do you think these myths persist?

3. Describe the three types of eligibility tests that a Canadian must meet in order to qualify for Social Assistance.

4. List the three federal pieces of legislation that have affected Social Assistance in Canada. What was the impact of the move from CAP to the CHST on Social Assistance?

5. List and describe the three key debates in discussions about Social Assistance.

6. Define *workfare*, and discuss criticisms put forward by social policy advocates.

Exploring Social Welfare

1. Find out more about the welfare or Social Assistance program where you live. Information can be found at www.canadiansocialresearch.net/welfare.htm. Determine the name of the program, the department responsible for the program, some demographic characteristics of recipients, the enabling legislation, and major current issues.

2. The National Council of Welfare produces annual *Welfare Incomes* summaries for Canada. The latest reports can be found at www.ncwcnbes.net. Look at the latest report and determine the amount of income by type of household for your province or territory. How does this compare to LICO (called the *Poverty Line* in the report)? How is your province or territory treating the National Child Benefit? With this information, write your own "Report Card on Welfare" for your province or territory.

3. The National Council of Welfare released a 2007 report entitled *Solving Poverty: Four Cornerstones of a Workable National Strategy for Canada*, which is available at www.ncwcnbes.net. After reading the report, write a 500-word essay outlining the major approaches to solving poverty. Discuss the approach that you think Canada should follow, and explain why.

Websites

National Council of Welfare
www.ncwcnbes.net

The National Council of Welfare is a citizen's group that advises the Minister of Human Resources and Social Development on issues relating to low-income Canadians. This is a one-stop location for information poverty in Canadian.

Canadian Social Research Links
www.canadiansocialresearch.net/welfare.htm

Gilles Séguin has collected an impressive selection of links to information about welfare reform.

Campaign 2000
www.campaign2000.ca

This is an extensive site that contains report cards on child poverty, publications and other resources, and suggestions for taking action. Campaign 2000 was an across-Canada public education movement that aimed at building Canadian awareness and support for the 1989 all-party House of Commons resolution to end child poverty in Canada by the year 2000.

References

Bohácek, Radim. 2002. The efficiency-equality tradeoff in welfare state economies (February 5). CERGE-EI Working Paper No. 193. http://ssrn.com/abstract=317862 or DOI: 10.2139/ssrn.317862.

Canadian Council on Social Development (CCSD). 1998. *Statistics: Estimates of Distribution of Social Assistance Cases and Recipients by Family Type, March 1998.* Ottawa: CCSD. www.ccsd.ca/factsheets/sadis98.htm.

Centre for International Statistics. 2002. *Incidence of Child Poverty among Children in Female Lone-Parent Families, by Province, Canada, 1990–1996.* Ottawa: Canadian Council on Social Development (using data from Statistics Canada, Cat. 13-569-XPB). www.ccsd.ca/factsheets/fscp90s.htm.

Clark, Christopher. 1995. Work and welfare: Looking at both sides of the equation. *Perception* 19 (1). www.ccsd.ca/perception/191/perchris.htmlt

Finnie, R. 2000. *Low Income (Poverty) Dynamics in Canada: Entry, Exit, Spell Durations, and Total Time.* Ottawa: Human Resources Development Canada. www.hrsdc.gc.ca/en/cs/sp/sdc/pkrf/publications/research/2000-000167/page00.shtml.

Government of British Columbia, Ministry of Employment and Income Assistance. 2007. *BC Employment and Assistance Month Statistics, February 1, 2007.* Victoria: Government of British Columbia. www.eia.gov.bc.ca/research/.

Government of Ontario, Ministry of Community and Social Services 2002. *Ontario Welfare Fraud Control Report 2001–2002.* No longer available online.

Guest, Denis. 1999. *The Emergency of Social Security in Canada*, 3rd ed. Vancouver: UBC Press.

Human Resources and Social Development Canada (HRSDC). 2006. *Provincial Social Assistance and Child Welfare Programs.* Ottawa: HRDC. www.hrsdc.gc.ca/en/cs/sp/sdc/socpol/tables/pre/tab435.shtml.

Human Resources Development Canada (HRDC). 2000. *Provincial Social Assistance Program Expenditures, 1996 to 2003.* Ottawa: HRDC.

Mitchell, Andrew, and Richard Shillington. 2004. *Federal Tax Relief for Low Income People.* Ottawa: National Anti-Poverty Organization. www.napo-onap.ca/en/issues/tax_cuts.php.

National Council of Welfare. 1998. *Profiles of Welfare: Myths and Realities.* Ottawa: National Council of Welfare. www.ncwcnbes.net.

National Council of Welfare. 2001. *The Cost of Poverty.* Ottawa: National Council of Welfare. www.ncwcnbes.net.

National Council of Welfare. 2002. *Welfare Incomes 2000 and 2001.* Ottawa: National Council of Welfare. www.ncwcnbes.net.

National Council of Welfare. 2006. *Welfare Incomes 2005.* Ottawa: National Council of Welfare. www.ncwcnbes.net.

Phipps, Shelley, and Lynn Lethbridge. 2002. *Fitting kids in: Children and inequality in Canada.* Luxembourg Income Study Working Paper No. 322.

Rice, J.J., and M.J. Prince. 2000. *Changing Politics of Canadian Social Policy.* Toronto: University of Toronto Press.

Statistics Canada. 2006a. *Income and the Outcomes of Children.* Ottawa: Minister of Industry. Cat. no. 11F0019MIE, No. 281.

Statistics Canada. 2006b. *Women in Canada: A Gender-Based Statistical Report,* 5th ed. Ottawa: Statistics Canada. www.statcan.ca/english/freepub/89-503-XIE/0010589-503-XIE.pdf.

Vozoris, N., B. Davis, and V. Tarasuk. 2002. The affordability of a nutritious diet for households on welfare in Toronto. *Canadian Journal of Public Health* 93 (1):36–40.

12 Children and Families in Poverty

A Call to Action

The persistence of child poverty in Canada is a threat to our future. Financial and social supports for families and children have recently changed, with decreasing welfare rates in many provinces and the addition of the National Child Benefit and Universal Child Care Benefit. But what is lacking is a comprehensive and integrated approach to family income policy. Without it, children and working families in Canada will remain in a precarious position.

For most Canadians, child poverty is considered something that happens in another country. However, as of 2003, one in six Canadian children (17.5 percent) lives in poverty. This translates into 1,201,000 Canadian children. Canadian governments have recognized that Canada's children need help — not only is it the ethical thing to do, but our economic and social well-being depends on it. But not all attempts to

> *" . . . while all children are born equal, they don't all have the same opportunities to flourish. This is as true for children here as it is for children in the third world."*
>
> *— Her Excellency the Right Honourable Michaëlle Jean, Governor General, September 27, 2005*

A World Fit for Children

In 2002, the Special Session of the UN General Assembly on Children culminated in the official adoption, by some 180 nations, of the document *A World Fit for Children*. It emphasizes:

■ putting children's needs first
■ eradicating poverty and investing in children
■ committing to leaving no child behind
■ caring for every child
■ listening to children and ensuring their participation

This was the first session of the UN General Assembly to focus exclusively on issues affecting children, and the first to include children as official representatives.

effect change have been successful, as we will see in this review of Canada's income security for families with children.

One cannot examine the welfare of Canada's children without addressing the situation of families since, up to a certain age, children are dependent on the households in which they live. Not surprisingly, social researchers are finding that the income security of children's families in the early years of life is especially important for the children's health, education, and personal well-being.

Some of the income security benefits for families with children have been, and continue to be, delivered through the tax system in the form of tax credits and exemptions. Others have been distributed through direct cash transfers. In 1944 a universal benefit called the *Family Allowance* was instituted, and this benefit went to all families with children regardless of income. Over time, this benefit became targeted towards middle- and low-income families. In 1993 it was eliminated entirely. The Canada Child Tax Benefit, the National Child Benefit, and the Universal Child Care Benefit are now used as the major child-related benefits for families with children. They are applied through the tax system, with eligibility determined by family income.

While Canada does not have an official family policy, it does have a collection of income security measures directed solely at families with children. In this chapter, we will examine these programs and explore their impact on Canada's children.

Canada's Children

Child poverty diminishes life chances for children. The National Council of Welfare and the Canadian Council on Social Development have reported extensively on the negative effect of poverty on children and their families. Good health and development during childhood are among the most important factors in making sure that individuals grow up healthy enough to learn, find work, raise families, and participate fully in society throughout their lives. Children in low-income families have higher risks of poor health and poor developmental outcomes than do children in middle-income and high-income families.

The less income a family has, the less they can afford health care costs not covered by public health insurance. Fewer educational opportunities exist for these children and their parents, which makes it difficult to secure employment or upgrade to better employment. Financial strain can also lead to family breakdown and contribute to social problems such as crime. As Children's Aid and group homes become involved, this can translate into higher social services costs. In short, there is a clear need for strong measures to eliminate child poverty in Canada.

In 1989, the House of Commons declared its commitment to eliminating poverty among Canadian children by the year 2000. At the time, the child poverty rate was estimated to be 14.5 percent.

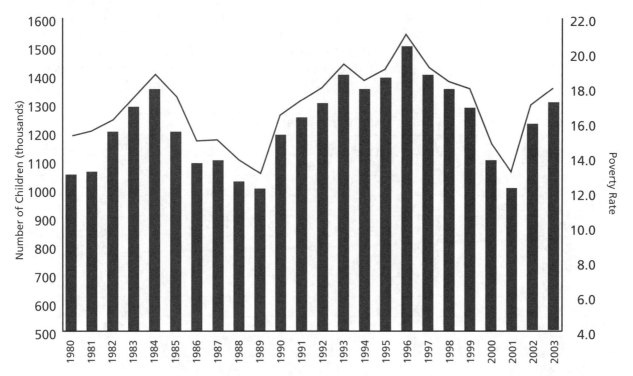

Figure 12.1: Child Poverty in Canada

Source: Based on data prepared by the Canadian Council on Social Development using Statistics Canada's Survey of Consumer Finances, microdata files (1996–2003), and Survey of Labour and Income Dynamics (2003).

Campaign 2000, an across-Canada public education movement to build Canadian awareness and support for the 1989 all-party House of Commons resolution, reports yearly on the progress towards the goal of eliminating child poverty. In their report on the situation of children in the year 2000, they found that about 1.1 million Canadian children live on incomes below Statistics Canada's Low Income Cut-off (LICO), and found that many families live far below these lines (see www. campaign 2000.ca/rc). The 2000 report notes that it is a positive sign that the rate of child poverty dropped for the fourth consecutive year, but goes on to point out that child poverty has actually increased since the resolution in 1989, when Canada's child poverty rate was 14.4 percent. It now stands at over 17 percent and has reached as high as 21 percent.

This dire situation exists despite the federal government's tax and income security policies. Many of these children live in modest-income households whose earnings have declined over the last decade. At the same time, the cost of raising children has increased, and the supply of secure, full-time employment has dropped.

Child poverty rates tend to rise in economic downturns and fall during economic growth. This trend is illustrated in Figure 12.1. In the 1980s, the child poverty rate rose with the 1981–82 recession, peaking in 1984 at 21 percent, and then declining for the rest of the 1980s. By the recession of 1990–91, child poverty was again on the rise. The percentage of children in poverty peaked in 1993 and 1996 at over 21 percent. Then, a modest decline began in 1997 and continued in 1998 as the child poverty rate fell to 19 percent. As the poverty rate declined, so did the number of poor children. In 2003, there were 1,201,000 Canadian children living in poverty (17.5 percent).

It is instructive to examine the extent to which poor families live below LICO — this is known as the poverty gap. The poverty gap

Table 12.1: Child Poverty in Canadian Provinces, 2003

	Rate	Number
Canada	17.6	1,201,000
Newfoundland	21.8	23,000
Prince Edward Island	11.3	-
Nova Scotia	20.7	40,000
New Brunswick	17.3	26,000
Quebec	16.7	254,000
Ontario	16.1	443,000
Manitoba	22.1	57,000
Saskatchewan	18.3	40,000
Alberta	15.6	114,000
British Columbia	23.9	201,000

Source: With permission from Campaign 2000, quoting its annual report card on child poverty (2005, Fig. 2). www.campaign2000.ca.

Table 12.2: Children Living Below Median National Income

	Percentage of Children Living Below		
	50% of Median National Income	40% of Median National Income	60% of Median National Income
Finland	2.8	1.3	8.0
Norway	3.4	1.6	7.5
Sweden	4.2	1.8	9.2
Belgium	7.7	3.2	13.7
Hungary	8.8	4.4	16.9
Luxembourg	9.1	2.1	18.3
Netherlands	9.8	5.9	14.2
Germany	10.2	6.2	16.9
Austria	10.2	6.1	21.4
Poland	12.7	6.5	17.3
Canada	14.9	7.7	23.3
UK	15.4	5.5	27.0
Italy	16.6	10.6	26.5
USA	21.9	14.1	30.2
Mexico	27.7	20.9	35.0

Source: UNICEF, "Child Poverty in Rich Countries, 2005," *Innocenti Report Card No. 6*. UNICEF Innocenti Research Centre, Florence.

for two-parent families with children increased from 1999 to 2000. As mentioned, 17.5 percent of children lived below the 2003 LICO. Within this number is a large discrepancy between children in two-parent families and children in single-parent families. The poverty rates for families headed by single-parent mothers have consistently been five to six times higher than the poverty rates for two-parent families. According to Statistics Canada, about 11.6 percent of children in two-parent families and about 52.1 percent of children in female-led single-parent families lived below LICO in 2004.

For families with wage earners making minimum wage, it is necessary to have more than one wage earner in the family. For example, a single mother in Ottawa who works full-time as a cashier at minimum wage ($7.75 per hour in 2007) does not make enough to be above the poverty line established by LICO. Based on a 40-hour work week, she earns just over $15,000 in one year. Even with only one child, she would need to make over $20,956 in gross income to be above LICO. This rate is based on the 2005 LICO for a family living in a city with 500,000 people or more. Even if she lived in a much smaller city with a population of less than 30,000 where living costs are lower, she would still be below the poverty line. To be above LICO she would need to live in a rural area and work more than 40 hours per week at minimum wage.

For single mothers with more than one child, it is even more difficult to get out of poverty. For example, a single mother of two children (a three-person family), living in a city with over 500,000 people, needs to earn over $26,095 to be above LICO. If she lives in a rural area (where the LICO level is the lowest), she would need to earn over $17,071. For a four-person family (a single mother with three children, or two adults and two children) living in a medium-sized city of 100,000–499,999, the LICO is $27,532. Clearly, work does not guarantee that families will not be living in poverty.

One might think that, in a country with enormous wealth and resources, child poverty would not be an issue. Yet, Canada's child poverty rates are higher than most other countries. Using a conservative measure of poverty to compare child poverty rates, the UNICEF study *Child Poverty in Rich Countries 2005* found that Canada's rate (14.9 percent) for children is the eighth worst, falling behind Russia, Australia, Japan, and Spain. Using the United Nations poverty measure of living on less than half of medium national income, Canada has the second-highest rate of single-mother poverty in the world, at 45.4 percent. Canada falls behind all countries except the United States, including Russia, Slovakia, and Taiwan (UNICEF 2005).

The face of child poverty is changing from the lone mother on welfare to that of the working-poor mother who is holding down at least one job. While just 6.8 percent of poor children lived with mothers who worked full-time in 1996, 11.5 percent of all poor children did

UNICEF's Measure of Poverty

The measure of poverty used by UNICEF is different from the Statistics Canada LICO measure, and therefore provides different rates.

The UNICEF measure calculates poverty as living below one-half of the median income in a country. This measure allows for international comparisons.

According to UNICEF's 2005 report, Child Poverty in Rich Countries, 2005, 23.3 percent of children in Canada lived below 60 percent of the median national income, 14.9 percent of children lived below 50 percent, and 7.7 lived below 40 percent.

so in 1998. Unfortunately, single mothers who are taking up the challenge of welfare departments across the country in trading a welfare cheque for a pay stub are not finding that the transition raises them out of poverty.

The downward trend in child poverty since 1997 is encouraging, but many analysts are concerned that child poverty may increase again the next time there is an economic crisis. To achieve a sustained reduction in child poverty, governments need a multi-pronged strategy. Delineating such a strategy would be complex, not least of which because it should include consistent and adequate income security for families with children, improvements in the availability of living-wage jobs, early childhood education and care, and affordable housing programs that provide housing for the most vulnerable families.

Market Poverty: Children in Working Poor Families

Not all children who live in families with a low income are on Social Assistance. Many families struggling to survive on low income are employed. Increasingly, the marketplace is not providing adequate income for Canadian families.

Market poverty

■ when a household meets the characteristics of poverty, despite one or more household members being employed

Market poverty refers to a situation in which a household remains below some measure of poverty, even though one or more members of the household earn a market income or are employed. These are referred to as the "working poor." There are two basic causes of market poverty: low wages and lack of access to the labour market. Low wages contribute to market poverty when wages do not provide an adequate income to support families. Lack of access to the labour market can be due to either a lack of skills and training or particular barriers

Table 12.3: Prevalence of Persons in Low Income Before Tax and After Tax, 2000, 2002, and 2004

	Before Tax 2000	After Tax 2000	Before Tax 2002	After Tax 2002	Before Tax 2004	After Tax 2004
Persons under 18 in two-parent families	12.6%	9.5%	11.8%	7.2%	11.6%	8.1%
Persons under 18 in female single-parent families	50.0%	40.1%	55.7%	43.0%	52.1%	40.0%
Persons under 18 in all other economic families	22.9%	14.4%	17.7%	10.9%	22.6%	14.8%

Note: Prevalence of low income shows the proportion of people living below the LICO within a given group. It is expressed as a percentage. The before-tax incidence does not include tax-based income security transfers such as the CCTB, CPP, OAS, etc.

Source: Adapted from Statistics Canada. 2006. *Table 202-0802 Persons in low income (before and after tax), by prevalence in precent.* CANSIM (database) Last modified: 2006-03-28. http://www40.statcan.ca/l01/cst01/famil19a.htm and http://www40.statcan.ca/l01/cst01/famil41a.htm

such as a lack of recognition of education as is the case with some immigrants or the lack of accommodation for a disability, to name a few. Market poverty continues to exist, despite people's commitment to seek paid employment.

Increasingly, the expectation is that families should become more self-reliant through labour market participation, whether it is a lone-parent or two-parent family. There is little consideration as to how realistic this is, in terms of the level of minimum wage and the high costs of daycare for these families. For example, a single mother with a very young child that is not in school needs full-time daycare if she has a full-time job. At the Ontario general minimum wage of $8.00 per hour (2007), the cost of daycare takes up a large percentage of her earnings, particularly since full-time daycare can cost from several hundred to several thousand dollars per month, depending on the daycare provider. Even when her child is in school and she works full-time during the school hours, her income is so low that the family still falls below the LICO. Two-parent families are not much better off, especially if both parents earn wages at a low hourly rate and have to pay for daycare. Even if their combined income places the family above the LICO, the cost of daycare can be enough to plunge them into poverty.

Government policies tend to be based on the idea that if people can get a job, they won't be living in poverty. However, the quality of the job is often more significant than the job itself. According to Campaign 2000's 2005 Report Card, in Ontario one-third of the children from families living below the LICO have one or more parents who works full-time, full year.

Many people have little sympathy for those on welfare; they are seen as lazy and undeserving. Since the mid-1990s, many government welfare reforms have reinforced these perceptions, and they have become ingrained in the thinking of a large segment of society. But people don't turn to welfare because they want to; they turn to it because they have no other options. Who would choose to live on such a meagre income? People are on welfare because they have lost their jobs, are widowed, are separated or divorced and are raising their children alone, are fleeing abusive relationships, or have a disability that prevents them from accessing a job.

The current poverty statistics raise many questions. Why are so many working families still left with inadequate incomes? Does Canada have an official government policy that is addressing the problem?

Approaches to Children's Social Welfare

It is helpful to examine where Canada's policy fits within the two main approaches to children's social welfare. These two approaches are: (1) the family responsibility approach and (2) the investing in children approach.

Many children living in poverty have parents who work in low-paying jobs.

According to the family responsibility approach, parents are solely responsible for making decisions and providing for their children's well-being. The role of income security and social services is to facilitate decision making and provide support when the family's ability to provide fails. Within this approach there is little recognition of the contribution of parents to the future of society. This approach, therefore, sees labour force attachment for family members as the primary focus of concern. Programs are designed to intervene only when the family resources and abilities fail. Programs using this approach provide tax deductions for families with children, employment leaves, and targeted minimum-income programs.

The investing in children approach, on the other hand, believes in building supports for families and households that enable them to attain positive outcomes for children. This approach holds that social spending on income supports and child education and care is an investment that benefits all of society in the long run. There is a recognition that the decisions open to families are increasingly limited and that the options for parents have narrowed insofar as most families need two incomes to adequately provide for themselves. The market is also increasingly unable to provide sufficient incomes for families; hence, the increase in children living in low-income situations. This approach parallels aspects of the social responsibility model discussed in Chapter 6.

The Canadian government's focus on child poverty is generally consistent with a family responsibility approach to social welfare. Many social workers and policy analysts have been at the forefront in advocating a policy shift in the direction of the social responsibility model. The social responsibility approach recognizes that parents cannot always stay at home full-time, so there is a need for daycare and early childhood development programs. There is also recognition that not all parents are employable and that they may require income assistance or child care assistance in order to access education and attend programs (to develop their skills so that they can become employable).

Four Purposes of Child-Related Income Security

Amazingly, in a society in which we repeatedly hear about the importance of the family, there is no direct national family-related social policy, only indirect programs. At times, Canada's collection of programs has had aspects of the approaches outlined above. The 1944

Family Allowance, for example, tended towards an investing in children approach. Recently we have moved further towards a family responsibility approach, whereby policies such as the National Family Benefit emphasize incentives to get parents working. Today, Canada can be squarely placed within the family responsibility model.

Child-related income security benefits have four main purposes:

- **To deal with child poverty by providing a minimum income.** The labour market does not differentiate wages according to family size, so this has always disadvantaged households with children. The first purpose is to supplement the income of lower-income families with children, and help to fill the gap between wages and the poverty line.

- **To generate horizontal equity for households with children so that they have income equal to those without children.** Horizontal equity is based on the recognition that parents have heavier financial demands than childless households and single persons with the same income.

- **To act as an economic stimulus by putting money in the hands of those most likely to spend it.** The idea behind economic stimulus is that putting more money in the hands of parents who will spend it helps to stimulate consumer demand. This was one of the main purposes of the 1944 Family Allowance program. The idea was to give every mother a monthly cheque, which she would spend on necessities for her child or children, thereby stimulating the postwar economy.

- **To recognize parents as contributing to the future of society.** The children of today are the future leaders and workers of tomorrow, and families with children contribute something to society that people without children do not. Parental recognition is an acknowledgement by society of the contribution parents make to society in terms of raising future citizens, workers, and taxpayers. It is a way of assisting all parents.

At various times, Canadian governments have implemented programs that attempt to address one or more of the preceding purposes. An approach that emphasizes investing in Canada's children would involve programs that address all of these purposes simultaneously. In this regard, Canadian policies have been lacking. In the beginning, programs were intended to create economic stimulus, such as with the 1944 Family Allowance. Now, child poverty is increasingly being addressed with employment incentives and income security policies targeted at poor families.

History of Benefits for Families with Children

The current system of income security benefits directed specifically at children has had a long history in Canada. Indeed, the Family

Convention on the Rights of the Child

Since its adoption in 1989, 192 countries have signed on to the convention (which can be viewed at www.unicef.org/crc). Its basic premise is that children (below the age of 18) are born with fundamental freedoms and the inherent rights of all human beings. Article 27 requires that governments *"recognize the right of every child to a standard of living adequate for the child's physical, mental, spiritual, moral and social development"* and that when parents are unable to secure a child's standard of living, that governments should assist parents *"to implement this right and shall in case of need provide material assistance and support programmes, particularly with regard to nutrition, clothing and housing."*

Unfortunately, according to the Innocenti report on child poverty (UNICEF 2005), many of the world's richest countries, including Canada, are failing to ensure that the rights outlined in the convention are realized.

Allowance in 1944 was the first universal income security program, prior to being changed to an income-based program in 1978. The overall history can be divided into four phases.

Phase 1: Recognition of Family Needs, 1918–40

In the 1700s and early 1800s, children were treated harshly under the Common Law of England. Early legislation, such as the *Orphans Act* in 1799 and the *Apprentices and Minors Act* of 1874 gave town wardens the power to bind a child under the age of 14 as an apprentice or labourer. The *Indian Act* of 1876 demonstrated the colonizer's view of First Nations children, and many were placed in residential schools administered by Christian churches with the overriding aim of assimilation.

Income support to families with children began in 1918 with the introduction of the **Child Tax Exemption** in personal income tax. The exemption provided income tax savings that increased with taxable income. The after-tax benefit was of greatest absolute benefit to those in the highest tax brackets; the exemption provided no benefits to families that did not owe income tax. Concern about widowed mothers with small children after World War I led to Mothers' Allowance, first in Manitoba in 1916, Saskatchewan in 1917, and Ontario and BC in 1920. This provided a needs-tested monthly income support. All provinces followed suit within the next decade. Eligibility requirements varied between provinces, but one element remained steadfast — any mother deemed to be of bad character was not eligible, which was a throwback to the Poor Law concerns of distinguishing between the deserving and undeserving poor. Women's groups that wanted to avoid the stigmatizing effects of "assistance" demanded the term "pension" be used instead. They also demanded, but did not obtain, a non-discretionary pension.

Phase 2: Universal Benefits, 1941–74

The *Family Allowance Act* of 1944 introduced the universal **Family Allowance (FA)**, providing benefits to all Canadian families with dependent children. The FA was also popularly known as the "baby bonus," and it was the first universal income security scheme. The FA provided a monthly payment of $5.94 to the mother of every child under the age of 16 (changed to the age of 18 in 1973). If of school age, the child had to be attending school. The stated purpose of the plan was to assure children of their basic needs and to maintain purchasing power in the postwar era.

The Family Allowance provision was introduced one year after the Marsh Report, which indicated that an allowance for the parents of children was central to a social security system. The majority of social workers and the Canadian Association of Social Workers strongly supported the plan. Interestingly, Charlotte Whitton, a leading

Child Tax Exemption (1918)

■ provided income tax savings that increased as income increased; provided no benefit to families that did not owe income tax

Family Allowance (1944)

■ known as the "baby bonus," this provided monetary benefits to all Canadian families with dependent children; it remained universal until 1973 and was eliminated in 1993

Child welfare has changed drastically over the last century, abandoning the harsh treatment afforded children under the old common law.

social worker and director of the Canadian Welfare Council at the time, deemed the plan wasteful as both poor and wealthy families benefited. She believed that any such program should target the most needy with social utilities, such as health and housing, rather than cash. Perhaps surprisingly, many trade unions also tended to oppose the benefit, seeing it as a substitute for adequate wages.

Historians continue to debate why the Mackenzie King Liberal government introduced this universal children's benefit. Several factors have been suggested: (1) it would maintain purchasing power in the economy as a whole, (2) it was an alternative to the wage freeze that was in place at the time, (3) it would stave off the threat from the leftist Co-operative Commonwealth Federation (CCF) Party that was endorsing such a program, and (4) it would win Liberal support in Quebec where the conscription issue was problematic.

The Family Allowance remained completely universal until 1973, when various reforms made it taxable income in the hands of the recipients. In the 1973 amendments to the act, the benefit was made taxable and was indexed to the **Consumer Price Index (CPI)**. Indexation is an arrangement in which periodic adjustments are made to benefits based on changes to an index, usually the CPI. The CPI is an indicator of the consumer prices in Canada, calculated on a monthly basis using the cost of a fixed list of commodities purchased by a typical Canadian family. The CPI is used as an indicator of inflation. Why make the Family Allowance benefit taxable? The argument was that people with more income pay higher marginal tax rates and keep less of the benefit, which is the underlying idea behind a progressive income tax system. Reforms in 1989 increased the tax rate with a clawback, and the Family Allowance met its ultimate demise in 1993.

Phase 3: Erosion and Growing Poverty, 1975–90

Refundable Child Tax Credit (1978)

■ a credit targeted for families in need of government assistance; it resulted in a decrease in Family Allowance benefits

Beginning in 1978, Finance Minister Jean Chrétien announced a merging of social security programs and income tax provisions. The Liberal government introduced the **Refundable Child Tax Credit** as a way to target families in need of government assistance. Upon the creation of the Child Tax Credit, FA benefits were reduced from an average of $25.68 per month (which would have increased to $28 with indexing) to an average of $20 per month. The stated goal of the benefit was to help families meet the costs of raising children. It was income tested and varied according to the number of children in a family.

Unlike universal benefits, the use of the tax system to target low-income families was a fundamental shift in thinking from an institutional view of social welfare to a residual view. It was also the first time that the tax system was used to redistribute income.

The tax credit provided the maximum benefit to low-income families, a declining amount to middle-income families, and no benefit to wealthy families. It provided a credit in the income tax account with the federal government. The whole credit was payable to families with a net income below a certain threshold, and it was gradually reduced until the family's income reached the national average, at which point it was reduced to zero. If the family's tax credit was more than the amount they owed in taxes, the difference was paid to them in the form of a monthly cheque. This is what is meant by the term "refundable" – the tax credit is paid out if the taxpayer does not owe income tax.

Benefits paid in this way are called "tax expenditures." They are made up of foregone taxes, or taxes that go uncollected. In the case of a tax credit, it can become a reverse tax. This was the first major program of its type in the field of income security. Previously, it was used in the investment arena, in which governments would use it to induce certain types of investment behaviour and support for various industries.

Child Care Expense Deduction (1971)

■ intended for lone-parent families to help with the costs of child care for working parents

The **Child Care Expense Deduction** was first introduced in 1971 and was originally intended for lone-parent families. It was designed to offset the incremental costs of child rearing for parents in the labour force. When first introduced, the amount that parents could deduct from their personal income taxes for children was limited to $2,000 per child under the age of 14, subject to a maximum of $8,000 per family. In 1998, the deduction increased from $5,000 to $7,000 (and from $3,000 to $4,000 for children aged 7 to 16). Currently, approximately 1.2 million families use the deduction. In 1986, the FA benefit, which still existed in its reduced form, was "partially de-indexed," meaning that there were no increases in benefit levels until inflation reached 3 percent. This meant the value of the FA would lessen over time. In 1989, benefit clawbacks were introduced. The clawback came in the form of a higher tax rate for FA benefits, which meant that higher income earners would pay back their FA. This marked the end of FA as a universal program in all but name, and it eventually led to the elimination of the Family Allowance in 1993 — and, many argued, to the end of universality as a principle of Canadian social security.

Phase 4: Targeting Poverty and Work Incentives, 1991–Present

The idea of the welfare wall entered the government lexicon during this period. The term **welfare wall** refers to the disincentives that hinder the move from welfare to work because of the financial and other supports that are lost when families accept employment.

In 1993, the Government of Canada consolidated its child tax credits and the Family Allowance into a single **Child Tax Benefit (CTB)** that provided a monthly payment based on the number of children and the level of family income. In addition to a basic benefit, the Child Tax Benefit included a **Working Income Supplement (WIS)** to supplement the earnings of working poor families.

The CTB included a supplement of $213 per year for each child in a family who was under the age of seven. The maximum basic benefit was $1,020 per child per year, plus an additional $75 for the third child and each subsequent child in a family. The maximum basic benefit was payable to all families with annual incomes of less than $25,921. The benefit was reduced at a rate of 5 percent of family net income in excess of $25,921 for families with two or more children, and at a rate of 2.5 percent for families with one child. Families with one or two children no longer received basic benefits once the net family income exceeded $67,000.

The maximum Child Tax Benefit per child per year in 1994 was broken down as follows:

- Basic benefit: $1,020
- Supplement for third and each additional child: $75
- Supplement for children under age seven: $213
- Working Income Supplement: $500

The WIS gave an additional benefit to those working at low-income levels; the benefit was paid out at the rate of 8 percent of all earnings. This benefit was not available to unemployed parents. Families began to receive benefits from the WIS once their earnings exceeded $3,750. A maximum annual benefit of $500 was provided for families with annual incomes between $10,000 and $20,921, regardless of the number of children in the family. The WIS was reduced at a rate of 10 percent of family net income in excess of $20,921, and the benefits ceased when income reached $25,921.

In 1998 an initiative called the **Canada Child Tax Benefit (CCTB)** was introduced. The CCTB has two main elements: a Canada Child Tax Benefit (CCTB) basic benefit and the **National Child Benefit Supplement (NCBS)**. The NCBS is an additional tax credit that adds to the

Child Tax Benefit (1993)

■ a monthly payment based on number of children and income level; created when government consolidated child tax credits and the Family Allowance

■ included a Working Income Supplement for working poor families

CCTB — it is the federal contribution to the CCTB. The NCBS provides low-income families with additional child benefits on top of the basic benefit. The terminology is confusing as the federal government, at times, refers to the overall program (CCTB and NCBS) as the National Child Benefit, instead of the Canada Child Tax Benefit (see www.nationalchildbenefit.ca). Finance Canada refers to the overall program as the CCTB.

Since 1998, the federal investment in the CCTB has risen dramatically. It is the first joint federal/provincial/territorial initiative under the Social Union Framework Agreement (SUFA), and the first national social welfare program since medicare and the Canada Pension Plan in the 1960s. The 2000 federal budget announced that CCTB funding would automatically rise with inflation.

The critics contend that the reform discriminates against welfare families in particular, because they will see no net increase in their child benefits, and only the working poor and other low-income families (families not on welfare or collecting Employment Insurance) will enjoy an improvement in benefits.

In 2006 the **Universal Child Care Benefit** (UCCB) was introduced. The UCCB is a taxable $1,200 per year benefit that was introduced for each child under 6 years of age.

The Current System: CCTB, NCBS, and UCCB

By the end of 1997, there was a growing concern that many Canadian children did not have the opportunity for a healthy start to life and the support to reach a healthy, happy, and educated future. This growing consensus recognized that the previous child benefit system was lacking. As a result, Canada's first ministers and their governments examined various ways to improve assistance to children of low-income families.

Canada Child Tax Benefit (CCTB)

The CCTB program is currently the primary mechanism for addressing child and family low income and poverty in Canada. It attempts to reduce overlap between provinces and to promote labour market attachment by ensuring that families will always be better off as a result of working.

The CCTB has three stated objectives:

- to prevent and reduce the depth of child poverty
- to promote attachment to the labour market by ensuring that families will always be better off as a result of working
- to reduce overlap and duplication by harmonizing program objectives and benefits and simplifying administration

With these objectives, the CCTB aims to help low-income families by increasing federal benefits for families with children. The program provides a tax credit to those who qualify based on an income test. A **tax credit** is an amount deducted directly from income tax otherwise payable. Examples of tax credits include the disability tax credit and the married credit for individuals, and the scientific research and experimental development investment tax credit for corporations. This is different from a **tax deduction**, which is an amount deducted from total income to arrive at taxable income. Child care expenses and capital cost allowances are tax deductions. Tax deductions are worth more to people with higher incomes, as they are in a higher marginal tax bracket.

The CCTB basic benefit provides child benefits to all low- and middle-income families with children. More than 80 percent of Canadian families with children receive this basic benefit. In 2007, families with a net income under the threshold of $36,378 received the CCTB tax credit benefit of $1,255 per child, with additional amounts for children under age seven and for families with more than two children. The CCTB also includes the Child Disability Benefit (CDB) for families with children under age 18 who have a severe and prolonged disability. The CDB provides up to $191.66 per month and starts being reduced when income is more than $36,378.

Some families are eligible for an additional benefit – the National Child Benefit Supplement.

National Child Benefit Supplement (NCBS)

When it created the National Child Benefit Supplement, the federal government stated that the NCBS was designed to address the welfare wall phenomenon. As has been mentioned, it is difficult for families receiving Social Assistance to make the transition from welfare to work without losing financial and other supports. For example, many low-income working families may not be eligible for benefits and services, such as the prescription drug coverage that is provided through Social Assistance for families on welfare. These barriers create the welfare wall, preventing some families from leaving Social Assistance and making it difficult for low-income working families to obtain necessary support for their children.

The NCBS attempts to address this by augmenting family income only for low-income families not on welfare (such as the working poor and low-income families drawing from Employment Insurance). The NCBS is designed to promote labour force participation by funding significant income supplements for low-income working families, and supports and services, such as child care and extended health benefits. In essence, it encourages and supports parents who enter and stay in the workforce.

The NCBS provides low-income families with additional child benefits on top of the CCTB. The supplement provided almost $2,000 per child for families with a net income under the $20,435 threshold

The National Child Benefit

www. nationalchildbenefit.ca

This federal government website provides the government's perspective on the success of the NCBS.

The Universal Child Chare Benefit provides $1,200 per child under six to help offset the cost of child care. Critics argue that $100 a month is not nearly sufficient to deal with the child care concerns of the working poor.

in 2007. It is reduced with income above the threshold, and is fully phased out when family net income exceeds $36,378 (as of 2007). Over time the supplement has increased more than the CCTB, and as a result, the NCBS now exceeds the amount of the base benefit.

Though the NCBS is administered through the tax system (individuals must file a tax return to apply), the federal government says it is fundamentally an anti-poverty program rather than a tax provision. While it is a federal tax provision, it was designed as a joint initiative with provincial and territorial governments. The federal and provincial governments, with the exception of Quebec, support the NCBS.

Until 2002, neither the CCTB nor the NCBS were indexed, which enabled the government to ignore increases in the cost of living and thereby reduce the benefit surreptitiously. Non-indexation of benefits has the effect of reducing the benefit each year by the amount of any increases in the Consumer Price Index (CPI). The benefits are now indexed to the CPI.

Universal Child Care Benefit (UCCB)

In 2006 the newly elected federal Conservative government announced the Universal Child Care Benefit (UCCB). This new program was a replacement for the universal child care program that the previous Liberal government had negotiated with the provinces. The UCCB payment is paid on behalf of children under the age of 6 years in instalments of $100 per month per child. It is a taxable benefit (unlike the CCTB which is a tax credit). For two-earner households, the UCCB should be declared by the spouse having the lowest net income — this means that the non-earning spouse of a millionaire could get a much larger monthly benefit from this program than a single working parent. This benefit is not taken into account, however, in calculating the CCTB or the federal goods and services tax credit. As a replacement

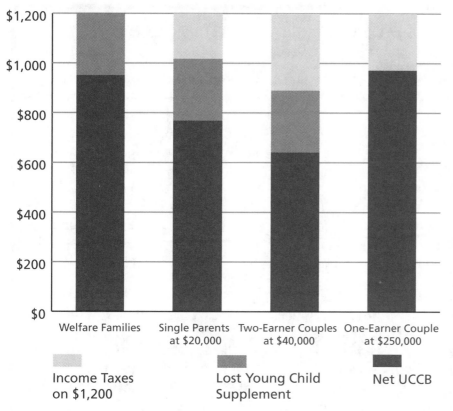

Figure 12.2: Net Universal Child Care Benefit, by Family Type and Income, Ontario, 2006

Source: Battle, Ken, Sherri Torjman, and Michael Mendelson. 2006. **More Than a Name Change: The Universal Child Care Benefit.** *Ottawa: Caledon Institute of Social Policy, 4. Reprinted with permission.*

for comprehensive child care, the UCCB payment is intended to help cover the costs of child care.

A recent report by the Caledon Institute entitled *More Than a Name Change: The Universal Child Care Benefit* argues that two flaws exist in the UCCB (Battle, Torjman, and Mendelson 2006). First, by taxing the payment in the hands of the lowest earner in a household, they punish working single parents, perhaps those who need the child care the most. Second, to help pay for the UCCB, the CCTB's young child supplement ($249 annually as of July 2006 for children under 7) was abolished. This again will be hardest felt by low-income families and single parents. The tax is complicated, and it is beyond the scope of this chapter to detail how the UCCB will affect all the different family configurations, but Figure 12.2 shows to some degree the results of these flaws.

Clawbacks and Drawbacks

In comparison to the basic benefit, the distinctive feature of the National Child Benefit Supplement is that, by agreement with the provinces and territories, there is an NCBS clawback for Social Assistance recipients. The money taken back by the provinces is then supposed to be used for other programs that benefit low-income persons. Newfoundland, Nova Scotia, Quebec, Manitoba, and New Brunswick have increased Social Assistance benefits using NCBS funds. In all other

A SUMMARY OF THE FEDERAL CHILD BENEFITS IN CANADA

1918 **Child Tax Exemption:** This exemption provided income tax savings that increased as taxable income increased. It provided no benefits to families that did not owe income tax.

1944 **Family Allowance (FA):** This benefit was provided to all Canadian families with dependent children.

1973 **Family Allowance:** The benefit levels of the FA were tripled, indexed to the cost of living, and made taxable.

1978 **Refundable Child Tax Credit:** This more targeted and income-tested approach to child benefits provided the maximum benefit to low-income families, a declining amount to middle-income families, and no benefit to upper-income families.

1993 **Child Tax Benefit (CTB):** This benefit consolidated child tax credits and the Family Allowance into a monthly payment based on the number of children and level of family income.

1993 **Working Income Supplement (WIS):** This additional benefit was provided to supplement the earnings of low-income working families with children. Federal child benefits in 1993 totalled $5.1 billion.

1998 **Canada Child Tax Benefit (CCTB) and National Child Benefit Supplement (NCBS):** The NCBS replaced the WIS and was provided to all low-income families as part of the renamed Canada Child Tax Benefit.

2006 **Universal Child Care Benefit (UCCB):** The UCCB was introduced to provide assistance for child care expenses; it consists of a taxable benefit of $100 per month for each child under 6 years of age.

Source: Human Resources and Social Development Canada. National Child Benefit Progress Report, 2002. Reproduced with the permission of Her Majesty the Queen in Right of Canada 2006.

provinces and territories, the supplement is clawed back from Social Assistance recipients in different ways. As of 2005, Saskatchewan, British Columbia, and all three territories have a full clawback of Social Assistance; in PEI, Ontario, and Alberta, the amount is partially clawed back. Ontario and Prince Edward Island treat the NCBS as non-exempt income and reduce Social Assistance by the full amount. According to a reinvestment agreement, the provinces that claw back the NCBS must use the money for provincially designed and delivered programs and services for families with children, particularly low-income families.

Nova Scotia and Manitoba initially treated the NCBS as non-exempt income, but have since allowed families to keep the benefit while cutting back in other areas. In the case of Nova Scotia, families are worse off, as they have lost other, more generous, provincial allowances. A few other provinces have since allowed some families on welfare to keep a fraction of the supplement. For example, Quebec no longer deducts annual increases to the supplement from the Family Allowance. More than anything, this treatment has allowed provinces to

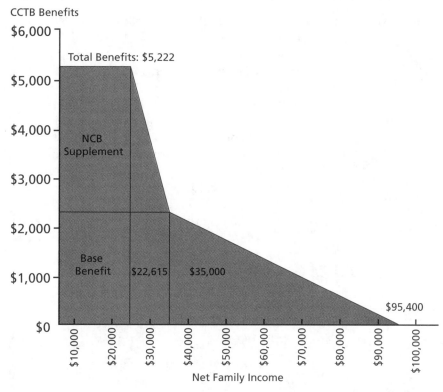

CCTB Benefits

Figure 12.3: The Canada Child Tax Benefit for a Two-Child Family: July 2004 to June 2005

Source: Human Resources and Social Development Canada. National Child Benefit Progress Report, 2004. Reproduced with the permission of Her Majesty the Queen in Right of Canada 2006.

publicly state that they are now allowing welfare families to keep the NCBS, but, in fact, no extra benefits are being paid.

While the clawback is the issue that receives the most attention, there are two other critical issues that negatively influence the effectiveness of the CCTB: the way it defines a family, and the use of net income as opposed to gross income in calculating benefits.

First, the CCTB calculation of benefit is based on net family income as reported on the income tax form. This is a compelling incentive not to report oneself as part of a couple on the tax form. In the case of a single mother, the tax rule stipulates that if she shares a dwelling with a person of the opposite sex for more than 12 months, her CCTB could be substantially reduced.

Second, basing the benefit calculation on net income, and not gross income, has negative consequences for low-incomes families. Many tax deductions exist that can lower the net income or taxable income of middle- and high-income earners. These include Registered Retirement Savings Plans (RRSPs), child care expenses, professional dues, employment expenses, interest expenses, investment losses, and even various tax shelters and investment funds. Low-income families are less likely to make these deductions. Basing the CCTB benefit calculation on net income, or income after these deductions, enables upper-income families to obtain the benefit, and may even mean that borderline eligible families do not receive benefits.

ADDITIONAL PROVINCIAL CHILD BENEFITS

The Canadian Revenue Agency administers the following provincial and territorial programs that assist families with children:

Alberta Family Employment Tax Credit

The Alberta Family Employment Tax Credit is a non-taxable amount paid to families with working income that have children under the age of 18.

You may be entitled to receive:

- $560 ($46.66 per month) for the first child;
- $510 ($42.50 per month) for the second child;
- $306 ($25.50 per month) for the third child; and
- $102 ($8.50 per month) for the fourth child.
- The maximum you can get is the lesser of $1,478 and 8% of your family's working income that is more than $2,760.

The credit is reduced by 4% of the amount of family net income that is more than $25,475.

BC Earned Income Benefit

Families whose earned income is more than $3,750 may also be entitled to the following:

- up to $20.25 per month for the first child;
- up to $17.58 per month for the second child; and
- up to $18.91 per month for each additional child.

Families whose net income is more than $21,480 may get part of the earned income benefit.

New Brunswick Child Tax Benefit

The New Brunswick Child Tax Benefit (NBCTB) is a non-taxable amount paid monthly to qualifying families with children under the age of 18. The New Brunswick Working Income Supplement (NBWIS) is an additional benefit paid to qualifying families with earned income who have children under the age of 18. Benefits are combined with the CCTB into a single monthly payment.

Under the NBCTB, you may be entitled to a basic benefit of $20.83 per month for each child. The amount of the basic benefit is reduced if your family net income is more than $20,000.

The NBWIS is an additional benefit of up to $20.83 per month for each family. It is phased in once family earned income is more than $3,750. The maximum benefit is reached when family earned income is $10,000.

Families with net income between $20,921 and $25,921 may get part of the supplement.

Newfoundland and Labrador Child Benefit

The Newfoundland and Labrador Child Benefit (NLCB) is a non-taxable amount paid monthly to help low-income families with the cost of raising children under the age of 18. The Mother Baby Nutrition Supplement (MBNS) is an additional benefit paid to qualifying families who have children under the age of one. Benefits are combined with the CCTB into a single monthly payment.

Under the NLCB, you may be entitled to a benefit of:

- $21.41 per month for the first child;
- $27.91 per month for the second child;
- $30.00 per month for the third child; and
- $32.16 per month for each additional child.

Families with net income between $17,397 and $22,397 may get part of the benefit.

Under the MBNS, you may be entitled to a benefit of $45 per month for each child under the age of one if your family net income is under $22,397.

Northwest Territories Child Benefit

The Northwest Territories Child Benefit (NWTCB) is a non-taxable amount paid monthly to qualifying families with children under the age of 18. The Territorial Worker's Supplement, part of the NWTCB program, is an additional benefit paid to qualifying families with working income who have children under the age of 18. Benefits are combined with the CCTB into a single monthly payment.

Under the NWTCB, you may be entitled to a basic benefit of $27.50 per month for each child. Families who have earned income of more than $3,750 may also get the Territorial Worker's Supplement of up to $22.91 per month for one child, and up to $29.16 per month for two or more children. Families with net incomes above $20,921 may get part of the benefit.

Nova Scotia Child Benefit

The Nova Scotia Child Benefit (NSCB) is a non-taxable amount paid monthly to help low- and modest-income families with the cost of raising children under the age of 18. Benefits are combined with the CCTB into a single monthly payment.

Under the NSCB, you may be entitled to a benefit of:

- $37.08 per month for the first child;
- $53.75 per month for the second child; and
- $60.00 per month for each additional child.

Families with net income between $16,000 and $20,921 may get part of the benefit.

Nunavut Child Benefit

The Nunavut Child Benefit (NUCB) is a non-taxable amount paid monthly to qualifying families with children under the age of 18. The Territorial Worker's Supplement, part of the NUCB program, is an additional benefit paid to qualifying families with working income who have children under the age of 18. Benefits

are combined with the CCTB into a single monthly payment.

Under the NUCB, you may be entitled to a basic benefit of $27.50 per month for each child. Families who have earned income of more than $3,750 may also get the Territorial Worker's Supplement of up to $22.91 per month for one child, and up to $29.16 per month for two or more children. Families with net income above $20,921 may get part of the benefit.

Ontario Child Care Supplement for Working Families

The Ontario Child Care Supplement (OCCS) is a tax-free monthly payment to help with the costs of raising children under the age of 7. . . . The program benefits low-to-middle income single- or two-parent families, families with one stay-at-home parent, or families with one or both parents studying or in training.

For each child under age 7, qualifying two-parent families can receive a monthly payment of up to $91.67 ($1,100 annually), and qualifying single-parent families can receive a monthly payment of up to $109.17 ($1,310 annually).

Yukon Child Benefit

The Yukon Child Benefit (YCB) is a non-taxable amount paid monthly to help low- and modest-income families with the cost of raising children under the age of 18. Benefits are combined with the CCTB into a single monthly payment.

Under the YCB, you may be entitled to a benefit of $37.50 per month for each child. Families with net income above $25,000 may get part of the benefit.

Source: **Your Canada Child Tax Benefit,** *(July 2006 to June 2007).* **Canada Revenue Agency.** *Reproduced with permission of the Minister of Public Works and Government Services Canada, 2006. Ontario information from Ministry of Finance,* **Ontario Child Care Supplement for Working Families,** *Government of Ontario.* **www.fin.gove.on.ca/english/tax/credit/occs.**

Child Poverty and Social Spending

Every country that spends more than 10 percent of its national income on social spending for families with children has a child poverty rate below 10 percent. This includes Denmark, Norway, Finland, and Sweden, which all have child poverty rates below 5 percent. In contrast, Canada devotes a little over 5 percent of national income to social spending, and has a child poverty rate of 15 percent.

The value of social expenditures in preventing child poverty is clear. In 2003, 628,000 children were kept out of poverty as a result of social security. Without this, Canada's child poverty rate would have been 26.9 percent. Any serious strategy to reduce the depth and levels of child poverty requires additional income transfers. Earnings from employment have never been sufficient for families with jobs at the lower ends of the labour market to escape poverty. This is particularly true for families with children, as wages are not related to income needs.

Source: UNICEF, 'Child Poverty in Rich Countries, 2005,' Innocenti Report Card No. 6. UNICEF Innocenti Research Centre, Florence.

Policy Impacts on Poverty

Many critics believe the NCBS will not eliminate poverty because it is clawed back from recipients of Social Assistance (the CCTB is not clawed back). The result, argue the critics, is that the majority of single mothers, who are most in need of the benefit, are denied the supplement. As well, there is no evidence that programs are improved by the reinvestment of funds in the provinces that take back benefits from Social Assistance. Indeed, many view the clawback of the NCBS as more of a discriminatory denial of necessary benefits than a mechanism to address the difficulties of the transition from welfare to work.

Supporters of the program point out that the benefit simply levels the playing field by providing benefits to those who are working. Prior to the NCBS, parents on welfare were reluctant to take a job because it would lead to the loss of prescription drug and other benefits for their children. Supporters of the program argue that the process of determining eligibility is superior with the CCTB and the NCBS. Eligibility is determined through an income test as reported on the income tax return rather than through an intrusive needs test as used by welfare. The supporters believe that the chance of improving benefits under an income-tested program with wide public appeal is far superior to obtaining increases in welfare benefits.

The National Council of Welfare (NCW), a citizen's advisory body, provided pointed analysis of the 2006 Universal Child Care Benefit (UCCB), which provides $100 per child per month to families with children aged 6 or under. They believe that as a taxable benefit in the hands of the lowest earner in a family, that it heightens inequities between one- and two-earner families with the same annual income, and between one-earner families with two parents and employed lone parents who struggle as their family's sole or primary earner and caregiver. Further, they do not believe that it is adequate to really provide child care choices to low-income families. Therefore, they see it as an inequitable child benefit and not a child care benefit. On the positive side, the NCW views the lack of any clawback on Social Assistance recipients by the provinces and territories as commendable.

The Caledon Institute (www.caledoninst.org) and its president, Ken Battle, believe that the NCBS should not be passed through to families on Social Assistance. They believe that any successful anti-poverty strategy must be based on a diverse range of social programs that have broad appeal and acceptance. They see the lack of public response to the severe cuts to welfare as an indication that welfare programs do not have public support. Therefore, the Caledon Institute argues that replacing child benefits in the welfare system with a broad, income tax–based, non-stigmatizing system of benefits is the first step in building an acceptable anti-poverty program.

In their report *Child Benefit Reform in Canada: An Evaluative Framework and Future Directions* (1997), Ken Battle and Michael

Mendelson even say that the argument against the clawback is naive. They argue that the provinces know the other income of welfare recipients, and generally, with the current climate of cutbacks, it is unlikely that many provinces would have actually passed the extra child benefits through (see Battle and Mendelson 1997, Chapter 7). As of early 2007, the provinces and territories have chosen not to claw back the UCCB from welfare recipients.

Conclusion

In 1992, Canada ranked first among all countries in the world on the **Human Development Index** (see Chapter 5). Canada has recently dropped on this list primarily due to child poverty and single-mother poverty levels: in 2002, Canada ranked third behind Norway and Sweden, and in the 2006 report, Canada dropped to sixth. For nearly thirty years, one of the richest nations in the world has maintained an average child and family poverty rate of one in six children. According to Campaign 2000's 2005 report card on child poverty in Canada, 1,201,000 of Canada's children, or nearly one in six, remained in poverty. Despite strong economic growth, rising employment, and strong job creation, child poverty remains stuck at 17.6 percent and has remained at a rate over 16 percent for the past thirty years (UNICEF 2005, 3).

Child poverty still persists in Canada; as this protest sign at a Halifax rally in 2002 suggests, many attribute child poverty to government policies and failure to make good on promises.

The CCTB and NCBS were expressly directed at addressing the low-income situations of families, and the UCCB to help families with child care expenses. The poverty levels of children are inextricably linked with the incomes of their parents or guardians, and several factors appear to be keeping the child poverty rate high. First, the number of single mothers is increasing, and this family type is the most likely to live in poverty. It is clear that in today's economy most families require the income of two people. Second, increasing numbers of working poor translate into more children living in poverty. Finally, decreased levels of income security benefits, such as Social Assistance in Ontario, Alberta, and BC, and difficult eligibility criteria for Employment Insurance, have lowered the incomes of the poor in Canada.

Without a comprehensive and integrated approach to family income policy, it is unlikely that this situation will change. Canada must see that helping children is an investment in the future. Social workers frequently see the effects of poverty on children and families, and clearly the long-term costs far outweigh the investment that can be made today.

Chapter Summary

Key Concepts

- [ ] **Campaign 2000**
- [ ] **Canada Child Tax Benefit (CCTB)**
- [ ] **Child Care Expense Deduction**
- [ ] **Child Tax Benefit (CTB)**
- [ ] **Child Tax Exemption**
- [ ] **Consumer Price Index**
- [ ] **Family Allowance (FA)**
- [ ] **Family responsibility approach**
- [ ] **Horizontal equity**
- [ ] **Human Development Index**
- [ ] **Indexation**
- [ ] **Investing in children approach**
- [ ] **Market poverty**
- [ ] **National Child Benefit Supplement (NCBS)**
- [ ] **National Council of Welfare**
- [ ] **NCBS clawback**
- [ ] **Poverty gap**
- [ ] **Refundable Child Tax Credit**
- [ ] **Tax credit**
- [ ] **Tax deduction**
- [ ] **Universal Child Care Benefit (UCCB)**
- [ ] **Welfare wall**
- [ ] **Working Income Supplement (WIS)**

Review Questions

1. What is the current poverty situation of Canada's families and children?
2. What is market poverty, and what are its basic causes?
3. What are the two general approaches to children's social welfare? What approach most closely resembles the approach followed by the Canadian government?
4. Explain the four purposes of child-related income security.

5. List and describe four key changes that took place over the history of income security for children in Canada.

6. What federal programs currently provide income security for Canadian families with children? What are two of the criticisms of the programs as they pertain to families on Social Assistance?

7. What is the welfare wall?

Exploring Social Welfare

1. How does your province treat the NCBS? Does it claw the NCBS back, and if so, what does it do with the clawed-back funds? The federal government refers to spending of the clawed-back funds as "reinvestments," and such monies are supposed to be spent on programs for low-income people in your province. You can find government information about reinvestments at www. nationalchildbenefit.ca. Do some research on your own and see what you can find out about the NCBS in your province.

2. Go to the Progress of Canada's Children and Youth website at www.ccsd.ca/pccy/2006. This site contains substantial information on a variety of issues facing children and youth. Pick one of the key issues that the site addresses. Locate two additional sources that address this same issue. Try finding a book or journal article on the topic, which will likely not be found on the Internet. Write a short report using APA citations, complete with data portraying the issue and proposed solutions.

Websites

The Progress of Canada's Children and Youth
www.ccsd.ca/pccy/2006
This is the website for the Canadian Council on Social Development's *Progress of Canada's Children and Youth* report, presenting a portrait of family life and the social, educational, physical, and economic security of children and youth.

Child Poverty Overview
www.policy.ca/policy-directory/Policy_Articles/index.html
This site has a collection of public policy articles. In the Children & Family section there is a Poverty section containing articles on child poverty from a variety of authors.

Child Rights Information Network (CRIN)
www.crin.org
The CRIN is a global network that disseminates information about the Convention on the Rights of the Child and child rights among NGOs, UN agencies, IGOs, educational institutions, and other child-rights experts.

References

Battle, K., and M. Mendelson. 1997. *Child Benefit Reform in Canada: An Evaluative Framework and Future Directions.* Ottawa: Caledon Institute. www.caledoninst.org/cbr-toc.htm.

Battle, K., S. Torjman, and M. Mendelson. 2006. *More Than a Name Change: The Universal Child Care Benefit.* Ottawa: Caldeon Institute. www.caledoninst.org/Publications/PDF/589ENG.pdf.

Bradbury, B., and M. Jantti. 1999. *Child Poverty across Industrialized Nations.* Italy: UNICEF.

Campaign 2000. 2005. *Decision Time for Canada: Let's Make Poverty History: 2005 Report Card on Child Poverty in Canada.* Ottawa: Campaign 2000.

UNICEF. 2005. *Child Poverty in Rich Countries, 2005: Innocenti Report Card No. 6.* Florence, Italy: UNICEF Innocenti Research Centre. www.unicef-icdc.org.

13 Disability and Social Welfare

Income Security and Full Participation

Disability is part of the human experience. The 2001 Participation and Activity Limitation Survey (PALS) found that over 12 percent of Canadians have a disability — that means 3.6 million people, or one in eight Canadians. Social welfare policy is meant to promote and support the full participation of people with disabilities in all dimensions of Canadian society — a key aspect of citizenship. This support is found in a vast array of federal, provincial, and municipal programs, and tax policies and in both the non-profit and the private sectors.

The term disability applies to a wide range of so-called impairments including sensory impairments, such as blindness or deafness, physical disabilities impairing mobility, and psychiatric, developmental, learning, and neurological disabilities. The complexity of addressing the social welfare of persons with disabilities is complicated by

> **"** The full participation of persons with disabilities requires the commitment of all segments of society."
>
> — In Unison: A Canadian Approach to Disability Issues *(HRDC 1998)*

United Nations Enable

www.un.org/esa/
socdev/enable

This is the website of
the Secretariat for the
Convention on the Rights
of Persons with Disabilities,
the motto for which is "full
participation and equality."

Persons with Disabilities: Terminology Debate

Persons with disabilities
is considered a more
humanizing, person-first
term that has generally
replaced the use of the
term "disabled people."
However, some disability
theorists disagree with
this linguistic effort.
Paul Abberley, a British
economic professor, who
is also disabled, suggests
that by de-emphasizing
the word "disability," we
allow ourselves to ignore
the continuing separation
of disabled people from
society. To insist that
disabled people are "like
everyone else" may only
serve to justify society's
failure to meet the unique
needs of disabled people,
thereby continuing
to prevent their full
participation in society.

the fact that needs vary greatly, from needing assistance to participate in the workplace, to needing support when unable to work, to requiring in-home care. The issue of disability is further complicated by conflicting perceptions: one, the most common, sees disability as a physical impairment; another sees disability as a social construct that prevents individuals from full participation in society. However, to administer support programs and uphold laws, the federal government must ascribe to definitions of disability. A mobility impairment is the most common type of disability in Canada, and the older Canadians are, the more likely they are to have a disability.

This chapter highlights the social welfare issues of disability in Canada, the challenge of employment for **persons with disabilities**, and the various income security programs available.

Disability in Canada

In 1976 the United Nations declared 1981 the **International Year of Disabled Persons**. According to Human Resources and Social Development Canada, this year was the cornerstone for the development of the government's action on disability. Beginning in 1981, the special House of Commons Committee on the Disabled and Handicapped reviewed all federal legislation concerning those with disabilities. The result was a report entitled *Obstacles*, which outlined 130 public policy recommendations from providing funding for assisted living programs and employment equity, to encouraging diversity in government marketing and promotions.

Fifteen years later, a 1996 first minister's meeting identified persons with disabilities as a national priority for social policy renewal. In response to the meeting, the federal, provincial, and territorial governments published *In Unison: A Canadian Approach to Disability Issues* in 1998, which was the first joint effort to promote equity and inclusion in all parts of Canadian society for people with disabilities. As a follow-up, the Government of Canada produced a 1999 report called *Future Directions to Address Disability Issues for the Government of Canada: Working Together for Full Citizenship*, which outlined the government's agenda for dealing with disability issues.

All of this has culminated in the collection of programs that we have today. While far from perfect, the social welfare of persons with disabilities has come a long way since the early days of the United Nations International Year of Disabled Persons in 1981.

Accessibility, Opportunities, and Supports

Social welfare for persons with disabilities mostly concerns accessibility, opportunities, and supports. **Accessibility** refers to creating an environment that is free of or provides alternatives to barriers, both physical and systemic, that prevent full participation in society. This can include obvious things such as ramp access to buildings or more conceptual things such as policies regarding government information services and promoting employment programs. Disability supports "refer to a range of goods, services and supports tailored to the individual requirements for daily living" (HRDC 2000). Such supports range from technical aids and special equipment such as computer software, hearing aids, Braille readers, etc., and human services such as personal support workers, interpreter services, and physiotherapy.

An example of this approach to social welfare for persons with disabilities is Ontario's *Accessibility for Ontarians with Disabilities Act* (AODA), enacted in 2005. The goal of this legislation is to develop accessibility standards throughout Ontario. By the 2025 deadline outlined in the act, people with disabilities will be able to move around from place to place, go shopping, attend school, visit their doctor, or get a job without facing barriers that people without disabilities would not normally face.

Profile of Persons with Disabilities

The **Participation and Activity Limitation Survey** (PALS) is a post-censal survey conducted every five years. Previously, the government conducted the Health and Activity Limitation Survey, but in 2001 the survey was renamed PALS to reflect the focus on examining barriers to participation among persons with disabilities. The survey is based on the World Health Organization's understanding of disability as a relationship between body structures and functions, daily activities, and social participation, and also recognizes the role of environmental factors.

The 2001 survey identified 3.6 million Canadians as having a disability; that is more than 10 percent of the population. Of that number, 5 percent are under 15 years of age, 55 percent were of working age (15 to 64), and 40 percent were 65 and older (see Table 13.1). The PALS also showed that disability rates increase with age and that disability rates are higher for women. Research also tells us Aboriginal people experience a rate of disability that is more than one and a half times the rate of the non-Aboriginal population. In the 2001 census, about 165,000 Aboriginal people reported having a disability (HRSDC 2004, 9).

Difficulty with mobility is the most commonly reported disability, comprising 12.2 percent of women and 8.6 percent of men. Often closely related is pain and lack of agility with similar although slightly

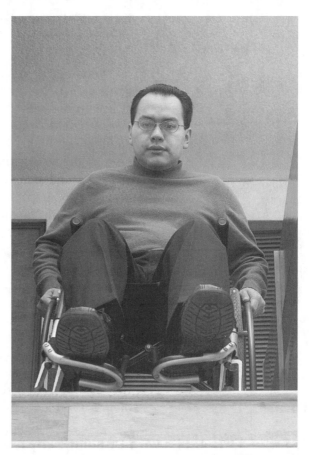

Barriers to full participation in society can come in many forms; physical barriers are the most well-known. The *Accessibility for Ontarians with Disabilities Act* aims to make Ontario barrier free by 2025.

lower rates. Sensory impairments such as hearing and seeing are the next most prevalent. The vast majority of adults with disabilities (82 percent) have more than one type of disability (CCSD 2005a, 1).

Psychological disabilities (also called *mental illness* within the health care field) affect 2 percent of men and 2.5 percent of women, according to Statistics Canada measures. This type of disability is characterized by alterations in thinking, mood, or behaviour, or some combination of the three. It includes conditions such as mood disorders (major depression and bipolar disorder), schizophrenia, anxiety disorders, and personality disorders. Health Canada estimates that 20 percent of Canadians will experience a mental illness during their lifetime (Health Canada 2002, 7). Major depression is most commonly reported. In their survey of the literature, Health Canada found that approximately 8 percent of adults will experience a major depression at some time in their lives (33).

The 2001 PALS found that working-age adults with disabilities are at higher risk of having a low income. In 1998, 48 percent of persons with disabilities relied on government programs as their primary source of income (Department of Finance Canada 2006, 5). In 2002, 15 percent of adults with disabilities lived in households below the after-tax Low Income Cut-off (LICO). This is more than double the proportion for Canadians without disabilities (6.6 percent) (HRSDC 2004, 54).

Table 13.1: Adults with Disabilities by Age Groups, by Sex, 2001

Age Groups	Total Number in Age Group	Number in Age Group as % of Total Population	Number of Men	Men as % of Total Population	Number of Women	Women as % of Total Population
Total—Aged 15 and over	3,420,340	14.6%	1,526,900	9.4%	1,047,470	15.7%
15–64	1,968,490	9.9%	921,020	9.4%	1,047,470	10.4%
15–24	151,030	3.9%	74,500	3.8%	76,530	4.0%
25–54	1,206,660	9.2%	555,420	8.6%	651,240	9.7%
55–64	610,800	21.8%	291,100	21.1%	319,700	22.4%
65 and over	1,451,840	40.5%	605,880	38.5%	845,970	42.0%
65–74	649,180	31.2%	296,310	30.2%	352,860	32.0%
75 and over	802,670	53.3%	309,570	52.1%	493,100	54.1%

Note: The Canada total excludes the Yukon, Northwest Territories, and Nunavut; the sum of the values for each category may differ from the total due to rounding.

Source: Human Resources and Social Development Canada. 2006. *Advancing the Inclusion of People with Disabilities 2006*. Ottawa, p. 86. http://www.hrsdc.gc.ca/en/hip/odi/documents/advancingInclusion06/index.shtml. Adapted from Statistics Canada publication *A Profile of Disability in Canada, 2001—Tables*. Catalogue 89-579. Release date: December 3, 2002, p. 6. http://www.statcan.ca/bsolc/english/bsolc?catno=89-579-X

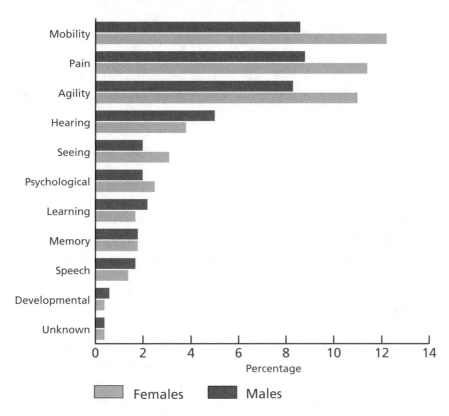

**Figure 13.1:
Prevalence of
Disability among
Adults Aged 15
Years and Over, by
Type of Disability
and Sex, 2001**

*Source: Statistics Canada.
2003.* **Participation and
Activity Limitation Survey.**
*Catalogue 89-577-XWE.
Ottawa, p. 18. http://
www.statcan.ca/english/
freepub/89-577-XIE/index.
htm*

Theories of Disability

Our understanding of disability has undergone a significant shift in
the last two decades. Historically, disability was a social and legal
issue, where individuals with disabilities were deemed objects of pity
and categorized as the deserving poor. Eventually, as medical science
advanced, disability became a medical health issue, and people with
disabilities were viewed as tragedy, and often kept away from public
view. Today, society is starting to develop a more inclusive understanding of disability, with an emphasis on the full participation in
society by people with disabilities.

History of Disability

In Canada, before the beginning of modern medicine, "disability" was
viewed as a social and legal category based on the English Poor Laws
of 1601 (Stone 1984). As was explained in Chapter 2, the Poor Laws
differentiated between the deserving poor and the undeserving poor.
The deserving poor included lepers, those who were bedridden, the
impotent (or those unable to work), and people above the age of 60.
The socio-legal criteria of disability established by the English Poor
Laws in Britain were adapted in the British colonies of North America, and the social and/or legal determination of disability lasted until
the early years of the twentieth century. Persons deemed unable to
work because of a disability by a local magistrate were considered

deserving of charitable support. Various methods of support, such as outdoor relief, indoor relief, and charity, were utilized throughout Canada from the late eighteenth to the early twentieth centuries.

Outdoor relief was a common form of assistance provided for persons with disabilities when their families could not take care of them; begging was the most prevalent form of outdoor relief. Through the Poor Laws, deserving poor persons, such as persons with disabilities, were given license to beg, and as time passed, other forms of outdoor relief supplemented begging. Persons with disabilities were housed in private homes, and funds to cover expenses for food, clothing, shelter, and medical care were often provided through municipal taxes, charitable organizations, and religious organizations. In essence, outdoor relief basically meant that persons with disabilities were cared for through non-institutional methods of relief and were more or less part of the community.

By the mid-nineteenth century, outdoor relief came to be seen as a mechanism that created rather than relieved dependency, and institutions such as asylums, poorhouses, and workhouses replaced the former methods of outdoor relief (Splane 1965). This change represents a significant shift in the philosophy regarding charitable relief. Persons with disabilities, who were once considered part of the social order, were now viewed as nuisance populations, to be removed from society and placed in segregated institutions. Disability was often considered a source of shame, and those who were not sent to institutions were often hidden away in the home by their family members.

Broad social, political, economic, and cultural changes took root in Canada during the mid- to late nineteenth century, including a shift in the public attitude towards social dependency and social relief. The social rejection of "defective" populations was so severe that many persons with disabilities were treated as common criminals and banned from the streets of many cities in Canada. Many were charged under vagrancy laws and sent to jail. Others were sent to a local poorhouse, a workhouse, or an asylum.

By the mid-twentieth century, the institutionalization of people with disabilities was the dominant method of care, and most provinces across Canada had established large facilities for this purpose. Many provinces had "special" residential schools for blind and deaf children as well as institutions for people with psychiatric disabilities and for people with developmental disabilities. In addition to the provincial institutions, specialized hospitals were established for many different disabled populations, including tuberculosis hospitals, orthopaedic hospitals, and rehabilitation hospitals. Within a few decades, the institutionalization of people with disabilities was so widespread that it became the common belief that this was the natural order of things, and that people with disabilities had always been separated from their communities (Bowe 1978).

The social model of disability considers the disadvantages facing persons with disabilities to be caused by society, not the disability itself. Changes in society help remove those disadvantages.

Because of this history of institutionalization and stigma, people with disabilities became social outcasts. However, this particular view changed with World War I when many young men from all levels of society returned home with significant impairments. The enormous effect of the war changed the public's attitude towards disability. The war also brought many advances in medicine, especially in the areas of surgery, follow-up care, and rehabilitation. Because of these factors, disability stopped being categorized as a socio-legal issue and became a medical issue. With the end of World War II, science advanced even further, and the welfare state emerged. This created the rehabilitation team, which included physician, nurse, occupational therapist, physiotherapist, and eventually such professionals as social worker, psychologist, and vocational counsellor.

The Medical versus Social Model of Disability

Perspectives on disability have shifted over the past three decades, moving from a strictly medical approach to a social model. The **medical model** views disability as a medical condition or personal tragedy or unfortunate life event; it focuses on limitations and advocates helping the individual to adapt to his or her situation. As the Legal Resource Centre for Persons with Disabilities explains, "Traditionally, disabilities were viewed through a medical lens and defined as a 'health problem' or 'abnormality' that must be cured. Most people are familiar only with this outmoded 'medical model' of disability." In contrast, the social model views disability within a social and environmental context, emphasizing the need for society to change so as to remove the barriers that prevent "disabled" persons from fully participating in social life.

The shift in model was due primarily to advocacy work done by the disability rights movement throughout the 1980s. The social model redefined the concept of disability as a social construct, that is, as a

Models of Disability

■ **Medical model:** the view that disability is a health problem to be dealt with medically and which consequently separated people from full participation in society

■ **Social model:** the view that disability is a social construct, existing only as long as society maintains barriers to full participation of people who are physically or mentally different

consequence of historical, material, and social conditions, which create a disabling society that marginalizes and excludes people with a disability (Mays 2006; Oliver 1996). In other words, some people may have physical and psychological differences from the statistical norm, but these only become disabilities when society fails to accommodate the differences and include the individuals in society to the same extent as those who are considered "normal." As part of the social model, disability advocates such as Michael Oliver (1996) forward a social oppression theory or a political rights model, arguing that the disadvantages faced by persons with disabilities are not merely due to a perceived impairment, but are caused by social and political inequality between those without disabilities (the majority) and those with disabilities (the minority). This model views disability as a form of social oppression.

Social scientist Paul Abberley added to the theoretical construction of the social model in the 1980s, building on his own experience living with a disability. He explains that he, as a disabled person, felt oppressed because he was regarded as inferior to other members of society. At an empirical level, Abberley argues that the disadvantages faced by persons with disabilities are dialectically related to an ideology or group of ideologies that justify and perpetuate the barriers (Abberley 1987, 7). In other words, persons with disabilities are only disadvantaged because people without disabilities believe they are and therefore perpetuate the disadvantages.

Throughout the 1990s, the disability rights movement in Canada has challenged the medical model, advocating a social model. By exploring the ways in which disability is socially produced, proponents of the social model have succeeded in shifting public perception and debates about disability from the traditional medical model to consideration about citizenship and social equality. In Canada, these challenges have often taken place within a human rights framework. A variety of tools exist to support disability advocacy: the *Canadian Charter of Rights and Freedoms* guarantees equality and prohibits discrimination based on mental or physical disability across all jurisdictions in Canada; the *Canadian Human Rights Act* protects the rights of people who face discrimination on a number of grounds, including a physical or mental condition. The *Canadian Human Rights Act* also requires federal employers and service providers to accommodate special needs.

Charity or Citizenship?

Disability theorists and activists are now emphasizing the notion of inclusion and full citizenship, which emphasizes the removal of barriers to full participation in social life. This participation goes beyond employment to include social, cultural, and recreational activities. This theory draws attention to the ways that our society's notion of

ARCH Disability Law Centre

www.archlegalclinic.ca

Funded by Legal Aid Ontario, ARCH provides support to persons with disabilities, from advice on applying for benefits to litigation on disability rights.

what makes a citizen is what precludes people with disabilities from achieving equality. For example, disability theorists highlight both the physical barriers (architectural and infrastructural) and discriminatory attitudes that dehumanize persons with disabilities. We are all familiar with the concept of making public buildings accessible to people with mobility impairment; however, many barriers are formed by society's prejudice, ignorance, and assumptions.

The social justice approach to equality advocates for both the public and private sector to meet the special needs of people of disabilities. But social model theorists have criticized the mainstream social justice approach because it tends to characterize persons with disabilities as deserving of public charity, rather than as full-fledged citizens. Being viewed collectively as recipients of charity only serves to reinforce the stereotypes of persons with disabilities as dependent, incapable of providing for themselves, and objects of pity. Indeed, much of the theoretical work on social justice has assumed that people with disabilities are incapable of gainful employment. Social justice theories rarely regard disability as an economic or citizenship issue; instead, persons with disabilities are seen as having special needs that lie outside of the circumstances of justice (Status of Women Canada 2001, 10–11).

Employment

We as Canadians have generally overcome the notion that persons with disabilities are unable to work. Two main reasons underlie this shift. The first, and most commonly understood reason is the advance in overall human rights legislation: legislation such as employment equity, the *Canadian Charter of Rights and Freedoms*, and the

Social justice approach

■ aims to create systems and policies that help meet the needs of persons with disabilities

■ some worry that it characterizes persons with disabilities as "charity cases" without emphasizing full citizenship

Table 13.2: Theories of Disability — Contrasting Approaches

	"Personal Tragedy" Theory (Medical Model)	"Social Oppression" Theory (Political Rights Model)
Definition of problem	Physical impairment, lack of employment skills	Dependent on professionals, relatives, etc.
Locus of problem	In the individual	In the environment and rehabilitation process
Solution to problem	Professional intervention by physician, therapist, occupational therapist, vocational rehabilitation counsellor, etc.	Peer counselling, advocacy, self-help, consumer control, removal of barriers
Social role	Patient/client	Citizen/consumer
Who controls	Professional	Citizen/consumer
Desired outcome	Maximize activities, living skills, and gainful employment	Independent living

Source: Hick, Steven. 2006. *Social Work in Canada*, 2nd ed. Toronto: Thompson Educational Publishing, 307. Reprinted with permission.

Human Rights Legislation

■ *Canadian Charter of Rights and Freedoms*
■ *Canadian Human Rights Act*

Canadian Human Rights Act have all worked to open opportunities for persons with disabilities. The second reason is that Canada is experiencing a shortage of skilled labour, and due to our aging population, this shortage is expected to get worse. Governments view persons with disabilities as one possible way to alleviate this impending shortage. While many people with disabilities can become self-sufficient if given the opportunity, some face workplace barriers and discrimination, and others are unable to participate in the labour market.

The percentage of people with disabilities who were employed full-time, full-year increased from 42.4 percent in 1999 to 46.4 percent in 2004, compared to an increase from 62.8 percent to 65.3 percent for people without disabilities in the same period (HRSDC 2006, 48). About 50 percent of persons with disabilities are not in the labour force compared with only 16 percent for persons without a disability. According to PALS 2001, only 27 percent of working-age adults with disabilities are employed all year, full-time. This is half the rate of 52 percent for other Canadians (as reported in HRSDC 2004, 40). Further, the report finds people with more severe disabilities are less likely to work all year: 41 percent of working-age adults with mild disabilities work all year and full-time, compared to 28 percent of those with moderate disabilities and 17 percent of those with severe disabilities. Only 10 percent of people with very severe disabilities work all year and full-time (HRSDC 2004, 40).

Even those individuals with jobs may find that they are earning less than their counterparts without disabilities; in 2004, the average earnings for persons with disabilities was 85.8 percent of the average for other Canadians (HRSDC 2006, 66). Some individuals, both employed and unemployed, must therefore rely on public income security programs. As such, people with disabilities are three times more likely than other Canadians to have income from government sources

Table 13.3: Labour Force Activity by Disability Status

	Total Adults		Adults with Disabilities		Adults without Disabilities	
	Count	%	Count	%	Count	%
Total	17,135,540		1,832,250		15,303,290	
Employed	12,764,420	74.5%	765,510	41.8%	11,998,900	78.4%
Unemployed	1,249,810	7.3%	468,120	25.5%	781,690	5.1%
Not in labour force	3,048,200	17.8%	525,830	28.7%	2,522,380	16.5%
Not specified	73,110	0.4%	72,790	4.0%	0	0.0%

Note: Total count excludes full-time students.

Source: Human Resources and Social Development Canada. *Advancing the Inclusion of People with Disabilities (2006).* Reproduced with the permission of Her Majesty the Queen in Right of Canada 2006.

as their major source of income: 27 percent as compared to 9 percent (HRSDC 2006, 67). In 2003, persons with disabilities received 54.2 percent of their income from wages and 26.8 percent from public income security programs (HRSDC 2006, 67).

Persons with disabilities were more likely than those without disabilities to have had no employment in 2000 in every province and territory. The rates were particularly high for women with disabilities, with wide variances between provinces. Women had an unemployment rate of 61 percent in Newfoundland and Labrador and 59.3 percent in Quebec, while some regions had rates just above or below 30 percent. The worst employment gap was for men in Prince Edward Island, where the percentage of those with disabilities who were without employment for the full year was nearly four times (3.89) that of men without disabilities (44.4 percent compared with 13.4 percent). New Brunswick, Nova Scotia, Quebec, and Ontario had rates for men that were over three times that of their non-disabled counterparts. The gap was smaller for women in every province due primarily to the high rates for women without a disability (CCSD 2005a, 8).

Barriers in the Workplace

The *Canadian Human Rights Act* ensures the right to accommodation in the workplace for people with disabilities. Beyond the legislative necessity of accommodation, ensuring access to the labour market for people with disabilities will also help alleviate an impending labour shortage caused by an aging population; making minor changes to the workplace can increase the supply of workers with individuals who would not otherwise be able to participate. There are 2 million Canadians aged 15 to 64 with disabilities, and about 45 percent of these are in the labour force. Of those who were employed in 2001, about 35 percent had no perceived workplace limitation; the others required some accommodation (Williams 2006, 23).

There are numerous types of workplace accommodation, and needs will be different for each individual in each context. Accommodation needs can be categorized as either job modifications or workplace modifications. **Job modifications** refer to the personal help that workers need to participate in the labour market, whereas **workplace modifications** are changes in the workplace environment.

Examples of job modifications could include human supports such as readers, sign language interpreters, and job coaches; technical aids such as voice synthesizers and portable note-takers; computers with Braille; communication aids such as recording equipment; and job redesign. **Job redesign** refers to an adjustment or modification of duties. According to the Canadian Council on Social Development (CCSD), about 30 percent of persons with disabilities who are employed require a work aid or job modification. Modified work hours and job redesign are the most common types of job modification, with

---

Workplace Accommodation

■ **Job modifications:** refers to the personal help that workers need to participate in the labour market, such as job redesign

■ **Workplace modifications:** refers to changes in the workplace, such as assistive software

The modern workplace can pose many barriers to individuals with disabilities; the government has various programs that assist employers in adapting the workplace to remove or reduce those barriers, such as providing technologies like Braille writers.

Discrimination in the Workplace

According to HRSDC, more than one in five people report that they have been the victim of discrimination when trying to obtain and maintain employment. Almost 80 percent of Canadians agree that equally qualified persons with disabilities are less likely to be hired for jobs, and more than 50 percent of Canadians state that they would hide a non-visible disability from their employers (SDC 2004, 28–29).

19 percent of employed persons with disabilities requiring an adjustment in work hours, and 17 percent requiring job redesign. The CCSD also reports that 29 percent of employed people with disabilities have an unmet need for "other" unspecified work aids and 27 percent for technical aids (CCSD 2005b, 2).

Workplace modifications are changes in the workplace environment. Fifteen percent of employed people with disabilities report that they need a "modified work structure" such as handrails, ramps, accessible parking, accessible elevators, modified workstations, accessible washrooms, or accessible transportation (CCSD 2005b, 2). The highest unmet work structure need is accessible transportation; this need goes unmet 26 percent of the time. Other unmet needs are as follows: 20 percent require handrails, ramps, accessible parking, accessible elevators, or accessible workstations, and 12 percent require accessible washrooms (CCSD 2005b, 3).

Employment Programs

There are many Canadians with disabilities who are not employed but who can and want to work. Most of these individuals would be able to contribute more fully to the Canadian economy and become more self-sufficient if they had some assistance in overcoming various barriers to employment.

Through the Employment Insurance program, the federal government is funding programs designed to assist people with disabilities to return to work even if they are otherwise ineligible for EI. The Opportunities Fund for Persons with Disabilities is a $30-million-a-year employability program for people with disabilities who have had little or no attachment to the labour force. People with disabilities who are unemployed (or working less than 20 hours per week) and are not normally eligible for Employment Insurance are eligible for this program. The fund has assisted approximately 36,000 people since its inception in 1997.

The Opportunities Fund helps people with disabilities prepare for and obtain employment; it also provides for ongoing skill development to help individuals keep working. One of the objectives of the fund is to encourage employers to hire people with disabilities. The fund also provides work experience that can lead to more stable employment and provides personal support to people accessing employment services.

Other initiatives include the **Labour Market Agreements for Persons with Disabilities (LMAPD)**. This is a multilateral agreement created in 2003 between the provinces and the federal government, and it replaced the 1998 Employability Assistance for People with Disabilities (EAPD) initiative. Under the agreement, the federal government provides funding to the provinces to help improve the employability of persons with disabilities. The provinces use the agreement to fund various programs such as job coaching and mentoring, pre-employment training and skills upgrading, employment counselling and assessment, and accessible job placement networks as well as post-secondary education, assistive aids and devices, wage subsidies and earning supplements, and supports for self-employment. In 2004 total federal funding for the LMAPD was $223 million (HRSDC 2004, 46).

Income Security Programs

Income security for persons with disabilities is about as complex as it gets. Programs are provided by multiple layers of government, and the rules for eligibility are complicated and inconsistent. The primary program for people with labour force attachment is the Canada/Quebec Pension Plan, or if the disability was the result of a workplace accident or illness, Workers' Compensation. Those individuals who cannot or are prevented from participating in the labour force must rely on provincial social assistance programs that provide minimal amounts. Disabled veterans are eligible for a Veterans Pension. Other benefits are available through the tax system, providing medical expense deductions and tax credits. Table 13.4 outlines federal expenditures in various disability support programs.

Canada Pension Plan Disability (CPPD) Benefit

The **Canada Pension Plan Disability (CPPD)** Benefit program is the largest long-term disability insurance program in Canada. The CPPD benefit provides a disability benefit to those with "severe and prolonged disabilities" and who meet the CPP contribution requirements. The Canada Pension Plan (CPP) has been in effect since 1966 and is a national plan based on contributions from workers and employers. It

---

Employment Programs

■ **Opportunities Fund for Persons with Disabilities:** funded through the EI program

■ this fund is intended to help persons with little or no attachment to the workforce find and keep jobs

■ **Labour Market Agreements for Persons with Disabilities (LMAPD):** agreements between the federal government and the provinces to provide funding for employment programs

Federal Benefit Programs

- Canada Pension Plan Disability (CPPD)
- Employment Insurance (EI)
- Disability Tax Credit (DTC)
- Veterans Disability Pension

is most commonly known as providing retirement pensions to workers in Canada, but it also provides survivor, death, and disability benefits to CPP contributors and their families.

In 2005/06, 296,000 adults and 89,000 of their dependent children received $3.3 billion in CPPD benefits; the maximum monthly benefit was $1,031 in 2006 with an average payout of $775 per month. The monthly benefit for each eligible child during this period was $200.40 (HRSDC 2006, 71). Disability pensions are paid until a recipient reaches age 65 and the benefits are converted to a retirement pension. Since disability benefits were first introduced in 1970, the CPP has seen steadily increasing caseloads. The disability caseload grew from 27,000 in 1970 to 283,508 beneficiaries by 2000 (Torjman 2002, 2).

In addition to having a "severe and prolonged disability," to qualify for the CPPD you must be under 65, have earned a specified minimum amount, and contributed to the CPP while working for a minimum number of years (usually at least four of the last six years). The CPP defines "disability" as a physical and/or medical condition that is "severe and prolonged." "Severe" means that you have a mental or physical impairment that regularly makes you incapable of doing *any* type of work. This is different from most other long-term disability insurance systems, which often base eligibility for benefits on incapacity to return to your former job. The CPP bases eligibility on the applicant's incapacity to do any type of paid work on a regular basis. "Prolonged" means your disability is likely to be long-term, or is likely to result in your death.

Table 13.4: Disability-Related Income Security Expenditures

Income Support Benefits	$ Millions
Canada Pension Plan Disability (CPPD) (HRSDC)	3,300.0
Canada Pension Plan Disability, vocational rehabilitation program (HRSDC)	2.8
Federal workers compensation benefits (HRSDC)*	155.1
Employment Insurance sickness benefits (HRSDC)**	813.2
Assisted Living Program (INAC)	682.3
Child Disability Benefit (FC and CRA)	90.0
Total	5,043.4

*This includes Compensation Benefits, Workers' Compensation Boards Administrations costs, and injury on-duty leave.

**EI sickness amount is for 2004/05 as 2005/06 figures were not yet available.

Source: Human Resources and Social Development Canada. *Advancing the Inclusion of People with Disabilities (2006).* Reproduced with the permission of Her Majesty the Queen in Right of Canada 2006.

The CPPD benefit has several important advantages over private insurance or most other income security programs. All working Canadians are covered by the program, including self-employed individuals who contribute. The program does not exclude people on the basis of medical history, and does not charge higher premiums for contributors deemed to be high risk. Unlike many private insurance plans, the CPPD program also provides full inflation protection (Torjman 2002, 10).

Other Federal Supports

In addition to the CPP disability benefit, the federal government provides Employment Insurance (EI) sickness benefits, the Disability Tax Credit (DTC), and the veterans disability benefits.

EMPLOYMENT INSURANCE SICKNESS BENEFITS

Intended as a temporary measure, Employment Insurance provides up to fifteen weeks of benefits for people who cannot work due to short-term illness, injury, or quarantine. Called *sickness benefits*, these are meant to fill the gap before people become eligible for longer-term illness and disability benefits from employer-sponsored group insurance plans, private plans held by individuals, or CPPD. Annual spending for EI Sickness Benefits in 2004/05 was $813.2 million (HRSDC 2006, 71).

DISABILITY TAX CREDIT

All Canadians with a severe and prolonged disability are eligible for the **Disability Tax Credit**. In 2003, 370,000 people met the eligibility criteria for the credit, which is a disability that "markedly restricts" activities of daily living. People that qualify for the credit claim a Disability Tax Credit on their income tax return, but must have a treating physician complete a form outlining the nature of the disability. Canadians who support someone with a disability may also claim the tax credit; in 2003 another 186,000 Canadians made such a claim.

In order to claim a Disability Tax Credit, a person with a disability or a supporting individual must have sufficient income to be taxable. For many Canadians this is not the case (Department of Finance Canada 2006, 5). Many disability activists consider the tax form to be unnecessarily complicated and argue that the program is restrictive; however, a recent court case (*Buchanan v. the Queen*) ruled that people with mental disabilities can qualify for the credit, and the decision was upheld in appeals. This led to revisions in the program for the 2006 tax year.

VETERANS DISABILITY BENEFITS

Veterans Affairs Canada administers the *Pension Act*, which provides a monthly disability pension designed to compensate veterans and their dependants if the veteran becomes permanently disabled or dies as a result of military service. Canadian veterans are eligible for the

Persons with Disabilities Online

www.pwd-online.ca

This excellent government site provides access to a wide variety of information for persons with disabilities, family members, caregivers, and all Canadians.

BUCHANAN V. THE QUEEN: THE DISABILITY TAX CREDIT

In 2006, the Disability Tax Credit system was revised, as a result of *James W. Buchanan v. the Queen* in 2000, which determined that individuals who have mood disorders that significantly interfere with their daily activities were eligible for the Disability Tax Credit.

The *Income Tax Act* provides a credit to individuals who have a "severe and prolonged mental or physical impairment." The act requires that "the effects of the impairment are such that the individual's ability to perform a basic activity of daily living is markedly restricted." There are six basic activities defined in the act: perceiving, thinking, and remembering; feeding and dressing oneself; speaking; hearing; bowel or bladder functions; and walking. To qualify for the Disability Tax Credit, a treating physician has to complete a form, responding to questions concerning these criteria.

Mr. Buchanan was diagnosed with bipolar affective disorder and had been exhibiting symptoms of the disease for decades — while he often exhibited coping skills, and above average intelligence, evidence given at court described his delusional behaviour. However, after qualifying for the credit for several years, Mr. Buchanan's doctor did not believe that he met the conditions of the tax credit, and completed the tax form such that the credit would be denied. The Buchanans took the case to tax court, with Mrs. Lembi Buchanan, having power of attorney, appearing on her husband's behalf.

The physician argued that Mr. Buchanan was not impaired in the basic activities of life, and asserted that, in his opinion, most patients with mood disorders don't qualify for the credit "which is intended for persons so severely disabled that they have difficulties with very basic self-care activities."

The judge in the case decided that the doctor was not offering an unbiased medical opinion when completing the tax forms for his psychiatric patients, and was misinterpreting the law with his own preconceived notions of who should qualify. In her judgment, the judge explained that the doctor misinterpreted the law and misinterpreted his responsibility in determining eligibility: "He clearly did not understand that the six items defining a basic activity of daily living, as contained in subsection 118.4(1)(c) are not to be read together, but each activity is treated separately."

Evidence presented to court outlining his mood swings and delusional behaviour made it very clear that Mr. Buchanan did indeed meet the criteria of being markedly restricted in his perceiving, thinking, and remembering.

Before the judge's decision, Lembi Buchanan also submitted a brief to the Sub-Committee on the Status of Persons with Disabilities regarding her husband's situation. The overall result of this case was a recognition that individuals with mental disorders do have long-term disabilities requiring some form of life management and are therefore eligible for the Disability Tax Credit.

Source: Memo to patients and their doctors on the recent changes to the Disability Tax Credit (DTC) Certificate Form T2201 for persons with mental impairments. Fighting for Fairness, June 16, 2006, www. disabilitytaxcredit.com/news.php; and Buchanan v. Queen (2001), Tax Court of Canada, http://decision.tcc-cci. gc.ca/en/2001/html/2001tcc20001865.html.

disability pension benefits if they have a permanent disability resulting from disease or injury incurred during a war or in a special duty area. Veterans with disabilities directly related to peacetime service in the Canadian Forces are also eligible. In March 2005 there were over 258,490 war service veterans in Canada, the large majority of whom are veterans of World War II and the Korean War. Over 90,000 veterans made use of Veterans Affairs services, and almost one-quarter (62,139) received a veterans disability pension (HRSDC 2005, 11).

Provincial Programs

Individuals who do not qualify for any other public or private income security programs are left with provincially delivered Social Assistance programs. Like the welfare system, these programs differ in each province and territory. The programs provide minimum income to those who pass a needs test and meet strict disability eligibility criteria. Both the benefit rates and the criteria are different in each province or territory. Canadians with disabilities access these programs only when all other public and private means of support are exhausted. For example, to qualify for benefits, persons with disabilities must liquidate their assets if they are over a certain value. Table 13.5 demonstrates the liquid assets levels for regular welfare qualification and for disability qualification across Canada.

The assets that persons with disabilities are allowed to keep while collecting benefits varies widely across Canada as Table 13.5 indicates. The asset exemptions are higher for persons with disabilities in most regions. The National Council of Welfare believes that having such asset limitations is bad public policy, because it doesn't allow households to maintain a cushion against unforeseen emergencies. This may be even more crucial for persons with disabilities, as they may face extra financial needs, such as assistive devises or accessibility needs.

Mental or psychiatric conditions are also considered disabilities under the law; in 2001 the Tax Court of Canada confirmed that mental disorders do qualify as disabilities if they interfere with basic activities of daily living.

Each of Canada's ten provinces and three territories designs, administers, and delivers its own disability income support program. In their review of welfare incomes, the National Council of Welfare (2006) outlines eligibility criteria and benefit amounts for each province and territory and compares these amounts with LICO. Table 13.6 illustrates the inadequacy of income support provided to persons with disabilities who do not qualify for CPPD or private insurance programs. With a few exceptions, the total annual support is less than 50 percent of LICO, with Alberta providing the lowest benefit amount.

ONTARIO DISABILITY SUPPORT PROGRAM (ODSP)

The ODSP is designed to meet the unique needs of people with disabilities who are in financial need, or who want and are able to work and need support. The benefit is available to Ontario residents who can prove they have a disability that meets the legislated definition: "A substantial physical or mental impairment that is continuous or recurrent, is expected to last one year or more and results in a substantial restriction in his/her ability to: attend to personal care; function in the community or function in the workplace." Applicants must prove they qualify by obtaining a health status report from a registered health professional, and they must undergo a needs test. This means that an applicant's income and assets must be below a certain amount to qualify. Individual applicants must have assests totalling less than $5,000, but this includes cash, RRSPs, or insurance policies. ODSP benefit amounts are higher than they are for other Ontario Works (OW) recipients. As of 2006, a single person with a disability would get $543 towards basic needs and $436 maximum for shelter. A couple with one child under 12 would get $912 for basic needs and $744 maximum for shelter. Some believe that the difference between regular welfare payments and disability payments has its origins in the Elizabethan Poor Law concepts of the deserving and undeserving poor (see Chapter 2).

Table 13.5: Provincial Liquid Asset Exemption Levels as of January 2005 for Single Persons with and without Disabilities

	Single Employable Person	Single Person with a Disability
Newfoundland and Labrador	$500	$3,000
Prince Edward Island	$50 to $200	$900
Nova Scotia	$500	$500
New Brunswick	$1,000	$3,000
Quebec	Applicants: $816 Recipients: $1,500	Applicants: $816 Recipients: $2,500
Ontario	$520	$5,000
Manitoba	Applicants: $0 Recipients: $400	$2,000
Saskatchewan	$1,500	$1,500
Alberta	$402	$1,114
British Columbia	Applicants: $660 Recipients: $1,500	$3,000
Yukon	$500	$1,500
Northwest Territories	$0	$5,000
Nunavut	$0	$5,000

Source: National Council of Welfare. *Welfare Incomes 2005*. Reproduced with the permission of the Minister of Public Works and Government Services Canada, 2007.

Manitoba Income Assistance for Persons with Disabilities Program

Manitoba's Income Assistance for Persons with Disabilities Program provides financial assistance for adults enrolled in the Employment and Income Assistance program, and it also provides employment assistance. The purpose of the program is to support the additional costs associated with living in the community for persons with disabilities. The program also provides extra assistance for various things. For example, there is an allowance of $80 for people living in the community, transportation passes for wheelchair users, a telephone rental allowance, a coin laundry allowance, and additional financial assistance to support employment (child care, transportation, clothing). Basic assistance for one person is $295.90. If a single person also receives shelter assistance, the amount is $331.40 plus rental costs.

Alberta Assured Income for the Severely Handicapped (AISH)

Alberta's AISH program is for adults with permanent disabilities that diminish their ability to participate in the workforce. The level of benefits depends on income and assets. The maximum living allowance is $1,000 per month, and additional benefits (personal income support benefits) may be provided to meet clients' special needs. The personal income support benefits can be used for such continuous costs as child care, special diets, guide dogs, as well as one-time costs ranging from emergencies to children's school supplies. The health benefits include eye care, dental, prescriptions; if individuals no longer qualify for AISH due to increased income, they may still qualify for the health benefits.

Canadian Caregiver Coalition

www.ccc-ccan.ca

This organization supports caregivers across Canada and advocates for the importance of recognizing caregivers' contributions to the society at large.

Table 13.6: Annual Disability Support Income as a Percentage of LICO

Province/Territory	Annual Disability Income, Single Individual (2005)	Percentage of LICO (%)
Newfoundland and Labrador	$9,728	54%
Prince Edward Island	$8,084	45%
Nova Scotia	$8,897	50%
New Brunswick	$7,995	45%
Quebec	$10,063	48%
Ontario	$12,057	58%
Manitoba	$8,601	41%
Saskatchewan	$48,893	50%
Alberta	$7,851	38%
British Columbia	$10,656	51%
NWT	$17,275	NA
Nunavut	$13,225	NA

Source: Adapted from National Council of Welfare. 2006. *Welfare Incomes 2005*. Ottawa: National Council of Welfare, 4. www.ncwcnbes.net/htmdocument/reportWelfareIncomes2005/WI2005ENG.pdf.

The Cost of Care

In late 2006, a severely disabled girl known as Ashley underwent a medical treatment to stunt her growth, at the behest of her parents. One of the reasons for the treatment was to keep the little girl small to facilitate her in-home care. The case inspired great debate about the rights of the severely disabled and the rights of their caregivers, exposing the challenge that many Canadians face in providing care for severely disabled children and adults. Many news stories outlined the financial strain families face when providing constant care in the home; often caregivers are prevented from earning an income, and government benefits only go so far.

Some countries provide an income to family or other volunteers. For example, Australia provides a twice-monthly carer allowance of $178 (CDN) to family caregivers, which is meant to provide partial compensation; there is also a twice-monthly carer payment of $459 for caregivers who cannot participate in the workforce due to their caregiving responsibilities. Norway, Sweden, and the United Kingdom also have similar income support programs for caregivers (White and Keefe 2005).

BRITISH COLUMBIA EMPLOYMENT AND ASSISTANCE FOR PERSONS WITH DISABILITIES PROGRAM (EAPD)

The Government of British Columbia has recently redesigned its income assistance programs. The new system, while focusing on employment for those clients who are able to work, ensures that assistance is there for persons with disabilities. This program provides qualifying persons with disabilities a higher income assistance rate, supplementary assistance, and specialized employment supports. A single person with disabilities would be eligible for $531.42 in basic assistance and a $325 maximum shelter allowance as of 2006. Currently persons with disabilities receive the highest rate of assistance available in British Columbia and the third-highest among Canadian provinces.

Aging and Disability

About 40 percent of Canadians over the age of 65 have a disability. The increase in the numbers of Canadians with disabilities is due partly to the aging population. Canadians are also living longer, and the chances of having a disability greatly increase with age. Those aged 65 and over have about a one in three chance of developing a disability, and that likelihood continues to increase as we grow older. By the time we are over 75, more than half of us will experience at least one disability (HRSDC 2005, 8).

The most common types of disabilities among older Canadians are mobility: in 2001, 43 percent of those age 75 and over, and 25 percent of those 65 to 74 years of age had mobility disabilities. A similar number experience agility limitations (40 percent and 23 percent), which are frequently accompanied by pain-related limitations (31 percent and 22 percent) (HRSDC 2005, 10).

Conclusion

If you have a disability in Canada and require income support, you could live comfortably if you are eligible for C/QPP, Workers' Compensation, or private disability insurance. Otherwise you are left with little access to income. The various provincial disability programs are part of the provincial welfare or Social Assistance systems and provide extremely low benefits rates, often well below LICO. Often people with disabilities only want the same opportunities to participate in society as other Canadians. This involves removing barriers that might be within infrastructure, attitudes, or job design, to name a few. More and more, the social model of disability is raising awareness about barriers that prevent the full participation of people with disabilities. In the end, it is a matter of treating people with dignity and respect, not discounting their potential contribution to society. Currently, the federal government is working to develop a *National Disability Act* to improve accessibility and inclusion for Canadians with disabilities. It appears that we are at another important historical juncture for people with disabilities.

Chapter Summary

Key Concepts

- **Accessibility**
- **Accessibility for Ontarians with Disabilities Act (AODA)**
- **Canada Pension Plan Disability (CPPD) Benefit**
- **Disability**
- **Disability Tax Credit**
- **Employment Insurance Sickness Benefits**
- **International Year of Disabled Persons**
- **Job modifications**
- **Job redesign**
- **Labour Market Agreements for Persons with Disabilities (LMAPD)**
- **Medical model**
- **Opportunities Fund for Persons with Disabilities**
- **Participation and Activity Limitation Survey (PALS)**
- **Persons with disabilities**
- **Psychological disabilities**
- **Social justice approach**
- **Social model**
- **Veterans disability benefits**
- **Workplace modifications**

Review Questions

1. Disability refers to a range of so-called impairments. What are the various difficulties or impairments included under the term *disability*?
2. What are psychological disabilities, and how widespread are they?
3. How has our conception of disability changed since the mid-nineteenth century, and what have been the implications for social policy?
4. Describe and compare the medical and social models of disability.
5. What is the employment situation of people with disabilities, and how can employment opportunities be increased?

6. What income security programs for people with disabilities exist in your province? Do they offer an income that provides an adequate standard of living?

7. What is the primary federal income security program for people with disabilities, and how does it operate?

Exploring Social Welfare

1. Go to the Canada Benefits website (www.canadabenefits.gc.ca) and look up the benefits for persons with disabilities in your region. How do the benefits in your province or territory stack up against other provinces? Consider the cost of living in your area. How would a person with disabilities fare in your area, if he or she were unable to work? Worked in a low-income job? Worked in a middle-income job?

2. Major depression can cause significant disruptions in people's lives, both financially and personally. When one compares Statistics Canada prevalence data on psychological disabilities with other research on "mental illness," it appears that major depression may be unreported. Analyze this disability, including the prevalence, types, causes, and potential treatments, by visiting the Canadian Mental Health Association (www.cmha.ca), Mood Disorders Society of Canada (www.mooddisorderscanada.ca), and The Public Health Agency of Canada's *Report on Mental Illnesses in Canada* (www.phac-aspc.gc.ca/publicat/miic-mmac/index.html).

Websites

Disability Research Information Page (DRIP)
www.ccsd.ca/drip/research
The site provides centralized access to Canadian Council on Social Development (CCSD) information about disability research.

Persons with Disabilities (HRSDC)
www.hrsdc.gc.ca/en/gateways/individuals/audiences/pd.shtml
This federal government website provides extensive information about programs and services, including income security programs.

***Advancing the Inclusion of People with Disabilities* 2006 Report**
www.hrsdc.gc.ca/en/hip/odi/documents/advancingInclusion06/toc.shtml
This report on disability issues covers more than fifty programs and initiatives that some thirty federal departments and agencies deliver in order to facilitate the participation of people with disabilities in all aspects of Canadian society.

References

Abberley, P. 1987. The concept of oppression and the development of a social theory of disability. *Disability, Handicap, and Society* 2 (1): 5–19.

Bowe, Frank. 1978. *Handicapping America: Barriers to Disable People.* New York: Harper and Row.

Canadian Council on Social Development (CCSD). 2005a. *Combinations of Disabilities.* Disability Information Sheet 19. www.ccsd.ca/drip/research.

Canadian Council on Social Development (CCSD). 2005b. *Employment and Persons with Disabilities in Canada.* Disability Information Sheet 18. www.ccsd.ca/drip/research.

Department of Finance Canada. 2006. *A New Beginning: The Report of the Minister of Finance's Expert Panel on Financial Security for Children with Severe Disabilities.* Ottawa: Department of Finance Canada. www.fin. gc.ca/activty/pubs/disability_e.html.

Health Canada. 2002. *A Report on Mental Illnesses in Canada.* Ottawa: Health Canada. www.phac-aspc.gc.ca/publicat/miic-mmac/index.html.

Human Resources and Social Development Canada (HRSDC). 2004. *Advancing the Inclusion of People with Disabilities, 2004.* Ottawa: Social Development Canada. Cat. no. SD13-6/2004E. www.hrsdc.gc.ca/en/ gateways/nav/top_nav/program/odi.shtml.

Human Resources and Social Development Canada (HRSDC). 2005. *Advancing the Inclusion of Persons with Disabilities, 2005.* Ottawa: Social Development Canada. Cat. no. SD23-4/2005-1. www.hrsdc.gc.ca/ en/gateways/nav/top_nav/program/odi.shtml.

Human Resources and Social Development Canada (HRSDC). 2006. *Advancing the Inclusion of People with Disabilities, 2006.* Ottawa: Social Development Canada. Cat. no. HS4-27/2006E. www.hrsdc.gc.ca/en/ gateways/nav/top_nav/program/odi.shtml.

Human Resources Development Canada (HRDC). 1998. *In Unison: A Canadian Approach to Disability Issues.* Ottawa: HRDC. www.socialunion. gc.ca/pwd/unison/unison_e.html.

Human Resources Development Canada (HRDC). 2000. *In Unison 2000: Persons with Disabilities in Canada.* Ottawa: HRDC. www.socialunion. gc.ca/pwd/unison/unison_e.html.

Mays, Jennifer. 2006. Feminist disability theory: Domestic violence against women with a disability. *Disability & Society* 21 (2): 147–58.

National Council of Welfare. 2006. *Welfare Incomes 2005.* Ottawa: National Council of Welfare. www.ncwcnbes.net/htmdocument/ reportWelfareIncomes2005/WI2005ENG.pdf.

Oliver, M. 1996. *Understanding Disability: From Theory to Practice.* Houndsmills: Macmillan.

Social Development Canada (SDC). 2004. *Canadian Attitudes towards Disability Issues: 2004 Benchmark Survey, Prepared for the Office for Disability Issues.* Ottawa: Social Development Canada.

Splane, Richard. 1965. Review: The role of public welfare in a century of social welfare development. In *Perspectives on Canadian Health and*

Social Services Policy: History and Emerging Trends, ed. Carl. A Meiliche and Janet A. Storch. 1980. Ann Arbour, MI: Health Administration Press.

Status of Women Canada. 2001. *Disability-Related Support Arrangements: Policy Options and Implications for Women's Equality.* Toronto: The Roeher Institute.

Stone, D. 1984. *The Disabled State.* Philadelphia: Temple University Press.

Torjman, S. 2002. *The Canada Pension Plan Disability Benefit.* Ottawa: Caledon Institute.

White, Sheri, and Janice Keefe. 2005. Paying caregivers: A briefing paper. Maritime Data Centre for Aging Research and Policy Analysis. Mount Saint Vincent University in partnership with the Canadian Caregiver Coalition. www.ccc-ccan.ca/pdf/caregiverCompensationEng2005.pdf.

Williams, C. 2006. Disability in the workplace. *Perspectives on Labour and Income* 7 (2): 16–24. Statistics Canada cat. no. 75-001-XIE.

The Elderly and Retired

Pensions, Health Care, and an Aging Population

Although income security for the retired and elderly in Canada expanded rapidly in the 1950s and 1960s, leading to a large reduction in old age poverty, the current system may be strained over the next thirty-five years by the doubling of the percentage of persons over age 65. In particular, the challenge of combatting old age poverty for elderly unattached women, people with disabilities, and Aboriginal peoples still remains. Continuing vigilance will be needed if we are to maintain recent gains and resolve these outstanding concerns.

A Canadian born in 1960 can expect to live twenty years longer than a Canadian who was born in 1900. Birth rates have been declining, and a growing proportion of the population is over 65. By the year 2031, approximately 20 percent of Canada's population — one in five — will be seniors. These facts have important consequences for

❚❚ Old age pensions have been a recurring issue in Canadian politics since the beginning of the twentieth century and now have more government resources devoted to them than to any other single public program."

— *Kenneth Bryden, author of* Old Age Pensions and Policy-Making in Canada *(1974)*

Canadian society and income security programs. What are the needs of these older Canadians? How will they be taken care of? What are their income security needs?

Good health and financial security help to ease the changes that aging and retirement require. Factors such as forced retirement, ill health, and lack of money all contribute to lessened satisfaction with this period of life. Canada's income security system for the elderly and retired consists of three main "pillars" or components: basic minimum income allowances, such as Old Age Security (OAS), Guaranteed Income Supplement (GIS), and Spouse's Allowance (SPA); social insurance benefits, such as the Canada/Quebec Pension Plan; and private pensions and publicly supported and regulated private savings plans, such as Registered Retirement Savings Plans (RRSPs).

Canada's income security programs have had significant impacts on low income rates for the elderly and retired. The percent of elderly living below the Statistics Canada Low Income Cut-off (LICO) after tax fell from 14.7 percent in 1985, to 10.8 percent in 1990, to 7.3 percent in 2004. For men, the rate between 1992 and 2004 fell from 5.1 to 3.5 percent (Statistics Canada 2006a).

Nevertheless, Canadians still have much to learn about the special issues of aging. This chapter looks at the various income security programs that are currently in place for old age and retirement with a view to maintaining and improving the system for the challenging years that lie ahead.

The Aging Population

The percentage of persons over age 65 will almost double over the next thirty-five years — from 12 percent today to 23 percent by the year 2030. As the "baby boomers" (born between 1946 and 1965) age, the senior population is expected to reach 6.7 million in 2021 and 9.2 million in 2041 (nearly one in four Canadians). The fastest growth is occurring among those 85 years of age or older. In 2001, over 430,000 Canadians were 85 years of age or older — more than twice as many as in 1981. The proportion of Canadians aged 85 or older is expected to grow to 1.6 million in 2041 (Health Canada 2002, 3).

A number of social changes have affected the needs and composition of the retired population in Canada. These include:

- improvement in health care and extension of life expectancy
- long-term decline in the birth rate
- establishment of the retirement age
- establishment of the value that the elderly deserve a rest

The first change has been the improvement in health care, which has resulted in a large extension of life expectancy. In 1997, life expectancy for Canadians was 75.8 years for men and 81.4 years for women. Life expectancy is expected to continue to grow, although

The Challenge of Aging Populations

Around the world, headlines are warning that when the "baby boom" generation starts retiring in earnest, the labour force will shrink and economic growth and material well-being will be threatened. To limit the impact, some policy analysts believe that innovative policies are needed to allow people to spread work across the full span of their lives — people can increase their leisure time in their early years and spend more time working and learning in their later years.

more slowly, reaching 81 years for men and 86 years for women in 2041. This will continue to contribute to an increase in the number of elderly people in Canada (Health Canada 2002, 5).

The second change is the long-term decline in the birth rate. In 2001, Canada's fertility rate reached a record low at 1,512 births per 1,000 women aged 15 to 49. It now stands at less than half of the peak reached in 1959, when there were 3,935 births per 1,000 women. The current fertility rate of 1.5 children per woman is expected to remain relatively constant in the near future (Health Canada 2002, 4). Combined with the extension of life expectancy, this has resulted in an increase in the proportion, or the relative size, of the older population, and these trends are expected to increase for several decades. Furthermore, female life expectancy is higher than that of males – women are living longer – and this too has implications for the income security system.

Third, a retirement age to leave the labour force was established in the age of industrialization. Initially, it was set at 70 years of age, and now it is set at 65. The concept of retiring from paid employment at an elderly age came about because people eventually reach an age when their level of productivity does not sufficiently maintain the demand for their labour. Whereas previously, with extended families, the elderly relied on their family for support, industrialization also changed the traditional nature of the family.

Finally, Canadian society realized that, when a person's productivity becomes insufficient, they should be given a phase in their lives in which they can rest. This notion is also tied to the concern that older workers should make way for the younger generation of more productive workers.

All of these social changes have significant implications within Canada's income security system. By 2030, for each person receiving income security benefits, there will only be three working Canadians to support these benefits, compared to the five of today. As the proportion of retired Canadians receiving benefits keeps increasing, economic expenditures will continue to rise steadily.

Women and Old Age

Due to their longer life expectancy, women form the majority of the Canadian elderly population. In 2001, women comprised 56 percent of the elderly, and their proportion increases with age. In 2001, women made up 60 percent of those aged 75 to 84, and 70 percent of those aged 85 or older (Health Canada 2002, 6). The effects of a variety of factors inhibit women from amassing adequate resources to support their later life and retirement. The present economic trends of downsizing, of enforcing involuntary retirement, and of the growth in the service sector (where many women work) mean fewer benefits and pension coverage for many workers, particularly women. Many

Mandatory Retirement

As of 2006, Ontarians are no longer required to quit working at age 65. Alberta, Manitoba, Quebec, Prince Edward Island, Nunavut, the Yukon, and the Northwest Territories have also abolished mandatory retirement. Many groups support this trend because it opens up options for people in their senior years. But workers' unions warn against increasing the age at which people can qualify to collect pensions (both government and workplace), and the Canadian Union of Public Employees (CUPE) believes that permitting people to work longer because they feel financially obligated to work does not really expand workers' options when it comes to retirement.

Due to longer life expectancies, the majority of Canada's elderly population is women; with less consistent work histories, elderly women often have limited retirement incomes.

elderly and retired women find themselves living with low income and insufficient income security for a number of reasons:

■ The labour force itself is aging, and a large proportion of women workers are aged 45 to 64; thus there are sizeable numbers of women "pre-retirees." There has been a longstanding trend for men to take early retirement, and many Canadian women retire at ages 60 to 62.

■ Women work in lower paying occupations and sectors, such as community, business, and personal services and trade. Women working full-time earn approximately 65 percent of male earnings (full-time workers). Contrasted with 10 percent of men, 28 percent of women work part-time.

■ Many women are unattached or single in old age – the risk of widowhood increases with age; 30 percent of Canadian women are widowed at age 65 and 50 percent by age 75. Older men are nine times more likely to remarry than older women, so more women grow older alone, and many find themselves living below the Low Income Cut-off (LICO). The rate for unattached women aged 65 or over living below LICO (after tax) in 2004 was 38.4 percent (Statistics Canada 2006).

■ Fewer women are covered by their employer's pension plans than men, and many such plans have no survivor's benefits. Compared with 52 percent for men, 70 percent of the income of women aged 65 and over is from government transfers. Of persons collecting C/QPP retirement benefits (in September of 1995), women averaged $274 per month while men averaged $477 per month.

WOMEN CONTRIBUTING TO PENSION PLANS

There have been some interesting changes in the pattern of women and men contributing to the various forms of retirement pension plans in recent years. On the one hand, a slightly greater proportion of women are now covered by employer-sponsored pension plans than two decades ago. In 2002, 39% of all employed women were members of such plans, compared with from 38% in 1980.

In contrast, the proportion of men covered by employer-sponsored plans has dropped sharply in the same period, falling from 54% in 1980 to 40% in 2002. As a result, the proportion of female workers currently covered by a private pension is virtually the same as that for men. Indeed, by 2002, women made up 46% of all workers covered by employer-sponsored pensions, compared with just 31% in 1980.

The overall long-term increase in the proportion of employed women contributing to an employer-sponsored pension plan, though, masks the fact that the share of women participating in these plans has declined in the past decade. Indeed, the proportion of employed women contributing to a private pension plan peaked at around 42% in the early 1990s and dropped to the current figure of 39% by the late 1990s. On the other hand, there has been almost no change in the share of women participating in these plans in the 2000s. In contrast, the share of employed men participating in these plans declined fairly consistently right through this period.

There has also been an increase in the proportion of women in Canada contributing to the Canada/Quebec Pension Plan in the past two decades as more women have joined the paid workforce. In 2002, 68% of all women aged 20 to 64 contributed to this program, up from 57% in 1981. In contrast, the share of working-aged men participating in this program has fallen in the same period, although the share of men currently contributing to these plans (74%) is still higher than that for women.

Source: Statistics Canada. 2006. Women in Canada: A Gender-based Statistical Report. Fifth Edition. Catalogue 89-503. Ottawa, p. 137. http://www.statcan.ca/english/freepub/89-503-XIE/0010589-503-XIE.pdf

Elderly Poverty Rates

The rate of low income among the elderly in Canada has declined noticeably since 1980, primarily to the effect of income security transfers. In 1982, 17.5 percent of seniors had after-tax incomes below Statistics Canada's LICO. The rate had fallen to 5.6 percent by 2004 (Statistics Canada 2006a). Low-income rates for Canadian seniors are

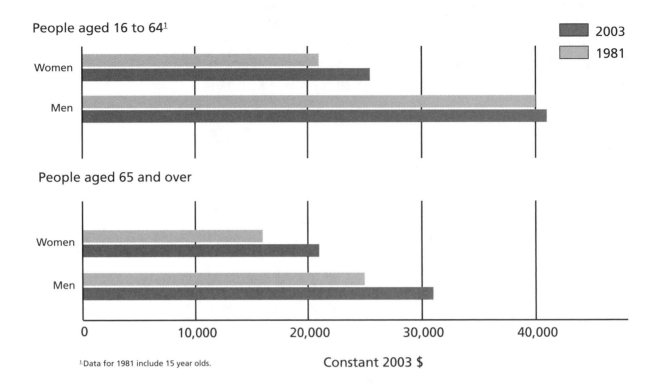

People aged 16 to 64[1]

People aged 65 and over

Constant 2003 $

[1]Data for 1981 include 15 year olds.

Figure 14.1:
Average Income of Women and Men, by Age, 1981 and 2003

Source: Statistics Canada. 2006. **Women in Canada: A Gender-based Statistical Report.** *Fifth Edition. Catalogue 89-503. Ottawa, p. 279. http://www.statcan. ca/english/freepub/89-503-XIE/0010589-503-XIE.pdf*

among the lowest in all countries studied by the Organisation for Economic Co-operation and Development (OECD 2001).

In 2004, the after-tax below LICO rate was 5.6 percent, compared to a before-tax rate of 14 percent. When measuring low income rates for the elderly population in Canada it is important to consider after-tax income. In 2001, elderly households received on average an estimated $19,900 in government transfers, accounting for 43 percent of their total income before taxes. According to Statistics Canada, the after-tax income of elderly households remained stable for the last decade, in part because of the high proportion of government transfers in their income.

Nevertheless, there is a particularly wide gap in the likelihood of unattached senior women and unattached senior men having low incomes. In 2001, about half of these women (45.6 percent) lived in a low-income situation, compared with 33 percent of unattached senior men. The after-tax incidence of low income among both unattached senior women and men, however, has dropped sharply since the early 1980s. Among women, the figure fell from 70 to 38.4 percent between 1980 and 2004, while among men it dropped from 52 to 31.5 percent (Statistics Canada 2006a).

Elderly poverty rates have decreased over the past few decades, largely due to the development of comprehensive income security programs for seniors. To a large extent, this has resulted from political pressure brought to bear by this powerful and growing lobby group.

The first income security program for the elderly was the *Old Age Pensions Act* of 1927; in Ottawa on May 18, 1928, the prime minister signed the pension agreement between the Dominion and the Province of Saskatchewan.

History of Income Security for the Elderly and Retired

As the caring capacities of families shifted, pensions became a major issue in many industrializing countries. The elderly could no longer rely on an extended family support structure, as they once had within an agrarian society. Denmark led the way in 1891 with its means-tested plan, and New Zealand followed in 1901. Social advocates and reform-minded politicians in Canada argued that the federal government should use its new power and financial capacities to extend the pension provisions that were currently offered only to war veterans.

In 1921, a minority government was elected federally for the first time in Canadian history, making it impossible to pass any pension legislation. The 1925 election saw similar results, and Prime Minister William Lyon Mackenzie King needed the support of the Progressive Party and the only two elected Labour members of Parliament — James S. Woodsworth and Abraham A. Heaps. Woodsworth and Heaps, in cooperation with Progressive leader Robert Forke, presented Mackenzie King with a number of policy initiatives, including an Old Age Pension program. The prime minister agreed to pursue the reforms in return for the support of the two parties, thus ensuring his government would not fall. In 1926, Mackenzie King won a majority Liberal government and was able to undertake reforms. This led to the first major piece of income security legislation for the elderly — the *Old Age Pensions Act* of 1927.

The 1927 plan authorized the federal government to form agreements with the provinces to pay half of the costs of pensions paid under provincial legislation that met the requirements of the federal act. Administration was to be entirely a provincial responsibility. The pension was not to be available to Aboriginal people, as defined by the

Canada's First *Old Age Pensions Act*

The 1927 *Old Age Pensions Act* provided a maximum pension of $20 per month or $240 per year, available to British subjects aged 70 or over who had lived in Canada for twenty or more years. As a means-tested provision of benefits, it was given only to the elderly whose income was less than $365 per year, including the pension benefits, and it excluded Status Indians.

Child Rearing Drop-out Provision (CRDO)

The amount of your CPP benefit is based on how long and how much you have contributed. Historically, this has negatively affected women who opt to stay at home and care for newborn children. Periods when they had no earnings or their earnings were low resulted in a lower benefit. The CPP now has a special provision to prevent this. Months of low or zero earnings spent caring for children under the age of seven are excluded from the calculation of a pension.

Seniors Canada On-line

www.seniors.gc.ca

This federal government web resource provides access to information and services that are relevant to seniors, their families, caregivers, and supporting service organizations.

Indian Act. The amount of the pension was set at $240 a year, subject to a means test. The pensioner was allowed to have a total income of $365 per year, meeting what the government of the day determined to be an adequate income of $1 per day.

Kenneth Bryden, a CCF politician and professor of economics, wrote the definitive history of Old Age Pensions (Bryden 1974). He attributes the emergence of public pension policy in Canada to two opposing forces: the social and economic needs of an emerging urban-industrial society, and the influence of a deep-rooted set of cultural values, referred to as the market ethos. He argues that the struggle between these two forces — one demanding pensions and the other resisting — led to means-tested pensions in 1927, universal pensions in 1951, and contributory pensions in 1965.

The *Old Age Security Act* and *Old Age Assistance Act* in 1951 moved the government into universal pensions. The exclusion of Aboriginal people was dropped with these acts. The *Old Age Security Act* established a universal pension for those over 70, subject only to a twenty-year residency requirement. The federal government funded and administered the program. The decision to institute a universal plan was made with some reluctance by the government, but any attempts to substitute a different design were resisted by seniors. The program remained universal until 1989, and a special old age security tax was implemented to fund the program. The *Old Age Assistance Act*, on the other hand, was a provincially administered means-tested benefit with partial funding from the federal government.

Income Security for the Elderly and Retired

Canada's old age income security system balances public and private retirement benefits. It guarantees a minimum income for all seniors and allows Canadians to avoid serious disruptions in living standards upon retirement.

The two government-stated objectives of the retirement income system are to ensure that elderly people have sufficient income regardless of their preretirement income, and to maintain a reasonable relationship between working and retirement income to avoid drastic income reduction.

To accomplish these objectives, the government has devised a variety of income security measures that can be divided into three levels of income security for the retired and elderly:

1. Basic minimum: Old Age Security, Guaranteed Income Supplement, and provincial/territorial supplements
2. Social insurance: public pensions — Canada/Quebec Pension Plan (C/QPP)
3. Private plans: occupational pensions and private savings

Total federal expenditures in 2002 for Canada's retirement income system were $25 billion for the OAS, GIS, and SPA (up from $17 billion in 1990), and $26.4 billion for C/QPP (up from $14 billion in 1990), for a total federal cost of $51.4 billion (Health Canada 2002, 23). These programs account for the largest share of federal income security spending. Added to this are foregone tax revenues such as those diverted by RRSPs, which amounted to $16 billion in 2002. Given the changing demographics discussed earlier, this amount will increase in the future.

Basic Minimum: Old Age Security, Guaranteed Income Supplement, and Provincial/Territorial Supplements

The first level of income security for the retired and elderly comprises the following public programs:

- Old Age Security (OAS)
- Guaranteed Income Supplement (GIS)
- Allowance (previously the Spouse's Allowance)
- Provincial/territorial supplements

The Old Age Security (OAS) program provides a basic pension (adjusted for inflation) to virtually everyone over 65 years of age who has lived in Canada for a required length of time. It is a universal monetary benefit payable to Canadians over a specified age (though some would argue that it is no longer universal due to the clawback for higher-income Canadians). It is an income transfer program paid out of the general revenue of the federal government. The OAS program includes the income-tested Guaranteed Income Supplement (GIS), which provides extra money to OAS recipients who have little or no other income, and the Allowance, which pays benefits to low-income spouses or partners of an OAS pensioner, or widows/widowers between the ages of 60 and 64. Annual OAS program expenditures

War Veterans Pensions and Allowance

Veterans' Affairs Canada (VAC) administers the *Pension Act*. It provides pensions to those suffering from disabilities related to military service, either during peace or wartime. When a disability pensioner dies, the spouse or common-law partner will receive a Survivor's Pension. Surviving children may be eligible for Orphan's Benefits following a pensioner's death. In addition, an income-tested War Veterans Allowance is available for those in financial need. It is meant to increase a minimum income to meet basic needs. Eligibility is based on wartime service, age, health, income, and residence.

Level 3: Private Plans

Occupational Pensions and Private Savings

Level 2: Social Insurance

Public Pension Plans — Canada and Quebec Pension Plans (C/QPP)

Level 1: Basic Minimum

Old Age Security, Guaranteed Income Supplement, and Provincial/Territorial Supplements

Figure 14.2: The Three Levels of Income Security for the Retired and Elderly

In 1951 the Old Age Security program was created (it was implemented in 1952). It was the first major federal program without a cost-sharing arrangement with the provinces. Before it could be legislated, an amendment to the *British North America Act* was required to allow the federal government jurisdiction in the area of Old Age Pensions. It was the second universal income transfer program in Canada, after the *Family Allowance Act* of 1944. It was financed from federal general revenues, and it was paid out to every person 65 years of age and older if they met certain residency requirements.

The OAS remained a universal program until 1989, when the Conservative government of Brian Mulroney introduced the clawback of benefits for people with higher incomes. Pensioners with an individual net income above $62,144 (as of 2006) must repay part or all of the Old Age Security pension amount. The repayment amounts are deducted from monthly payments before they are issued. The full OAS pension is eliminated when a pensioner's net income is $101,118 or above. Strictly speaking, the OAS is therefore no longer a universal program. The federal government argues that it is essentially still a universal program, as only about 5 percent of seniors receive reduced OAS benefits, and only 2 percent lose the entire benefit.

OLD-AGE INCOME SECURITY: 75 YEARS IN THE MAKING

1927: The *Old Age Pensions Act* was enacted, permitting the federal government to give assistance to provinces that provided a pension to British subjects aged 70 and older.

1952: The *Old Age Security Act* came into force, establishing a federally funded pension. It replaced the 1927 legislation that required the federal government to share the cost of provincially run, means-tested old age benefits.

1965: Amendments to the *Old Age Security Act* lowered the eligible age for the OAS pension to 65, one year at a time, starting in 1966 at the age of 69.

1966: The CPP and QPP came into force on January 1, 1966.

1967: The Guaranteed Income Supplement was established under the Old Age Security program.

1972: Full annual cost-of-living indexation was introduced for OAS.

1973: Quarterly indexation was introduced for the Old Age Security program.

1974: Full annual cost-of-living indexation was introduced for the CPP.

1975: The Spouse's Allowance was established as part of the Old Age Security program.

1975: The same Canada Pension Plan benefits became available to male and female contributors, as well as to their surviving spouses or common-law partners and dependent children.

1975: The retirement and employment earnings test for Canada Pension Plan retirement pensions at the age of 65 was eliminated (a contributor can, upon application, receive his or her retirement pension the month following his or her 65th birthday, but can no longer contribute to the CPP).

1977: The payment of partial Old Age Security pensions was permitted, based on years of residence in Canada.

The Guaranteed Income Supplement (GIS) was implemented in 1966 as a selective, income-tested benefit paid to OAS recipients with no other income. The GIS was introduced in conjunction with the C/QPP in 1966. It was intended as a "guaranteed annual income" program and is the only such program in Canada; it is one of the few guaranteed income programs operating in industrialized countries. With this program, every Canadian over the age of 65, except for those who do not meet the residency requirement, have an income that is at least equal to OAS plus the maximum GIS. With this equation, the program guarantees a minimum income for elderly Canadians. The GIS stops being paid at an income of $34,368 (as of 2006).

There has been some debate about whether or not the GIS, when taken together with the OAS, actually provides an adequate income. For example, the maximum GIS for a single pensioner was $4,937 a year in 2006, and when this was combined with the OAS, a single person would have an annual income of $10,495.92. This was far below the LICO of $17,219 for a city with a population of 500,000 or more, and just below the $11,264 LICO for a rural area. Analysis finds a similar pattern for couples, thereby showing that a poverty gap still exists for the elderly in Canada.

1978: Periods of zero or low earnings while caring for the contributor's child under the age of 7 were excluded from the calculation of Canada Pension Plan benefits.

1978: Canada Pension Plan pension credits could be split between spouses in the event of a marriage breakdown (CPP credit splitting).

1985: Under OAS, the Spouse's Allowance was extended to all low-income widows and widowers aged 60 to 64.

1987: Several new CPP provisions came into effect, including flexible retirement benefits payable as early as the age of 60, increased disability benefits, continuation of survivor benefits if the survivor remarries, sharing of retirement pensions between spouses or common-law partners, and expansion of credit splitting to cover the separation of married or common-law partners.

1989: The repayment of OAS benefits or "clawback" was introduced.

1992: Three major amendments to the CPP came into effect: a new twenty-five-year schedule for employer-employee contribution rates was established, children's benefits were increased, and provision was made for individuals who were denied disability benefits because of late application.

1995: The period of retroactivity for OAS benefits changed from five years to one year. Individuals were permitted to request that their OAS benefits be cancelled.

1998: The CPP moved from pay-as-you-go financing to fuller funding. Contribution rates were increased. A new investment policy was introduced.

2000: All OAS and CPP benefits and obligations were extended to same-sex, common-law couples.

Pension Timeline from The History of Canada's Public Pensions, 2002, www.civilization.ca © Canadian Museum of Civilization

The other basic minimum income program, the Spouse's Allowance (SPA) (now called "the Allowance"), was created to deal with a hardship-creating anomaly in the OAS/GIS. In some cases, an elderly couple consisting of a woman under age 65 and an income-earning husband aged 65 would receive OAS and GIS intended for one person. When the woman reached age 65, their income would jump to the OAS/GIS amount intended for married couples. The 1975 SPA intended to correct the anomaly by providing an income-tested benefit to those between 60 and 65 years of age, when one spouse is over 65.

The Allowance provides money for low-income seniors who meet the following conditions:

- His or her spouse or common-law partner (same-sex or opposite-sex) receives or is entitled to receive the Old Age Security pension and the Guaranteed Income Supplement.
- He or she is 60 to 64 years old.
- He or she is a Canadian citizen or a legal resident at the time the Allowance is approved or when he or she last lived here.
- He or she has lived in Canada after the age of 18 for at least ten years.

In addition, the Allowance for the survivor provides benefits for those who are 60 to 64 years old and whose spouse or partner has died. The Allowance for the survivor stops when a recipient remarries or lives in a common-law relationship for at least one year. The Allowance is stopped at an income of $26,496 (as of 2006).

Federal benefits are supplemented with provincial and territorial benefits in Ontario, Manitoba, Saskatchewan, Alberta, British Columbia, the Yukon, the Northwest Territories, and Nunavut. The provincial programs are generally means- or income-tested and are administered by local Social Assistance or welfare departments. Finally, there are several other benefits available to seniors through the tax system.

Social Insurance: Public Pensions — Canada/Quebec Pension Plan (C/QPP)

The earnings-based Canada/Quebec Pension Plan (C/QPP) makes up the second level of income security for the retired and elderly. The plan provides a pension upon retirement to persons who have contributed to it. It is a social insurance type of income security program; it insures the contributor against loss of income due to retirement. All employed or self-employed Canadians over the age of 18 make compulsory contributions to the plan (matched by their employer) throughout their working careers. The plan also offers disability, survivor, and death benefits, as well as inflation protection. The plan is fully portable from job to job. (Human Resources and Social Development Canada 2006, 2). In the 2004/05 fiscal year, 4.5 million Canadians received $23.8 billion in C/QPP benefits (Human Resources and Social Development Canada 2006, 3).

The Canada/Quebec Pension Plan began in 1966. The mandate was to provide all members of the labour force in Canada and their families with retirement income and death and disability benefits. Although we discuss the plans in tandem, the Quebec Pension Plan (QPP) is a separate plan legislated by the province of Quebec — it has similar benefits and identical contribution rates to the Canadian Pension Plan (CPP). The QPP is closely associated with the CPP and is coordinated through a series of agreements between the federal government and Quebec. This ensures that Canadians who move in and out of Quebec carry all the pension benefits with them. The *Canada Pension Plan Act* allows any province to create its own program as Quebec has done.

Before the C/QPP was instituted, all pensions were administered by private insurance companies. A public contributory pension was a new way to provide income for retired persons. The basic-minimum programs (discussed previously) addressed the income needs of the retired by transferring income to the retired from taxes collected every year. Within these programs, income is redistributed from those who are of working age to retired people. Public contributory pensions, on the other hand, help people save from their earnings during their working years, and then use the accumulated funds to provide income during retirement.

As mentioned, all employed persons over the age of 18 must make compulsory C/QPP contributions while employed. Therefore, all Canadians who have participated in the paid labour force are eligible for benefits, even a person with only one contribution. Benefits are payable at age 65 and are equal to 25 percent of a contributor's average earnings. Benefits are adjusted downward by 0.5 percent for each month for people who begin drawing benefits before 65 years of age. The plan is fully indexed annually to the cost of living as measured by the Consumer Price Index (CPI).

The C/QPP is used as a vehicle for other non-retirement based contingencies: disability benefits, death benefits, and survivor benefits. The plan only provides disability benefits to contributors if they are unable to work due to a "severe" and "prolonged" disability — meaning that they are unable to regularly pursue any substantial gainful employment for an indefinite period. Survivor benefits are paid to the surviving spouse of a deceased contributor. Finally, a death benefit (a lump-sum benefit equal to six times the contributor's monthly pension, up to a specified maximum) is paid upon the death of a contributor.

In 1998, Parliament amended the Canada Pension Plan through Bill C-2. The changes resulted in a larger reserve fund to help ensure that the future pensions of the growing retirement population can be funded. Contribution rates were increased from the 1998 5.85 percent of contributory earnings to 9.9 percent. These changes will increase

Quebec Pension Plan

www.rrq.gouv.qc.ca/ an/accueil/00.htm

Although the option of having a separate, but highly linked, pension plan is open to all provinces, Quebec is the only province to take the option.

the size of the fund of money that is put aside to pay for future retirement pensions. The CPP reserve fund stood at $103 billion in 2006. The aim is to avoid a situation where younger working age Canadians are left financing the pensions of their parents.

Private Plans: Occupational Pensions and Private Savings

The private pension plans component of the retirement income system consists of pensions from employers, and publicly supported and regulated private savings plans such as Registered Retirement Savings Plans (RRSPs), Registered Pension Plans (RPPs), and Deferred Profit Sharing Plans (DPSPs).

The federal government provides tax assistance on savings in RRSPs, RPPs, and DPSPs — taxes are deferred on the contributions and investment income in these plans until the savings are withdrawn or received as pension income. This tax assistance is intended to encourage Canadians to save privately for retirement.

Private savings and assets also contribute to retirement incomes. As noted earlier, the tax-assisted private pension system accounts for an increasingly large share of retirement income system payments. Private occupational pension plans were an outcome of the escalating economy after World War II, and the demand by labour unions for pension coverage within their collective agreements. Now private pension capital pools are the largest pools of capital in industrialized nations.

Governments are relying on these private forms of savings, and are increasing the deductions allowed for contributors. Critics argue that a reliance on such plans is dangerous, as they only benefit those with high incomes.

Private occupational pension plans plans covered 39 percent of the labour force in 2002, but only one-third of the pensions are indexed to inflation. Most public sector employees are covered, but just over 30 percent of private sector employees are covered. Many people with low-paying jobs do not have occupational pensions. People with irregular employment histories could also end up without a pension. Still, in 1997, 20.6 percent of retirement income was derived from private retirement pensions. This almost equals the importance of the C/QPP (21.4 percent) as a source of retirement income.

Most of the gains in the overall average incomes of seniors, however, have come from work-related pensions. Between 1981 and 1997, for example, the proportion of the income of seniors coming from C/QPP more than doubled, rising from 10 to 21 percent, while the share coming from private employment pensions rose from 12 to 21 percent. In contrast, the share of income of seniors coming from the OAS program fell from 34 to 29 percent in the same period. Men and women are now equally covered by employer-sponsored pension plans, with women having a 39 percent coverage rate and men 40 percent. This equality is due to a large drop in male coverage — falling from

54 percent in 1980 to 40 percent in 2002. The rate for women has remained constant (Statistics Canada 2006b, 137).

Retirement Income Security Reform

Like other areas of income security, new reforms to the system for the retired and elderly have been widely discussed. In 1996 the federal government proposed the Seniors Benefit. This new program would combine the OAS, the GIS, and the Allowance into one benefit that would be more targeted at seniors with low incomes. In short, the Seniors Benefit would slightly increase benefits for couples with incomes up to $30,000 and sharply reduce benefits for all others. The stated objective of the new program was to make the system more sustainable as the baby boom generation reaches retirement age. Due to extensive pressure from seniors and advocacy groups, the government announced in 1998 that the plans for the Seniors Benefit had been scrapped.

Efforts to reform Canada's old age income security system will probably not end with the Seniors Benefit. The OAS is not paid to those with incomes over $102,865, (as of 2007) and is reduced on a sliding scale for those with incomes between $63,551 (as of 2007) and $102,865, so according to the exact definition of a universal program, the OAS does not qualify. But according to the federal government,

Table 14.1: Old Age Security Benefit Payment Rates, January to March 2007				
Type of Benefit	**Recipient**	**Average Monthly Benefit (October 2006)**	**Maximum Monthly Benefit**	**Maximum Annual Income**
Old Age Security pension	All recipients	$467.21	$491.93	See note
Guaranteed Income Supplement	Single person	$418.87	$620.91	$14,904
	Spouse of pensioner	$261.30	$410.04	$19,728
	Spouse of non-pensioner	$406.46	$620.91	$35,712
	Spouse of Allowance recipient	$337.29	$410.04	$35,712
Allowance	All recipients	$354.69	$901.97	$27,600
Allowance for the survivor	All recipients	$559.05	$999.81	$20,064
Note: Pensioners with an individual net income above $63,511 must repay part or all of the maximum Old Age Security pension amount. The repayment amounts are normally deducted from their monthly payments before they are issued. The full OAS pension is eliminated when a pensioner's net income is $102,865 or above.				
Source: Service Canada. "Old Age Security (OAS) Payment Rates," modified 2006-10-17. www.hrsdc.gc.ca/en/isp/oas/oasrates.shtml. Reprinted with permission.				

only a few Canadians actually lose the benefit. The concept of universality is being seriously challenged in Canada. The OAS (and the new Universal Child Care Benefit) is the only remaining income security program with any aspect of universality (health care and education are universal, but they are not income security programs). This will, no doubt, lead to further debate about the retirement system.

Another challenge to the retirement system stems from the demographic trends discussed earlier. Some refer to this as the demographic time bomb. As the baby boom generation retires, pension plan payouts will dramatically increase. Bill C-2 attempted to address this and ensure the sustainability of old age income security, but some say that the system will not be able to afford future pensions. Others point out that retirees have been paying contributions to the plan and that these invested contributions should finance the benefits. Unlike the OAS and GIS, which are paid out of general government revenues, the C/QPP payments are covered by contributions made by those who are retiring. This is meant to avoid an intergenerational transfer of wealth, whereby the young who are working finance the pensions of the old who are retired.

A problem arises, however, due to the commitment in law that the federal government loans the surplus CPP contributions to the nine provinces, at low interest rates. In most cases, the provinces are not in a hurry to pay back the low interest loans. When the funds are finally needed to pay pensions to the aging population, the provinces will have to obtain the needed funds through current taxation. In this way, indirectly, the CPP becomes an intergenerational transfer, as the current working generation must pay the increased provincial taxes to enable the provinces to repay the loans to the CPP fund.

Conclusion

Canada should be applauded for the substantial gains it has made in the income security of seniors. Such gains were made largely as a result of public pressure for retirement programs by this large and vocal section of the population.

Federal and provincial governments have recognized that the aging of Canadian society will put pressure on the Canada Pension Plan, and they have undertaken important reforms to ensure long-term sustainability. Their reforms include accelerating higher contribution rates, adopting a new investment strategy, and benefit measures to reduce the growth in benefit expenditures. The changes must ensure that the system will be fair across generations and not place an unfair burden on contributors.

As further pressure mounts, Canada will have to make some choices. Do we break down a public system that has been recognized worldwide as exemplary, or do we make the necessary changes to maintain a viable and comprehensive public system? The workforce of tomorrow will also be significantly affected. Currently, Canadians retire between the ages of 55 and 65, and most stop working at the age of 65. The aging of the population will eventually lead to a reduced growth of the labour force and a proportionally smaller workforce. The need for a workforce in the future may mean that fewer people have the option to retire, and the majority of older adults can still work productively. Therefore, it may become increasingly necessary that people who wish to work beyond the typical retirement age are given the opportunity to do so.

Chapter Summary

Key Concepts

- Bill C-2
- Canada/Quebec Pension Plan (C/QPP)
- Guaranteed Income Supplement (GIS)
- Occupational pension plans
- Old Age Security (OAS)
- Private pension plans
- Seniors Benefit
- Spouse's Allowance (SPA)

Review Questions

1. What are the future trends regarding aging and retirement in Canada?
2. How will these trends affect the old age income security system? What has the federal government done to try to ensure the sustainability of the pension system, for example?
3. List and describe the three levels of income security for old age and retirement.
4. Briefly describe the history of income security for the elderly, in particular the *Old Age Pensions Act* of 1927.
5. Calculate the total old age security benefits for an individual earning $58,000 per year. Explain.
6. Describe two key debates regarding old age income security reform.

Exploring Social Welfare

1. The number of people over the age of 65 is projected to dramatically increase. Today there are six workers in Canada for every retired person. By 2020 there will be three workers for every retired person. What do you think the implications of this will be for our social welfare programs? Which programs will be most affected? What do you think the government should do to prepare for this?

2. Explore the debates surrounding mandatory retirement age restrictions. What are the labour unions saying about the issue, and how does this differ from the government's viewpoint? You can begin with the websites of the Canadian Labour Congress (http://canadianlabour.ca) and the Canadian Union of Public Employees (www.cupe.ca).

Websites

Human Resources and Skills Development Canada
www.hrsdc.gc.ca

Go to the Human Resources and Skills Development Canada and click on "Seniors." This link provides an overview of our retirement income system.

Caledon Institute of Social Policy
www.caledoninst.org

The Caledon Institute of Social Policy is a non-profit think tank focusing on social policy research and analysis. Its goal is to "inform and influence opinion and to foster public discussion on poverty and social policy." Several reports and publications on social policy issues are available through this site.

Canadian Policy Research Networks
www.cprn.org/cprn.html

Canadian Policy Research Networks is a network of policy researchers with an extensive collection of online reports about social policy.

Seniors Canada On-line
www.seniors.gc.ca

Seniors Canada On-line provides access to web-based information and services. There are sections on finances and pensions that provide information on income security.

References

Bryden, Kenneth. 1974. *Old Age Pensions and Policy-Making in Canada.* Montreal: McGill-Queen's University Press.

Health Canada. 2002. *Canada's Aging Population.* Ottawa: Health Canada. www.hc-sc.gc.ca/seniors-aines/index_pages/publications_e.htm.

Human Resources and Skills Development Canada. 2006. *Annual Report of The Canada Pension Plan, Fiscal Year 2004-2005.* Ottawa: Government of Canada.

Organisation for Economic Co-operation and Development (OECD). 2001. *Ageing and Income: Financial Resources and Retirement in 9 OECD Countries.* Paris: OECD.

Social Development Canada. 2006. *Old Age Security, Canada Pension Plan.* January 2006. ISPB-258-01-06E. www.hrsdc.gc.ca/en/isp/statistics/rates/pdf/janmar06.pdf.

Statistics Canada. 2002. *Population Projections for 2001, 2006, 2011, 2016, 2021 and 2026.* Ottawa: Statistics Canada. www.statcan.ca/english/Pgdb/People/Population/demo23b.htm.

Statistics Canada. 2006a. *Persons in Low Income after Tax, by Prevalence in Percent (2000 to 2004).* Ottawa: Statistics Canada. CANSIM Table 202-0802. www40.statcan.ca/l01/cst01/famil19a.htm

Statistics Canada. 2006b. Women in Canada: A Gender-Based Statistical Report, 5th ed. Ottawa: Statistics Canada. www.statcan.ca/english/freepub/89-503-XIE/0010589-503-XIE.pdf.

Appendix A

Canada Health Transfer and Canada Social Transfer Regulations

SOR/2004-62
Registration March 30, 2004
FEDERAL-PROVINCIAL FISCAL ARRANGEMENTS ACT
Canada Health Transfer and Canada Social Transfer Regulations
P.C. 2004-331 March 30, 2004

Her Excellency the Governor General in Council, on the recommendation of the Minister of Finance, pursuant to section 40[a], of the *Federal-Provincial Fiscal Arrangements Act*[b], hereby makes the annexed *Canada Health Transfer and Canada Social Transfer Regulations*.

[a] S.C. 1999, c. 31, s. 93[b] S.C. 1995, c. 17, s. 45(1)

Canada Health Transfer and Canada Social Transfer Regulations

Interpretation

1. The following definitions apply in these Regulations.

"Act" means the *Federal-Provincial Fiscal Arrangements Act*. (*Loi*)

"population of a province for a fiscal year" means the population of a province for a fiscal year as determined in accordance with section 2. (*population d'une province pour un exercice*)

"taxation year" means a taxation year within the meaning of the *Income Tax Act*. (*année d'imposition*)

"transfer payment" means payment of the Canada Health Transfer or Canada Social Transfer under the Act, as the case may be. (*paiement de transfert*)

Determination of Population of a Province

2. Subject to subsection 4(7), the population of a province for a fiscal year shall be determined by the Chief Statistician of Canada on the basis of Statistics Canada's official estimate of the population of that province on June 1 of that fiscal year.

Calculation of Equalized Tax Transfer

3. (1) For the purposes of clause 24.7(1)(*b*)(ii)(A) of the Act, the relevant revenue bases for a province for a fiscal year shall be determined as follows:

(*a*) with respect to personal income taxes, by aggregating

(i) 75% of the assessed federal individual income tax applicable to the province for the taxation year ending in the fiscal year, as determined by the Minister of National Revenue, and

(ii) 25% of the assessed federal individual income tax applicable to the province for the taxation year beginning in the fiscal year, as determined by the Minister of National Revenue; and

(*b*) with respect to corporation income taxes, by aggregating

(i) 75% of the aggregate of taxable income earned in the taxation year in the province, as determined by the Minister of National Revenue under subsection 124(4) of the *Income Tax Act*, for all corporations having a taxation year ending in the calendar year that ends in the fiscal year, and

(ii) 25% of the aggregate of taxable income earned in the taxation year in the province, as determined by the

Minister of National Revenue under subsection 124(4) of the *Income Tax Act*, for all corporations having a taxation year ending in the calendar year that begins in the fiscal year.

(2) For the purposes of clause 24.7(1)(*b*)(ii)(B) of the Act, the amount of equalization referred to in subparagraph 24.7(1)(*b*)(ii) of the Act shall be increased by the amount determined by the following formula, if subsection 4(6) of the Act applies in respect of a province for a fiscal year:

$$P \times [A \times C/B]$$
where

P   is the population of the province for the fiscal year;

A   is the average per capita yield in the provinces of Ontario, Quebec, Manitoba, British Columbia and Saskatchewan for the revenue sources referred to in subsection 24.7(2) of the Act for the fiscal year;

B   is the average per capita yield in the provinces of Ontario, Quebec, Manitoba, British Columbia and Saskatchewan for all revenue sources for the fiscal year, under subsection 4(1) of the Act; and

C   is the amount by which

  (*a*) the equalization payment for the province determined in accordance with subsection 4(6) of the Act divided by the population of the province for that fiscal year

  exceeds

  (*b*) the equalization payment for the province, determined in accordance with subsection 4(1) of the Act, divided by the population of the province for that fiscal year.

Interim Estimates

4. (1) In respect of each fiscal year,

(*a*) the Minister shall make an estimate of the amount, if any, of the transfer payment to a province for the fiscal year

(i) before April 16 of that fiscal year,

(ii) during the period beginning on September 1 and ending on October 12 of that fiscal year,

(iii) during the period beginning on January 12 and ending on the last day of February of that fiscal year,

(iv) during the period beginning on September 1 and ending on October 12 of the first fiscal year following the end of that fiscal year,

(v) during the period beginning on January 12 and ending on the last day of February of the first fiscal year following the end of that fiscal year,

(vi) during the period beginning on September 1 and ending on October 12 of the second fiscal year following the end of that fiscal year, and

(vii) during the period beginning on January 12 and ending on the last day of February of the second fiscal year following the end of that fiscal year; and

(*b*) if, in the opinion of the Minister, there is new information available that may have a significant effect on the amount of the transfer payment to one or more provinces, the Minister may alter an estimate of the amount, if any, of the transfer payment to be made for the fiscal year to a province

(i) during the second quarter of that fiscal year,

(ii) during March of that fiscal year, and

(iii) during any period beginning on the first day of the final month of a quarter and ending on the twelfth day of the subsequent quarter, other than the periods specified in paragraph (a), following the end of the fiscal year, until such time as the final computation under subsection 5(2) is completed.

(2) If an estimate made under subparagraph (1)(*a*)(i) establishes that a transfer payment is to be made to a province for a fiscal year, the Minister shall pay to the province, on account of the final payment in respect of the fiscal year, an amount equal to one twenty-fourth of the amount so estimated on the first and third working days following the fifteenth calendar day of each month in that fiscal year.

(3) If an estimate made under subparagraph (1)(*a*)(ii) or (iii) or (*b*)(i) establishes that the amount payable to the province under the immediately preceding estimate in respect of that fiscal year should be revised, the Minister shall

(*a*) if any amount remains payable to the province, adjust the remaining payments referred to in subsection (2) in respect of that fiscal year in accordance with the new estimate, beginning with the first payment in the month following the month during which that estimate was calculated; and

(b) if an overpayment has been made to the province, recover the amount of the overpayment before the end of the fiscal year.

(4) If an estimate made under any of subparagraphs (1)(*a*)(iv) to (vii) or (*b*)(iii) establishes that

(*a*) an underpayment has been made to the province, the Minister shall pay the amount of the underpayment to the province within the four months following the month during which the estimate was made; and

(*b*) an overpayment has been made to the province, the Minister shall recover the amount of the overpayment within the four months following the month during which the estimate was made.

(5) If an estimate made under subparagraph (1)(*b*)(ii) establishes that the amount payable to the province under the immediately preceding estimate in respect of that fiscal year should be revised, the Minister shall

(*a*) if any amount remains payable to the province, pay to the province the amount in the month during which the estimate was made or, if the province so requests, pay the province that amount within the four months following the month during which the estimate was made; and

(*b*) if an overpayment has been made to the province, recover the amount of the overpayment in the month during which the estimate was made or, if the province so requests, recover the amount within the four months following that month.

(6) If an estimate establishes that an overpayment has been made to a province in respect of a fiscal year, the Minister may, subject to paragraph (3)(*b*), (4)(*b*) or (5)(*b*), recover the amount of the overpayment

(*a*) from any amount payable to the province under the Act; or

(*b*) from the province as a debt due to Her Majesty in right of Canada.

(7) For the purpose of making an estimate under subsection (1), the population of a province for a fiscal year is the population of that province on June 1 of that fiscal year as estimated by the Minister on the basis of population statistics made available to the Minister by the Chief Statistician of Canada.

Final Computation

5. (1) The Chief Statistician of Canada shall, in respect of each fiscal year, prepare and submit to the Minister, not later than 30 months after the end of the fiscal year, a certificate in respect of that fiscal year based on the most recent information prepared by Statistics Canada for that fiscal year, setting out, in respect of each province, the population of the province for the fiscal years required by the Act.

(2) Within 30 days after the receipt by the Minister of the certificate submitted by the Chief Statistician of Canada under subsection (1) in respect of a fiscal year, the Minister shall make the final computation on the basis of the information contained in that certificate of the amount, if any, of the transfer payment that is payable for that fiscal year under the Act to a province, and the Minister shall subsequently furnish each province with tables setting out the details of that computation.

(3) If a final computation made under subsection (2) establishes that there remains an outstanding amount payable to a province in respect of a fiscal year, the Minister shall pay to the province the outstanding amount.

(4) If a final computation made under subsection (2) establishes that an overpayment has been made to a province in respect of a fiscal year, the Minister shall recover the amount of the overpayment

(a) from any amount payable to the province under the Act; or

(b) from the province as a debt due to Her Majesty in right of Canada.

Coming into Force

6. These Regulations come into force on the day on which they are registered.

Appendix B

International Covenant on Economic, Social and Cultural Rights

G.A. res. 2200A (XXI), 21 U.N.GAOR Supp. (No. 16) at 49, U.N. Doc. A/6316 (1966), 993 U.N.T.S. 3, entered into force Jan. 3, 1976.

[Note: This copy is for information only.]

Preamble

The States Parties to the present Covenant, considering that, in accordance with the principles proclaimed in the Charter of the United Nations, recognition of the inherent dignity and of the equal and inalienable rights of all members of the human family is the foundation of freedom, justice and peace in the world,

Recognizing that these rights derive from the inherent dignity of the human person,

Recognizing that, in accordance with the Universal Declaration of Human Rights, the ideal of free human beings enjoying freedom from fear and want can only be achieved if conditions are created whereby everyone may enjoy his economic, social and cultural rights, as well as his civil and political rights,

Considering the obligation of States under the Charter of the United Nations to promote universal respect for, and observance of, human rights and freedoms,

Realizing that the individual, having duties to other individuals and to the community to which he belongs, is under a responsibility to strive for the promotion and observance of the rights recognized in the present Covenant,

Agree upon the following articles:

PART I

Article 1

1. All peoples have the right of self-determination. By virtue of that right they freely determine their political status and freely pursue their economic, social and cultural development.

2. All peoples may, for their own ends, freely dispose of their natural wealth and resources without prejudice to any obligations arising out of international economic co-operation, based upon the principle of mutual benefit, and internatonal law. In no case may a people be deprived of its own means of subsistence.

3. The States Parties to the present Covenant, including those having responsibility for the administration of Non-Self-Governing and Trust Territories, shall promote the realization of the right of self-determination, and shall respect that right, in conformity with the provisions of the Charter of the United Nations.

PART II

Article 2

1. Each State Party to the present Covenant undertakes to take steps, individually and through international assistance and co-operation, especially economic and technical, to the maximum of its available resources, with a view to achieving progressively the full realization of the rights recognized in the present Covenant by all appropriate means, including particularly the adoption of legislative measures.

2. The States Parties to the present Covenant undertake to guarantee that the rights enunciated in the present Covenant will be exercised without discrimination of any kind as to race, colour, sex, language, religion, political or other opinion, national or social origin, property, birth or other status.

3. Developing countries, with due regard to human rights and their national economy, may

determine to what extent they would guarantee the economic rights recognized in the present Covenant to non-nationals.

Article 3

The States Parties to the present Covenant undertake to ensure the equal right of men and women to the enjoyment of all economic, social and cultural rights set forth in the present Covenant.

Article 4

The States Parties to the present Covenant recognize that, in the enjoyment of those rights provided by the State in conformity with the present Covenant, the State may subject such rights only to such limitations as are determined by law only in so far as this may be compatible with the nature of these rights and solely for the purpose of promoting the general welfare in a democratic society.

Article 5

1. Nothing in the present Covenant may be interpreted as implying for any State, group or person any right to engage in any activity or to perform any act aimed at the destruction of any of the rights or freedoms recognized herein, or at their limitation to a greater extent than is provided for in the present Covenant.

2. No restriction upon or derogation from any of the fundamental human rights recognized or existing in any country in virtue of law, conventions, regulations or custom shall be admitted on the pretext that the present Covenant does not recognize such rights or that it recognizes them to a lesser extent.

PART III

Article 6

1. The States Parties to the present Covenant recognize the right to work, which includes the right of everyone to the opportunity to gain his living by work which he freely chooses or accepts, and will take appropriate steps to safeguard this right.

2. The steps to be taken by a State Party to the present Covenant to achieve the full realization of this right shall include technical and vocational guidance and training programmes, policies and techniques to achieve

steady economic, social and cultural development and full and productive employment under conditions safeguarding fundamental political and economic freedoms to the individual.

Article 7

The States Parties to the present Covenant recognize the right of everyone to the enjoyment of just and favourable conditions of work which ensure, in particular:

(a) Remuneration which provides all workers, as a minimum, with:
   (i) Fair wages and equal remuneration for work of equal value without distinction of any kind, in particular women being guaranteed conditions of work not inferior to those enjoyed by men, with equal pay for equal work;
   (ii) A decent living for themselves and their families in accordance with the provisions of the present Covenant;

(b) Safe and healthy working conditions;

(c) Equal opportunity for everyone to be promoted in his employment to an appropriate higher level, subject to no considerations other than those of seniority and competence;

(d) Rest, leisure and reasonable limitation of working hours and periodic holidays with pay, as well as remuneration for public holidays.

Article 8

1. The States Parties to the present Covenant undertake to ensure:

(a) The right of everyone to form trade unions and join the trade union of his choice, subject only to the rules of the organization concerned, for the promotion and protection of his economic and social interests. No restrictions may be placed on the exercise of this right other than those prescribed by law and which are necessary in a democratic society in the interests of national security or public order or for the protection of the rights and freedoms of others;

(b) The right of trade unions to establish national federations or confederations and the right of the latter to form or join international trade-union organizations;

(c) The right of trade unions to function freely subject to no limitations other than those prescribed by law and which are necessary in a democratic society in the interests of national security or public order or for the protection of the rights and freedoms of others;

(d) The right to strike, provided that it is exercised in conformity with the laws of the particular country.

2. This article shall not prevent the imposition of lawful restrictions on the exercise of these rights by members of the armed forces or of the police or of the administration of the State.

3. Nothing in this article shall authorize States Parties to the International Labour Organisation Convention of 1948 concerning Freedom of Association and Protection of the Right to Organize to take legislative measures which would prejudice, or apply the law in such a manner as would prejudice, the guarantees provided for in that Convention.

Article 9

The States Parties to the present Covenant recognize the right of everyone to social security, including social insurance.

Article 10

The States Parties to the present Covenant recognize that:

1. The widest possible protection and assistance should be accorded to the family, which is the natural and fundamental group unit of society, particularly for its establishment and while it is responsible for the care and education of dependent children. Marriage must be entered into with the free consent of the intending spouses.

2. Special protection should be accorded to mothers during a reasonable period before and after childbirth. During such period working mothers should be accorded paid leave or leave with adequate social security benefits.

3. Special measures of protection and assistance should be taken on behalf of all children and young persons without any discrimination for reasons of parentage or other conditions. Children and young persons should be protected from economic and social exploitation. Their employment in work harmful to their morals or health or dangerous to life or likely to hamper their normal development should be punishable by law. States should also set age limits below which the paid employment of child labour should be prohibited and punishable by law.

Article 11

1. The States Parties to the present Covenant recognize the right of everyone to an adequate standard of living for himself and his family, including adequate food, clothing and housing, and to the continuous improvement of living conditions. The States Parties will take appropriate steps to ensure the realization of this right, recognizing to this effect the essential importance of international cooperation based on free consent.

2. The States Parties to the present Covenant, recognizing the fundamental right of everyone to be free from hunger, shall take, individually and through international cooperation, the measures, including specific programmes, which are needed:

(a) To improve methods of production, conservation and distribution of food by making full use of technical and scientific knowledge, by disseminating knowledge of the principles of nutrition and by developing or reforming agrarian systems in such a way as to achieve the most efficient development and utilization of natural resources;

(b) Taking into account the problems of both food-importing and food-exporting countries, to ensure an equitable distribution of world food supplies in relation to need.

Article 12

1. The States Parties to the present Covenant recognize the right of everyone to the enjoyment of the highest attainable standard of physical and mental health.

2. The steps to be taken by the States Parties to the present Covenant to achieve the full realization of this right shall include those necessary for:

(a) The provision for the reduction of the stillbirth-rate and of infant mortality and for the healthy development of the child;

(b) The improvement of all aspects of environmental and industrial hygiene;

(c) The prevention, treatment and control of epidemic, endemic, occupational and other diseases;

(d) The creation of conditions which would assure to all medical service and medical attention in the event of sickness.

Article 13

1. The States Parties to the present Covenant recognize the right of everyone to education. They agree that education shall be directed to the full development of the human personality and the sense of its dignity, and shall strengthen the respect for human rights and fundamental freedoms. They further agree that education shall enable all persons to participate effectively in a free society, promote understanding, tolerance and friendship among all nations and all racial, ethnic or religious groups, and further the activities of the United Nations for the maintenance of peace.

2. The States Parties to the present Covenant recognize that, with a view to achieving the full realization of this right:

(a) Primary education shall be compulsory and available free to all;

(b) Secondary education in its different forms, including technical and vocational secondary education, shall be made generally available and accessible to all by every appropriate means, and in particular by the progressive introduction of free education;

(c) Higher education shall be made equally accessible to all, on the basis of capacity, by every appropriate means, and in particular by the progressive introduction of free education;

(d) Fundamental education shall be encouraged or intensified as far as possible for those persons who have not received or completed the whole period of their primary education;

(e) The development of a system of schools at all levels shall be actively pursued, an adequate fellowship system shall be established, and the material conditions of teaching staff shall be continuously improved.

3. The States Parties to the present Covenant undertake to have respect for the liberty of parents and, when applicable, legal guardians to choose for their children schools, other than those established by the public authorities, which conform to such minimum educational standards as may be laid down or approved by the State and to ensure the religious and moral education of their children in conformity with their own convictions.

4. No part of this article shall be construed so as to interfere with the liberty of individuals and bodies to establish and direct educational institutions, subject always to the observance of the principles set forth in paragraph I of this article and to the requirement that the education given in such institutions shall conform to such minimum standards as may be laid down by the State.

Article 14

Each State Party to the present Covenant which, at the time of becoming a Party, has not been able to secure in its metropolitan territory or other territories under its jurisdiction compulsory primary education, free of charge, undertakes, within two years, to work out and adopt a detailed plan of action for the progressive implementation, within a reasonable number of years, to be fixed in the plan, of the principle of compulsory education free of charge for all.

Article 15

1. The States Parties to the present Covenant recognize the right of everyone:

(a) To take part in cultural life;

(b) To enjoy the benefits of scientific progress and its applications;

(c) To benefit from the protection of the moral and material interests resulting from any scientific, literary or artistic production of which he is the author.

2. The steps to be taken by the States Parties to the present Covenant to achieve the full realization of this right shall include those necessary for the conservation, the development and the diffusion of science and culture.

3. The States Parties to the present Covenant undertake to respect the freedom indispensable for scientific research and creative activity.

4. The States Parties to the present Covenant recognize the benefits to be derived from the encouragement and development of international contacts and co-operation in the scientific and cultural fields.

PART IV

Article 16

1. The States Parties to the present Covenant undertake to submit in conformity with this part of the Covenant reports on the measures which they have adopted and the progress made in achieving the observance of the rights recognized herein.

2. (a) All reports shall be submitted to the Secretary-General of the United Nations, who shall transmit copies to the Economic and Social Council for consideration in accordance with the provisions of the present Covenant;

   (b) The Secretary-General of the United Nations shall also transmit to the specialized agencies copies of the reports, or any relevant parts therefrom, from States Parties to the present Covenant which are also members of these specialized agencies in so far as these reports, or parts therefrom, relate to any matters which fall within the responsibilities of the said agencies in accordance with their constitutional instruments.

Article 17

1. The States Parties to the present Covenant shall furnish their reports in stages, in accordance with a programme to be established by the Economic and Social Council within one year of the entry into force of the present Covenant after consultation with the States Parties and the specialized agencies concerned.

2. Reports may indicate factors and difficulties affecting the degree of fulfilment of obligations under the present Covenant.

3. Where relevant information has previously been furnished to the United Nations or to any specialized agency by any State Party to the present Covenant, it will not be necessary to reproduce that information, but a precise reference to the information so furnished will suffice.

Article 18

Pursuant to its responsibilities under the Charter of the United Nations in the field of human rights and fundamental freedoms, the Economic and Social Council may make arrangements with the specialized agencies in respect of their reporting to it on the progress made in achieving the observance of the provisions of the present Covenant falling within the scope of their activities. These reports may include particulars of decisions and recommendations on such implementation adopted by their competent organs.

Article 19

The Economic and Social Council may transmit to the Commission on Human Rights for study and general recommendation or, as appropriate, for information the reports concerning human rights submitted by States in accordance with articles 16 and 17, and those concerning human rights submitted by the specialized agencies in accordance with article 18.

Article 20

The States Parties to the present Covenant and the specialized agencies concerned may submit comments to the Economic and Social Council on any general recommendation under article 19 or reference to such general recommendation in any report of the Commission on Human Rights or any documentation referred to therein.

Article 21

The Economic and Social Council may submit from time to time to the General Assembly reports with recommendations of a general nature and a summary of the information received from the States Parties to the present Covenant and the specialized agencies on the measures taken and the progress made in achieving general observance of the rights recognized in the present Covenant.

Article 22

The Economic and Social Council may bring to the attention of other organs of the United Nations, their subsidiary organs and specialized agencies concerned with furnishing technical assistance any matters arising out of the reports referred to in this part of the present Covenant which may assist such bodies in deciding, each within its field of competence, on the advisability of international measures likely to contribute to the effective progressive implementation of the present Covenant.

Article 23

The States Parties to the present Covenant agree that international action for the achievement of the rights recognized in the present Covenant includes such methods as the conclusion of conventions, the adoption of recommendations, the furnishing of technical assistance and the holding of regional meetings and technical meetings for the purpose of consultation and study organized in conjunction with the Governments concerned.

Article 24

Nothing in the present Covenant shall be interpreted as impairing the provisions of the Charter of the United Nations and of the constitutions of the specialized agencies which define the respective responsibilities of the various organs of the United Nations and of the specialized agencies in regard to the matters dealt with in the present Covenant.

Article 25

Nothing in the present Covenant shall be interpreted as impairing the inherent right of all peoples to enjoy and utilize fully and freely their natural wealth and resources.

PART V

Article 26

1. The present Covenant is open for signature by any State Member of the United Nations or member of any of its specialized agencies, by any State Party to the Statute of the International Court of Justice, and by any other State which has been invited by the General Assembly of the United Nations to become a party to the present Covenant.

2. The present Covenant is subject to ratification. Instruments of ratification shall be deposited with the Secretary-General of the United Nations.

3. The present Covenant shall be open to accession by any State referred to in paragraph 1 of this article.

4. Accession shall be effected by the deposit of an instrument of accession with the Secretary-General of the United Nations.

5. The Secretary-General of the United Nations shall inform all States which have signed the present Covenant or acceded to it of the deposit of each instrument of ratification or accession.

Article 27

1. The present Covenant shall enter into force three months after the date of the deposit with the Secretary-General of the United Nations of the thirty-fifth instrument of ratification or instrument of accession.

2. For each State ratifying the present Covenant or acceding to it after the deposit of the thirty-fifth instrument of ratification or instrument of accession, the present Covenant shall enter into force three months after the date of the deposit of its own instrument of ratification or instrument of accession.

Article 28

The provisions of the present Covenant shall extend to all parts of federal States without any limitations or exceptions.

Article 29

1. Any State Party to the present Covenant may propose an amendment and file it with the Secretary-General of the United Nations. The Secretary-General shall thereupon communicate any proposed amendments to the States Parties to the present Covenant with a request that they notify him whether they favour a conference of States Parties for the purpose of considering and voting upon the proposals. In the event that at least one third of the States Parties favours such a conference, the Secretary-General shall convene the conference under the auspices of the United Nations. Any amendment adopted by a majority of the States Parties present and voting at the conference shall be submitted to the General Assembly of the United Nations for approval.

2. Amendments shall come into force when they have been approved by the General

Assembly of the United Nations and accepted by a two-thirds majority of the States Parties to the present Covenant in accordance with their respective constitutional processes.

3. When amendments come into force they shall be binding on those States Parties which have accepted them, other States Parties still being bound by the provisions of the present Covenant and any earlier amendment which they have accepted.

Article 30

Irrespective of the notifications made under article 26, paragraph 5, the Secretary-General of the United Nations shall inform all States referred to in paragraph I of the same article of the following particulars:

(a) Signatures, ratifications and accessions under article 26;

(b) The date of the entry into force of the present Covenant under article 27 and the date of the entry into force of any amendments under article 29.

Article 31

1. The present Covenant, of which the Chinese, English, French, Russian and Spanish texts are equally authentic, shall be deposited in the archives of the United Nations.

2. The Secretary-General of the United Nations shall transmit certified copies of the present Covenant to all States referred to in article 26.

Appendix C

Committee on
Economic, Social and Cultural Rights

Thirty-sixth session
Geneva, 1-19 May 2006

**Consideration of Reports Submitted by States Parties
Under Articles 16 and 17 of the Covenant**

**Concluding observations of the
Committee on Economic, Social and Cultural Rights
CANADA**

1. The Committee on Economic, Social and Cultural Rights considered the fourth and fifth periodic reports of Canada on the implementation of the International Covenant on Economic, Social and Cultural Rights (E/C.12/4/Add.15 and E/C.12/CAN/5) at its 9th to 12th meetings, held on 5 and 8 May 2006 (E/C.12/2006/SR.9-12), and adopted, at its 29th meeting, held on 19 May 2006, the following concluding observations.

A. Introduction

2. The Committee welcomes the submission of the fourth and fifth periodic reports of the State party, as well as the written responses provided in advance to the Committee's lists of issues (E/C.12/Q/CAN/2 and E/C.12/CAN/Q/5). The Committee also welcomes the dialogue with the State party's delegation, composed of experts in the various fields covered by the Covenant, as well as of representatives from some provinces and territories of the State party. The Committee notes, however, that the submission of the fifth periodic report at a time when the fourth periodic report had not yet been considered did not facilitate the consideration of the situation in the State party.

B. Positive aspects

3. The Committee notes that Canada still ranks near the top of the Human Development Index of the United Nations Development Programme. On the average, Canadians enjoy a high standard of living and Canada has the capacity to achieve a high level of realization of all Covenant rights.

4. The Committee welcomes the relatively low level of unemployment in the State party, and the decrease in the proportion of persons living below the Low-Income Cut-Off (as defined by Statistics Canada) from 13.7 per cent in 1998 to 11.2 per cent in 2004.

5. The Committee notes with appreciation the reduction in disparities between Aboriginal people and the rest of the population in the State party with regard to infant mortality and secondary education.

6. The Committee welcomes the measures taken by the State party in the area of equal pay for equal work, in particular the payment of retroactive adjustments to women who had suffered discrimination.

7. The Committee welcomes the extension of maternity and parental benefits from six months to one year.

8. The Committee notes with satisfaction the numerous health programmes conducted by the State party, such as the 10-Year Plan to Strengthen Health Care and the launch of the Public Health Agency.

9. The Committee notes that Canada's level of official development assistance was raised from about 0.27 per cent of GDP in 2004 to a current estimated level of 0.33 per cent of GDP.

C. Factors and difficulties impeding the implementation of the Covenant

10. The Committee notes the absence of any factors or difficulties preventing the effective implementation of the Covenant in the State party.

D. Principal subjects of concern

11. The Committee regrets that most of its 1993 and 1998 recommendations in relation to the second and third periodic reports have not been implemented, and that the State party has not addressed in an effective manner the following principal subjects of concern, which are still relevant:

    (a) The State party's restrictive interpretation of its obligations under the Covenant, in particular its position that it may implement the legal obligations set forth in the Covenant by adopting specific measures and policies rather than by enacting legislation specifically recognizing economic, social and cultural rights, and the consequent lack of awareness, in the provinces and territories, of the State party's legal obligations under the Covenant;

    (b) The lack of legal redress available to individuals when governments fail to implement the Covenant, resulting from the insufficient coverage in domestic legislation of economic, social and cultural rights, as spelled out in the Covenant; the lack of effective enforcement mechanisms for these rights; the practice of governments of urging upon their courts an interpretation of the Canadian Charter of Rights and Freedoms denying protection of Covenant rights, and the inadequate availability of civil legal aid, particularly for economic, social and cultural rights;

    (c) The absence of a legally enforceable right to adequate social assistance benefits for all persons in need on a non-discriminatory basis and the negative impact of certain workfare programmes on social assistance recipients;

    (d) The disparities that still persist between Aboriginal peoples and the rest of the Canadian population in the enjoyment of Covenant rights, as well as the discrimination still experienced by Aboriginal women in matters of matrimonial property;

    (e) The absence of an official poverty line;

    (f) The insufficiency of minimum wage and social assistance to ensure the realization of the right to an adequate standard of living for all;

    (g) The authorization given to provinces and territories to deduct the amount of the child benefit under the National Child Benefit Scheme from the amount of social assistance received by parents on welfare.

12. The Committee is concerned that, despite the consultations and sharing of information between federal, provincial and territorial governments through the federal/provincial/ territorial Continuing Committee of Officials on Human Rights, effective procedures to follow-up on the Committee's concluding observations have not been developed.

13. The Committee, while noting the State party's Court Challenges Program, regrets that this programme has not been extended to permit funding with respect to challenges to provincial and territorial legislation and policies, as previously recommended by the Committee.

14. The Committee notes with concern the cuts in financial support to civil legal aid services with regard to economic, social and cultural rights in a number of jurisdictions of the State party. This leads to a situation where poor people, in particular poor single women, who are denied benefits and services to which they are entitled to under domestic law, cannot access domestic remedies. The drastic cuts in British Columbia raise particular concern in this regard.

15. The Committee is concerned that, despite Canada's economic prosperity and the reduction of the number of people living below

the Low-Income Cut-Off, 11.2 per cent of its population still lived in poverty in 2004, and that significant differences in levels of poverty persist between provinces and territories. The Committee also notes with particular concern that poverty rates remain very high among disadvantaged and marginalized individuals and groups such as Aboriginal peoples, African Canadians, immigrants, persons with disabilities, youth, low-income women and single mothers. In a number of jurisdictions, including British Columbia, poverty rates have increased among single mothers and children in the period between 1998 and 2003. The Committee is also concerned by the significant disparities still remaining between Aboriginal people and the rest of the population in areas of employment, access to water, health, housing and education, and by the failure of the State party to fully acknowledge the barriers faced by African Canadians in the enjoyment of their rights under the Covenant.

16. The Committee, while noting that the State party has withdrawn, since 1998, the requirement for an express reference to extinguishment of Aboriginal rights and titles either in a comprehensive claim agreement or in the settlement legislation ratifying the agreement, remains concerned that the new approaches, namely the "modified rights model" and the "non-assertion model", do not differ much from the extinguishment and surrender approach. It further regrets not having received detailed information on other approaches based on recognition and coexistence of rights, which are currently under study.

17. The Committee notes with concern that the long-standing issues of discrimination against First Nations women and their children, in matters relating to Indian status, band membership, and matrimonial real property on reserve lands have still not been resolved. The Committee notes that such discrimination has had a negative impact on the enjoyment of economic, social and cultural rights of some First Nations women and their children under the Covenant.

18. The Committee notes with concern that the minimum wages in all provinces and territories of the State party are below the Low-Income Cut-Off and are insufficient to enable workers and their families to enjoy a decent standard of living.

19. The Committee is concerned that some categories of workers, such as public servants and employees of Crown corporations, public school teachers and college and university professors, are excluded from the right to strike in Canada. The Committee considers that the explanation provided by the State party that these workers provide essential services, is not satisfactory under articles 4 and 8 of the Covenant.

20. The Committee reiterates its concern that federal transfers for social assistance and social services to provinces and territories still do not include standards in relation to some of the rights set forth in the Covenant, including the right to social security. The Committee is also concerned that while the federal Government has increased its contribution to the costs of health care through the Canada Health Transfer, its support for post-secondary education, social assistance and social services through the Canada Social Transfer has not been restored to 1994-1995 levels, in spite of the sustained economic growth in the State party during these last years.

21. The Committee is concerned that the State party has not provided detailed information as to whether current provincial and territorial social assistance rates allow recipients to enjoy an adequate standard of living. It notes with concern that in most provinces and territories, social assistance benefits are lower than a decade ago, that they do not provide adequate income to meet basic needs for food, clothing and shelter, and that welfare levels are often set at less than half the Low-Income Cut-Off.

22. The Committee expresses concern about the significantly low proportion of unemployed workers eligible for receiving insurance benefits, and notes that the State party has not provided detailed responses to the Committee's previous concerns on this issue. The Committee notes with concern that in 2001, only 39 per cent of unemployed Canadians were eligible for benefits; that in some provinces, such as

Ontario, eligibility rates are even lower; that the number of youth receiving employment insurance benefits has decreased; that migrant workers and many part-time workers, predominantly women, contribute to the plan but have great difficulties in accessing benefits; and that the replacement rate of income which has been reduced to 55 per cent in 1997, is the lowest ever.

23. The Committee is deeply concerned by the discriminatory impact of the National Child Benefit "clawback system" on the poorest families in Canada, in particular single-mother-led families.

24. The Committee notes with concern that low-income families, single-mother-led families and Aboriginal and African Canadian families, are overrepresented in families whose children are relinquished to foster care. The Committee is also concerned that women continue to be forced to relinquish their children into foster care because of inadequate housing.

25. The Committee regrets that domestic violence as a specific offence has not been included in the Criminal Code.

26. The Committee notes with concern that women are prevented from leaving abusive relationships due to the lack of affordable housing and inadequate assistance.

27. The Committee notes with concern that about 7.4 per cent of the population, amounting to about 2.3 million people, suffer from food insecurity in the State party, that about 40 per cent of food bank users are children and young people, and that about 51 per cent of food bank users while receiving social assistance benefits in 2005, still had to resort to food banks because of the insufficient level of these benefits.

28. The Committee, while welcoming the National Homelessness Initiative and the adoption of numerous measures on housing, regrets that the information provided was not sufficient to assess the results of such measures. In particular, the Committee is concerned that the estimated number of homeless persons in Canada still ranges from 100,000 to 250,000. The Committee, while welcoming the decrease in the proportion of households with core housing need, notes with concern that in 2001 such households still represented about

13.7 to 16 per cent of all households. The Committee is further concerned that shelter allowances and social assistance rates continue to fall far below average rental costs, and that waiting lists for subsidized housing remain very long, for example, in Hamilton and Montreal.

29. The Committee notes with particular concern that many evictions occur on account of minimal arrears of rent, without due consideration of the State party's obligations under the Covenant.

30. The Committee regrets that the State party does not recognize the right to water as a legal entitlement, which is implicitly provided for under articles 11 and 12 of the Covenant, as outlined in the Committee's general comment No. 15 (2002) on the right to water.

31. The Committee, while noting that scholarships, bursaries, loans and other types of supports are provided to disadvantaged and marginalized individuals and groups, expresses concern about the discriminatory impact of tuition fee increases on low-income persons in many provinces and territories since 1998.

32. The Committee is concerned about information that African Canadian students face difficulties in accessing education and that they experience a disproportionately high dropout rate from secondary school.

33. The Committee, while noting the numerous programmes adopted to preserve Aboriginal languages in the State party, as well as the studies conducted in the area of the protection of traditional knowledge, regrets that no time frame has been set up for the consideration and implementation of the recommendations of the Task Force on Aboriginal Languages and Cultures, and that no concrete measures have been adopted in the area of intellectual property for the protection and promotion of ancestral rights and traditional knowledge of Aboriginal peoples.

E. Suggestions and recommendations

34. The Committee calls upon the State party to address the specific subjects of concern that date back to its second and third periodic reports and strongly reiterates that the State party should consider implementing the Committee's suggestions and recommendations in this regard.

35. The Committee reiterates its recommendation that the federal Government take concrete steps to ensure that provinces and territories are made aware of the State party's legal obligations under the Covenant, that the Covenant rights should be enforceable within provinces and territories through legislation or policy measures, and that independent and appropriate monitoring and adjudication mechanisms be established in this regard. In particular, the State party should establish transparent and effective mechanisms, involving all levels of government as well as civil society, including indigenous peoples, with the specific mandate to follow up on the Committee's concluding observations.

36. The Committee recalls that, within the limits of the appropriate exercise of their functions of judicial review, courts should take account of Covenant rights where this is necessary to ensure that the State party's conduct is consistent with its obligations under the Covenant, in line with the Committee's general comment No. 9 (1998) (see for example *Chaoulli v. Quebec - Attorney General*).

37. The Committee urges the State party to reexamine its policies and practices towards the inherent rights and titles of Aboriginal peoples, to ensure that policies and practices do not result in extinguishment of those rights and titles.

38. The Committee strongly recommends that the State party resume negotiations with the Lubicon Lake Band, with a view to finding a solution to the claims of the Band that ensures the enjoyment of their rights under the Covenant. The Committee also strongly recommends that the State party conduct effective consultation with the Band prior to the grant of licences for economic purposes in the disputed land, and to ensure that such activities do not jeopardize the rights recognized under the Covenant.

39. The Committee recommends that federal, provincial and territorial legislation be brought in line with the State party's obligations under the Covenant, and that such legislation should protect poor people in all jurisdictions from discrimination because of their social or economic status.

40. The State party should take immediate steps, including legislative measures, to create and ensure effective domestic remedies for all Covenant rights in all relevant jurisdictions.

41. The Committee, drawing the State party's attention to its general comment No. 9 (1998), reiterates its recommendation that the federal, provincial and territorial governments promote interpretations of the Canadian Charter of Rights and other domestic law in a way consistent with the Covenant.

42. The Committee reiterates its recommendation that the State party extend the Court Challenges Programme to permit funding of challenges with respect to provincial and territorial legislation and policies.

43. The Committee recommends that the State party ensure that civil legal aid with regard to economic, social and cultural rights is provided to poor people in the provinces and territories, and that it be adequate with respect to coverage, eligibility and services provided.

44. The Committee recommends that the State party fully abide by its obligations under article 2, paragraph 1, of the Covenant to take all possible measures to the maximum of its available resources to ensure the enjoyment of economic, social and cultural rights for all and reminds the State party, in line with its general comment No. 3 (1990), that steps to that end "should be deliberate, concrete and targeted as clearly as possible towards meeting the obligations recognized in the Covenant". The Committee also recommends that the State party eliminate gaps in the area of poverty as a matter of priority, bearing in mind the immediate nature of the obligations contained in articles 2 and 3 of the Covenant. The Committee further recommends that the State party assess the extent to which poverty is a discrimination issue in Canada, and ensure that measures and programmes do not have a negative impact on the enjoyment of economic, social and cultural rights, especially for disadvantaged and marginalized individuals and groups.

45. The Committee recommends that the State party, in consultation with First Nations and including Aboriginal women's groups, adopt measures to combat discrimination against First Nations women and their children in matters relating to Indian status, band membership and matrimonial property. In particular, the Committee urges the State party to repeal section 67 of the Canadian Human Rights Act, which prevents First Nations people from filing complaints of discrimination before a human rights commission or tribunal. The Committee also urges the State party to amend the Indian Act to remove any residual discrimination against First Nations women and their children.

46. The Committee recommends that the State party take into consideration the right to work of women and the need of parents to balance work and family life, by supporting their care choices through adequate childcare services.

47. The Committee urges the State party to adopt all necessary measures to ensure that minimum wages are increased throughout Canada to a level enabling workers and their families to enjoy a decent standard of living.

48. The Committee recommends that the State party take steps to ensure access to employment insurance benefits, enjoyment of trade union rights and effective protection by labour standards for workers in precarious, part-time and temporary low wage jobs in the State party, particularly women.

49. The Committee urges the State party to adopt effective measures, legislative or otherwise, to eliminate exploitation and abuse of migrant domestic workers who are under the federal Live-in Caregiver Program.

50. The Committee recommends that legislation be adopted at the provincial and territorial levels, where necessary, to ensure equal remuneration for work of equal value in both the public and private sectors. In this regard, the Committee reminds the State party that the principle of non-discrimination provided for in article 2, paragraph 2, is an immediate obligation.

51. The Committee strongly recommends that the compatibility of restrictions on the right to strike imposed at the federal, provincial and territorial levels with articles 4 and 8 of the Covenant be re-examined. Such restrictions should be eliminated where they are not strictly necessary for the promotion of the general welfare in a democratic society, for the protection of the interests of national security or public safety, public order, public health or the protection of the rights and freedoms of others, and where no other alternative can be found.

52. The Committee recommends that the State party undertake a detailed assessment of the impact of the reduction of federal transfers for social assistance and social services to provinces and territories, on the standard of living of people depending on social welfare, in particular women, children, older persons, persons with disabilities, Aboriginal people, African Canadians and members of other minorities. The Committee strongly recommends that the State party reconsider all retrogressive measures adopted in 1995.

53. The Committee urges the State party to establish social assistance at levels which ensure the realization of an adequate standard of living for all.

54. The Committee recommends that the State party reassess the Employment Insurance scheme with a view to providing greater access and improved benefit levels to all unemployed workers.

55. The Committee reiterates its recommendation that the National Child Benefit Scheme be amended so as to prohibit provinces and territories from deducting child benefit from social assistance entitlements.

56. The Committee recommends that the State party gather disaggregated statistical data in relation to the relinquishment to foster care of children belonging to low-income families, single-mother-led families, and Aboriginal and African Canadian families in order to accurately assess the extent of the problem. The Committee further recommends that, in accordance with the provisions of article 10 of the Covenant on the protection of families, the federal, provincial and territorial governments undertake all necessary measures including through financial support, where necessary, to avoid such relinquishment.

57. The Committee recommends that the State party give special attention to the difficulties faced by homeless girls, who are more vulnerable to health risks and social and economic deprivation, and that it take all necessary measures to provide them with adequate housing and social and health services.

58. The Committee recommends that domestic violence be included as a specific offence in the Criminal Code.

59. The Committee recommends that the State party ensure that low-income women and women trying to leave abusive relationships can access housing options and appropriate support services in keeping with the right to an adequate standard of living.

60. The Committee reiterates its recommendation that the State party establish an official poverty line. The Committee also recommends that the State party integrate economic, social and cultural rights in its poverty reduction strategies. In this regard, the State party is referred to the Committee's statement on poverty and the International Covenant on Economic, Social and Cultural Rights, adopted in May 2001.

61. The Committee recommends that the State party significantly intensify its efforts to address the issue of food insecurity and hunger in Canada. In this regard, the Committee reminds the State party of its core obligation to fulfil (provide) the right to food when disadvantaged and marginalized individuals or groups are, for reasons beyond their control, unable to realize these rights for themselves through all means possible at their disposal.

62. The Committee reiterates its recommendation that the federal, provincial and territorial governments address homelessness and inadequate housing as a national emergency by reinstating or increasing, where necessary, social housing programmes for those in need, improving and properly enforcing anti-discrimination legislation in the field of housing, increasing shelter allowances and social assistance rates to realistic levels, and providing adequate support services for persons with disabilities. The Committee urges the State party to implement a national strategy for the reduction of homelessness that includes measurable goals and timetables, consultation and collaboration with affected communities, complaints procedures, and transparent accountability mechanisms, in keeping with Covenant standards.

63. The Committee strongly recommends that, before forced evictions are carried out, the State party take appropriate measures, legislative or otherwise, to ensure that those affected by forced evictions are provided with alternative accommodation and thus do not face homelessness, in line with the Committee's general comment No. 7 (1997).

64. The Committee strongly recommends that the State party review its position on the right to water, in line with the Committee's general comment No. 15 (2002) on the right to water, so as to ensure equal and adequate access to water for people living in the State party, irrespective of the province or territory in which they live or the community to which they belong.

65. The Committee recommends that the State party ensure by every appropriate means that higher education be made equally accessible to all, on the basis of capacity.

66. The Committee recommends that an overall assessment of the situation of African Canadians be conducted, particularly in the area of education, in order to adopt and effectively implement a targeted programme of action to realize their rights under the Covenant.

67. The Committee recommends that the State party undertake the adoption and implementation of concrete plans, with relevant benchmarks and time frames, for the consideration and implementation of the recommendations of the Task Force on Aboriginal Languages and Cultures, as well as in the area of intellectual property for the protection and promotion of ancestral rights and traditional knowledge of Aboriginal peoples.

68. The Committee reminds the State party that, although trade liberalization has a wealth-generating potential, such liberalization does not necessarily create and lead to a favourable environment for the realization of economic, social and cultural rights. In this regard, the Committee recommends that the State

party consider ways in which the primacy of Covenant rights may be ensured in trade and investment agreements, and in particular in the adjudication of investor-State disputes under chapter XI of the North American Free Trade Agreement (NAFTA).

69. The Committee requests the State party to include in its sixth periodic report, detailed information on any measures taken and progress made, particularly with regard to the suggestions and recommendations made by the Committee in the present concluding observations.

70. The Committee requests that the succeeding State party's reports focus primarily on its follow-up to the Committee's previous concluding observations, and structured by articles of the Covenant. The Committee also requests the State party to provide, in addition to information on measures adopted, details on the substantive impact of such measures on the realization of economic, social and cultural rights. In this regard, the Committee also wishes to receive comparative statistical data disaggregated by year, as well as information on percentages of budget allocations to programmes relevant under the Covenant.

71. The Committee encourages the State party to actively engage non-governmental organizations and other members of civil society in a meaningful process of discussions, at the federal, provincial and territorial levels, prior to the submission of its next periodic report to the Committee.

72. The Committee requests the State party to disseminate the present concluding observations widely among all levels of society, particularly among government officials and judicial authorities, and to inform the Committee on all steps taken to implement them in its next periodic report.

73. The Committee requests the State party to submit its sixth periodic report by 6 June 2010.

Glossary

Aboriginal peoples. Aboriginal peoples are a diverse population of distinct peoples with unique heritages, languages, cultural practices, and spiritual beliefs. The Aboriginal peoples of Canada are the descendants of the original inhabitants of North America. Three groups of Aboriginal people are recognized by the Canadian *Constitution Act, 1982*: Indians, Métis, and Inuit. We now generally use the term First Nations in place of Indian except in a legal capacity, such as in the *Indian Act.*

Absolute homelessness. Absolute homelessness is a situation in which an individual or family has no housing at all, or is staying in a temporary form of shelter.

Absolute measure of poverty. The absolute measure of poverty is based on an essential basket of goods and services deemed necessary for survival (relative to cultural context). Those who cannot afford the "basket" are considered to be living in poverty. This types of measure is open for debate because people do not agree on what should be included in the "basket."

Accessibility. The quality of being free of or providing alternatives to barriers, both physical and systemic, that prevent full participation in society.

Accessibility for Ontarians with Disabilities Act (AODA). Enacted in 2005, this legislation outlines Ontario's goals to develop accessibility standards by 2025.

Administrative eligibility. In order to qualify for Social Assistance, applicants are normally required to meet certain administrative criteria. In most provinces, this entails the completion of a formal application, providing evidence that they meet other eligibility criteria (e.g., bank books, pay stubs, or doctors' notes), agreeing to meet with a worker in order to discuss his or her situation, etc.

Anti-racist approach. This Marxist approach helps us to understand the economic roots of racism and discrimination, and how these processes continue to be at play today, creating high levels of unemployment and underemployment among racialized groups.

Assembly of First Nations (AFN). The AFN is the national organization representing First Nations citizens in Canada, providing them with a national voice through their leaders, advocating for issues such as Aboriginal and treaty rights, economic development, education, languages and literacy, health, housing, social development, justice, taxation, land claims, and the environment.

Assimilation. In past federal government Indian policy, assimilation was the central pillar or goal. It was desired and expected that eventually all Indians would give up their traditional customs, culture, and beliefs and become like the dominant society.

Basic Needs Lines (BNLs). In 1992, the Fraser Institute published the Basic Needs Lines (BNLs) based on the basic subsistence requirements needed for survival (an absolute approach). They were widely criticized for being below most Canadians' survival expectations.

Beverage Report. The Beverage Report came out of Britain in 1943, the same year as the subsequent Canadian Marsh Report. These reports established the baseline for the rapid expansion of social welfare.

Bill C-2. In 1998, Parliament amended the Canada Pension Plan through Bill C-2. The changes resulted in a larger reserve fund to help ensure that the future pensions of the growing retirement population can be funded. Contribution rates were increased from the 1998 5.85 percent of contributory earnings to 9.9 percent. These changes will increase the size of the fund of money that is put aside to pay for future retirement pensions.

Bill C-12, the *Employment Insurance Act*. On January 5, 1995, changes to the Employment Insurance system took effect with Bill C-12, the new *Employment Insurance Act*. The new system replaced the previous Unemployment Insurance system on July 1, 1996.

Bill C-21. The introduction of Bill C-21 in 1990 reversed several of the enhancements of Bill C-229. The bill increased the number of weeks of work required to receive Unemployment Insurance benefits, reduced the maximum duration of benefits for most regions, and reduced the replacement rate from 60 to 50 percent of insurable earnings for those who declined "suitable employment," quit "without just cause," or were fired.

Bill C-229. Bill C-229, introduced early in 1971, completed a revamped UI that followed many of the White Paper recommendations. This was part of Prime Minister Pierre Elliott Trudeau's Just Society initiative. Due to these changes, 80 percent of unemployed workers were covered by UI.

B/U ratio. One way to measure the extent to which unemployed Canadians are covered by Employment Insurance is to calculate the proportion of unemployed who actually receive EI benefits. This is known as the B/U ratio — the ratio of unemployed EI beneficiaries to the unemployed without benefits.

Campaign 2000. In 1989, the House of Commons declared its commitment to eliminating poverty among Canadian children by the year 2000. Campaign 2000, an across-Canada public education movement to build Canadian awareness and support for the 1989 all-party House of Commons resolution, reports yearly on the progress towards the goal of eliminating child poverty.

Canada Assistance Plan (CAP). In an effort to consolidate Social Assistance and other income security and social services programs, the federal government introduced a new cost-sharing arrangement with the provinces in 1966 — the Canada Assistance Plan (CAP). CAP brought together a range of cost-shared income security, social services, education, and health programs into one system. It also included several national standards.

Canada Child Tax Benefit (CCTB). In 1998 a new initiative called the Canada Child Tax Benefit (CCTB) was introduced. The CCTB has two main elements: a CCTB basic benefit, and the National Child Benefit Supplement (NCBS). The NCBS is an additional tax credit that adds to the CCTB and is the federal contribution to the CCTB. It provides low-income families with additional child benefits on top of the basic benefit.

Canada Health and Social Transfer (CHST). Replacing the Canada Assistance Plan (CAP) and Established Programs Financing (EPF), the 1996 CHST set the funding formula for Social Assistance, social services, health care services, and post-secondary education.

Canada Health Transfer (CHT). Replacing the CHST, the Canada Health Transfer provides federal funding to the provices for health care services.

Canada Pension Plan Disability (CPPD) Benefit. The CPPD benefit provides a disability benefit to those with "severe and prolonged disabilities" who meet the CPP contribution requirements. It is most commonly known as providing retirement pensions to workers in Canada, but it also provides survivor, death, and disability benefits to CPP contributors and their families.

Canada/Quebec Pension Plan (C/QPP). The earnings-based Canada/Quebec Pension Plan (C/QPP) provides a pension upon retirement to persons who have contributed to it. It is a social insurance type of income security program; it insures the contributor against loss of income due to retirement. All employed or self-employed Canadians over the age of 18 make compulsory contributions to the plan (matched by their employer) throughout their working careers. The plan also offers disability, survivor, and death benefits, as well as inflation protection. The plan is fully portable from job to job.

Canadian Multicultural Policy (1971). Enacted by the Trudeau government, the policy's reframed ethnic or racial difference as a national agenda of "unity within diversity," recognizing the right all the cultural groups to participate within the greater Canadian society.

Canada Social Transfer. Replacing the CHST, the Canada Social Transfer provides federal funding to the provinces for Social Assistance, social services, and post-secondary education.

Capitalism. Capitalism is an economic and social system based on a monopoly of the ownership of capital rather than the ownership of land, as in the case of feudalism. Ownership of or access to capital (machinery and equipment, private property, and money) provided industrialists with the basis for employing workers at a wage.

Categorical eligibility. Categorical eligibility refers to the different types of reasons why applicants might request Social Assistance. While all applicants are presumed to be in need, different criteria for needs are considered. Criteria can depend on whether the applicant is elderly, disabled, a single parent, or otherwise employable.

Child Care Expense Deduction. The Child Care Expense Deduction was first introduced in 1971 and was originally intended for one-parent families. It was designed to offset the incremental costs of child rearing for parents in the labour force.

Child Tax Benefit (CTB). In 1993, the Government of Canada consolidated its child tax credits and the Family Allowance into a single Child Tax Benefit (CTB) that provided a monthly payment based on the number of children and the level of family income. It has now been changed to the CCTB and NCBS.

Child Tax Exemption. Income support to families with children began in 1918 with the introduction of the Child Tax Exemption in personal income tax. The exemption provided income tax savings that increased with taxable income. The after-tax benefit was of greatest absolute benefit to those in the highest tax brackets. The exemption provided no benefits to families that did not owe income tax.

Chinese Head Tax. A "tax" of $50 imposed on all incoming persons of Chinese origin, with very few exceptions, under the *Chinese Immigration Act* (1885). The tax was eventually increased to $100 in 1900, and $500 (the equivalent of 2 years of wages for a Chinese labourer) in 1903.

Christianization. Christianization was a process that supported the core assimilation policy. To the colonial government, the civilizing of the Indians was synonymous with their Christianization. Aboriginal ceremonies and cultural practices were officially discouraged or outlawed. Education through church residential schools was seen as a way to destroy the social, spiritual, and cultural systems and relations of the Indians and replace them with the beliefs of mainstream Canadian society.

Claim period. The claim period is the allowed amount of time you can be on EI and varies depending on the number of weeks you have worked and the local unemployment rate. The maximum claim period is forty-five weeks.

Clawback rule. Programs such as EI, the NCBS, and OAS take money back from certain beneficiaries. In the cases of EI and OAS, those with income over a certain level lose the benefit. With the NCBS, people on welfare have the benefit taken away.

Collective rights. This category of human rights defines rights at a collective level. This type of rights generally has roots in anti-colonial struggles, environmental activism, and the efforts for self-determination of indigenous peoples.

Congress of Aboriginal Peoples (CAP). CAP is an organization that represents the interests of Aboriginal people who are not legally recognized under the *Indian Act*, including non-Status Indians and Métis people.

Conservative ideology. The basic values of the conservative ideology are freedom, individualism, and the inevitability of inequality. According to the conservative ideology, the role of government (including its interference in the free market economy) should be limited, and the role of private property and private enterprise should be paramount.

Conservative/corporatist continental welfare states. Germany, Austria, and France typify the conservative/corporatist continental welfare state model. Welfare states following this model provide income maintenance to uphold the status quo and maintain income difference between classes. They are not concerned with eradicating poverty or creating a more egalitarian society.

Consumer Price Index (CPI). The CPI is an indicator of the consumer prices in Canada. It is calculated, on a monthly basis, using the cost of a fixed "basket" of commodities purchased by a typical Canadian consumer during a given month. The CPI is a widely used indicator of inflation (or deflation) and indicates the changing purchasing power of money in Canada.

Continuous Journey Requirement. Permitted entry to immigrants *only* if they arrived directly from their home country on tickets purchased before leaving the country. This policy was developed to limit immigration from the Indian subcontinent, from which a continuous journey was next to impossible.

Contributory negligence. Contributory negligence states that if the injured worker's own conduct contributed to the injury in even the slightest way, the employer completely escapes legal responsibility. This occurred up until the early 1900s when Workers' Compensation was introduced.

Culturally biased hiring practices. Practices that favour certain skills and behaviours which can make it difficult for newcomers to find appropriate employment. For example, here in North America, "selling yourself" and your skills is not only desirable, but necessary when searching for a job. Members of some cultural groups, however, see this behaviour as rude and boastful, and find it uncomfortable to act with such assertiveness.

Culture. Culture is the set of ideals, norms, beliefs, and values that are shared by a group of individuals. This shapes the way people interpret the world, and informs the way they live their day-to-day lives. It is important to remember that cultures shift and change over time, and that members of a particular cultural group might differ from one another in terms of their specific customs and traditions.

Cyclical unemployment. Cyclical unemployment occurs due to a temporary downturn in the job market. The most common form of cyclical unemployment occurs when workers are temporarily laid off.

Demogrants. These are universal flat-rate payments made to individuals or households on the sole basis of demographic characteristics, such as number of children or age, rather than on the basis of need. The Family Allowance program, benefiting all families with children under the age of 18, was Canada's first widespread demogrant.

Department of Indian Affairs. This department was established by the federal government as the main vehicle for regulating and controlling Aboriginal movement and ways of living. It administered the reserve system and gained its authority through the *Indian Act* of 1876.

Deserving poor. A term, originating with the English Poor Laws, used to describe those not physically able to work — that is, the deserving poor or paupers. Many

believe that this idea still informs much of social welfare policy towards the poor today.

Devaluation of credentials. When Canadian organizations and institutions do not recognize, or undervalue, a person's qualifications obtained in other countries.

Disability. Disability applies to a wide range of so-called impairments including sensory impairments, such as blindness or deafness, physical disabilities impairing mobility, and psychiatric, developmental, learning, and neurological disabilities.

Disability Tax Credit. The DTC is an income tax credit for individuals who have a disability that "markedly restricts" activities of daily living. A treating physician must complete a form outlining the nature of the disability.

Discouraged workers. *Discouraged workers* is the term used to refer to those individuals who are no longer looking for a job because they believe they will not find one. Discouraged workers are classified as not being in the labour force.

Dual-earner families. Currently, families that rely on the income of both partners predominate in Canada. This change has led to a complete revision of family obligations in a very short time and, hence, a great deal of uncertainty.

Economic class. This is an immigration category in which applicants can be either skilled workers, business owners or entrepreneurs.

Economic efficiency. Economic efficiency refers to the existence of optimal and stable economic growth with a flexible and productive labour market.

Economic globalization. The growing integration of international markets for goods, services, and finance, characterized by free trade and investment expansion, concentrated transnational corporation power, enforcement and rights protection.

Economic theory approach. The economic theory approach, as its name implies, focuses on the influence of economic theories. Economists have differing theories about the root causes of unemployment and poverty that generally derive from the three economic theories: Keynesian economics, monetarism, and political economy. Each body of economic theory has a different view of the role of government and the effects of social spending on the economy.

Elizabethan Poor Laws. The famous Elizabethan Poor Laws provided the bedrock of the modern welfare states in England, the United States, and Canada. In 1601 England passed the Elizabethan *Poor-Relief Act*, mainly to suppress vagrancy and begging. The act recognized the state's obligation to those in need, provided for compulsory local levies, and required work for the able-bodied poor. Institutional relief was provided by poorhouses and workhouses. The subsequent amendments of 1834 were based on the belief that pauperism was rooted in an unwillingness to work (rather than resulting from inadequate employment opportunities), and the relief provided to the poor had to be set at a level below that of the poorest labourer.

Employment. Employment includes any legal activity carried out for pay or profit. It also includes unpaid family work, when it is a direct contribution to the operation of a farm, business, or professional practice owned or operated by a related member of the household. Some employed people are self-employed.

Employment Insurance (EI). This social insurance type of income security program provides a level of income replacement to those workers who are temporarily out of work and meet strict eligibility conditions.

Employment Insurance Sickness Benefits. Employment Insurance Sickness Benefits are meant to fill the gap before people become eligible for longer-term illness and disability benefits from employer-sponsored group insurance plans, private plans held by individuals, or the Canada Pension Plan Disability Benefit. Annual spending for EI Sickness Benefits in 2004/05 was $813.2 million.

Employment population ratio. The employment population ratio is the ratio of employed to the working-age population.

Enfranchisement. Enfranchisement was the method envisioned for Indians to obtain citizenship and thus be fully recognized as Canadians, a process which required the loss of Indian status. In 1966 all Status Indians gained full citizenship and the right to vote in federal elections.

Ethnicity. Ethnicity describes a group of people who share a common descent, language, religion, and traditions. Although people might be members of the same racial grouping, they can differ in terms of ethnicity. For example, people who identify themselves racially as "black" may identify themselves *ethnically* as African, Jamaican, or Caribbean. Each of these ethnic groupings is linked to particular values and behaviours that differ considerably from one another, despite the perceived commonality in race.

Export processing zone (EPZ). An export processing zone is a particular area in a country from which benefits come in the form of preferential financial regulations and special investment incentives. There are export processing zones all over the world.

Family. This textbook uses the term *family* with some caution. Many definitions of families exclude common-law couples, most exclude lone-parent families, and pretty well all still exclude same-sex relationships. In Canada today, the term *family* is defined according to either structural criteria (what they look like) or functional criteria (what they do).

Family Allowance (FA). The *Family Allowance Act* of 1944 introduced the universal Family Allowance (FA), providing benefits to all Canadian families with dependent children. The FA was also popularly known as the "baby bonus." It was the first universal income security scheme. It was ended in 1993.

Family class. This is an immigration category in which applicants must be sponsored by family members who are already citizens.

Family responsibility approach. According to the family responsibility approach, parents are solely responsible for making decisions and providing for their children's well-being. The role of income security and social services is to facilitate decision making and provide support when the family's ability to provide fails.

Federalism. Federalism is a system of government in which a number of smaller states (in Canada's case, provinces and territories) join to form a larger political entity while still retaining a measure of political power.

Fellow servant rule. The fellow servant rule maintained that if a worker's injury was related to a co-worker's negligence, the employer was not responsible. The injured worker could sue the co-worker, but considering the income levels of workers at the time, this was an ineffective option. It also pitted worker against worker. This rule generally applied up until the early 1900s, when Workers' Compensation was introduced.

Feminization of poverty. Currently, almost 16 percent of adult women live below the Statistics Canada Low Income Cut-off, or LICO. Women are falling further and further into poverty. The term now commonly used to capture this social phenomenon is the *feminization of poverty.*

Feudalism. Prior to the fourteenth century, society was based largely on a system of obligations in a primarily agricultural society. This kind of social organization was known as *feudalism.* Feudalism was both an economic and a social system in which the owner of the property was responsible for the peasants working on the land.

Financial eligibility. To meet the financial eligibility requirement, an applicant must show the need for Social Assistance. A needs test compares the household's assets with its needs. When the cost of a household's needs is greater than its available income, Social Assistance may be granted.

First Nations. This is a term used in place of *Indian.* Together First Nations, Métis, and Inuit make up the Aboriginal peoples of Canada.

Food banks and feeding programs. With cutbacks in many income security programs, Canadians are having to rely on food banks and feeding programs in order to survive. Food banks are charities that provide groceries, whereas feeding programs provide cooked meals.

Free trade. Free trade refers to the lowering and dismantling of the barriers and regulations that might impede the international flow of capital and products, or restrict marketplace demand. Free trade is embodied in the growing collection of free trade agreements and international trade organizations, including the General Agreement on Tariffs and Trade (GATT), the Asia-Pacific Economic Cooperation (APEC), and the North American Free Trade Agreement (NAFTA).

Frictional unemployment. Frictional unemployment occurs when people move between jobs. This includes new labour force entrants, such as those returning to the labour force after completing school or raising children.

Full-time employment. Full-time employment refers to people who usually work 30 or more hours per week, or to people who work fewer than 30 hours per week but consider themselves to be employed full-time.

G8. The G8 (Group of 8) is a group of eight wealthy countries: Canada, France, Germany, Italy, Japan, Russia, the United Kingdom, and the United States. Each year, G8 leaders and representatives from the European Union meet to discuss broad economic and foreign policies.

Gender-based approach. The gender-based approach to social welfare identifies two regime types based on an analysis of the family and unpaid labour: the male-bread-winner regime and the individual earner-carer regime.

Gini coefficient. The Gini coefficient measures the degree of inequality in income distribution. Values of the Gini coefficient can range from 0 to 1. A value of 0 indicates that income is equally divided among the population, with all persons receiving exactly the same amount of income. At the opposite extreme, a Gini coefficient of 1 denotes a perfectly unequal distribution, where one unit possesses all of the income in the economy. A decrease in the value of the Gini coefficient can be interpreted as reflecting a decrease in inequality, and vice versa.

Global poverty. According to the World Bank, about one-quarter of the world's population lives on less than $1 per day and over half live on $2 per day. While some people can adequately survive on such meagre incomes given the cost of living in their home countries, many suffer with health problems, low life expectancies, high infant mortality rates, low levels of education, and malnutrition.

Global social welfare. Given the new era of globalization, the traditional concerns of social welfare will need to be broadened to include a concern with the issue of global human rights. As noted earlier, global social welfare (a concern with justice, social regulation, social provision, and redistribution between nations) is already a part of the activities of various supranational organizations or international governmental organizations of the United Nations.

Great Depression. The economic depression of the late 1920s and early 1930s was an important event in the rise of income security and social services in Canada. Public perception of the poor began to shift. Massive numbers of people were unemployed, and Canadians began to see that this could not possibly be due to individual fault, but had more to do with the operation of the economy. The idea that help for the poor should be a local or family responsibility was replaced with the idea that the government should be responsible for providing relief to the unemployed.

Guaranteed Income Supplement (GIS). The Guaranteed Income Supplement (GIS) provides extra money to OAS recipients who have little or no other income.

Horizontal equity. Horizontal equity is based on the recognition that parents have heavier financial demands than childless households and single persons with the same income.

Human capital perspective. This perspective views an immigrant's attributes, specific skills, and personal resources as shaping her/his level of employment success.

Human Development Index. In 1992 Canada ranked first among all countries in the world on a composite Human Development Index (created by the United Nations Development Programme) that combined life expectancy, educational attainment, and standard of living. Canada has recently dropped on this list, primarily due to child poverty and single-mother poverty levels.

Human rights. The inherent rights without which we cannot truly live as human beings. A right is a justified claim or entitlement by someone or some institution in society, and human rights are a standard by which we define human dignity from all peoples.

Income security. Income security provides monetary or other material benefits to supplement income or maintain minimum income levels (e.g., Employment Insurance, Social Assistance, Old Age Security, and Workers' Compensation).

Income Security Reform (ISR). This was an INAC initiative that ended in 2003. The objective of the ISR initiative was to transform the passive on-reserve welfare system to a dynamic system that promotes opportunities and self-sufficiency.

Income supplementation. These are programs that supplement income that is obtained elsewhere, through paid employment or through other income security programs. They are not intended to be the primary source of income. The National Child Benefit Supplement (NCBS) and the Guaranteed Income Supplement (GIS) are income supplementation programs.

Indexation. Indexation is an arrangement in which periodic adjustments are made to benefits based on changes in an index of some kind, most often the Consumer Price Index (CPI). Non-indexation of benefits has the effect of reducing the benefit each year by the amount of any increases in the Consumer Price Index (CPI).

Indian Act of 1876. This act provided for the government's guardianship over Indian lands. It is a piece of social legislation of very broad scope that regulates and controls virtually every aspect of Aboriginal life. The act has been amended throughout the years, but remained largely intact until major changes in 1996. The *Indian Act* strictly defines who is and who is not an Indian by setting out the requirements for determining who is a Status Indian.

Indian and Northern Affairs Canada (INAC). This is the federal government department responsible for policy and administration of programs and relations with Aboriginal peoples. It was created in October 1966 and was formerly known as the *Department of Indian Affairs and Northern Development*.

Individual earner-carer regimes. Individual earner-carer regimes are based on shared roles between men and women leading to equal rights. In this model, both sexes have equal rights to social entitlements as earners and caregivers. Paid work in the labour market and unpaid caregiving work have the same benefit entitlements, thereby neutralizing gender differentiation with respect to social rights. The state plays a central role in the provision of services and payments, whether it be caring for children, elderly relatives, the sick, or people with disabilities.

Individual responsibility model of the family. The individual responsibility model of the family consists of three main elements: formal gender equality, gender-neutral policies, and equalized caregiving. Within this model, the family unit is still treated as the normal unit of administration, but the husband and wife are seen as equally responsible for the economic well-being of themselves, each other, and any children.

Indoor relief. Indoor relief was provided to able-bodied men who were deemed employable. These recipients were obligated to live in a workhouse and undertake work duties in order to receive assistance. The objective was to limit relief and use work as a form of punishment.

Inequality. Inequality is linked to the differences between income groups. The way in which total income in a country is divided between households is a measure of inequality.

Institutional view. In the institutional view, social welfare is a necessary public response that helps people attain a reasonable standard of life and health. Within this view, it is accepted that people cannot always meet all of their needs through family and work. Therefore, in a complex industrial society, it is legitimate to help people through a set of publicly funded and organized systems of programs and institutions. The institutional model attempts to even out, rather than promote, economic stratification or status differences.

International Bill of Human Rights. This bill is the primary basis of United Nations activities to promote, protect, and monitor human rights and fundamental freedoms. The bill comprises three texts: the *Universal Declaration of Human Rights (1948)*; the *International Covenant on Economic, Social, and Cultural Rights (1966)*; and the *International Covenant on Civil and Political Rights* (1966) and its two optional protocols.

International Monetary Fund (IMF). Created in 1945, this international organization aims to promote international monetary cooperation, exchange stability, and orderly exchange arrangements to foster economic growth and high levels of employment, and to provide temporary financial assistance to countries to help ease balance of payments adjustment. Their structural adjustment programs have had many negative impacts on developing countries. At present the IMF has $107 billion loaned out to fifty-six countries.

International Year of Disabled Persons. In 1976 the United Nations declared 1981 the International Year of Disabled Persons, which led to the development of Canada's action on disability.

Inuit Tapiriit Kanatami (ITK). ITK is a national organization, founded in the 1970s, that represents the four Inuit regions in Canada: Nunatsiavut (Labrador), Nunavik (northern Quebec), Nunavut, and the Inuvialuit Settlement Region in the Northwest Territories.

Investing in children approach. This approach entails building supports for families and households that enable them to attain positive outcomes for children. There is a recognition that the decisions open to families are increasingly limited and that the options for parents have narrowed insofar as most families need two incomes to adequately provide for themselves.

Job modifications. These modifications include the personal help that persons with disabilities need to participate in the labour market, such as sign language interpreters, job coaches, voice synthesizers, computers with Braille, recording equipment, and job redesign.

Job redesign. Job redesign refers to an adjustment or modification of duties, such as flexible work hours; this is a type of job modification.

Keynesian. A Keynesian is a follower of the economic theory of the British economist John Maynard Keynes (1883–1946). Keynes' economic theories provided the intellectual rationale for the intervention of governments in economies and the transformation of social policy.

Labour force. The official definition of the labour force is the number of people in the country 15 years of age or over who either have a job or are actively looking for one. This excludes people living on Indian reserves, full-time members of the armed forces, and institutional residents (e.g., prison inmates and patients in hospitals or in nursing homes who have resided there for more than six months). Retired people, students, people not actively seeking work, and people not available for work for other reasons are also not considered part of the labour force, although they may be part of the working-age population.

Labour force participation rate. The ratio of the labour force to the working-age population (age 15 and over) is referred to as the labour force participation rate.

Labour Market Agreements for Persons with Disabilities (LMAPD). Agreements between the federal government and the provinces to provide funding for employment programs for persons with disabilities.

Labour market approach. This approach to immigrant employment suggests that characteristics of the local job market, (such as the demand for certain skills and other specific qualities of the geographic location) are key factors that determine the level of unemployment or underemployment experienced by newcomer groups.

Land surrender. Land surrender is the means by which the government obtained land held by Aboriginal peoples for the settlement of non-Aboriginal people.

Liberal ideology. The primary values of a liberal ideology are pragmatism, liberty, individualism, the inevitability of inequality, and humanism. Pragmatism means that, as a government or an individual, you do what needs to be done. Liberals have often been described as less ideological than conservatives, which means they are willing to do things that suit the circumstances, but may not exactly follow "liberal" principles. Liberty, individualism, and social inequality are tempered by a concern for justice for the poor. So competition and markets are tempered by a concern for people and the need for a certain basic level of social security.

Liberal welfare regimes. Liberal welfare regimes include countries such as Canada, the United States, Australia, the United Kingdom, and Ireland. "Liberal," as used here, refers to classical liberalism that is concerned with laissez-faire economics and minimal government interference.

Low Income Cut-off (LICO). This Statistics Canada measure of poverty is a combined relative and absolute measure often referred to as a "relative necessities" approach. It is based on the percentage of income that individuals and families spend on basic needs or necessities in comparison with the rest of Canadians. LICO is not explicitly put forth as a poverty line by the Canadian government, but rather as a level of low income.

Low Income Measure (LIM). A Statistics Canada relative poverty indicator that measures low-income rates as one-half of the median income of the country. Because it is a straightforward calculation and can be collected in all nations, it allows for simple comparisons between countries.

Low-paid worker. An individual whose annual earnings are low or works in a low-paying job. A low-paid worker may be among the working poor, depending on household circumstances.

Male-breadwinner families. Over the past thirty years, the proportion of male-breadwinner families has decreased drastically, and they now constitute less than 25 percent of the total of all Canadian families.

Male-breadwinner regimes. The male-breadwinner regime is characterized by an ideology of male privilege based on a division of labour between the sexes and resulting in unequal benefit entitlements. Men are seen as the family providers and thereby are entitled to benefits based on their labour force participation or their position as "head of the household."

Market Basket Measure (MBM). This new absolute measure of poverty calculates the amount of income needed by a given household to meet its needs based on "credible" community norms.

Market poverty. Market poverty refers to a situation in which a household remains below some measure of poverty, even though one or more members of the household earn a market income or are employed.

Marsh Report. The *Report on Social Security for Canada* by Leonard Marsh became commonly known as the *Marsh Report* and detailed the need for comprehensive and universal social welfare programs.

Medical model. The medical model views disability as medical condition or personal tragedy or unfortunate life event; it focuses on limitations and recommends helping the individual to adapt to their situation.

Meredith principle. The Meredith principle, also called the *historic compromise*, is a compromise in which workers give up the right to sue for work-related injuries, irrespective of fault, in return for guaranteed compensation for accepted claims.

Minimum income. This is a type of income security that provides monetary assistance to those with no other source of income. Social Assistance or welfare is a minimum income program.

Minimum wage. This is the lowest wage rate, by law, that an employer can pay employees to perform their work. Canada's provinces have all set a standard minimum wage.

Monetarists. The monetarists are a group of economists known for their preoccupation with the role and effects of money in the economy. Monetarist theory asserts that managing the money supply and interest rates (monetary policy) – rather than focusing on fiscal policy – is the key to managing the economy.

National Child Benefit Supplement (NCBS). The National Child Benefit Supplement is an additional tax credit that adds to the Canada Child Tax Benefit (CCTB). The NCBS is the federal contribution to the CCTB. It provides low-income families with additional child benefits on top of the basic benefit.

National Council of Welfare. The National Council of Welfare is a citizens' advisory body on matters of concern to low-income Canadians. It released a 1998 report entitled *Child Benefits: Kids Are Still Hungry.*

Natural unemployment. A combination of frictional and structural unemployment results in what is referred to as natural unemployment or NAIRU (non-accelerating inflation rate of unemployment). According to monetarist economists, attempts to lower unemployment below NAIRU will risk the acceleration or increase of inflation.

NCBS clawback. The distinctive feature of the National Child Benefit Supplement is that, by agreement with the provinces and territories, there is an NCBS clawback for Social Assistance recipients. Newfoundland, Nova Scotia, Quebec, Manitoba, and New Brunswick have increased Social Assistance benefits using NCBS funds. In all other provinces and territories, the supplement is clawed back from Social Assistance recipients in different ways.

Negative rights. The emphasis of negative rights is on protection. They are rights that need to be protected rather than realized through social security or provision. These rights call for inaction on the part of the person or institution fulfilling the rights. The right is met by merely refraining from acting in a way that would violate the right.

Non-profit and for-profit welfare agencies. With government cutbacks in recent years, more and more sources of income security protection are being provided by non-profit and for-profit welfare agencies. Food banks and emergency shelters are increasingly helping people with low incomes, while people with more material means are turning to private (for-profit) pensions and insurance programs to ensure their economic security in the future.

Occupational pension plans. Occupational pension plans are linked to an employment or professional relationship between the pension plan member and the entity that establishes the plan. They may be established by employers and labour or professional associations. They are the largest pools of capital in industrialized nations.

Old Age Security (OAS). The Old Age Security (OAS) program provides a basic pension (adjusted for inflation) to virtually everyone over 65 years of age who has lived in Canada for a required length of time. It is a universal monetary benefit payable to Canadians over a specified age. It is an income transfer program paid out of the general revenue of the federal government.

Opportunities Fund for Persons with Disabilities. Funded through the Employment Insurance program, this program provides assistance to people with disabilities who have had little or no attachment to the labour force. People with disabilities who are not eligible for Employment Insurance are eligible for this program.

Outdoor relief. Outdoor relief was provided to a select category of recipients in their place of residence: the sick, the aged, the disabled, the orphaned or the widowed — all groups that were seen as deserving of aid. The relief generally came in kind, meaning it was in the form of food, second-hand clothing, or fuel.

Parental leave benefits. Important changes to the *Employment Insurance Act* in 2000 increased parental leave benefits from ten weeks to thirty-five weeks, increasing the total maternity and parental paid leave time from six months to one year. In addition, the threshold for eligibility was lowered from 700 to 600 hours of insurable employment.

Participation and Activity Limitation Survey (PALS). PALS is a post-censal survey of persons with disabilities; it is based on the World Health Organization's understanding of disability as a relationship between body structures and functions, daily activities, and social participation, and also recognizes the role of environmental factors.

Part-time employment. Part-time employment refers to people who usually work fewer than 30 hours each week. The involuntary part-time worker prefers full-time work but can only find part-time employment.

Patriarchal model of the family. This model is based on perceptions that were dominant at the beginning of the twentieth century, whereby the husband was considered the undisputed master of the family, and the wife was economically and socially beneath her husband. Children were also treated as economic dependants of the husband/father. The wife/mother was seen as responsible for providing care and services to family members without pay. Finally, divorce did not exist (although there were separations not recognized by law).

Pay equity legislation. Legislation (in Canada since the 1970s) that ensures people receive equal pay for work of equal value.

Permanent residents. Immigrants, or "non-Canadians" who have lived in Canada legally for at least two consecutive years during any five-year period. These individuals enjoy the same rights and privileges as Canadian citizens, but are not allowed to vote or hold positions in public office until they are granted citizenship.

Personal resources. Additional factors that help a person obtain and keep employment; these can include a person's ability to know where to look for work, how to write a resume, and how to prepare for an interview.

Persons with disabilities. This is considered a more humanizing, person-first term that has generally replaced the use of the term "disabled people."

Points system. This current immigration policy awards points to potential immigrants based on a variety of qualities such as education, fluency of English or French, demand for occupation, number of relatives already in Canada. The sytem is intended to make the immigration system more transparent and objective.

Political economy theorists. Political economy theorists believe that the operation of economic markets is tied to private concentrations of ownership and is essentially exploitative. Most adherents, while not opposed to providing support to those in need, would argue that social spending serves to prop up and justify an unjust economic system. The welfare state, in their view, is one of the contradictions of capitalism: it increases well-being, but it also frustrates the pursuit of a just society. It reinforces the very institutions and values that the welfare state was established to do away with.

Political ideology approach. The political ideology approach situates social welfare in the context of economic, social, and political theory — in Canada, this is normally distinguished according to conservative, liberal, social democratic, and socialist beliefs.

Poor Law of 1834. The rather harsh Poor Law of 1834 had three main features: it forbade outdoor relief (relief outside the almshouses) for able-bodied persons and their families, it aimed to dramatically cut relief rates, and it aimed to tighten administrative rules and clean up what it saw as abuses of the system.

Positive rights. Positive rights imply that the state plays a more positive and active role in ensuring that these rights are realized. A positive right requires action, rather than inaction, on the part of the duty-bearer or the person or institution fulfilling the right. These rights require the state to play an active role in providing income security and services.

Poverty duration. Poverty duration refers to the length of time that people experience low income. The Statistics Canada Survey of Labour and Income Dynamics (SLID) enables analysis of the duration of poverty. SLID follows the same set of people for six consecutive years and is designed to capture changes in the economic well-being of individuals and families over time.

Poverty gap. The poverty gap is a measurement of how much additional income would be required to raise an individual or household above the LICO or some other measure of poverty. It measures the depth of poverty.

Poverty headcount. Poverty headcount measures the number and proportion of persons in poverty.

Poverty rate. A variety of measures have been proposed for measuring the rate of poverty. In discussing how much poverty exists, three dimensions need to be considered: how many people are poor (the headcount measure), by *how much* they fall below the poverty line (the poverty gap measure), and for *how long* they are poor (the poverty duration measure).

Principle of less eligibility. This principle is based on the idea that the amount of assistance has to be less than that of the lowest-paying job. It stipulated that the "able-bodied pauper's" condition be less eligible (that is, less desirable or favourable) than the condition of the independent labourer. The intention is to stigmatize relief.

Private pension plans. The private pension plans component of the retirement income system consists of pensions from employers, and publicly supported and regulated private savings plans such as Registered Retirement Savings Plans (RRSPs), Registered Pension Plans (RPPs), and Deferred Profit Sharing Plans (DPSPs).

Private welfare. Private welfare can be non-profit or for-profit, and provides "in-kind" benefits to those lacking income. In-kind benefits include such things as food, emergency shelter, and other bare necessities. By law, organizations that provide these benefits are often registered, and rules and regulations govern their activities.

Psychological disabilities. Called *mental illnesses* within the healthcare field, psychological disabilities are characterized by alterations in thinking, mood, or behaviour, or some combination of the three and can include conditions such as mood disorders (major depression and bipolar disorder), schizophrenia, anxiety disorders, and personality disorders.

Public welfare. Public welfare takes place at the three levels of government: the federal or national government, the provincial and territorial governments, and the regional and municipal governments. The various levels of government fund and deliver monetary benefit programs.

Quintile income distribution. Quintiles are used to provide a window into the income levels of people at various levels of society. There are five quintiles, each measuring 20 percent of the population, usually referred to as the lowest, second, third (or middle), fourth, and highest quintiles. The *quintile income distribution* calculates the share of total income that goes to each quintile. If the Canadian population is divided into quintiles, the highest quintile of Canadians receives around 40 percent of the total income; the lowest fifth receives only 6 percent of the income.

Race. Race is defined as the observable, physical features that are shared among several people, but that distinguish them from members of other groups. For example,

if we orient to skin colour and hair texture, people who are labelled "black" differ visibly from those identified as "white."

Racism. Racism is the collection of actions, attitudes, beliefs, and practices that reflect a negative view of people in particular racial groups. *Individual* racism describes negative attitudes that people might have about others who are members of a different racial group. *Institutional* racism involves the "official" policies and regulations of an organization or institution that allows people from different racial groups to be treated differently in that setting. *Structural* racism describes how deeply rooted inequalities in the structure of society prevent the full participation of people of colour in major social and cultural institutions.

Refugee class. This is an immigration category in which applicants are permitted to enter Canada based on the threat of persecution, torture, or cruelty in their home countries.

Refundable Child Tax Credit. Beginning in 1978, Finance Minister Jean Chrétien announced a merging of social security programs and income tax provisions. The Liber*al g*overnment introduced the Refundable Child Tax Credit as a way to target families in need of government assistance. The stated goal of the benefit was to help families meet the costs of raising children. It was income tested and varied according to the number of children in a family.

Relative homelessness. Relative homelessness is a situation in which people's homes do not meet the United Nations' basic housing standards, which are that a dwelling must have adequate protection from the elements, provide access to safe water and sanitation, provide secure tenure and personal safety, and not cost more than 50 percent of total income.

Relative measure of poverty. The relative measure of poverty is based on how low one's income is relative to that of other people. This measure reflects the differences in income between the poor and the majority of society, rather than an abstract standard.

Reserve system. The reserve system is a by-product of the land-surrender treaties. Reserves are parcels of land that have been set aside for exclusive occupation and use by Aboriginal communities.

Residential schools. This term refers to a range of historical institutions including industrial schools, boarding schools, student residences, hostels, billets, and residential schools tasked with educating Aboriginal children and the overall assimilation of Aboriginal peoples.

Residual view. In the residual view, social welfare is a limited, temporary response to human need, implemented only when all else fails. It is based on the premise that there are two natural ways through which an individual's needs are met: through the family and the market economy. The residual model is based on the idea that government should play a limited role in the distribution of social welfare.

Royal Commission on Aboriginal Peoples (RCAP). RCAP, in 1996, was an extensive study that focused on the current situation of Aboriginal people in Canada. It included an examination of the need for Aboriginal people to heal from the consequences of domination, displacement, and assimilation. The foundation for a renewed relationship, according to the report, involves recognition of Aboriginal nations as political entities. This report was followed by the 1998 government response: *Gathering Strength: Canada's Aboriginal Action Plan.*

Selective programs. Selective programs target benefits at those who are in need or eligible, based on a means test (sometimes called an *income test*) or a needs test.

Self-employment. Self-employed people rely on their own initiative and skills to generate income, and undertake the risks and uncertainties of starting and operating their own businesses.

Seniors Benefit. In 1996 the federal government proposed the Seniors Benefit. This new program would have combined the OAS, the GIS, and the Spouse's Allowance into one benefit that would be more targeted at seniors with low incomes. Due to extensive pressure from seniors and advocacy groups, the government announced in 1998 that the plans for the Seniors Benefit had been scrapped.

Social Assistance (SA). When a person has no source of income, he or she is entitled to what is commonly known as *Social Assistance* (SA), also known as *welfare*. SA is a province-based minimum income program for people defined as "in need." Strict eligibility criteria, known as a *needs test*, are applied to determine whether people are in need. Social Assistance is a program of last resort with roots in early charity relief and the English Poor Laws.

Social democratic ideology. The key values of social democratic ideology are social equality, social justice, economic freedom, and fellowship and cooperation. To the social democrat, social inequality wastes human ability and is inefficient in its distribution of resources. Freedom for social democrats is not only political, it is economic — the kind of freedom that results from government intervention in maintaining a stable economy and stable employment.

Social democratic welfare regimes. Social democratic welfare regimes include countries such as Sweden, Finland, and Norway. This model emphasizes citizenship rights and the creation of a universal and comprehensive system of social benefits. The model is focused on optimum conditions for the citizen — as a right.

Social equity. Social equity refers to the existence of adequate levels of health and security for all people, and a reasonably equal distribution of income and wealth.

Social exclusion. Many scholars, particularly in Europe, are increasingly conceptualizing poverty in terms of social exclusion. The concept refers to marginalization — having limited opportunities or abilities to participate in the social, economic, and cultural activities of society. In short, social exclusion views poverty not as a matter of a low degree of well-being, but as the inability to pursue well-being because of the lack of opportunities.

Social inclusion. This concept challenges social welfare scholars to consider the non-economic aspects of society that lead to social disadvantages or social exclusion, such as education, community life, health care access, and political participation.

Social insurance schemes. The fundamental element of a modern welfare state is a social insurance scheme. You pay premiums and then have a right to benefits. Employment Insurance and Workers' Compensation are examples.

Social investment state. The social investment state focuses on social inclusion by strengthening civil society and providing equality of opportunity rather than equality of outcomes. Also known as the "third way," it claims that jobs that are not low-paying and dead-end are essential to attacking involuntary social exclusion. Nevertheless, an inclusive society must also provide for the basic needs of those who cannot work, and must recognize the wider diversity of goals that life has to offer.

Social justice approach. This approach aims to create systems and policies that help meet the needs of persons with disability. Some worry that it characterizes persons with disabilities as "charity cases" without emphasizing full citizenship.

Social model. The social model views disability within a social and environmental context, emphasizing the need for society to change so as to remove the barriers that prevent "disabled" persons from fully participating in social life.

Social problem. This is a situation that is incompatible with some standard or norm held by a significant number of people in society, who agree that action is needed to alter the situation.

Social responsibility model of the family. The social responsibility model of the family directly addresses gender inequality, gender-sensitive policies, and the social dimension of caregiving. The model contains minimal gender inequality or stratification. The goal with this model shifts from moving towards a society based on equality to one where inequality is minimized.

Social services. Social services (personal or community services) help people improve their well-being by providing non-monetary help to persons in need. Offered by social workers, services include probation, addiction treatment, youth drop-in centres, parent-child resource centres, child care facilities, child protection services, shelters for abused women, and counselling.

Social Union Framework Agreement (SUFA). This 1999 government act affecting income security and social services aims to smooth out federal-provincial/territorial relations after the fallout from the unilateral discontinuation of CAP and the implementation of the CHST. The SUFA refers to a range of programs such as medicare, social services, and education. It also addresses how these programs are funded, administered, and delivered.

Social welfare system. The social welfare system consists of a combination of income security programs and social services.

Socialist ideology. Socialist ideology could be described as emphasizing freedom, collectivism, and equality. Socialists believe in equality and a society that operates to meet people's needs. Marx's saying, "From each according to their abilities, to each according to their needs" summarizes this view. In short, production should be organized according to social criteria and distributed according to need. Here, equality means the absence of special privilege.

Spouse-in-the-house rule. A welfare-related rule that considers individuals who co-habit to be "spouses." Previously, this would lead to a termination of benefits if the "spouse" were an income-earner. A *Canadian Charter of Rights and Freedoms* challenge to the definition of spouse prompted the Ontario government in 1987 to allow welfare recipients a three-year grace period of co-habitation before it affects assistance programs. However, in 1995 the Ontario government redefined spouse, declaring that economic interdependence is deemed to exist as soon as there is evidence of cohabitation, thus a welfare recipient's benefits are reassessed after he or she has lived with an income-earner for three months.

Spouse's Allowance (SPA). The Spouse's Allowance (SPA) was created to deal with a hardship-creating anomaly in the OAS/GIS. In some cases, an elderly couple consisting of a woman under age 65 and an income-earning husband aged 65 would receive OAS and GIS intended for one person. When the woman reached age 65, their income would jump to the OAS/GIS amount intended for married couples. The 1975 SPA was intended to correct the anomaly by providing an income-tested benefit to those between 60 and 65 years of age when one spouse is over 65.

Status or Registered Indians. Status or Registered Indians are persons who are listed in the federal government's Indian Register.

Statute of Labourers. The Black Death ravaged Europe between 1347 and 1351 and brought about a serious labour shortage. English labourers took advantage of the situation and demanded higher wages. One response was the *Statute of Labourers*, which was issued by Edward III in 1351 and directed against the rise in prices and wages.

Structural adjustment. Structural adjustment policies (SAPs) have been imposed by the International Monetary Fund (IMF) on poor countries to ensure debt repayment and economic restructuring. With the stated goals of helping to reduce poverty and promoting economic health, SAPs have often had negative impacts.

Structural approach. The structural approach to social welfare considers the operation of economic markets to be essentially exploitative: while social welfare is necessary to assist those in need, it only further perpetuates the inherently oppressive capitalist structure, rather than forcing a chance in society.

Structural unemployment. Structural unemployment is due to mismatches between the skills of the unemployed and the skills necessary for available jobs.

Tax credit. A tax credit is an amount deducted directly from income tax otherwise payable. Examples of tax credits include the disability tax credit and the married credit for individuals, and the scientific research and experimental development investment tax credit for corporations.

Tax deduction. A tax deduction is an amount deducted from total income to arrive at taxable income. Child care expenses and capital cost allowances are tax deductions. Tax deductions are worth more to people with higher incomes, as they are in a higher marginal tax bracket.

Tax expenditures. Tax expenditures are foregone tax revenues resulting from special exemptions, deductions, rate reductions, rebates, credits, and deferrals that reduce the amount of tax that would otherwise be payable.

Trade unions. Trade unions are organizations that represent those individuals working in particular industries or industrial sectors and that work to defend and advance the interests of these workers in terms of wages and working conditions, as well as broader welfare concerns.

Transnational corporations. Transnational corporations (TNCs) are organizations that possess and control the means of production or services outside of the country in which they were established.

Treaties. Treaties between the Canadian government and First Nations generally served to establish peaceful relations, institute payments, and gain the surrender of land. The treaties generally stipulated the relinquishment of the Indian right and title to specific land and provided for the annual payment of five dollars per person (this amount has not changed and was never indexed to inflation).

Types of Employment Insurance benefits. EI benefits include regular benefits, paid to people who have lost their jobs and are actively looking for work; maternity/parental benefits for new parents, including adoptive parents; compassionate care benefits for people who must leave work temporarily to care for a gravely ill family member; the family supplement for low-income families with children; and fishing benefits for self-employed persons engaged in fishing who earn insufficient earnings from that activity.

Underemployment. Underemployment occurs when the education and training required for the job are less than the education and training of the worker who is doing the job. Evidence indicates that underemployment increases as higher quality jobs become relatively fewer in number.

Undeserving poor. In early English Poor Laws, those physically able to work were considered undeserving and were forced to work by law. Today, a similar concept persists.

Unemployment rate. The unemployment rate is the percentage of the labour force that is unemployed.

Universal Child Care Benefit (UCCB). The UCCB is a taxable $1,200 per year benefit that was introduced in 2006 and can be claimed by parents for each child under 6 years of age.

Universal Declaration of Human Rights (UDHR). The 1948 *Universal Declaration of Human Rights* defines the fundamental expectations for freedom and dignity in a free and just society. Accepted human rights include freedom of expression, freedom of association, freedom from fear and persecution, and freedom of religion, as well as the right to shelter, education, health, and work, among others.

Universal programs. These programs are for everyone in a specific category (such as people over age 65 or children), on the same terms and as a right of citizenship.

Vanier Institute of the Family. The Vanier Institute of the Family is a national, charitable organization dedicated to promoting the well-being of Canadian families. It uses a functional definition of the family that emphasizes the activities of family members.

Veterans disability benefits. Canadian veterans are eligible for disability pension benefits if they have a permanent disability resulting from disease or injury incurred during a war or in a special duty area. Dependants of veterans are also eligible to collect the benefit.

Visible minority. Visible minorities are minority groups that are visually distinct from the mainstream, dominant group, and include people who are non-white in skin colour. According to Canada's *Employment Equity Act*, the ten visible minority groups identified are Chinese, South Asian, Black, Filipino, Latin American, Southeast Asian, Arab, West Asian, Japanese, and Korean groups.

Voluntary assumption of risk. This is one of the early principles used to define the relationship between employers and employees. The voluntary assumption of risk meant that the worker assumed the usual risks of the job, and the rate of pay for each job was assumed to reflect its level of risk. The principle is based on the assumption that contracts between workers and their employers are the same as commercial contracts between people of equal bargaining power.

Welfare fraud. Often exaggerated, fraud within the Social Assistance or welfare systems occurs when applicants are being deceptive in order to receive benefits. Almost half of the fraud cases in Ontario were instances of people collecting welfare while in prison. Many of the other reported frauds were overpayments and administrative errors, or cases where documents were missing.

Welfare state. The welfare state is a system in which the state protects the health and well-being of its citizens, especially those in social and financial need. The key functions of the welfare state are (1) using state power to achieve desired goals (powers include government, bureaucracy, the judiciary, and political parties); (2) altering the normal operation of the private marketplace; and (3) using grants, taxes, pensions, social services, and minimum-income programs such as welfare and social insurance.

Welfare state regimes approach. The welfare state approach classifies welfare states according to how social welfare is provided in a given society. Also referred to as *welfare state approach* and *welfare state models approach*.

Welfare wall. The term *welfare wall* refers to barriers that hinder the movement from relying on Social Assistance to participating in the labour market.

Workers' Compensation. Workers' Compensation is a collection of provincial social insurance programs for employers and workers, established to replace the tort system (the courts) in determining compensation for workplace injuries and health-related risks. It provides no-fault compensation.

Workfare. Workfare takes many different forms – it could mean that a person must take a job to get their Social Assistance cheque or it could mean that people receive a smaller cheque if they refuse to work. It could also involve mandatory community volunteer work or self-employment.

Workhouses. Erected as private enterprises, seventeenth-century workhouses were officially called *almshouses*. Able-bodied applicants for poor relief were forced to report to the workhouse to complete work tasks in order to obtain assistance.

Working Income Supplement (WIS). In addition to a basic benefit, the 1993 Child Tax Benefit included a Working Income Supplement (WIS) to supplement the earnings of working poor families.

Working poor. The low-wage earners or working poor are people who are participating in the labour force through paid employment, but do not earn enough income to lift them above the poverty line.

Workplace modifications. These modifications include changes in the workplace environment for persons with disabilities, such as handrails, ramps, accessible parking, accessible elevators, modified workstations, accessible washrooms, or accessible transportation.

World Bank. The World Bank Group's mission is to fight poverty and improve the living standards of people in the developing world. It provides loans, policy advice, technical assistance, and knowledge-sharing services to low- and middle-income countries to reduce poverty.

World Trade Organization (WTO). The WTO is a global international organization dealing with the rules of trade between nations. In this new era of globalization, the rules for the global economy that were once made by national governments are increasingly being made by international organizations such as the WTO (www.wto.org).

Youth unemployment. Youth unemployment refers to Canadians under the age of 18 who are without a job, but want one.

Index

Credits